Publications of the American Folklore Society
Bibliographical and Special Series
General Editor, Kenneth S. Goldstein
Volume 18 1967

THE ***NEGRO*** *AND HIS* ***FOLKLORE*** *IN NINETEENTH-CENTURY PERIODICALS*

Edited with an Introduction by

Bruce Jackson

Published for the AMERICAN FOLKLORE SOCIETY by the
UNIVERSITY OF TEXAS PRESS, Austin & London

Standard Book Number 292–73662–2
Library of Congress Catalog Card No. 67–21894

Manufactured in the United States of America

Second Printing, 1969

for my father, Irving Jackson
May 31, 1908–March 11, 1967

and nothing quite so least as truth
—i say though hate were why men breathe—
because my father lived his soul
love is the whole and more than all

e. e. cummings

Poll-cats are coming, hurrah, hurray.
I votes in my hole.

John Berryman, *Dream Songs*

"De white man done drive off de Injun,
done mos' drive off de fox,
but Brer Rabbit, he say he gwine stay."

Atlantic Monthly, 1891

Contents

ACKNOWLEDGMENTS

I want to thank Professor Kenneth S. Goldstein, of the Folklore Department, University of Pennsylvania, for suggesting that I undertake this collection; Henry David Shapiro, of the History Department, Ohio State University, who first called my attention to five of the articles included; B. A. Botkin, who offered several suggestions about useful material in obscure volumes; the participants in the proofreading bee—Alan, Candy, Julia, Judy, and Sue Jackson; and the Society of Fellows of Harvard University, whose financial support has afforded me time to engage in fruitful research in folklore. Professor Roger D. Abrahams, of the English Department, University of Texas, read the manuscript and offered many useful suggestions for which I am particularly grateful.

Most of all, I want to thank Professor Herbert Halpert, of the English Department, Memorial University, St. Johns, Newfoundland, who more than anyone else, is responsible for the publication of this collection. Thirty years ago, when he was co-editing the National Service Bureau's "American Folk-Song Publications" series, he had stencils cut for a volume of nineteenth-century articles on Negro folksong. The man who carried the stencils to George Herzog, hearing that the WPA project had closed that day, celebrated by getting drunk; he lost the stencils. Halpert's interest in the project continued, but there was never time and occasion to begin all over again. Not long ago, he suggested to Dr. Goldstein that someone be found to redo the collection, and when the suggestion was passed on to me I decided to expand the contents to include articles on nonmusical folklore forms. After the manuscript was finished, Halpert read it and sent me a six-thousand-word letter that demonstrated his skills as fine editor and scholar; it is my hope that both the collection and editor profited from it. Many of Halpert's remarks in his letter appear in the Prefaces to the various articles; many others influenced my comments on the contents of the articles. His valuable counsel saved me from many errors of fact and lapses in discretion. For those that remain, I bear full responsibility.

BRUCE JACKSON

Harvard University
Cambridge, Massachusetts

Introduction

The thirty-five articles, letters, and reviews in this anthology represent but a fraction of the literature on Negro folklore published in nineteenth-century periodicals. I have tried to present as wide a range of material and attitudes as possible; the intention has been to offer a representative group of articles that present basic folklore materials, without undue concern about the prejudices of the authors, except where the prejudice seems to have distorted the materials. The articles present and discuss folksong, speech, belief, custom, and story; the authors range from militant abolitionists to dedicated slaveholders, and their attitudes toward the Negro and his folklore reflect their positions.

Although I have taken stage minstrelsy to be outside the scope of this anthology—for that is another problem with its own controlling social framework—a few minstrelsy articles are included to give some idea of the confusion in terms facing anyone beginning to study Negro folklore in the nineteenth century. Just as today, a broad audience thought what it was getting from the popular stage was folklore or something like it, and its attitude is not without importance. "Negro song" did not mean the same thing in 1829 that it meant in 1827, for in the intervening period Daddy Rice had burst upon the Louisville stage with a stereotype that still hasn't quit twitching. The great achievement of the early collectors of Negro folksong and speech was not that they collected good material (they did), but that they were able to write down what they saw and heard instead of seeking to verify the image pictured by the minstrels.

Minstrelsy, remember, was immensely popular for more than a half century. By 1850 it was big business, and during the next two decades dozens of minstrel companies traveled wherever American roads or rivers or railroads struck a city. Printed versions of minstrel songs were everywhere available (even the pages of the *Southern Workman*, a monthly magazine published by Hampton Institute, the Virginia college for Negroes and Indians, carried mail-order advertisements for *Minstrel Songs Old and New* and similar titles). As big-time minstrelsy went into its well-earned decline, blackface and banjo moved to the vaudeville stage, presenting still more excessive parodies of the real Negro. In the 1890's, "coon songs" compounded the image.[1] It is still difficult to evaluate the extent of influence exercised by these entertainments on collectors.[2]

With a few exceptions, serious collecting did not begin until the Civil War, when for the first time many Northern abolitionists came to know the slaves as something more corporeal than a good cause. There were problems from the start. Many of the people taking down the folklore were white Yankees, new to the material and the dialect. But, as D. K. Wilgus has observed:

> Considering the sympathies and understandable ignorance of these collectors, their conclusions are surprisingly moderate. They were not folklorists, anthropologists, or musicologists. They knew little of the South, their acquaintance with the "Western and Southern Camp-meetings" must have been superficial, and they knew nothing of folksongs among the white population. But they recorded a body of song, religious and secular, that differed from any they knew. They discovered the shout and the work song. They described the nonpart harmony of the singers. They heard irregularities, *slides,* and *turns,* and noted what they could. They recognized adaptations of camp-meeting hymns, such as "The Ship of Zion," and rejected some songs paralleled in Methodist hymnals. For the rest, they turned to the only authorities they knew, the Negroes themselves.[3]

We are not likely to discover how representative were the songs and stories the white man heard, or what proportion he decided to print. It seems peculiar that nowhere in any of the accounts do we find any mention of bawdry; even though such material could not be printed, it could have been referred to. There must have been nongroup songs in circulation, but perhaps those whites who could record with ease while their informants were in church or at work could not do so in a more private situation. W. G. Allen wrote, in his preface to *Slave Songs of the United States*: "Our intercourse with the colored people has been chiefly through the work of the Freedmen's Commission, which deals with the serious and earnest side of the negro character. It is often, indeed, no easy matter to persuade them to sing their old songs, even as a curiosity, such is the sense of dignity that has come with freedom."[4] When collecting be-

[1] See Paul Charosh, "Slander in Song," *Listen,* I (December 1963), 3–7.

[2] For a demonstration of how fruitful a careful examination of the old minstrel collections might be, see the annotations to the songs in Newman I. White, *American Negro Folk-Songs* (Cambridge, Mass., 1928; reprinted Hatboro, Pa., 1965).

[3] *Anglo-American Folksong Scholarship since 1898* (New Brunswick, N. J., 1959), p. 34.

[4] (New York, 1867), p. x.

came more sophisticated the problem remained, for the friends of the freedman were not likely to put things in print that would show him in a bad light, and the enemies rarely bothered to put the Negro in print at all.

We must read the transcriptions with some care and occasionally wonder what the white men did when they were confronted by sounds strange to their ears. Some tried to transcribe the actual sounds, but others, assuming mispronunciation, made editorial corrections; others assumed African origins for some words and produced weird orthographies; and some, *expecting* alien sounds, misinterpreted and misheard. How much and what kind of error occurred we cannot tell, but we should assume there were some. What is surprising is the relative absence of obvious gross errors from this source.

To get some idea of the kind of distortion that could occur, consider the following item printed by Thomas W. Talley, a Negro collector, in 1922:

Shool! Shool! Shool!
  I rule!
Shool! Shool! Shool! I
  rule!
Shool! Shacker-rack!
I shool bubba cool.

Seller! Beller eel!
Fust to ma tree'l.
Just came er bubba.
Buska! Buska-reel![5]

The line breaks are Talley's. He titles the item "Tree Frogs," and parenthetically remarks, "Guinea or Ebo Rhyme." With his spelling, one might easily assume a West African provenience, particularly if one were unfamiliar with West African languages and white American folksong. The song is, of course, the Irish "Shule Agra," well known in the United States as "Johnny Has Gone for a Soldier."[6]

Ironically enough, some of the most accurate text transcriptions in the nineteenth-century articles probably appear in those written

[5] *Negro Folk Rhymes* (New York, 1922), p. 168.

[6] Some versions by whites are easily as corrupt or were as strangely transcribed. In the *Frank C. Brown Collection of North Carolina Folklore* (II [Durham, 1952], 362) one finds for instance, the following:

Scheel-di-scheel-di scheel I ru
Sche-li-schackle-i-lack-i
Schil-i-bal-i-coo
The first time I saw my il-li-bil-i-bee
This come bib-ie-lapie slowree.

by hostile observers, for the anti-Negro or antifolklore writers had no desire to make the Negro's syntax appear neat or exotic.

The sense of discovery that pervades many of the essays may be somewhat misleading. These writers were by no means the first to notice that slaves sang and told stories; they *were* the first to take such practices with much seriousness. Although earlier accounts described happy dancing throngs of carefree blacks,[7] few writers bothered to write down more than a few lines, and most were content to stop with the observation that the slaves did on occasion sing; few realized that they were observing phenomena more complicated than simple manifestations of uncomplicated happiness. A Southern slaveholder would no more have thought of publishing his slaves' songs than he would have considered paying them a salary or acknowledging his mixed progeny.

It was fashionable, in the early part of the nineteenth century, to say the Negro had a natural sense of rhythm and a natural ear for music; he wasn't particularly bright, but he sure did swing. The epitome of this notion was poor Blind Tom, the ugly and idiotic child pianist from Georgia.[8] Tom could not carry on a conversation, but he could repeat anything he ever heard—anything. One night he found his way to a piano and amazed his owners; later he amazed audiences and critics who came from all over the world to hear him play extremely complicated duets, either part, after one hearing. Blind Tom: musical prodigy and physical horror rolled neatly into one grotesque attraction. And everyone *knew* that every old slave could pat time and dance and sing and . . .

That passed, but parts of the fiction lasted until quite recently. Now, everything seems to have gone to quite the other extreme and it is gauche to say the Negro is musical at all. Some moderation is in order. American Negroes, particularly those who grow up in rural communities or first-generation urban ghettos, are generally more

[7] See Dena J. Epstein, "Slave Music in the United States before 1860, A Survey of Sources," Music Library Association *Notes* (1936), pp. 195–212 and 377–390.

[8] See *Dwight's Journal of Music*, XIX (May 18, 1861), 55. An article by the "Author of 'Margaret Howth'" offers a lavish description of Tom's extraordinary career; see "Blind Tom," *Atlantic*, X (November 1862), 580–585; reprinted in *Dwight's Journal of Music*, XXII (November 8, 1862), 250–252. Tom, the semipseudonymous author tells us, could repeat verbatim a fifteen-minute speech, without understanding a word (much as John Steinbeck's Johnny Bear). Because Perry Oliver, his owner, did not want to risk Tom in the free states, he never performed north of Baltimore.

musical than whites. Not all of them—but many. There is nothing racist in that kind of comment, and a visit to a few Negro storefront or rural churches will supply empirical support. The reason is environmental, not genetic. If anyone matures in a milieu in which music exists as a participant activity, he has an excellent chance of at least sharpening latent abilities; in a milieu in which music is a passive activity, such abilities atrophy or never come to maturity. Certainly at this late date we need no justification for admitting the influence of environment. In this regard, articles such as "'The Persimmon Tree and the Beer Dance," "A Georgia Corn-Shucking," "Creole Slave Songs," and many of the others here recorded are particularly valuable, for they give us rare contemporary accounts of the folklore in its own context.

If we are to appreciate the articles presented here both as historical documents and as folklore reports, we must note some of the attitudes toward the Negro current in the nineteenth century, for though all our writers use the word "Negro," they mean by the word quite different things: serf, chattel, stage caricature, human being.

II

Gunnar Myrdal has observed that captured Indians and imported Negroes

> originally were kept in much the same status as white indentured servants. When later the Negroes gradually were pushed down into chattel slavery while the white servants were allowed to work off their bond, the need was felt in this Christian country, for some kind of justification above mere economic expediency and the might of the strong. The arguments called forth by this need were, however, for a time not biological in character, although they later easily merged into the dogma of natural inequality. The arguments were broadly these: that the Negro was a heathen and a barbarian, an outcast among the peoples of the earth, a descendant of Noah's son Ham, cursed by God himself and doomed to be a servant forever on account of an ancient sin.[9]

There is an obvious conflict between this view of the Negro and the views of humanity expressed in the basic documents of the American Revolution. For the Northern abolitionists, there was no conflict; to them, "human slavery was an offense against the fundamental moral law. Their spiritual ground was puritan Christianity and the

[9] *An American Dilemma* (New York, 1964). pp. 84–85.

revolutionary philosophy of human rights."[10] The ante bellum Southerner solved the dilemma by accepting the American Creed only

> as far as whites were concerned; in fact, they argued that slavery was necessary in order to establish equality and liberty for the whites. In the precarious ideological situation—where the South wanted to defend a political and civic institution of inequality which showed increasingly great prospects for new land exploitation and commercial profit, but where they also wanted to retain the democratic creed of the nation—*the race doctrine of biological inequality between whites and Negroes offered the most convenient solution.*[11]

Ironically, the belief in equalitarianism held by both the North and the South created the great intellectual schism between the two areas. In the North, equalitarian beliefs negated the arguments of racial inferiority, but in the South equalitarianism

> indirectly calls forth the same dogma to justify a blatant exception to the Creed. The race dogma is nearly the only way out for a people so moralistically equalitarian, if it is not prepared to live up to its faith. A nation less fervently committed to democracy could, probably, live happily in a caste system with a somewhat less intensive belief in the biological inferiority of the subordinate group. *The need for race prejudice is, from this point of view, a need for defense on the part of the Americans against their own national Creed, against their own most cherished ideals.* And race prejudice is, in this sense, a function of equalitarianism. The former is a perversion of the latter.[12]

Once the illogical leap required by this perversion is made, the rest of the Southern argument follows logically. Before the Civil War, the Negro was regarded legally and socially as a mere chattel. If he is satisfactorily dehumanized, as he is by the racist argument, this is easy, and there are no complications. Frederick Olmsted, who visited the South in 1853–1854, wrote that "as a general rule, the larger the body of negroes on a plantation or estate, the more completely they are treated as mere property, and in accordance with a policy calculated to insure the largest pecuniary returns."[13]

We see, even before the Civil War, several major changes in the Negro's status in this country. He begins as something like an indentured servant, then approaches freedom when there is a weak-

[10] *Ibid.*, p. 87.
[11] *Ibid.*, pp. 87–88. Italics in original.
[12] *Ibid.*, p. 89. Italics in original.
[13] *A Journey in the Back Country* (New York, 1907), I, 64, quoted in E. Franklin Frazier, *The Negro in the United States*, rev. ed.; New York, 1957), p. 48.

ening in the proslavery forces as the institution becomes unprofitable. Manumission requirements in the South are made easier and many Northern states legislate complete abolition at this stage. Then industrial innovation, such as Whitney's cotton gin, again makes slavery profitable and there follows a sequence of rationalizations which forces the Southern Negro into a role of dehumanized chattel, a role affirmed by the Dred Scott decision in 1857.

With the Negro's subordinate role expounded in philosophical theory and ratified by judicial process, the time was ripe for scientific treatises to explore the implications. A Dr. Cartwright, professor at the University of Louisiana, "thought that running away from slavery was a peculiar mental disease, called by him *Drapetomania,* to which Negro slaves were subject. He described the symptoms as follows: 'Before negros run away, unless they are frightened or panic-struck, they become sulky and dissatisfied. The cause of this sulkiness and dissatisfaction should be inquired into and removed, or they are apt to run away or fall into negro consumption.' "[14]

Reconstruction and awarding the Negro civil rights struck the South a greater blow than had military defeat in the war. One explosive reaction was voiced by the Fairfield *Herald* (South Carolina), which opposed

> the hell-born policy which has trampled the fairest and noblest States of our great sisterhood beneath the unholy hoofs of African savages and shoulder-strapped brigands—the policy which has given up millions of our free-born, high-souled brethren and sisters, countrymen and countrywomen of Washington, Rutledge, Marion, and Lee, to the rule of gibbering, louse eaten, devil worshipping barbarians, from the jungles of Dahomey, and peripatetic buccaneers from Cape Cod, Memphremagog, Hell, and Boston.[15]

The editor did not have to rave for long. Negro enfranchisement survived in the North but it died quickly in the South.

There were several reasons why the South won, some political and others economic. Unlike most European serf-freeings, there was no land reform after our Civil War, and the Negroes found themselves without property, power, or function. The North, after the heavy costs of the war, did not feel up to compensating the landowners of the property that might have been confiscated and redistributed. "Under these circumstances," writes Myrdal, "the road to the national compromise of the 1870's was actually well paved from the

[14] Frazier, *The Negro in the United States,* p. 94.
[15] *Ibid.,* p. 138.

beginning. Except for a Republican party interest in the Negro vote and the general craving for revenge against the Southern rebels, there seems not to have been much interest among most Northerners in helping the Negroes."[16] He says also:

> For a decade after the War, the aim of protecting Negro freedom retained its importance in Northern ideology. It gained strength by its capacity to furnish a rationalization for Republican party interests. After the national compromise of the 1870's, the Negro problem dropped out as a national issue. The great majority of Southerners have an interest in keeping it out as long as possible. On the surface, there seem to be no signs that the dominant North will break the compromise and start again trying to reform the South.[17]

When the Supreme Court in 1883 declared unconstitutional the Civil Rights Bill of 1875, the Negro's gains were all gone, and he found he had exchanged his status as chattel for the lowest role in a rigid caste structure.[18]

Against this background, the articles relating to Negro culture and folklore in the nineteenth century form a coherent pattern. Early in the century the Negro is a curiosity to be described with humor or paternalistic condescension, such as we find in "The Persimmon Tree and the Beer Dance" and "Uncle Sam's Peculiarities . . ." Minstrelsy was for many Northerners a way to shelve the problem posed by the free Negro: hide him in a caricature. But by the middle of the century a reaction to this had set in, and Kinnard and Nathanson published articles suggesting they have realized that the Negro may have a very real contribution to make. Just before, during, and immediately after the war, the Northern Abolitionists—C. W. D., the McKims, Spaulding, Higginson—comment on the Negro's spirituals. It is not surprising that they should find this one aspect of his culture most worthy of public attention, for it helped make their point that the Negro is a human being, one with a soul. Later, during Reconstruction days, there are several "discovery" articles—for the first time the Negro is regarded as a bearer of culture, and we are

[16] Myrdal, *American Dilemma,* p. 226.

[17] *Ibid.*, p. 431. The twenty-five years that have elapsed since Myrdal wrote this have seen great charges in both the attitude of the North and the status of the Negro, but this time the Negro himself has been largely responsible for the changes.

[18] Robert Ezra Park sees the change as one from a feudal state to caste structure. See his article "The Etiquette of Race Relations in the South," in *Race and Culture* (New York, 1964), pp. 177–178, especially p. 181. The article appeared originally as the Introduction to Bertram W. Doyle, *The Etiquette of Race Relations in the South* (Chicago, 1937), pp. xi–xxiv.

given accounts of his church services, his speech, his superstitions and, finally, his stories.

During this period, America was still digesting the European Romanticism and the notion of the Noble Savage. As had the Europeans a short while before, the Americans included folklore in their romantic reaction. "Suddenly important literary figures (Cable, Harris, Thomas Nelson Page, etc.) started writing about the Negro and his folklore. In the past, the only important figures were socially and politically oriented, not literarily."[19] The interminable love affair between the American reading public and the image of the ante bellum South was taking hold at just about the same time the Negro was demoted from freedman to serf. A chattel is not a fit subject for literature, but a serf, it seems, is. The old attitudes, safely distant in theory in the North and safely operational in the South, formed the matter of a new literature of nostalgia, and in that literature the folksy plantation Negro had his place. That nostalgic view was helped along by groups such as the Fisk and Hampton singers, who sang nice old plantation songs in palatable white harmonies.

With the last decade of the century we move into modern times. The Negro discovers the value of his folklore himself and, as the "Folk-Lore and Ethnology" series in *Southern Workman* indicates, begins to take seriously his own cultural heritage. This discovery was helped by scholarly attention, such as found in the articles that appeared in *Journal of American Folklore* beginning with its first volume in 1888, and the great psychic boost supplied by Dvorak, whose praise and use of Negro folk music helped make it fully respectable. This anthology ends with an article that is modern in intent, if not in method: Jeanette Robinson Murphy's serious attempt to identify—without opprobrium—cultural links between American Negro and African folklore.

19 Dr. Roger D. Abrahams (private communication).

THE NEGRO AND HIS FOLKLORE IN NINETEENTH-CENTURY PERIODICALS

1838

The Persimmon Tree and the Beer Dance

by William B. Smith

Farmers' Register, VI (Shellbanks, Va., April 1838), 58–61.

In the previous volume of Farmers' Register, *Smith had described in lavish detail the multiple glories of the persimmon tree (V, 596–597). His letter was followed by one by James Garnett, which informed us that we could make molasses from the tree "at the rate of a gallon from less than a bushel of the fruit—and that the third watering of the casks would produce excellent vinegar for table use, although too dark for pickling" (p. 597). It is to this letter that Smith refers in his opening paragraph.*

Smith's article is worth reprinting for his description of the beer dance and the Negroes clapping "juber" to the music supplied by the priestlike "banjo-man." "Juber" was picked up by the blackface minstrels and still survives in Negro folklore in the form of "Hambone." (For a discussion of "Hambone," see Lydia Parrish, Slave Songs of the Georgia Sea Islands *[New York, 1942], pp. 80–84; Roger D. Abrahams,* Deep Down in the Jungle *[(Hatboro, Pa., 1964), p. 37] notes the presence of the rhythmic play in Philadelphia in 1958.) The sequence of letters indicates that* Diospyros virginiana *is surely one of the most cornucopian growths on record: the writers claim to derive from it ink, vinegar, beer, shoe lasts, bed posts, molasses, sugar, brandy, pie, pudding, ersatz coffee, and bread.*

Smith lived in Cumberland, Virginia, a circumstance which may in part explain his naïve attitude regarding the slave's estate: Virginia was breeding territory and no slaveholder would consider damaging a slave when he could just as easily sell him in Georgia at a profit. To Smith, the slave's lot seemed perfectly satisfactory and he could calmly dash off lines like ". . . if a northern abolitionist, with his pocket filled with inflammatory documents and resolutions, could have witnessed such a scene in Virginia, he would, in my opinion, have consigned them to the flames; his great love for the blacks, to the con-

trary notwithstanding," and "as I left the house, I thought to myself, that Virginia slaves, were the happiest of the human race—and I still think so."

To the Editor of the *Farmers' Register:*

When I found my "Persimmon Tree," grouped with the "Persimmon Tree" of James M. Garnett, Esq., in your January No. of the *Farmers' Register,* I drank his health in a glass of persimmon beer. I am not only pleased with his remarks, but highly gratified that the gentleman has employed his able pen on the subject of this valuable tree. I find very little difference between his opinions and mine, and it rarely happens that two communications on the same subject, accidentally falling together, should correspond in so many particulars. We agree perfectly, as it regards the use and value of the persimmon tree. It will be seen, however, by the reader, that he has discovered an astringent acid quality, in the leaves and unripe fruit, which, when combined with iron, gives a black color for ink. To make amends for this, I have given the medicinal properties of the bark. He has discovered vinegar for table use; to meet this, I have given a good receipt for making beer. He has also informed us, that the wood of this tree makes shoe-lasts; and I have told you, the wood of the persimmon tree makes bed-posts. His molasses and sugar stand ready to sweeten my coffee and tea, and the two communications are so nicely poised and equally balanced, that it is impossible to tell which will kick the beam. I regret, however, that the learned gentleman has obtained brandy by the distillation of persimmon beer; for it may have a very demoralizing effect in eastern Virginia; the brandy drinkers will require such a demand on the product of this tree next fall and winter, that we may lose our sugar, molasses, pies and puddings. Should this be the case, there will, I suspect, be a tumultuous scuffle, and all make a simultaneous movement in order to obtain the great prize. Then, as Jim Black would say, *"the longest pole takes the simmons."* I am of the opinion, that persimmon beer contains no alcohol, and although it is found in most fermented fluids, I have never witnessed any intoxicating effects from the use of this beverage. Our slaves make it in great perfection, and use it freely without any appearance of inebriation. An old servant in my family was remarkable for making good persimmon beer, and whenever I would pass the door of his house, he never failed to invite me in to taste his beer. "Come, master, drink some beer; simmon beer and ash-cake is equal to *cash*; but it don't make *glad* come like whiskey."

Although the old man was a movable swill-tub as long as his beer lasted, yet I never knew him to be intoxicated. I differ with Mr. Garnett, as it regards the presence of alcohol in ripe fruit. Speaking of the persimmon, he says "it contains so much of the alcoholic principle as never to freeze." I have been educated to believe, that alcohol is never present in ripe fruit; its components, oxygen, hydrogen and carbon, are not developed or properly evolved, previous to fermentation. Alcohol forms the true characteristic of vinous liquors, and is obtained from wine and other fermented fluids by distillation.

I will call your attention again to the persimmon seed, as a substitute for coffee. It has not the genuine coffee taste, and some individuals may not like it at first; but if they will continue its use, with one-third or one-fourth West-India coffee, they must be pleased with it, and but few can distinguish the taste from genuine coffee. Much depends on parching the seed; they should be carefully stirred with a stick while parching, in order to prevent them from burning, which never fails to give the coffee a bitter taste. Twelve gallons of water, to eight gallons of persimmons, makes the beer luscious, rich and very fine; it may be too brisk and sharp for delicate palates; the beer we generally meet with, has double the quantity of water. Although I am of the opinion that persimmon beer is not intoxicating, yet I have witnessed great glee, and highly pleasurable sensation, produced in our slaves, over a jug-gourd of beer; but I ascribe this reverie or pleasurable hilarity, to the wild notes of the "banjor," which gives zest to the beer. There is an indescribable something in the tones of this rude instrument, that strikes the most delicate and refined ear with pleasing emotion; the uninterrupted twang or vibration of its strings, produces a sound as it dies away, that borders on the sublime. I never could account for its wonderful effect on a well-organized ear, capable of distinguishing and appreciating agreeable sounds; unless it be admitted, that concord and discord are so completely blended as to produce perfect harmony. This opinion, however absurd it may seem at first view, is not without its supporters. Pope says, "all discord is harmony not understood."

The honorable gentleman, Mr. Garnett, has indulged in a little innocent merriment in giving us a "Munchausen story"—a "mutton machine," which would really be invaluable if reduced to practice. With all due respect for your valuable columns, I must ask the privilege of being indulged in a similar strain, in giving an account of a "beer dance" that came under my observation.

Some years ago, I rode in the night to visit a patient, and as I passed the house of Mr. Samuel Poe, in the lower end of Prince Edward, I heard the tones of a banjor, and was told by the old gentleman, (Mr. Poe,) that his servants had brewed a barrel of persimmon beer, and he gave them the privilege of having what they called a "beer dance." Curiosity induced me to ride to the door, accompanied by Mr. Poe, and the other gentleman. And here we saw rare sport! "an unco sight!" Not, however, such a sight as Tam O'Shanter saw when he peeped into "Kirk-Alloway," for the dancers there were "*warlocks* and witches"; here they were Virginia slaves, dancing jigs and clapping "juber," over a barrel of persimmon beer. It occurred to me, that if Tam could have made his appearance about this time on his gray mare *Meg*, the scene would have frightened *Maggie* more than the "*bleeze*" of "Kirk-Alloway"; and Tam might have roared out, "weel done Cutty Sark!" a thousand times, and the torch-lights would not have been extinguished.

The ball was opened with great ceremony by singing a song known to our Virginia slaves by the name of "who-zen-John, who-za."

Old black bull come down de hollow,
He shake hi' tail, you hear him bellow;
When he bellow he jar de river,
He paw de yearth, he make it quiver.
Who-zen-John, who-za.

This was a sky-rocket thrown out, as a prelude to the grand exhibition, and will give the reader some idea of what is to follow. Those who could not get seats in the house, took their stand outside, peeping in the door and through the logs, making remarks on the dancers; and here I will observe, that there was a complete Babel jargon, a confusion of tongues!

"Down the road, come show me de motion." "Set to your partner, Dolly."— "Cut him out, Gabe."—"Sal, *does* put her foot good."—"Yonder come de coal-black horse."—"The yallow roan's up! hear how he lumbers! he's a *rael* stormer, ring clipper, snow-belcher and *drag out*."—"Congo is a *scrouger*; he's up a gum, and no bug-eater I tell you; he carries a broad row, weeds out every thing—hoes de corn, and digs de taters."—"Molly look like kildee; she move like handsaw —see how she shake herself."—"Hello! in there, I wish you all sen' us out some simmon beer." "Lor! *see* how Aggy shake her foot! she *ken* pull the whip-saw down."—"Nick? come here and see Ben cross hi' bow-legs! look at hi' mouf! when he grin, hi' mouf and teeth like hen-ness full o' eggs."—"Nick? I reckon if Tamar's cat stay in there much longer, they will mash her guts out; her skin *'ont* hold peas."—"Come here, Gabe; come, if you please; Jackson's Dick is dancing with Ellington's Nance! see how she quivers! *Now*, Nance!—*Try*, Nance!—She *does* but look pretty.—When she sets and turns, she is like a *picter*—and she is fine form, back. Dick shan't have Nance; I'll kick him high as the meat house first." [*Sings.*] "She *bin* to the north, she *bin* to the south, she *bin* to the east, she *bin* to the west, she *bin* so far *beyond* the sun, and she is the *gal* for me."—"Dick had'nt no business dancing with Nance; he ain't a man of *gumption.* I tried him, and he can't be made to understand the *duramatical* part of the function, the function of the fundamental, and the *imperality* of ditrimental things. Gabe? Dick's a fool, and you may tell him Sambo says so: he is knock-knee'd, and ugly enough to eat *Gumbo.*" "Well, I know that; sing on Sambo."

I went from the great-house, down to the kitchen,
To get a knot of light-wood to see to go fishing,
To treat granny Dinah;
I went to the stable, I cotch master gray horse,
I clap the saddle *pon* him and he trot like *do'nk* care.
He *do'nk* care, he *do'nk* care.

Having become tired of this out of door conversation, we concluded to view the group in the house. Here the banjor-man, was seated on the beer barrel, in an old chair. A long white cowtail, queued with red ribbon, ornamented his head, and hung gracefully down his back; over this he wore a three-cocked hat, decorated with peacock feathers, a rose cockade, a bunch of ripe persimmons, and to cap the climax, three pods of red pepper as a top-knot. *Tumming* his banjor, grinning with ludicrous gesticulations and playing off his wild notes to the company. Before him stood two athletic blacks, with open mouth and pearl white teeth, clapping "Juber" to the notes of the banjor; the fourth black man held in his right hand a jug gourd of persimmon beer, and in his left, a dipper or water-gourd, to serve the company; while two black women were employed in filling the fire-place, six feet square, with larded persimmon dough. The rest of the company, male and female, were dancers, except a little squat wench, who held the torch light. I had never seen Juber clapped to the banjor before, and you may suppose I looked upon such a novel scene, with some degree of surprise. Indeed I contemplated the dancing group, with sensations of wonder and astonishment! The clappers rested the right foot on the heel, and its clap on the floor was in perfect unison with the notes of the banjor, and palms of the hands on the corresponding extremities; while the dancers were all jigging it away in the merriest possible gaiety of heart, having the most ludicrous twists, wry jerks, and flexible contortions of the body and limbs, that human imagination can divine.

The whole world is a ball we find,
The water dances to the wind;
The sea itself, at night and noon,
Rises and dances to the moon.

The earth and planets round the sun,
Still dance; nor will their dances be done,
Till nature in one blast is blended;
Then may we say the ball is ended.

The rude ballad set to Juber, corresponds admirably with the music and actors in this wild fantastic dance. While the clappers were laboring in the performance of their office, they responded at the same to the notes of the banjor.

Juber up and Juber down,
Juber all around de town,
Juber dis, and Juber dat,
And Juber roun' the simmon vat.
Hoe corn, hill tobacco,
Get over double trouble, Juber boys, Juber.

Uncle Phil, he went to mill,
He suck de sow, he starve de pig,
Eat the *simmon,* gi' me de seed,
I told him, I was not in need.
Hoe corn! hill tobacco!
Get over double trouble, Juber boys, Juber.

Aunt Kate? look on the high shelf,
Take down the husky dumplin,
I'll eat it wi' my *simmon* cake.
To cure the rotten belly-ache.
Hoe corn! hill tobacco!
Get over double trouble, Juber boys, Juber.

Racoon went to *simmon* town,
To choose the rotten from de soun,
Dare he *sot* upon a sill,
Eating of a whip-poor-will.
Hoe corn! hill tobacco!
Get over double trouble, Juber boys, Juber.

When supper was announced, the banjor-man, was first served; then the clappers and beer bearer, and lastly, the beaux and their partners. Each had a huge loaf of larded persimmon bread with a gourd of beer.

Thus ended the beer dance, and as I left the house, I thought to myself, that Virginia slaves were the happiest of the human race—and I still think so.

> The learn'd is happy, nature to explore,
> The fool is happy that he knows no more.

Solomon the wisest man, says—"in much wisdom, there is much grief: and he that increaseth knowledge, increaseth sorrow."

The beer dance, I have attempted to describe, is a faint representation of what actually occurred. It requires an abler pen to do it justice; I feel mortified that I cannot give a more vivid and glowing description of these black beaux, who acted so conspicuous a part with their partners in the persimmon junket. The broad grin, the smile of the little squat wench, seen through her torch-light, the humid lip, the twist of the tongue, the white teeth, the oblique look, the glance of the eye, the toss of the head, the quaint bow, the curved shin, the bandy leg, the nimble jig, the affected air of the wenches, the profuse perspiration, the cloud of dust, the lurid room, the phiz of the banjor man, the banjor's *tum, tum, tum,* and Juber's song and clap, would call forth the combined talents and lively imagination of a Wirt, an Irving, a Burns, an Addison, and Dryden. And if a northern abolitionist, with his pocket filled with inflammatory documents and resolutions, could have witnessed such a scene in Virginia, he would, in my opinion, have consigned them to the flames; his great love for the blacks to the contrary notwithstanding.

In conclusion, I offer no apology for introducing in your columns, and bringing before your intelligent readers, such a novel, rude production, as the *beer dance.* We are to derive from such scenes in this life, much useful instruction; the poet, divine, statesman, philosopher, and all mankind, may be benefited by looking *down* in life, in order to explore the dark corners of nature.

There is this consolation to be derived from the scene I have described; the pleasing recollection that God has placed us high in the scale of human beings; and we should all appreciate its worth.

I drink you the following sentiment, in a glass of persimmon ale: May the product of persimmon tree, substitute foreign wines, molasses, sugar, tea, and coffee, and save the "old dominion" thousands annually.

With sentiments of regard, and esteem, I am,

Your obedient servant,

William B. Smith.

1839

Uncle Sam's Peculiarities. American Niggers.—Hudson River Steam-Boat Dialogues

(Unsigned article)

Bentley's Miscellany, VI (London, 1839), 262–271.

A body of folklore about *the Negro and his folklore runs through many of the nineteenth-century accounts; with humor fairly typical for the period, this article from a British journal illustrates that folklore at length. Two Negro stereotypes are operative here, one created by the minstrels, the other maintained by the slaveholders. Although the geriatric epithets of the obnoxious Western Merchant are obviously contrived, we should note that the* treatment *of Negroes is described straightforwardly—it is still too early in the nineteenth century for many people to express concern over such descriptions. If the stereotypes presented here had much currency, and it is quite likely they did have, one hardly wonders that the first serious collectors chose to focus their attention upon religious songs.*

In a recent letter, Roger D. Abrahams drew my attention to the fact that "the American did not have to make up the stereotype of the Negro. The English have had it for the 'dark peoples' for a long time. . . . Among the dark peoples to the English were the Celts, and over and over they have used this stereotype as a rationale for their prejudice against the Welsh 'Taffy' ('Taffy was a Welshman, Taffy was a thief . . .'), the Scot and the Irish (especially). Yet it is from these groups that the English have over and over again found cultural stimulation when their repressed expression ran dry, just as we have from the Negro." Among the characteristics the English ascribed to the Irish were that they were "dirty, oversexual, producing too many children, unable to care for themselves, overemotional, little children. This was the consistent rationale for subjugation." The parallels to our American situation are obvious.

Sir Harry Johnston's description of the Negro in Africa could have been written by any number of partisan Americans in the last hundred years:

He is possessed of great physical strength, docility, cheerfulness of disposition, a short memory for sorrows and cruelties, and an easily aroused gratitude for kindness and just dealing. He does not suffer from homesickness to the over-bearing extent that afflicts other peoples torn from their homes, and provided he is well fed, he is easily made happy. Above all, he can toil hard under the hot sun and in the unhealthy climates of the torrid zone. He has little or no race-fellowships—that is to say, he has no sympathy for other negroes; he recognizes, follows and imitates his master independently of any race affinities, and, as he is usually a strong man and a good fighter, he has come into request not only as a labourer but as a soldier.[1]

There is not the least exchange of feeling between the white and black population of America. In some of the slave States, to teach a slave to read and write is an offence punishable with death, and a *free* black sailor arriving in port is consigned to a prison until his ship is again ready for sea. The following observations refer exclusively to the "free States"; in which the blacks and mulattoes are proprietors of their own persons, but have not all the social and political privileges of the republic:—

Nature has created a difference in physical formation, colour, and mental capacity between the *real negro*, with retiring forehead, projecting jaws and large heels, and the European, or Caucasian variety of the genus homo, which nothing can ever set aside. American physiologists declare that there are upwards of fifty different anatomical developments by which the existence of negro blood in any individual can be tested. But, if no difference were perceptible except the rank odour of a nigger, *that one* difference would be quite sufficient, in my humble opinion, to place an insuperable bar against the "amalgamation"—odious word!—which the blacks, and some eccentric white enthusiasts, in the United States, are professing to desire. The zealous "abolutionist" is pleased to think that at a future age of the world, some thousands of years hence, no *black* man will be in existence; the negro blood being all "amalgamated" with the white, so that mankind will assume a sober whity-brown appear-

[1] *A History of the Colonization of Africa by Alien Races* (Cambridge, England, 1913), pp. 151–152, quoted in E. Franklin Frazier, *The Negro in the United States* (rev. ed.; New York, 1957), p. 82.

For discussion of aspects of American forms of the stereotype, see Gunnar Myrdal, *An American Dilemma* (New York, 1964), especially the subchapter "Specific Rationalization Needs," pp. 106–108.

ance. There can be no doubt that when this process shall be completed, our descendants of the thousandth generation will commence an amalgamation between the aforesaid Negro-Caucasian, whity-browns, and the Tartarian inhabitants of the "Celestial Empire."

The treatment of the blacks by the whites in the "free" States is simply founded on the conventional opinions that the blacks are *not* the brethren of the whites; that it is a "curse" to the country that so many blacks are in existence in it, elbowing their superiors; and that the only way to make these two distinct races of mankind live peaceably together is to draw a line of demarcation beween them, and allow *all* the whites to say to *all* the blacks, "keep your distance, confess your inferiority, and do not attempt to associate with us." Although this state of things may be called ungenerous, and even cruel, towards the few blacks who have more than an average amount of intelligence, yet it has puzzled all the Philadelphia lawyers to invent more than two systems of government for a free state with niggers in it: one system being to rest satisfied with the *distinctive die* of nature, and to enforce obedience from the blacks; the other is sacrilegiously to break down the law,

> Whereto we see in all things nature tends,

and "amalgamate" the two species.

I shall conclude this exordium with remarking, that I never met an Englishman, who, after being six months in the States, did not agree that the plan of treating the blacks as natural inferiors was unavoidable, and that the amalgamation doctrine is an abomination too hideous ever to be entertained except by the blacks themselves, and the most degenerate and frantic white men.

Passing on a summer evening one of the African churches in New York, I listened at an open window to the following snatches of the minister's discourse. I should have ventured within doors, but the steam at the window forewarned me.

"My belobed brebren," said the parson, "ebery ting tells me de molgamation assoity mus triump. I wab at Bosson toder day, an hard a bootiful sarmen frum de Reberend Missa Rae. He said de Queen ob Sheba wab a dark lady, may be bery dark—'spose black. Yet de Queen ob Sheba cum to Sollymun, who raise her, and pud her on a chair by em side. Reberend Missa Rae guess Sollymun wad hab made her Queen ob Israel only he wab married afore. Dis Sollymun wab a king sarten; but not like a king ob de present day. He wab so wise dat he wab the wisest man as eber live on dis circular globe as is continually surrounding the heabens. De heabens tell de glory ob heaben, and dis circular globe tell de anjust 'havior ob man to hisself, for man to man is man to hisself, or his own fam'ly." (*A pause.*) "Yas, I say de anjust 'havior ob man to hisself, or his own likeness. Are we not broders? I say we is. I say so wid a loud voice to ma fellow white Chrestian brebren. Em cannot answer dat. Em say *no*, but a say *yas*." (*A pause.*) "I dine wid de white men in Bosson—de obilition assoity—an' dey did not turn up 'em nose at me. No; but gabe me one ob de tob seats, an' a sat wib de white men an' ma colo'd frens, wib de univarsal feelen ob ooman natur on ma soul." (*A pause.*) "Some say too we shall hab de militiee-law ultered, and de black and white will go fort to battle togeder side by 'em side, at de next war."

After the sermon I heard the congregation singing a hymn, the concluding line of the verses, which was repeated twice, being

We shall be de soldiers in de army by and by.

The laws of New York State disqualify the blacks from serving in the militia, or voting as citizens, unless they have freehold property of the value of two hundred and fifty dollars. No doubt there are many thus qualified, but no American mob would permit a nigger to take part with it in an election. A coloured man is not allowed to enter any part of a theatre but the gallery, and there he is carefully excluded by wooden palings from the whites. Black men are not permitted to work a fire-engine at a conflagration, although they *may* take up the water-plugs, and busy themselves with the hose. No nigger must enter the public grounds, called the Park and the Battery, in New York, on "celebration days." I saw a drunken nigger who had offended in this respect, when a balloon was about to ascend from the Battery, chased by the mob, and nearly murdered. The mob caught him by some iron railing, against which they beat his head and face until the poor creature was covered with blood and wounds. Certainly no English mob would have used a dog so. Some constables were on the spot, but did not interfere; the sovereign people were merely having a *nigger hunt!* After the balloon had ascended, their majesties, pleased with the sport they had enjoyed in "whipping" the nigger, commenced a general hunt, and obliged every coloured man "to clear out" of the streets, under pain of being brutishly knocked down and trampled on. Sometimes, on such occasions, the niggers collect together and show fight, which is then called a *nigger riot*; the blacks defending themselves are taken before the squires, and sent to cut stones at the State's prison: thus, a nigger riot helps the State to some valuable labour.

The river Schuylkill, near Philadelphia, is much used by the anti-poedo-Baptist niggers, for *total* immersion, in their "baptisms for riper years"; and the favourite season for this religious ablution is the depth of winter. I was witness to the baptism, or dipping, of about twenty niggers one Sunday morning, when the river was frozen over. Some grinning labourers were breaking the ice with pickaxes, while a procession of six hackney-coaches was approaching; the white coachmen looking all sorts of unutterable fun. The black minister let himself out of the first coach, and immediately commenced a discourse, the aim of which was to convince the bystanders that there was nothing ridiculous in what they were about to perform. He concluded by informing the troop of unhappy bathers that, if they trusted in the Lord, they would certainly not catch cold. The poor fellows, dressed like Spanish monks, were, however, shivering with the damp expectation. The minister walked first into the water, and, as his congregation followed him, he gave each the *coup de grace* by sousing the head under water so low as to make the fullest assurance of the total immersion being perfect. While this was being acted, the following colloquy ensued between three white Philadelphians and two of the black Baptists.

1st Phil.: What on airth can these black fellows be communicating in the water?

2nd Phil.: Can't say, if they aint washing themselves agin the summer comes on.

3rd Phil.: Those on the airth are shaking quaking Baptists, kind of Mother Ann people, a-going to be dipped present-*ly*. Those in the water under the airth have caught cold, and are coming out quite cured of the excruciating enthusiasm that made them go in.

1st Phil. (*to one of the blacks.*): How is it you choose winter for this here washing?

3rd Phil.: Who gave that coloured man in the black cap leave to have the ice broke? It shouldn't be done near here. It spoils sleighing and skating frolics, and don't ought to be done by any.

1st Nigger: We are anti-poedo Baptists.

1st Phil.: Are you?

2nd Phil.: Howoo? (how?)

3rd Phil.: What's that to do with washing yourselves, and using cakes of ice for soap?

1st Nigger: For total 'mersion.

2nd Nigger: Don't 'terrupt de cerem'ny.

3rd Phil.: Ceremony, you curious nigger! I should call it a frolic, only you look so eternal shivered. You should have brought some apple-jack with you.

1st Nigger: Jamaky sperets is best.

2nd Phil.: Well said, old 'un.

1st Nigger: Ole enough to be oo fader.

2nd Phil.: Father? you precious nigger! Do you say I'm a baboon, or a Hottentot monkey!

1st Nigger: No, sa; but oo shouldn't make fun of 'ligious cerem'ny.

2nd Phil.: I make fun? What's the use of that when the whole gang of you are making so much fun of yourselves, you don't give anybody a chance to strike out a funny idea in addition?

The following dialogues will serve to introduce a variety of niggers.

FIRST PART.—DECK OF A HUDSON RIVER STEAM-BOAT.

A dandy nigger, technically termed a "Long-tailed Blue," dancing Jim Crow's pattern dance, of which Mr. T. D. Rice has afforded the denizens of London an exact portraiture. It must be remarked, however, that the dance on deck does not include the song with which Mr. Rice accompanies it. A very old nigger is selling fruit to the passengers, who are laughing at "Long-Tailed Blue"; a good-looking mulatto lad is selling hot Indian corn; two very ugly niggers are at the steam-engine, looking on with a peculiar scowl, expressive of animosity to the "whites," of whom they are conversing; and two black stewards occasionally make their appearance at the companion door.—Time, dusk of the evening.

Mulatto *(chaunts)*:

Hot corn, hot *corn,*
Here's your nice hot *corn,*
All hot!

Tennessee: The owners of this boat ought to be ashamed of themselves for having such abominable niggers on board. I shall complain. I overheard one of them say, that if all the blacks were of his mind they would not leave a white man on the face of the earth.

Spectator: What an atrocious idea! Yet the generality of white men would agree in the wish that no *black* men darkened the face of nature.

Tennessee: If he were in Tennessee his back should be warmed as soon as we reached the shore. I don't know how you Englishers feel, but really my republican blood boils when these black rascals dare to utter a disrespectful word in my presence, and I not to be able to punish them for it. The license these niggers have in these infernal free States sickens any one from the south. Look at that fellow eating clams.* You don't see such an ugly nigger as that every day.

SPECTATOR: A monstrous ill-looking fellow, indeed! With some long hair, and a bear-skin, he would make a perfect representative of Shakspeare's Caliban.

TENNESSEE: There's the other too! Why, sir, I wouldn't give a hundred dollars for both of them in one lot. What a broken-winded, spavined pair! What a sprawling, lame-handed, loose-jointed pair! Shame on the proprietors to have such rascals on board! I shall patronize the Mohawk Company next trip.

MULATTO:

> *Hot* corn, hot *corn*,
> *Here's* your nice hot *corn*,
> *All* hot!

TENNESSEE: There's a likely young fellow, that corn-dealer there!

SPECTATOR: What may be the value of such a hand as that in the south?—two hundred dollars?

TENNESSEE: Oh, ay! dirt cheap at that. Now, there's a tight nigger—that one dancing; he figures it well, too. How proud he seems that the whites are looking on. Astonishing the pride of some of those fellows! That black devil has been jumping Jim Crow ever since we have been on board, I expect. What a capital hand for a light-footed messenger on a plantation! Now some of our gentlemen from the south couldn't see that fellow without wishing to kidnap him. He'd fetch a high price, *he* would! If he'd sell himself he might raise a little fortune.

CALIBAN *(sings)*:

> Ole Jim Crow has sole hisself to de debil.

TENNESSEE: Do you hear that, sir? The scoundrels are listening.

[The Tennessee and myself here separated, and I went to another part of the boat, and overheard the following conversation]:

WESTERN FARMER: What kind is it for a fix?

WESTERN MERCHANT:† They know how to go a-head pretty bustling.

W. FARMER: Did you go far out of Liverpool?

* Shell-fish resembling cockles, but about as large as a London oyster.

† An American "Western Merchant" is a similar trader to an English village shopkeeper; an epitome of linendraper, shoe-dealer, grocer, and ironmonger.

W. Merchant: Yes; right into the bowels of the land, as Hamblin says when he plays Richmond.

W. Farmer: And what did you see?

W. Merchant: Why I went to Hull, and see the most considerable black, ugly-looking steamers, as ever were created on the entire globe. I was crossing a ferry when I first saw one, and I was tee-totally amazed. So I set to, and laughed rather loud, until all the passengers came to the side of the vessel to see what was the matter. "You're in a fit," says the boatman.—"I can't help it," says I; "that there steamer is enough to give a man from the States the cholera-morbus, or Vitus's dance, for three weeks; only from good manners I disguise my feelings."—"Disguise," says the ferryman, "why, I expect you laughed out loud a-purpose."—"No," says I, "I didn't; I only smiled a leetle. When I laugh out loud you'll hear it two or three times over, like an echo. I laugh like a forge-bellows at a foundry, and it gets easier to me the longer I'm at it. My lungs are real American, *they* are; springy, tough, and curious bendible." If I wasn't struck powerful amazed, then that nigger as is helping himself to his own apples doesn't know he's born yit.

The nigger alluded to was a white-headed, stout-looking, old fellow, who, as I afterwards understood, was of the great age of one hundred and two. He had a deep and full-toned voice, and such a laugh as would not have disgraced Sir John Falstaff before the neglect of Prince Hal, heartburn, and potations of sack-posset or "sherris," put him under the care of Dame Quickly. The old nigger—who did not object to be known by the *sobriquet* of *Old Horse*,—on finding he was spoken of, said he was his own *bos* (master), and he had given himself leave to take two cents' worth to set the passengers an example.

W. Farmer: Never mind. It's nothing to us. You are your own nigger, I guess, and nobody has a better right to the apples, if you have leave.

W. Merchant: What! Nigger *Hundred-per-cent*, is that you? Are you quite sure you're alive yet? A young child said you put it in mind of a coffin as much as ten years ago. How do you manage to fix yourself in this way, out of all reasonable calcylation?

Ole Hoss: Lo'd lub oo, sa! it wab the tumperance assoity as dib it,—ha! yah!

W. Merchant: Ah! Good things those temperance institutions are sometimes; but can't say as they done much good keeping such an old nigger as you alive, that ought to have been buried comfortable twenty years ago, short reckoning.

OLE HOSS: A wab an ole boy den, sa, twenty years ago; a wab called Ole Hoss cos a wab so tarnation strong. Diff'rence ma loife,—ha! yah!

W. MERCHANT: Well then, *Old Horse*, as you keep a-head with the temperance, you'll have no rum, I calcylate, the next time you help me with my luggage at the Federal Wharf.

OLE HOSS: Much as oo please to pay for, sa; ole ooman hab join de temperance; *a* habn't; so a hab double 'lowance sperets, an' keep aloive a consequence,—ha! yah!

W. MERCHANT: Oh! that's the constitution-ticket, is it, *Old Horse*, you rum Hottentot nigger, you? If I had as many cents as I've spent in rum on your throat these twenty years, they'd buy me a span of new Bosson hats.

OLE HOSS: Recollect when oo gained 'lection for 'special Caucus man, what a treat oo gabe at Jerusalem,—ha! yah!

W. MERCHANT: To be sure I do, Old *Never-die*.

OLE HOSS: Had twenty-tree glasses Jamaky sperets maself. Seberal ole niggas dere; all dead since. Pore fallows! ole field niggas! ole slabes! Diff'rence ma loife,—ha! yah!

W. MERCHANT: How long have you been free, old *Dodge-at-death*?

OLE HOSS: Ah! long time, sa,—long time. Ma aunt nuss Gen'ral Washenton. Recollect when no house furder den de park in New York. Diff'rence ma loife,—ha! yah! When a little snub,—dis high—at school, taught catechism,—ha! yah! Taught to say "Kingdom come; king, queen, an' all de royal fam'ly." Gen'ral Washenton kill all ob 'em; and den, "kingdom come, royal fam'ly," and all taken out ob de prayer. Dat wab 'fore oo wab born, sa. Diff'rence ma loife,—ha! yah!

W. MERCHANT: Where were you raised, you exaggerated piece of darkness, eh?

OLE HOSS: Africa, sa. Come ober as an emigrant wid fader and moder in two vessels. Bery oncomfortable cos ob no steam-boats in dose days. Diff'rence ma loife,—ha! yah!

W. MERCHANT: And, how long were you a slave?

OLE HOSS *(evidently offended)*: A don't 'member dates, sa. A am not a common nigga.

W. MERCHANT: Who said you were, old Bumpos? Do you think I wish to offend your dignity, eh, old Grim death and cross-bones?

OLE HOSS: Not at all, sa. A am not offended. Dis nigga salls apples and things for amoosement; but a am a suspectible fam'ly. Ma grandaughter quite white, all but de hair an' eyes. Diff'rence ma loife,—ha! yah!

W. MERCHANT: So you've been amalgamating, eh, you extravagant piece of blubber?

OLE HOSS: Ma grandaughter married an English nobleman's 'prentis.

W. MERCHANT: His apprentice, eh, you woolly tortoise? What trade does he carry on?

OLE HOSS: Can't say, sa. Same trade as 'em bos. 'Em go gunning togeder.

W. MERCHANT: And, which carries the bag, old Flourhead?

OLE HOSS: 'Prentis.

W. MERCHANT: By the living Jingo! he has the best place of it. Why didn't he invite you over to England?

OLE HOSS: A am too ole, sa; would hab made a fus-rate nobleman's 'prentice fifty years ago; but lost a good deal ob time. Too ole! too ole; Diff'rence ma loife,—ha! yah!

MULATTO:

> *Hot* corn, hot *corn*,
> *Here's* your nice hot *corn*,
> *All* hot!

W. MERCHANT: *(to the Spectator)*: This old fellow, sir, has seen *all* the celebration days, and was forty-years old when they began.

OLE HOSS: Fifty-eight celebration days for de white people, and forty-seben for de black genelmen.* Diff'rence ma loife,—ha! yah! Plenty of nigga hunts in the Battery since niggas made free. A hab been hunted sebenteen times. Nar kill me sebrel times.

W. MERCHANT: How could you live so long, you live elephant's leg, you?

OLE HOSS: No tumperance assoity in dose days, when 'em a young man. Diff'rence ma loife,—ha! yah!

W. FARMER: No; but the boses took care the niggers didn't drink too much.

W. MERCHANT: But, tell us how you swindle death in this manner. Let us know the patent. How do you fix it, you immortal nigger, eh?

OLE HOSS: Four 'sicians once a-board dis boat, sa, an' held consultation. 'Zamined me, all four. Den one says, we can't *cross*-zamine dis nigga, cos 'em good oomard. No make dis nigga cross no way, 'em

* The Declaration of Independence is celebrated on the *fourth* of July by the white natives, or Anglo-Americans, and on the *fifth*—the day *after* the fair—by the black natives, or Africo-Americans; but sometimes the blacks have omitted the celebration. This fact is highly characteristic of the American *social* system, and deserves to be the cue for a political thought or two; but this is not the place for its introduction.

calcylate. 'Em lib so long eder cos 'em drink so much Jamaky sperets, or, cos 'em laugh so much. So a says, "a laugh cos ob de rum, an' a has good sperets cos a allaws take de best Jamaky": 'em both go togeder,—ha! yah!

W. Farmer: You're a rum one, *you* are, you extraordinary specimen, you!

A Sailor (*sings.*):

> Come, nigger, ferry me over
> To the good ship called the "Fame,"
> For I've got a husband on board her,
> But, blow me, if I know his name!

Ole Hoss: Buy ma apples, sa?

W. Merchant: Why, you unconscionable nigger, how dare you enter into conversation with me, and then ask me to buy apples? How much will you charge for the entire whole of this specylation, all but the basket? And, will you take a grocery order in payment?

Ole Hoss: Quarter dullar, hard Jackson.

W. Merchant: Well, here it is, you wonderful patriarch. Hand the apples round, and contrive not to pocket any yourself, you curious sample of another generation, you.

Mulatto:

> *Hot* corn, hot *corn*,
> *Here's* your nice hot *corn*,
> *All* hot!

SECOND PART

Long-tailed Blue, Caliban, and Zip Coon (three niggers), near the engine hatchway.

Caliban: Dis rum too 'trong; a put some more water to it.

Zip Coon: Let me say too 'trong fust. Den water it for oosalf,—yah! yah! Last night a dream of being in 'Lisium.

Caliban: 'Lysian fields, opposite New York?

Zip Coon: No, real 'Lisium; an' saw Adam; an' a said a wab a coloured genelman, an' all de fam'ly, till 'em had de yallow fever—yah! yah!

Caliban: A dream, too; saw debil, an' said 'em quite white, onny painted black by de fust settlers in dis country.

Long-tailed Blue (*theatrically*): " 'Tis de eye ob chilehood fears painted debil."

Zip Coon: But, some say de debil's dead an' buried in Cole Harbour,—yah! yah!

CALIBAN: In ma dream 'em said 'em kept a plantation in New Orleans.

ZIP COON: A had a dream once, so tarrible a couldn't remember it, no way.

LONG-TAILED BLUE (*theatrically*): "Onny a dream; but, den, so tarrible, it shakes ma soul."

CALIBAN: A had a dream so exasperating, couldn't wake for laughing at it, and kep sleepen all Sunday.

ZIP COON: Dat wab de day when two charity sermons preached, —yah! yah!

CALIBAN: A waked in de evenen.

ZIP COON: Cos de boat wab going to Albany,—yah! yah!

LONG-TAILED BLUE: One of oo niggas at de blazen embas, 'blige by gibing som fia for ma sega.

(*Caliban brings a log of blazing wood.*)

LONG-TAILED BLUE: Dat's not de way to breng a genelman fia for a sega. 'Low me to hab it in a 'spectable manner.

CALIBAN: Why, a allaws breng fia to white men in dat way.

LONG-TAILED BLUE: Do oo? Den larn better noder time. Knock off a small bit at de side; dat's de 'spectable way ob it.

CALIBAN: Oo a some man's servant, oo a.

LONG-TAILED BLUE: A am not anybody's servant. A wab a help to a person once, but gabe him notice to quit, an' clared out. A am a genelman, an' no low trade. A am not a common nigga.

CALIBAN: A store-porter.

LONG-TAILED BLUE: No; I isn't in any low trade, a tell ye. A am a profession.

ZIP COON: What a long-tailed blue dis nigga hab to be sure,—yah! yah!

CALIBAN: A stole it ready made.

ZIP COON: Look at ma varagated buttons. Dese are de patent crush buttons; onny two parcels come ober in four ships,—yah! yah!

LONG-TAILED BLUE: Vulga cretturs! Dat inferna' opposition ball, at de low price of fifty cents, make dese common niggas horrible familia.

CALIBAN: None of oo kitchen pride here. A am a coloured genelmen as well as ooself, a calcylate.

Long-tailed Blue begins to dance.

ZIP COON: A know 'em now; a dibn't afore. Oo ib de master ob de cerem'nies at de social congress ob all nations, coloured genelmen and ladies in pertickler,—yah! yah!

LONG-TAILED BLUE: Dat's quite correc. Hab de hona to be 'pointed by de female committee of pattern ladies. Here's ma card. "Sebenty-foive, Erclese-street, end of de dird avenue," whare de fust-rate secon' han' costume ib at de lowest mark price.

CALIBAN: Why, you inferna' nigger! dat wab oo den dat cheat me ob seben dullars wid de grocery order a breng in exchange.

LONG-TAILED BLUE: Don't stroike! Oo'll pud oosalf into a bushel ob nettles ib oo stroike me.

CALIBAN: Oo are a wicker-basket ob bumposity, oo are, wid a liddle dash ob aggrawation.

ZIP COON: 'Em a secon' han' tailor's goose, wid cabbage wegetables for the lining ob 'em pockets,—yah! yah!

LONG-TAILED BLUE: A call dat a blow. Ib oo stroike dat way, ma blood will be up. Dib oo see dat blow?

ZIP COON: No; but a see oo teeth threatened addaciously.

Enter upon the scene the skipper of the steam-boat.

SKIPPER: What's the matter with you black devils there? You'll be splitting your tongues some of these days with your eternal jaw. I'll not have it on board my boat for any nigger as ever walked on four legs. If you can't be quiet, I'll give you such a hint that you'll jump into taking it. I'll pitch you two a couple of hundred miles into that en-*jine* fire! and, this long-tailed blue shall go ashore in his own hat, with that cambric-handerchief for a mainsail! I expect you take me for an English figure-head, a wooden man, with a sham telescope. If you want to jaw, keep ashore, and be hanged to you! D' ye think I'm going to turn my boat into a zoological institute, and have nothing but chattering scratching apes in her? Keep her to, there!—keep her to! Slue up the extra, and pull the boat-line taut.

[This reprimand from the captain had the desired effect: the quarrel which had just commenced was immediately discontinued; and, as I was making my way into the cabin, I heard Zip Coon singing]:

THE STOKER'S CHAUNT

The ebben tide ib floating past,
  Fire down below!
The arrival time ib coming fast,
  Fire down below!
Racoon cry in de maple tree,
  Fire down below!
The wood ib on fire, and the fire a see,
  Fire down below!
Oo a oo oh! fire down below!

1845

Who Are Our National Poets?

by J. K[innard], Jr.

Knickerbocker Magazine, XXVI (New York, October 1845), 331–341.

The slapstick and sarcasm in this article grow tedious quickly, but parts are well worth preserving. Kinnard's sarcasm is mixed: he is obviously rather cynical about the rage for so-called "Negro song," or the greedy capitalizing on it, but at the same time he is heir to the images of his time and offers for some of his examples lines no more rooted in tradition than the ones he professes to despise. And he is not immune to stereotypes—notice that the one Negro who does not sing in the boat is (of course) fated to be a runaway and a traitor. James Crow and Scipio Coon are the well-known minstrelsy figures Jim Crow and Zip Coon. But Kinnard does notice isochronism in the worksongs, and his description of the worksong situation is apparently straight reportage. His picture of the folk composer hacking away in the swamp while the white collector alters the text and finds an eager publisher is not without recent parallel.

BY OUR 'SALT-FISH DINNER' CORRESPONDENT.

Who says we have no American Poetry? No American Songs? The charge is often made against us, but (as will be hereinafter proved) without the slightest foundation in truth. Foreigners read BRYANT, and HALLECK, and LONGFELLOW, and hearing these called our best poets, and perceiving nothing in their poems which might not just as well have been written in England, or by Englishmen, they infer that as the productions of those who stand highest among our poets have nothing about them which savors *peculiarly* of America, therefore America has no national poetry; a broad conclusion from narrow premises.

What are the prerequisites of national poetry? What is necessary to make the poet national?—this being, in the opinion of these foreign critics, the highest merit he can possess. Certainly, liberal education and foreign travel cannot assist him in attaining this desirable end; these denationalize a man; they render any but the narrowest soul cosmopolitan. By these means the poet acquires a higher standard than the national. By a kind of eclecticism, he appropriates forms and thoughts, images and modes of expression, from all countries and languages; by comparing the specific, the transient, and the idiosyncratic, he arrives at the general and the permanent; and when he has written in his own language a poem in accordance with his new ideal standard, he may have produced a noble work, but it can hardly be a *national* poem. He has striven to avoid the faults peculiar to his own countrymen, faults which he might have deemed beauties had he finished his education in his village school, and never ventured out of his native valley. He has become enamoured of the excellencies of the poets of other nations, the very knowledge of which prevents him from being national himself. He has become acquainted with the rules of universal poetry, as the linguist learns, in the study of foreign tongues, the principles of universal grammar. His standard is universal, not national.

From what has been said, it follows that if it be so desirable, as some people think, that poetry should smack of the locality in which it is written, then in order to obtain that end we must keep our poets at home, give them a narrow education, and allow them no spare money by which they might purchase books, or make excursions into other ranks of society than their own. If we could only pick out the born poets when they were a fortnight old, and subject them to this regimen, the nation would be able to boast of original poets in plenty, during the next generation. This is the way in which BURNS became Scotland's greatest national poet. If he had been born a lord, had been educated at Cambridge, and had made the grand tour of the world, does any one suppose he would have been a better poet? or half so good? At best, he could not have been so original nor so Scottish; and he might have proved to be only a tasteful HAYNES BAYLEY, or BARRY CORNWALL; or perhaps a miserable, moody, misanthropic LORD BYRON. Where would have been the glory of England, the immortal SHAKSPEARE, had the boy WILLIAM received an education like that given in the nineteenth century to lads of genius who have rich fathers?

Applying this rule to America; in what class of our population must we look for our truly original and American poets? What class is most secluded from foreign influences, receives the narrowest education, travels the shortest distance from home, has the least amount of spare cash and mixes least with any class above itself? Our negro slaves, to be sure! *That* is the class in which we must expect to find our original poets, and there we *do* find them. From that class come the Jim Crows, the Zip Coons, and the Dandy Jims, who have electrified the world. From them proceed our ONLY TRULY NATIONAL POETS.

When Burns was *discovered,* he was immediately taken away from the plough, carried to Edinburgh, and fêted and lionized to the "fulness of satiety." James Crow and Scipio Coon never were discovered, personally; and if they had been, their owners would not have spared them from work. Alas! that poets should be ranked with horses, and provided with owners accordingly! In this, however, our negro poets are not peculiarly unfortunate. Are not some of their white brethren owned and kept by certain publishing houses, newspapers, and magazines? Are not the latter class, like the former, provided with just sufficient clothing and food to keep them in good working condition, and with no more? And do not the masters, in both cases, appropriate all the profits?

Messrs. Crow and Coon could not be spared from the hoe, but they might be introduced to the great world by proxy! And so thought Mr. THOMAS RICE, a "buckra gemman" of great imitative powers, who accordingly learned their poetry, music and dancing, blacked his face, and made his fortune by giving to the world his counterfeit presentment of the American national opera; counterfeit because none but the negroes themselves *could* give it in its original perfection. And thus it came to pass, that while James Crow and Scipio Coon were quietly at work on their masters' plantations, all unconscious of their fame, the whole civilized world was resounding with their names. From the nobility and gentry, down to the lowest chimney-sweep in Great Britain, and from the member of Congress, down to the youngest apprentice or school-boy in America, it was all:

> Turn about and wheel about, and do just so,
> And every time I turn about I jump Jim Crow.

Even the fair sex did not escape the contagion: the tunes were set to music for the piano-forte, and nearly every young lady in the Union, and the United Kingdom, played and sang, if she did not *jump,* "Jim Crow." "Zip Coon" became a fashionable song; "Lubly Rosa, Sambo come," the favorite serenade, and "Dandy Jim, of Caroline" the established quadrille-music. White bards imitated the negro melodies; and the familiar song

> As I was gwine down Shinbone Alley,
> Long time ago!

appeared, in the following shape:

O'er the lake where drooped the willow,
Long time ago!

What greater proofs of genius have ever been exhibited, than by these our National Poets? They themselves were not permitted to appear in the theatres, and the houses of the fashionable, but their songs are in the mouths and ears of all; white men have blacked their faces to represent them, made their fortune by the speculation, and have been caressed and flattered on both sides of the Atlantic.

Humorous and burlesque songs are generally chosen for theatrical exhibition, and this fact may have led many to believe that the negroes composed no others. But they deal in the pathetic as well as the comical. Listen to the following, and imagine the hoe of Sambo digging into the ground with additional vigor at every emphasized syllable:

Massa an Misse promised me
When they died they'd set me free;
Massa an Misse dead an' gone.
Here's old Sambo hillin'-up corn!

Poor fellow! it seems a hard case. His "massa and misse" are freed from *their* bonds, but Sambo stills wears his. He might here very properly stop and water the corn with his tears. But no; Sambo is too much of a philosopher for *that.* Having uttered his plaint, he instantly consoles himself with the thought that he has many blessings yet to be thankful for. He thinks of his wife, and the good dinner which she is preparing for him, and from the depths of a grateful and joyous heart he calls out, at the top of his voice:

Jenny get your hoe-cake done, my darling,
Jenny get your hoe-cake done, my dear:

and Jenny, in her distant log hut, which is embowered in Catalpa and Pride-of-India trees, gives the hominy another stir, looks at the hoe-cake, and giving the young ones a light cuff or two in the side of the head, to make them "hush," answers her beloved Sambo in the same strain:

De hoe-cake is almost done, my darling,
De hoe-cake is almost done, my dear.

Now if that field of corn belonged to Sambo, and the hut and its inmates were his own, and he belonged to himself, that would be a delightful specimen of humble rural felicity. But perhaps his young master may be so unfortunate as to lose the ten thousand dollars which he has bet upon the race that is to take place to-morrow; and poor Sambo and his family may be sold, separated, and sent just where their new masters may please; possibly to labor on a sugar plantation—the hell of the blacks.

The greater portion of our national poetry originates in Virginia, or among involuntary Virginian emigrants. Slaves are worked very lightly in that state, comparatively speaking. They are raised chiefly for exportation. Every year thousands are sent to the far south and southwest for sale. The Virginian type of negro character therefore has come to prevail throughout the slave states, with the exception of some portions of Louisiana and Florida. Thus every where you may hear much the same songs and tunes, and see the same dances, with little variety, and no radical difference. Taken together, they form a system perfectly *unique*. Without any teaching, the negroes have contrived a rude kind of opera, combining the poetry of motion, of music, and of language! "Jim Crow" is an opera; all the negro songs were intended to be *performed*, as well as sung and played. And, considering the world-wide renown to which they have attained, who can doubt the genius of the composers? Was not the top of Mount Washington, once upon a time, the stage on which "Jim Crow" was performed, with New Hampshire and Maine for audience and spectators? So saith one of the albums at the foot of the mountain. And doth not William Howitt tell us that the summit of the Harz mountains was the scene of a similar exhibition?

These operas are full of negro life: there is hardly any thing which might not be learned of negro character, from a complete collection of these original works. A tour through the south, and a year or two of plantation life, would not fail to reward the diligent collector; and his future fame would be as certain as Homer's. Let him put his own name, as compiler, on the title-page, and (the real author's being unknown) after a lapse of a few centuries the contents of the book will be ascribed to him, as "the great American Poet," the object of adoration to the poetical public of the fiftieth century! What was Homer but a diligent collector? Some learned people *say* he was nothing more, at any rate. Thou who pantest for glory, go and do likewise!

While writing this, your city papers advertise: "Concert this evening, by the African Melodists." *African* melodists! As well might the Hutchinsons call themselves *English* melodists, because their ancestors, some six or eight generations back, came from England. Whether these performers are blacks, or whites with blacked faces, does not appear; but they are doubtless meant to represent the native colored population of "Old Virginny," and as such should be judged. They are *American* melodists, *par excellence*.

It is a true test of genius in a writer, that he should be able to put his sayings into the mouths of all, so that they may become household words, quoted by every one, and nine times in ten without knowledge of the author of them. How often do we find in Shakspeare, Sterne, and other celebrated old writers, the very expressions we have been accustomed to hear from childhood, without thought of their origin! They meet us every where in the old standard works, like familiar faces. And how often, when uttering one of these beautiful quotations, if questioned as to its origin, we feel at loss whether to refer the querist to Milton, Sterne, or the Bible! Proverbs are said to be "the wisdom of nations," yet who knows the author of a single proverb? How many, of the millions who weekly join their voices to that glorious tune Old Hundred, ever heard the name of the composer? How transcendent, then, must be the genius of the authors of our negro operas! Are not snatches of their songs in every body's mouth, from John O'Groat's to Land's End, and from Labrador to Mexico? Three hundred and fifty times a day, (we took the pains to count, once,) we have been amused and instructed with "Zip Coon," "Jim Crow," and the tale of a "Fat Raccoon, a-sittin on a rail." Let Webster tell of the tap of Britain's drum, that encircles the world! Compared with the time occupied by Great Britain in bringing this to pass, "Jim Crow" has put a girdle round about the earth in forty minutes. At no time does the atmosphere of our planet cease to vibrate harmoniously to the immortal songs of the negroes of America. At this present moment, a certain ubiquitous person seems to be in the way of the whole people of these United States simultaneously, (a mere pretender, doubtless, dressed up in some cast-off negro clothing,) and any one may hear him told, a hundred times a day, to "Git out ob de way, old Dan Tucker!" But if he gets out of any body's way, it is only that of "Dandy Jim, of Caroline." Oh, that he *would* obey the command altogether! but depend upon it, he will do no such thing, so long as the young ladies speak to him in such fascinating tones, and accompany their sweet voices with the only less sweet music of the piano. Dan takes it as an invitation to stay; and doubtless many a lover would like to receive a similar rejection from his lady-love; a fashion, by the way, like that in which the country lass reproved her lover for kissing her: "Be done, Nat!" said she, "and *(sotta voce)* begin again."

Who is the man of genius? He who utters clearly that which is dimly felt by all. He who most vividly represents the sentiment, intellect and taste of the public to which he addresses himself. He to whom all hearts and heads respond. Take our "national poets," for example, who being unknown individually, we may personify collectively as the

American SAMBO. Is not Sambo a genius? All tastes are delighted, all intellects are astonished, all hearts respond to his utterances; at any rate, all piano-fortes do, and a hundred thousand of the sweetest voices in christendom. What more convincing proof of genius was ever presented to the world? Is not Sambo the incarnation of the taste, intellect and heart of America, the ladies being the judges? Do not shrink from the answer, most beautiful, accomplished, delicate and refined lady-reader! You cannot hold yourself above him, for you imitate him; you spend days and weeks in learning his tunes; you trill his melodies with your rich voice; you are delighted with his humor, his pathos, his irresistible fun. Say truly, incomparable damsel! is not Sambo the realization of your poetic ideal?

But our national melodists have many imitators. Half of the songs published as theirs are, as far as the words are concerned, the productions of "mean whites"; but base counterfeits as they are, they pass current with most people as genuine negro songs. Thus is it ever with true excellence! It is always imitated, but no one counterfeits that which is acknowledged by all to be worthless. The Spanish dollar is recognized as good throughout the world, and it is more frequently counterfeited than any other coin. The hypocrite assumes the garb of virtue and religion; but who ever thought of feigning vice and infidelity, unless upon the stage? Every imitator acknowledges the superior excellence of his model. The greater the number of imitators, the stronger is the evidence of that superiority: the warmer their reception by the public, the more firmly becomes established the genius of the original.

But the music and the dancing are all Sambo's own. No one attempts to introduce any thing new *there*. In truth they, with the chorus, constitute all that is essentially permanent in the negro song. The blacks themselves leave out old stanzas, and introduce new ones at pleasure. Travelling through the South, you may, in passing from Virginia to Louisiana, hear the same tune a hundred times, but seldom the same words accompanying it. This necessarily results from the fact that the songs are unwritten, and also from the habit of extemporizing, in which the performers indulge on festive occasions. Let us picture one of these scenes, which often occur on the estates of kind masters, seldom on those of the cruel. So true is this, that the frequent sound of the violin, banjo, or jaw-bone lute, is as sure an indication of the former, as its general absence is of the latter.

Like the wits of the white race, the negro singer is fond of appearing to extemporize, when is fact he has every thing "cut and dried" beforehand. Sambo has heard that his "massa" is going to be put up as candidate for congress; that his "misse" has that day bought a new gold watch and chain; that Miss Lucy favors one of her lovers above the rest; that "massa and misse" have given their consent, and in fact that Violet, the chamber-maid, saw Miss Lucy looking lovingly on a miniature which she had that morning received in a disguised package. Sambo has learned all this, and he has been engaged the whole day, while hoeing corn, in putting these facts, and his thoughts thereon, into verse, to his favorite tune, "Zip Coon." He never did such a day's work in his life. He hoed so fast, that his fellow-laborers looked at him in astonishment, and said Sambo had "got de debbil in him; dumb debbil, too; no get a word out ob him all day." Sambo finished his hoeing task by three o'clock, but not his rhyming. He could not sit still, so he went to work in his little garden-patch; and just at sundown, having completed his verses to his satisfaction, and hummed them over till confident that he could sing them through without hesitation, he threw down his hoe, and shouted and capered for joy, like a madman.

Soon after tea, Violet enters the parlor: "Sambo sends compliments to Massa and Misse, and de young gemmen and ladies, and say he gwine to gib musical entertainment to company dis evening in de kitchen, and be happy to hab a full house." Sambo is a favorite servant, and so, with an air of kindness and dignity, the master replies: "Give our compliments to Sambo, and say that we will attend with pleasure"; and soon the whole family go out to the kitchen, which at the South is always a building by itself. The master's family occupy one end of the room, standing; the doors and windows are filled with black faces, grinning ivory, and rolling eyes. Sambo emerges from behind a rug, hung across the corner of the kitchen; and the orchestra, consisting of one fiddle, played by old Jupe, strikes up: "Clar de kitchen, old folks, young folks, old Varginny neber tire." This is a feint, skillfully planned by Sambo, just as if he intended nothing more than to sing over the well-known words of one or two old songs. He goes through this performance, and through two or three more, with the usual applause: at last old Jupe strikes up "Zip Coon," and Sambo sings two or three familiar stanzas of this well-known song; but suddenly, as if a new thought struck him, he makes an extraordinary flourish, looks at his master, and sings:

> Oh, my ole massa gwine to Washing*ton*,
> Oh, my ole massa gwine to Washing*ton*,
> Oh, my ole massa gwine to Washing*ton*,
> All 'e niggers cry when massa gone.

I know what I wish massa do,
I know what I wish massa do,
I know what I wish massa do,
Take me on to Washington to black him boot an' shoe.
  Zip e duden duden, duden duden da.

. . . .

Misse got a gold chain round her neck,
Misse got a gold chain round her neck,
Misse got a gold chain round her neck:
De watch on toder end tick tick tick,
De watch on toder end tick tick tick,
De watch on toder end tick tick tick,
Jus de same as Sambo when he cut up stick:
  Zip e duden duden, duden duden da.

Miss Lucy she hab a gold chain too,
Miss Lucy she hab a gold chain too,
Miss Lucy she had a gold chain too,
Miss Lucy she hab a gold chain too;
No watch on de toder end ob *dat*, I know,
No watch on de toder end ob dat, I know,
No watch on de toder end ob dat, I know,
I reckon it's a picture ob her handsome beau:
  Zip e duden duden, duden duden da.

Great tittering and grinning among the blacks; hearty laughter among the whites; blushes, and a playfully-threatening shake of the finger at Sambo, from Miss Lucy. Sambo meanwhile "does" an extra quantity of jumping at an extra height. His elation at the sensation he has produced really inspires him, and he prolongs his saltations until he has concocted a genuine impromptu stanza:

Who dat nigger in a door I spy?
Who dat nigger in a door I spy?
Who dat nigger in a door I spy?
Dat old Scip, by de white ob him eye:
  Zip e duden duden, duden duden da.

By de white ob him eye and he tick out lip,
By de white ob him eye and he tick out lip,
By de white ob him eye and he tick out lip,
Sambo know dat old black Scip:
  Zip e duden duden, duden duden da.

Exit Sambo, behind the rug. Great applause; and white folks *exeunt*.

The evening winds up with a treat of whiskey, all round, furnished by "massa" on the occasion, and in due time all disperse to their several log huts, and retire to rest, after one of the most joyous evenings they ever passed in their lives. All sleep soundly but Sambo; he lies awake half the night, so excited is he by the honors he has acquired, so full of *poetical thoughts*, seeking to shape themselves into words. Slumber at last falls on him; but his wife declares, next morning, that Sambo talked all night in his sleep like a crazy man. Thousands at the South would recognize the foregoing as a faithful sketch of a not infrequent scene:

> The man who has no music in his soul,
> Nor is not moved by concord of sweet sounds,
> Is fit for treasons, stratagems and spoils;
> Let no such man be trusted.

Shakspeare never uttered a more undeniable truth; and if he were living at the present day, and needed evidence to back his opinion, a short experience as a cotton planter would furnish him with the requisite proof. This thing is well understood at the South. A laughing, singing, fiddling, dancing negro is almost invariably a faithful servant. Possibly he may be lazy and idle, but "treasons, strategems and spoils" form not the subject of *his* meditations. He is a thoughtless, merry fellow, who sings "to drive dull care away"; sings at his work, sings at his play, and generally accomplishes more at his labor than the sulky negro who says nothing, but looks volumes. These last words have struck "the electric chain" of memory, and forthwith starts up a picture of by-gone days. "The time is long past, and the scene is afar," yet the mental daguerreotype is as fresh as if taken yesterday.

One day during the early part of the Indian war in Florida, we stepped into a friend's boat at Jacksonville, and with a dozen stout negro rowers, pushed off, bound up the St. Johns with a load of muskets, to be distributed among the distressed inhabitants, who were every where flying from the frontier before the victorious Seminoles. As we shot ahead, over the lake-like expanse of the noble river, the negroes struck up a song to which they kept time with their oars; and our speed increased as they went on, and became warmed with their singing. The words were rude enough, the music better, and both were well-adapted to the scene. A line was sung by a leader, then all joined in a short chorus; then came another solo line, and another short chorus, followed by a longer chorus, during the singing of which the boat foamed through the water with redoubled velocity. There seemed to be a certain number of lines ready-manufactured, but after this stock was exhausted, lines relating to surrounding objects were extemporized. Some of these were full of rude wit, and a lucky hit always drew a thundering chorus from the rowers, and an encouraging laugh from the occupants of the sternseats. Sometimes several minutes elapsed in silence; then one of the negroes burst out with a line or two which he had been excogitating. Little regard was paid to rhyme, and hardly any to the number of syllables in a line: they condensed four or five into one foot, or stretched out one to occupy the space that should have been filled with four or five; yet they never spoiled the tune. This elasticity of form is peculiar to the negro song. But among these negroes there was one who rowed in silence, and no smile lighted up his countenance at the mirthful sallies of his sable companions. When the others seemed merriest, he was unmoved, or only showed, by a transient expression of contempt, the bitterness which dwelt in his heart. In physiognomy he differed entirely from his companions. His nose was straight, and finely cut, his lips thin, and the general cast of his countenance strikingly handsome. He was very dark, and in a *tableau vivant* might have figured with credit as a bronze statue of a Grecian hero. He seemed misplaced, and looked as if he felt so. The countenance of that man, as he carelessly plied his oar, in silent contempt of the merry, thoughtless set around him, made an impression on my mind which will never be effaced. He spoke not, but "looked unutterable things." He had no "music in his soul"; he was not "moved by concord of sweet sounds"; but his thoughts were on "treasons, stratagems and spoils"; he was thinking of the muskets and ammunition which the boat contained, and of the excellent use that might be made of them, in the way of helping the Indians, instead of repelling them. "Let no such man be trusted!" would have been a proper precaution in this case. A few weeks after this he ran away and joined the Seminoles, and was suspected to have acted as a guide to the party that subsequently laid waste his master's plantation.

Comparatively speaking, however, there are few negroes at the South who have "no music" in their souls. The love of music and song is characteristic of the race. They have songs on all subjects; witty, humorous, boisterous and sad. Most frequently, however, specimens of all these classes are mingled together in the same song, in grotesque confusion. Variety is the spice of the negro melodies. Take the following as a fair specimen of negro humor and pathos:

Come all you jolly niggers, to you de truf I tell-ah;
Neber lib wid white folks, dey neber use you well-ah:
Cold frosty mornin', nigger bery good-ah,
Wid he axe on he shoulder, he go to cut de wood-ah;
  Dingee I otten dotten, balli' otten dotten,
  Dingee I otten, *who dar*?

Come home to breakfast, get somethin' to eat-ah;
And dey set down before him a little nasty meat-ah;

Den at noon poor nigger, he come home to dine-ah,
And dey take him in de corn-field, and gib him thiry-nine-ah!
Dingee I otten dotten, balli' otten dotten,
Dingee I otten, *who dar*?

Den de night come on, and he come home to supper-ah,
And dey knock down, and break down, and jump ober Juber-ah!
Den a little cold pancake, and a little hog-fat-ah,
And dey grumble like de debbil, if you eat too much ob dat-ah!
Dingee I otten dotten, balli' otten dotten,
Dingee I otten, *who dar*?

. . . .

Den oh! poor nigger, I sorry for your color-ah;
Hit you on de back-bone, you sound like a dollar-ah!
Cold frosty mornin', nigger bery good-ah;
Wid de axe on he shoulder, he go to cut de wood-ah!
Dingee I otten dotten, balli' otten dotten,
Dingee I otten, *who dar*?

The intelligent reader, conversant with Howitt's "Student Life in Germany," cannot have failed to note the close similarity of style between the foregoing and some of the student-songs, translations of which are therein given. The question arises, Who was the imitator? Surely not the negro: he knows not that there is in existence such a being as a German student. But the students know the whole history of the negroes, and doubtless are acquainted with their world-renowned songs. The inference is irresistible: the student is the imitator of the negro, just in the same way that he is the imitator of Homer, and Anacreon, and Sappho. The student is a man of discernment, able to recognize true genius, and not ashamed to emulate it, however lowly the circumstances in which it may be found. He remembers that Homer was a blind, wandering beggar, and knowing that simplicity and adversity are favorable to the growth of true poetry, he is not surprised to find it flourishing in perfection among the American negroes. Or, say that the student is *not* an imitator of the negro: then we have a case which goes to establish still more firmly the well-known truth that, human nature being the same every where, men of genius, living thousands of miles apart, and holding no communication with each other, often arrive at the same results!

Proofs of the genius of our American poets crowd upon us in tumultuous array from all quarters. A few of them only are before the reader, but enough, it is hoped, establish their claim beyond a doubt. Now let justice be done! Render to Caesar, and Pompey, and Scipio, and Sambo, the just honor which has been so long unjustly withheld; and render to America the meed of praise which has been so pertinaciously denied to her. Sambo claims honor for the fact that he *is* a true poet: America asks praise for bringing him up, with infinite pains, in the only way in which a true poet should go; which fact was demonstrated in the beginning of this article. Acknowledge, then, ye British critics! your sins of omission and commission; eat your own slanderous words, and proclaim the now undeniable truth, or else be branded as false prophets, and "for ever after hold your peace!"

A wise man has said, "Let me have the making of the songs of a people, and I care not who makes their laws." The popular song-maker sways the souls of men; the legislator rules only their bodies. The song-maker reigns through love and spiritual affinity; the legislator by brute force. Apply this principle to the American people. Who are our true rulers? The negro poets to be sure! Do they not set the fashion, and give laws to the public taste? Let one of them, in the swamps of Carolina, compose a new song, and it no sooner reaches the ear of a white *amateur*, than it is written down, amended, (that is, almost spoilt), printed, and then put upon a course of rapid dissemination, to cease only with the utmost bounds of Anglo-Saxondom, perhaps of the world. Meanwhile, the poor author digs away with his hoe, utterly ignorant of his greatness! "Blessed are they who do good, and are forgotten!" says dear Miss Bremer. Then blessed indeed are our national melodists! "True greatness is always modest," says some one else. How great then are our retiring Samboes! How shrinkingly they remain secluded, and allow sooty-faced white men to gather all the honors and emoluments! The works of great men are always imitated. Even those miserable counterfeits, "Lucy Long," and "Old Dan Tucker," have secured a large share of favor, on the supposition that they were genuine negro songs. With the music, no great fault can be found; that may be pure negro, though some people declare it to be Italian. Be that as it may, the words are far beneath the genius of our American poets: this any student, well-versed in negro lore, can perceive at a glance.

BRYANT, LONGFELLOW, HALLECK, WHITTIER, do you ardently desire fame? Give heed to foreign reviewers; doubt no longer that nationality is the highest merit that poetry can posses; uneducate yourselves; consult the taste of your fair countrywomen; write no more English poems; write negro songs, and Yankee songs in negro style; take lessons in dancing of the celebrated Thomas Rice; appear upon the stage and perform your own operas; do this, and not only will fortune and fame be yours, but you will thus vindicate yourselves and your country from the foul imputation under which both now rest! With *your* names on the list with CROW and COON, who *then* will dare to say that America has no National Poets?

1855

Negro Minstrelsy, Ancient and Modern

by Y. S. Nathanson

Putnam's Monthly, V (New York, January 1855), 72–79.

Nathanson was one of the earliest writers to distinguish intelligently between Negro song and the songs the minstrels sang. He presented several interesting secular songs (something which few of the later collectors would do), and he suffered from none of the offensive urbanity that characterizes so many of the authors who focused on minstrelsy. We can, therefore, excuse some of his soaring rhetorical excursions—though perhaps he goes a bit too far when he asks that we imagine "Hynd Horn" translated as a plantation song, and the digressions concerning poor Quash are somewhat gooey. Once we wade through the superfluous superlatives we realize that he was neither unintelligent nor unobservant: he appreciated the inadequacy of songs published without music, he noted the need for field collecting, he distinguished among several genres of Negro song, he damned epigonous misstrels and praised folksingers. A rather remarkable article.

For us, Nathanson's discussion raises what is probably the single most important question about nineteenth-century Negro song: what originated with the Negro and what was adapted from white sources? Academic warfare has raged over the religious songs and their sources, but only because so little secular material was collected. Was Dan Emmet lying when he claimed authorship of "Old Dan Tucker," or was Nathanson completely wrong when he proclaimed it authentic? We'll never know. Many minstrels claimed their material was still hot from the cottonfield; others said theirs was still wet from the inkwell. One suspects some dissembling on both sides. Observers like Nathanson couldn't have been completely wrong; some Negro material must have reached the stage. But most of the traffic seems to have been in the other direction—many demonstrably minstrel stanzas have been collected among the folk. Nathanson's description of the excitement that greeted the publication of a new song is paralleled in our time only by the release of a new single by the Beatles. It is not difficult to understand how the false had so great an influence upon the real.

"Quashie," Roger D. Abrahams told me recently, "is the British affectionate name for the Negro male. It comes from the naming procedure brought over from Africa, in which there were two sets of seven names, one male, one female, and a child might be named because of the day of the week on which he was born. Quashie was the male name for Monday. Because it carried certain qualities with the day, much as in 'Monday's child is fair of face,' the names eventually became synonymous with these (or other) qualities."

It is now some eighteen or twenty years since an enterprising Yankee, actuated, it is but charitable to suppose, by the purest love of musical art, by the enthusiasm of a discoverer, or by a proper and praiseworthy desire for posthumous fame, produced upon the boards of one of our metropolitan theatres, a musical sketch entitled "Jim Crow." Beyond the simple fact of its production by the estimable gentleman above referred to, the origin of this ancient and peculiar melody is beyond the reach of modern antiquarian lore. Whether it was first sung upon the banks of the Alatamaha, the Alabama, or the Mississippi; or, whether it is pre-American, and a relic of heathen rites in Congo, or in that mysterious heart of Africa, which foot of civilized man has never trod, is a problem whose solution must be left to the zeal and research of some future Ethiopian Oldbuck. It is sufficient for the present disquisition to know that it appeared in the manner above stated. To those (if there can be any such) who are unacquainted with its character and general scope, it may be proper to remark that "Jim Crow" is what may be called a dramatic song, depending for its success, perhaps more than any play ever written for the stage, upon the action and mimetic powers of the performer. Its success was immediate and marked. It touched a chord in the American heart which had never before vibrated, but which now responded to the skilful fingers of its first expounder, like the music of the Bermoothes to the magic wand of Prospero. The schoolboy whistled the melody on his unwilling way to his daily tasks. The ploughman checked his oxen in mid-furrow, as he reached its chorus, that the poetic exhortation to "do just so," might have the action suited to the word. Merchants and staid professional men, to whom a joke was a sin, were sometimes seen by the eyes of prying curiosity in private to unbend their dignity to that weird and wonderful posture, now, alas! seldom seen but in historic pictures, or upon the sign of a tobacconist;

and of the thoroughly impressive and extraordinary sights which the writer of this article has in his lifetime beheld, the most memorable and noteworthy was that of a young lady in a sort of inspired rapture, throwing her weight alternately upon the tendon Achillis of the one, and the toes of the other foot, her left hand resting upon her hip, her right, like that of some prophetic sybil, extended aloft, gyrating as the exigencies of the song required, and singing Jim Crow at the top of her voice. Popularity like this laughs at anathemas from the pulpit, or sneers from the press. The song which is sung in the parlor, hummed in the kitchen, and whistled in the stable, may defy oblivion. But such signal and triumphant success can produce but one result. Close upon the heels of Jim Crow, came treading, one after the other, "Zip Coon," "Long-tailed Blue," "Ole Virginny neber tire," "Settin' on a Rail," and a host of others, all of superior merit, though unequal alike in their intrinsic value, and in their participation in public approval. The golden age of negro literature had commenced. Thenceforward for several years the appearance of a new melody was an event whose importance can hardly be appreciated by the coming generation. It flew from mouth to mouth, and from hamlet to hamlet, with a rapidity which seemed miraculous. The stage-driver dropped a stave or two of it during a change of the mails at some out of the way tavern; it was treasured up and remembered, and added to from day to day, till the whole became familiar as household words. Yankee Doodle went to town with a load of garden vegetables. If upon his ears there fell the echo of a new plantation song, barter and sight-seeing were secondary objects till he had mastered both its words and music. Thereafter, and until supplanted by some equally enthusiastic and enterprising neighbor, Yankee Doodle was the hero of his native vale, of Todd Hollow. Like the troubadours and minstrels of ancient days, he found open doors and warm hearts wherever he went. Cider, pumpkin pie, and the smiles of the fair were bestowed upon him with an unsparing hand. His song was for the time to him the wand of Fortunatus.

The prevailing characteristics of the melodies which this period produced are their perfect and continual lightness, spirit, and good humor; but the true secret of their favor with the world is to be found in the fact that they are genuine and real. They are no senseless and ridiculous imitations forged in the dull brain of some northern self-styled minstrel, but the veritable tunes and words which have lightened the labor of some weary negro in the cotton fields, amused his moonlight hours as he fished, or waked the spirits of the woods as he followed in the track of the wary racoon. It is as impossible to counterfeit, or successfully imitate, one of these songs as it would be for a modern poet to produce a border ballad like Chevy Chase or Lord Jamie Douglas. It is not alone the patient and laborious student of negro minstrelsy that can detect the ring of the false metal. The shameless imitations carry their imposture upon their face. Walpole, with all his credulity, would never have been deceived, had Chatterton turned his attention to manufacturing plantation songs.

The allusion to ancient English and Scottish ballads cannot fail to bring to the mind of the poetical scholar, the striking similarity that exists between many of the "specimens" of Percy, Ritson and others, and the most approved poetry of the African school. In the terseness and fitness of the language, the oft repeated idiomatic expressions, the occasional looseness and negligence in respect to rhyme, the carelessness and license in the metre, and, above all, in the incoherence of the constantly recurring refrain; the lover of negro minstrelsy is continually reminded of the old, plain songs which Shakespeare loved, and "the spinsters and the knitters in the sun" did use to chant. I quote almost at random from Motherwell:

Oh! I never saw my love before
With a hey lilelu and a how lo lan;
Till I saw her through an auger bore,
And the birk and the brume blooms bonnie.

And she gave to me a gay gold ring,
With a hey lilelu and a how lo lan;
With three shining diamonds set therein,
And the birk and the brume blooms bonnie.

Let the words peculiarly Scottish in Hynd Horn, the ballad from which the above is taken, or in almost any other ancient ballad, be literally translated into the African dialect, and we have at once a plantation song. The birk and the brume may be more alliterative, but they are certainly not more poetic trees than the gum and the persimmon. In further illustration of this subject I cannot forbear quoting a portion of a banjo song from a volume now lying before me. Its genuineness, no one at all familiar with negro literature will presume to question, while its intrinsic worth and excellence will be perceived by the most indifferent or prejudiced observer. It is hardly possible to peruse it without thinking of Gil Maurice or Syr Charles Bawdin. Not inferior to the former in its simplicity and truthfulness, it is far above the feeble imitation of Chatterton in dramatic effect and artistic construction:

Oh, my boys I'm bound to tell you;
Oh! Oh!

Listen awhile, and I will tell you;
Oh! Oh!
I'll tell you little 'bout Uncle Gabriel;
Oh, boys, I've just begun.
Hard times in old Virginny.

Oh, don't you know old Uncle Gabriel?
Oh! Oh!
Oh, he was a darkey General,
Oh! Oh!
He was the chief of the insurgents,
Way down in Southampton.
Hard times in old Virginny.

It was a little boy betrayed him,
Oh! Oh!
A little boy by the name of Daniel
Oh! Oh!
Betrayed him at the Norfolk landing;
Oh, boys I'm getting done.
Hard times in old Virginny.

Says he, How d'ye do, my Uncle Gabriel?
Oh! Oh!
I am not your Uncle Gabriel,
Oh! Oh!
My name it is Jim McCullen;
Some they calls me Archy Mullin.
Hard times in old Virginny.

. . . .

They took him down to the gallows,
Oh! Oh!
They drove him down with four grey horses,
Oh! Oh!
Brice's Ben, he drove the wagon,
Oh, boys, I am most done.
Hard times in old Virginny.

And there they hung him, and they swung him,
Oh! Oh!
And they swung him and they hung him,
Oh! Oh!
And that was the last of the darkey General;
Oh, boys I'm just done.
Hard times in old Virginny.

Those of us who have for so many years been looking anxiously forward to the advent of the coming poet who is to take away from

America the sin and the shame of never having produced an epic, or a lyric, commensurate with Niagara and the Rocky Mountains, will do well to get up a subscription and buy the author of this song, if his owner can be persuaded to part with him. His noble, poetic nature must chafe in the cotton field like Pegasus in harness. The specimen above given, is simple, grand, and expressive. The picture it presents to the imagination is natural and life-like. The stream of song runs in a straight channel, and conducts us swiftly and directly to the catastrophe. There is no turning aside for flowery metaphors, or forcible expressions—no straining for effect—no lugubrious whining over the hero's downfall—no moralizing his unhappy fate. Even the jingle of rhyme is wanting. And yet, for severe beauty, perfect dramatic structure, and succinct impressive narration, it would be difficult in the whole range of ancient and modern ballad poetry, to find a worthy rival to "Uncle Gabriel."

The lightness and prevailing good humor of the negro songs, have been before remarked upon. A true southern melody is seldom sentimental, and never melancholy. And this results directly from the character and habits of the colored race. No hardships or troubles can destroy, or even check their happiness and levity. As I pen these words, the grinning image of the boy Quash rises up before me like a phantom. Light-hearted, witty, and gay, he was the very type of his race. His jests, his laughter, and his songs linger with me yet, though many a long year has passed since I gazed upon his shining face. It is but fitting that I should embalm his memory in these pages. Watching one day the embarkation of a few bales of cotton, I noticed Quash in the shadow of the steamboat as she lay alongside the dock. A foolish whim induced me to say, "Quash, what is the name of that boat?" Quash stepped deliberately up to the side of the boat, gazed knowingly at the large black letters on the wheel-house, shaded his eyes with his hand, and looked again, dropped his head between his shoulders, and peered earnestly into the unknown characters, stepped a few paces back, and went through the same manoeuvres, and at last turned to me with an arch leer upon his face; "I 'clar, Maussa," replied he, "I'se so near-sighted, dis mornin', I can't 'stinguish de letters."

Reading Othello one warm and quiet afternoon, in the shade of a spreading fig-tree, I became suddenly aware of the bright eyes of Quash, which were turned with a curious gaze upon me and my book, as if he were wondering at that strange and awful science, which discloses to us the thoughts and feelings of the dead. "Quash," said I, wishing to get, from a mind totally unbiased by the conflicting opinions of critics, a "first impression" upon a disputed passage, "which reading do you prefer, 'Put out the light, and then—Put out the light,' or, 'Put out the light, and then—put out *the* light'?" Quash scratched his woolly head, and putting on that same indescribable leer again, solved the difficulty at once. "I tink, Maussa," replied he, "I should make um blow de light out de fuss time." If the student of Shakespeare ponders as long and as deeply upon this answer as I did, the covert satire and the Aesopian wisdom which it displays will not be lost upon him. Alexander's solution of the Gordian knot was not more witty or more wise. But that rascal Quash is at his old trick, again, I find, of causing me to neglect my business. Let us return.

In or about the year 1841, a descriptive ballad, entitled "Ole Dan Tucker," first made its appearance, and speedily acquired a renown and popularity hardly excelled, even by that of "Jim Crow." This may be partly attributable to the fact that less histrionic talent is required to give it a fitting interpretation, and partly to its intrinsic worth. In some respects Ole Dan Tucker may be regarded as the best of what I have denominated, the ancient negro ballads. The melody* was far superior to anything that had preceded it. In its vivacity and liveliness, the music occasionally reminds us of some of Donizetti's happiest efforts, while its simplicity and quaintness at times breathe of Auber. The words, too, came more clearly home to the heart of the American people, than those of its predecessors. The song, it is needless to say, consists of a series of vivid pictures, disconnected in themselves, varying as rapidly as the changes in a kaleidoscope, and yet presenting to us the character of the hero, as a most artistic whole. The most searching test of popularity can be applied to "Ole Dan Tucker" with perfect confidence. It has been sung, perhaps, oftener than any melody ever written.

I have said that this was in some aspects the best of these songs. It was the last. With that ballad African minstrelsy may be said to have culminated. From that period its decline and fall was rapid and saddening. Hardly a song has been produced since that time which does not present the most glaring marks of barefaced and impudent imposition. The zealous student of this species of literature, as he wanders amongst the decaying ruins of its former grandeur, may well sigh at the rank and mildewed vegetation which is fast overspreading those noble relics of antiquity. If a buttress or a cornice of beauty meets his eye, he finds it but a portion of the old edifice degraded to a new position. If a gleam of the former light

* I have hitherto given to the word *melody* its technical signification of *a negroic song*. Of course, here, it has the ordinary meaning.

occasionally sparkles in his path, it is but the phosphoric glimmer which beams from loathsome and decaying putrescence. Vile parodies, sentimental love songs, dirges for dead wenches who are generally sleeping under the willow, on the bank of some stream, and melancholy reminiscences of negroic childhood fill the places once allotted to the grand old ballads of former days. From the volume before mentioned, I have not been able, after a most critical examination, to select more than ten which bear any trace of the cotton-field afflatus, and these ten, with only one exception, have been so patched and dressed up for drawing-room inspection, that they look like a bumpkin who has suddenly come into possession of a fortune. They have lost their country grace without acquiring a city polish. This inundation of trash has swept away in its might all the ancient landmarks of song. It is mortifying to be obliged to confess that I have searched unsuccessfully from Appleton's to the book stand in the rear of the post-office, for a copy of the original Jim Crow. The names, even, have lost their marked significance. The questionable taste which has given birth to appellations like Fanny Fern, Lotty Lee, Minnie Myrtle, and their long retinue of vegetable alliterations, has crept into this department of poetry and exhibits itself in such Africo-romantic fancies as Rosa Lee, Lilly Dale, Flora May, Nelly Bell or Etty Way.* Poetasters who never saw an alligator, or smelt the magnolia blossom in their lives, sit coolly down to write an African ditty as a pleasant after-dinner pastime, or a daily task; and, as a natural consequence of this reprehensible assumption, we find the banana growing wild in Tennessee, South Carolina slaves gorging themselves with pumpkin pie, a deceased negress buried upon the Lawrence river in the midst of a furious snow, and a Kentucky sugar mill in full blast in the month of June.

But ludicrous anachronisms, and unpardonable ignorance of to-

* Rosa Lee, if such a personage had ever existed, would have been known as "Massa Lee's Rosa." The prevailing ignorance at the North on the subject of negro names is remarkable and amusing. They seldom have pretty or common appellations, as they impose on their owners the office—on some plantations no sinecure—of dispensing the nomenclature; and as the gentlemen are naturally unwilling to confer upon a slave name borne by some member of the family or some friend. The fruitfulness of the women on the place of a planter whom I once visited, had on one occasion exhausted his vocabulary. "Please, Massa," said a hand to him one morning before he was out of bed, "Clementine sent me to ask you for a name. She had a little boy, last night." "Call him Last Night," said my friend, lazily catching at the last words; and "Last Night" he is, and will remain until the shadow of the last night of all shall gather round him. He blacked my boots, and it struck me as a curious anomaly to rise in the morning, and call for Last Night. It seemed as if, like the last poet out, I was "summoning before me the dark past."

pography, are not the worst evils of which we have to complain. Instead of the lyrics which once stirred the heart of the nation, our wives and children are daily and nightly compelled to listen to some such horrible parody as this—

> In a lone cypress swamp, where the *wild-roaring* bullfrog,
> The echoes *awake* with his deep thrilling tones—
> Old Pompey lies there, and the plantation watchdog
> A requiem howls o'er his deep sunken bones.

or sentimental trash like this—

> Etty was so gentle, kind, and good to all,
> She played the old banjo which hung upon de wall;
> Etty's voice was low and sweet, like de little bird;
> Them soft and gentle tones dat I've so often heard.

or this—

> Oh! I ne'er can lub anudder
> So fond, so true, again;
> I'm thine, and thine forebber,
> My charming Kate Loraine.

They are fortunate if they get to bed without being wearied and disgusted with some crude burlesque on a popular opera, served up with vulgar caricatures of the style and manner of well-known artists; and commended to popular favor by the vilest puns, of which "Lend her de Sham-money," or "Lucy did lam a Moor," are not exaggerated specimens. Now, all this may serve to make the unskilful laugh, but it cannot fail to make the judicious grieve. It is from the purpose of negroic minstrelsy, whose end at the first was, and now ought to be, to present to the lovers of original poetry and music, a class of songs peculiar, genuine, and unadulterated. A thoughtful, reflective man, can hardly leave one of the temples devoted to such barbaric sacrifices, without reasonable and just despondency and alarm. The decay of Athens and Rome was as marked and as melancholy in their literature as in their government.* The poet, the orator, and the statesman went down hand in hand into the shadowy valley, and disappeared together in the clouds of ignorance and superstition that veil for ever the Dark Ages. Is it treasonable to hint, for the warning of American minstrels and politicians, that there is something more than a striking coincidence in this simultaneous decline; and that the present diseased taste in popular poetry, may be but the first faint symptoms of another dark period, in which America

* Hallam's Middle Ages, Chapter ix, Part 1.

shall be hidden from the gaze of the world; never, perhaps, to emerge to her pristine dignity and splendor? I am no alarmist, and yet it seems to me that, in these views, the patriot may find matter for deep and serious consideration.

A proper diagnosis of the disease, however, is of no effect, unless a remedy is applied. Fortunately, in this case, we are not left without hope. The mine from which Jim Crow and Ole Dan Tucker were dug, is not yet exhausted, and a resort to it will be alike easy and successful. Why need we groan and grumble under the inflictions of ignorant and self-conceited song-writers, when every cotton-field teems with melody, and every slave hut, throughout the Southern country, has its little list of genuine ballads, which only need to be known, in order to be received to the heart of a nation. We talk with vague regret and sentimental longings, of the forgotten strains of Tasso, once chanted so commonly by the shrill-voiced gondoliers of Venice. Poets have mused dejectedly over the songless boatmen, travellers have feelingly bewailed the silence and desolation of those once gay canals; romanticists and serenaders are gradually ceasing to adjure us to "list to the voice of the gay gondolier." That malice which delights to slander the unresisting dead, has begun to deny both the gaiety of the gondolier, and the purity of his voice. He shares the fate of Memnon. Ever since the hush of those mysterious sounds which were wont to greet the dawn, there have not been wanting travelled Gradgrinds to assure us that the song from his lips was a humbug and a sham; and to degrade that majestic statue into a vulgar shoemaker with a musical lapstone, upon which the morning hymn was hammered by his knavish priests. So we are asked to believe that the voice of the gondolier was harsh and unmusical, and that "Tasso's echoes," chanted alternately, were such polite and complimentary remarks as may be heard to this day among the drivers on the Erie Canal. But as I seat myself in imagination, on this calm and moonlight night, by a certain wayside in the South, I leave these discussions to the prosy antiquary, and care not for the songs of Venice, or the music of Memnon. Up from the Sound comes a gentle south wind, rippling the water, and fanning my whiskers; the shore surge whispers low at my feet; afar in the distance I hear the hum of the plantation. The tumultuous harmony of the stock, mingled and blending with the faint shouts and cries of the "people," and the nameless and varied sounds of insect life lull my senses like the gentle susurrus of Tityrus. And now, faintly heard far over the water, I distinguish the soft thump of oars in the rowlock of an approaching boat. I listen with attentive ears—for I know by experience the gratification in store for me—and soon catch the distant tones of the human voice—and more faintly heard, and now entirely lost. A few minutes pass, and the breeze once more wafts to me the swelling notes of the chorus half buried in the measured cadence of the oars. The wind dies away, and my straining ears again hear nothing but the measured beat of the rowers, and the plashing of the restless sea. But now, anew, I hear the sound of those manly negro voices swelling up upon the evening gale. Nearer and nearer comes the boat, higher and higher rises the melody, till it overpowers and subdues the noise of the oars, which in their turn become subservient to the song, and mark its time with harmonious beating. And now the boat is so near, that every word and every tone comes to my ear, over the water, with perfect distinctness, and I recognize the grand old triumphal chorus of the stirring patriotic melody of "Gen'el Jackson":

Gen'el Jackson, mighty man—
   Whaw, my kingdom, fire away;
He fight on sea, and he fight on land,
   Whaw, my kingdom, fire away.

Gen'el Jackson gain de day—
   Whaw, my kingdom, fire away,
He gain de day in Floraday,
   Whaw, my kingdom, fire away.

Gen'el Jackson fine de trail,
   Whaw, my kingdom, fire away,
He full um fote wid cotton bale,
   Whaw, my kingdom, fire away.

But the boat touches the beach; the negroes with a wild cry quit their singing, tumble out into the shallow water, drag their dug-out up high and dry upon the sand, and I am left once more with the evening breeze and the quieter harmony of nature.

The song, a part of which I have just quoted, is fresh from the sable mint in which it was coined. Its originality and genuineness every one familiar with plantation life will at once perceive; while some Georgians may even be able to point to the very river on which the dusky troubadours still chant it. I am well aware that in depriving the words of their appropriate music, I rob it of much of its attractiveness, and still it is no bad sample of what may be called the Historic Plantation Ballad. The particular naval battle in which Old Hickory was engaged, I have not been able to discover; but the allusion to the bales of cotton in the third stanza may not be without its effect in settling one of the vexed questions relating to the defence of New Orleans; and it adds another to the many examples of the superiority of oral tradition over contemporaneous written history.

It is not alone, however, on the water that those quaint songs are produced. The annual corn-shucking season has its own peculiar class of songs, never heard but on that festival; their rhythmical structure or caesural pauses not being adapted to the measured cadence of the oars. Standing at a little distance from the corn heap, on some dark and quiet night, watching the sable forms of the gang, illuminated at intervals by the flashes of the lightwood knot, and listening to the wild high notes of their harvest songs, it is easy to imagine ourselves unseen spectators of some secret aboriginal rite or savage festival. Snatches of one or two songs which on such occasions I have heard, recur to me. Could I in the following specimen give you any idea of the wild grandeur and stirring music of the refrain, I should need no apology for presenting it to my readers.

De ladies in de parlor,
   Hey, come a rollin' down—
A drinking tea and coffee;
   Good morning, ladies all.

De gemmen in de kitchen,
   Hey come a rollin' down—
A drinking brandy toddy;
   Good morning, ladies all.

I place the above in a class to which I have given the name of descriptive songs. By this I do not mean to be understood as hinting that it is an accurate description of a "whitefolks," party. On the contrary, it probably originated in the tipsy brain of its dusky author; or, perhaps, in a moment of discontent may have been composed as an exaggerated satire. The allusion to the kitchen, as the place where the gentlemen are engaged in their pleasing and congenial occupation, goes to show that the minstrel had in his view a colored party, which I am inclined to think was in fact the case. But at this stage of our critical knowledge on the subject of negro literature, such speculations are alike tedious and unprofitable.

The comic ballads of the South, form a large and highly interesting class of songs, more especially as they are of a sort most readily transplanted, and most grateful to the public taste. Apart from their fun, however, they lack the merit which distinguishes many other kinds of African composition. The negro is humorous rather than witty, and his comic songs consist of ludicrous images, instead of witty conceits. I do not remember, in the whole course of my investigations, to have met with anything like a pun in a genuine plantation melody. The following shucking song has nothing to recommend it to public attention, save the questionable rhyme to "supper." The lovers of "Ole Dan Tucker" will be pleased and interested with a coincidence in which there cannot be the slightest ground for a suspicion of plagiarism:

Cow bog on middle e' island—
  Ho! meleety, ho!
Cow bog on middle e' island—
  Ho! meleety, ho!

Missis eat de green persimmon,
  Ho! meleety, ho! [*Repeat.*]

Mouf all drawd up in a pucker,
  Ho! meleety, ho! [*Repeat.*]

Staid so till she went to supper,
  Ho! meleety, ho! [*Repeat.*]

The main obstacle which the enthusiastic collector of these songs will have to contend against, will be the difficulty of thoroughly comprehending the negro dialect. So peculiar is it, that those even who have been familiar with it from their infancy, are often times at a loss to interpret such passages as the chorus in the last specimen. No assistance can be expected in such matters from the negroes, who, when called upon to repeat slowly and distinctly a line which they have just sung, will declare with the utmost gravity and solemnity that they have utterly forgotten it. I used to think that they were unwilling to show to the world the richest treasures of their literature; but subsequent investigations induced me to believe their assertion, and to conclude that their intellects could only retain the words when assisted by the music. An intelligent friend to whom I applied, suggested, though not without doubt, that the line in question was "Oh! my lady, oh!" And the fact that the ballad is principally devoted to the misfortune of the "mistress," gives some countenance to this interpretation. With the line "He full um fote wid cotton bale," in the ballad of Gene'l Jackson, I had an amount of trouble which will hardly be appreciated by those who see the line in print. I suppose it is hardly necessary to observe that "full um fote" means "filled" *i.e.*, constructed "his fort."

Autobiographic ballads hold a prominent position among Southern melodies; but as they are usually sung exclusively by the authors, and are regarded in a measure as private property, I do not feel at liberty to transfer any specimens to these pages; more especially as at this moment I find it impossible to bring any to my recollection. One melancholy chorus, "The long summer's day," I still remember. Its perpetually recurring sound never failed to have a singularly saddening and depressing effect upon me, whenever I heard it.

In speaking of this kind of literature the improvisations of the negroes must not be forgotten, but as they are usually but a running commentary on matters passing under the immediate notice of the minstrel, they possess but a local and transitory interest, and a single stanza taken at random will suffice. The reader will notice the chorus, which was a favorite one with the improvisator, and has served to string many thousand lines together:

> Ole Maus William, he gone to legislatur;
> Ah! chogaloga, chogaloga, chogalog.
> Young Maus John, he done come home from college,
> Ah! chogaloga, chogaloga, chagolog.

Those who are familiar with Southern life, and especially those who have participated in its hunting delights, will perhaps understand, without any explanation, that the foregoing refrain is intended to be an imitation of the gobble of the wild turkey. I have performed many orthographical experiments, in order to represent the sound more nearly on paper, but without success, and I am aware that no words can express the rich, unctuous, guttural flow of the line, when uttered in perfect time by a full gang at their corn-shucking task. All approximation to it, however, may be made by pronouncing the words rapidly in a deep tone, and at the same time violently agitating the body in a perpendicular direction. Having on one or two occasions essayed this mode with considerable satisfaction to myself, and no little commendation from a few privileged spectators, I am enabled to make this assertion with some confidence; but, as the movement is slightly fatiguing, and totally devoid of grace, I do not wish to be understood as recommending it either to invalids or ladies. It is, however, the only feasible method of "talking turkey," that I have yet been able to discover.

I have thus attempted, as calmly and dispassionately as my own strong feelings of the importance of the subject will permit, to call the public attention to a serious and growing evil, and humbly, as becomes me, to point out some means for its removal. My task is finished, and my duty accomplished. Henceforth, the duty of my guiding or correcting the public taste in these matters will devolve upon other pens than mine. I have endeavored to discharge my obligations to society fearlessly and sincerely. For this courage and sincerity alone I desire credit. If the considerations which I have presented shall have the effect of awakening public attention to the subject, I shall be sufficiently rewarded; if not, the consciousness of duty performed will sustain me. It is earnestly to be desired that collections of genuine plantation songs may be made. The grateful incense of posterity would embalm the memory of him who should hand down to them authentic ballads, which another generation may sweep from the face of the earth forever. There are men whose birth or long residence in the South, and whose knowledge of the negro dialect, and whose taste and accomplishments in polite literature, seem to have especially fitted them for this service. For the few and imperfect specimens which I have given above, I have been indebted to a treacherous memory of a few months' sojourn in Georgia some six or seven years ago when I had no reason to suppose that I should ever feel called upon to pen this article. Could I have foreseen its necessity, the collection would have been greatly larger and more perfect. But enough has been presented to show how much may be effected by a zealous scholar under more advantageous circumstances. Upon a rough, calculation, made with no statistics to refer to, I have concluded that there are, at least, thirty thousand slave plantations in the United States. Is it unreasonable to suppose that, on each of these plantations, one song may be found of undisputed genuineness and excellence? It will be a proud day for America when these thirty thousand songs are collected into several volumes, handsomely bound in Turkey morocco, and superbly embellished. Then negro minstrelsy will take its proper place in literature; then Ethiopian Serenaders, and Congo Minstrels will draw crowded houses at three dollars a seat, and one dollar for a promenade ticket; and then—but long ere that time the hand that writes these lines will have mouldered and become dust—will the eye of the student and antiquary linger reverently and delightedly over some time-worn manuscript as he deciphers the title "Jim Crow," or "Uncle Gabriel"?

1856

Songs of the Blacks

(Unsigned article)

Dwight's Journal of Music, IX:7 (Boston, November 15, 1856), 51–52; reprinted XV (1859), 178–180.

Dena Epstein says: "'Evangelist' at the end [of the present article] referred, not to the author, but to the journal where it originally appeared, The Evangelist, *a religious weekly edited in New York by William Bradford, Henry M. Field, and J. G. Craighead. 'Songs of the Blacks' appeared unsigned in the issue for October 23, 1856 (Vol. 27, p. [1])."*

The article presents an almost Continental portrait of the Noble Savage: "Inferior to the white race in reason and intellect, they have more imagination, more lively feelings and a more expressive manner. In this way they resemble the southern nations of Europe." The sentence might be paraphrased from De l'Allemagne. *It is quite in line with Abraham's observations on the similarities between the European and American stereotypes of the "dark races" (see Preface to "Uncle Sam's Peculiarities"). More surprising than the portrait of the artistic slaves is the Thoreauvian image of the joyless whites, working out lives of grim labor in quiet gloom. Most important, in retrospect, is the first sentence of the sixth paragraph: "But it is in religion that the African pours out his whole voice and soul." None of the previous commentators seems to have been impressed by this, but, with a very few exceptions, it could stand as topic sentence for the collectors for the next forty years.*

The only musical population of this country are the negroes of the South. Here at the North we have teachers in great numbers, who try to graft the love of music upon the tastes of our colder race. But their success is only limited. A few good singers are produced, and some fine instrumental performers, but the thing never becomes general. Music may perchance be the fashion for a winter. But it does not grow to a popular enthusiasm. It never becomes a passion or habit of the people. We are still dependent on foreigners for music. Italian singers fill our concert rooms, and German bands parade our streets.

Throughout the country the same holds true. Singing masters itinerate from village to village, giving instruction in the tuneful art, but the most they can muster is a score or two of men and maidens to sing in church on Sunday. Brother Jonathan is awkward at the business, and sings only on set occasions. Let him be enrolled in the ranks of the choir, and placed in the front of the gallery, and he will stand up like a grenadier, and roll out lustily the strains of a psalm. But all his singing is done in public. He makes little music at home, or at most only on the Sabbath day. During the week his melodies are unheard. He does not go to his labor singing to himself along the road. No song of home or country, of love or war, escapes his lips as he works in his shop or follows the plough. Our people work in silence, like convicts in a Penitentiary. They go to their tasks, not with a free and joyous spirit that bursts into song, but with a stern, resolute, determined air, as if they had a battle to fight, or great difficulties to overcome.

Even the gentler sex, who ought to have most of poetry and music, seem strangely indifferent to it. Young ladies who have spent years in learning to play on the piano, and sing Italian airs, drop both as soon as they are married. Enter their houses a few months later, and they tell you that they are out of practice; they have forgotten their music, their pianos are unopened, and their harps are unstrung.

Compared with our taciturn race, the African nature is full of poetry and song. The Negro is a natural musician. He will learn to play on an instrument more quickly than a white man. They have magnificent voices and sing without instruction. They may not know one note from another, yet their ears catch the strains of any floating air, and they repeat it by imitation. The native melody of their voices falls without art into the channel of song. They go singing to their daily labors. The maid sings about the house, and the laborer sings in the field.

Besides their splendid organs of voice, the African nature is full of poetry. Inferior to the white race in reason and intellect, they have more imagination, more lively feelings and a more expressive manner. In this they resemble the southern nations of Europe. Their joy and grief are not pent up in the heart, but find instant expression in their eyes and voice. With their imagination they clothe in rude poetry the incidents of their lowly life, and set them to simple melodies. Thus they sing their humble loves in strains full of tenderness. We at the North hear these songs only as burlesque by our Negro Minstrels, with faces blackened with charcoal. Yet even thus all feel that they have rare sweetness and melody.

Mingled with these love songs are plaintive airs which seem to have caught a tone of sadness and pathos from the hardships and frequent separation of their slave life. They are the Songs of their Captivity, and are sung with a touching effect. No song of a concert room ever thrilled us like one of these simple African airs, heard afar off in the stillness of a summer night. Sailing down the Mississippi, the voyager on the deck of the steamer may often hear these strains, wild, sad and tender, floating from the shore.

But it is in religion that the African pours out his whole voice and soul. A child in intellect, he is a child in faith. All the revelations of the Bible have to him a startling vividness, and he will sing of the judgment and the resurrection with a terror or a triumph which cannot be concealed. In religion he finds also an element of freedom which he does not find in his hard life, and in these wild bursts of melody he seems to be giving utterance to that exultant liberty of soul which no chains can bind, and no oppression subdue. As hundreds assemble at a camp meeting in the woods, and join in the chorus of such a hymn as

When I can read my title clear,
To mansions in the skies,

the unimpassioned hearer is almost lifted from his feet by the volume and majesty of the sound.

No voices of well trained choir in church or cathedral, no pealing organ, nor mighty anthem, ever moved us like these voices of a multitude going up to God under the open canopy of heaven. Blessed power of music! that can raise the poor and despised above their care and poverty. It is a beautiful gift of God to this oppressed race to lighten their sorrows in the house of their bondage.

Might not our countrymen all learn a lesson from these simple children of Africa? We are a silent and reserved people. Foreigners think us taciturn and gloomy. So we are, compared with the European nations. The Germans sing along the banks of the Rhine. The Swiss shepherd sings on the highest passes of the Alps, and the peasant of Tyrol fills his valleys with strains wild as the peaks and the torrents around him. But Americans, though surrounded with everything to make a people happy, do not show outward signs of uncommon cheerfulness and content. We are an anxious, careworn race. Our brows are sad and gloomy. Songless and joyless, the laborer goes to his task. This dumb silence is ungrateful in those who have such cause for thankfulness. Americans are the most favored people on earth, and yet they are the least expressive of their joy. So that we almost deserve the severe comment of a foreigner, who on seeing the great outward prosperity, and yet the anxious look of the people, said that "in America there was less misery, *and less happiness,* than in any other country on earth."

Let us not be ashamed to learn the art of happiness from the poor bondman at the South. If slaves can pour out their hearts in melody, how ought freemen to sing! If that love of music which is inborn in them, could be inbred in us, it would do much to lighten the anxiety and care which brood on every face and weigh on every heart. The spirit of music would beguile the toilsome hours, and make us cheerful and happy in our labor.

Nor would this light and joyous heart make us too gay, and so lead to folly and frivolity. On the contrary, it would prove a friend to virtue and purity. The sour and morose spirit, when it recoils from its oppressive gloom, is apt to plunge into the worst excesses. The absence of a cheerful buoyancy is one of the causes which drive men into vice and sin. If every family sung together at early morn, that lingering melody would render their spirits more elastic. With his children's voices in his ear, the hardworking man would go more cheerfully to his labor, and those melodies would make his spirit sunny and joyous through the day.

If common domestic joys, home, health and fireside love, can thus fill the heart with happiness, and cause it to break forth into singing; surely, when that heart is bounding with immortal hope, it may rise to the highest strains of exultation and of ecstasy.

Let those refuse to sing
  Who never knew our God,
But children of the heavenly King
  May speak their joys abroad.

Evangelist.

1861

Contraband Singing

by C. W. D.

Dwight's Journal of Music, XIX (Boston, September 7, 1861), 182.

One frequently reads that Lucy McKim's letter in Dwight's *first brought to public attention the qualities of slave songs. This may indeed have been the case, but it is not unlikely that many of her readers remembered the rather touching tableau described here.*

It is one of the most striking incidents of this war to listen to the singing of the groups of colored people in Fortress Monroe, who gather at their resorts after nightfall. Last evening, having occasion to "visit" an officer of the garrison sick in his tent, I passed around by the fortress chapel and adjacent yard, where most of the "contraband" tents are spread. There were hundreds of men of all ages scattered around. In one tent they were singing in order, one man leading, as extemporaneous chorister, while some ten or twelve others joined in the chorus. The hymn was long and plaintive, as usual, and the air was one of the sweetest minors I ever listened to. It would have touched many a heart if sung in the audiences who appreciate the simple melody of nature, fresh and warm from the heart. One verse ran thus:

Shout along, children!
Shout along, children!
  Hear the dying Lamb:
Oh! take your nets and follow me
For I died for you upon the tree!
  Shout along, children!
  Shout along, children!
    Hear the dying Lamb!

There was no confusion, no uproar, no discord—all was as tender and harmonious as the symphony of an organ.

Passing into the yard, I found a large company standing in the open air round a slow fire. One young man sat on the end of a rude seat, "with a little book in the hand." It had been much fingered, and he was stooping down towards the dim blaze of the fire, to make out the words, as he lined them for the singers. Where he had learned to read I know not, but where some of his companions *will* learn to read I *do* know. The singers were dressed in all manner of garbs and stood leaning around in all kinds of attitudes. As the reader progressed one young man threw a few fresh hoops on the fire, and then as the reading became more distinct, I caught the words:

Could I but climb on Pisgah's top
  And view the promised land,
My flesh itself would long to drop,
  At my dear Lord's command.

This living grace on earth we owe,
  To Jesus' dying love;
We would be only his below,
  And reign with him above.

At this moment the tattoo drum sounded the parade, and a distant bugle reminded me of my duty in another direction. With a word of counsel to the company, and a gentle encouragement, I withdrew.

Who shall dare say that these fellow-inheritors with us of the image of the Father and the love of the Son are fit only to be slaves?—C. W. D.—*N. Y. Com. Ad.*

1862

Negro Songs

by J[ames Miller] McKim

Dwight's Journal of Music, XIX (Boston, August 9, 1862), 148–149.

In partial contrast to "Songs of the Blacks," we are told here about songs without mirth and without joy—they express hope only. But McKim was a Pennsylvania minister, a dedicated abolitionist, and we cannot be sure he didn't have some filters obscuring his musical vision. In 1859, he had accompanied Mrs. John Brown to Harpers Ferry to pick up her husband's body; later, he was an organizer of the Port Royal Relief Society, which provided for freed slaves in 1862.

His daughter, Lucy, whose letter follows this article, was one of the editors of Slave Songs of the United States *(New York, 1867). In that volume appear variants of both songs published here—"'Poor Rosy" (p. 7), and "Many Thousands Go" (p. 48). The songs he describes are part of one of the oldest surviving genres in American tradition. In fact, most of the remarks about rowing songs and steamboat songs made by these early commentators may be applied to the worksongs found in Southern prison camps to this day.*

Mr. J. McKim, of Philadelphia, an agent of the Port Royal Relief Society, who last month visited the Sea Islands of South Carolina, makes the following remarks upon the negroes' songs:

That the present condition of these people is in favorable contrast with that under their masters is evident from their songs, which constitute a striking feature in their manifestations of character. They are a musical people. When they work in concert, as in rowing or grinding at the mill, their hands keep time to music. Their boat songs are the ones most frequently heard. The islands are made and permeated by rivers and creeks, and the boat furnishes the most common mode of locomotion.

When the negroes begin to row, they at the same time begin to sing. All their songs are in the minor key. If one chances to begin on the major, it quickly saddens and passes into the minor. Their songs are all religious, barcaroles and all. I speak without exception. So far as I heard or was told of their singing, it was all religious. None of their songs express mirth or present joy. The only joy expressed or implied is that of hope. "Rest at last" was their general burthen; "Heaven is my home"; "Have a little patience"; "God will deliver"—these and the like were the refrains of all their ballads.

There was one which on shore we heard more than any other, and which was irresistibly touching. It was a sort of ballad, known as "Poor Rosy, Poor Gal." It is almost impossible to give an idea of the effect of this or any of their songs by a mere recital or description. They are all exceedingly simple, both in sentiment and in music. Each stanza contains but a single thought, set in perhaps two or three bars of music; and yet as they sing it, in alternate recitatives and choruses, with varying inflections and dramatic effect, this simple and otherwise monotonous melody will, to a musical ear and a heart susceptible of impression, have all the charm of variety. Take, for instance, a few stanzas from the dirge of "Poor Rosy." Fancy the first line sung in the major key, and the two following changed by an easy transition, and with varying inflections, into the minor, and you will have some idea of the effect:

Poor Rosy, poor gal!
Poor–Rosy–poor–gal!
P-o-o-r R-o-s-y, p-o-o-r gal!
Heaven shall be my home.

Hard trial on my way!
Hard–trial–on–my–way!
H-a-r-d t-r-i-a-l o-n m-y w-a-y!
Heaven shall be my home.

Wonder what de people want of me,
Wonder–what–de–people–want–of–me,
W-o-n-d-e-r w-h-a-t d-e p-e-o-p-l-e w-a-n-t o-f m-e,
Heaven shall be my home.

When I talk I talk with God!
When–I–talk–I–talk–with–God!
W-h-e-n I t-a-l-k I t-a-l-k w-i-t-h G-o-d!
Heaven shall be my home.

I asked one of these blacks—one of the most intelligent I had met—where they got these songs. "Dey make em, sah." "How do they make them?" After a pause, evidently casting about for an explanation, he said, "I'll tell you; it's dis way. My master call me up and order me a short peck of corn and a hundred lash. My friends see it and is sorry for me. When dey come to de praise meeting dat night dey sing about it. Some's very good singers and know how; and dey work it in, work it in, you know; till dey get it right; and dat's de way." A very satisfactory explanation.

I said these songs were all in the minor key. This was a mistake. They have one that has a cheerful, and, as it sounded when I first heard it, a hilarious ring. It is a new one, made, as they said, "since secesh times." It runs thus:

No more driver call for me,
  No more driver call;
No more driver call for me,
  Many a thousand die!

No more peck of corn for me,
  No more peck of corn;
No more peck of corn for me,
  Many a thousand die!

No more hundred lash for me,
  No more hundred lash,
No more hundred lash for me,
  Many a thousand die!

and so on, recounting all the incidents of slave life.

When I first heard this song I was going up from Hilton Head to Beaufort in a boat rowed by a half dozen men detailed from the first regiment of South Carolina volunteers. They were in fine voice and spirits, and the echoes came back from the inlets of Ladies' and St. Helena with fine effect. As we passed along we encountered a boat load of black people rowing in the opposite direction. They were acquaintances of our oarsmen, and after the first salutation, asked what those clothes meant? Our crew were dressed in the blue blouse and pants and felt hat, which constitute the uniform of the regiment. They explained—one of them adding, in a tone of laughing triumph,

"We'se Uncle Sam's chil'n now; we'se Uncle Sam's chil'n; we're none of your fiel' hans."

The others looked envious and passed on. The fact that these people are thought worthy to be enlisted as soldiers, adds to their self-respect.

I dwell on these songs not as a matter of entertainment but of instruction. They tell the whole story of these people's life and character. There is no need after hearing them, to inquire into the history of the slave's treatment. Recitals of this kind one will hear enough of, whether he desires it or not; for these people, having now, for the first time in their lives, sympathetic listeners, pour out their hearts in narrations which nothing but flint can resist. I ought to add before leaving this subject, that their songs, like their talk, are couched in a barbarous, African sort of English, and are sometimes quite unintelligible. In the specimens I have here given I have not followed their pronunciation.

1862

Songs of the Port Royal Contrabands

by Lucy McKim

Dwight's Journal of Music, XXI (Boston, November 8, 1862), 254–255.

This brief letter was cited frequently during the nineteenth century and appears to have been extremely influential. Miss McKim crams quite a bit into a small space: she says the songs express the character and life of the race—they are wild and sad and reflect the misery of the race's lot and its faith in the future; she notes the way the songs may be adapted to various functions; she imposes political overtones on the already-rich structure of "Roll, Jordan, Roll." Her description of the irregularity of folk group-singing is excellent, and supplies a point of contrast with the polished European tradition of groups like the Fisk Jubilee Singers and their successors. With William Francis Allen and C. P. Ware, Lucy edited Slave Songs of the United States *(New York, 1867). She later married Wendell Phillips Garrison, managing editor of the* Nation *(see Preface to "Literature of the Day:* Slave Songs of the United States").

Philadelphia, Nov. 1st. 1862.

Mr. Dwight,

Sir:—In a recent number of your journal there appeared an article relating to the music of the slaves of Port Royal, taken from an address delivered by my father before the members and friends of the Port Royal Freed-men's Association of this city. The extract included the words of one of their songs, beginning "Poor Rosy, poor gal!"

My chief object in writing to you, is to say, that having accompanied my father on his tour to Port Royal, and being much struck with the songs of its people, I reduced a number of them to paper; among them, the ballad referred to. I send you herewith a copy of it, hoping it may interest you. Whether to have the others printed, is as yet, a question with me.

It is difficult to express the entire character of these negro ballads by mere musical notes and signs. The odd turns made in the throat; and that curious rhythmic effect produced by single voices chiming in at different irregular intervals, seem almost as impossible to place on score, as the singing of birds, or the tones of an Aeolian Harp. The airs, however, can be reached. They are too decided not to be easily understood, and their striking originality would catch the ear of any musician. Besides this, they are valuable as an expression of the character and life of the race which is playing such a conspicuous part in our history. The wild, sad strains tell, as the sufferers themselves never could, of crushed hopes, keen sorrow, and a dull daily misery which covered them as hopelessly as the fog from the rice-swamps. On the other hand, the words breathe a trusting faith in rest in the future—in "Canaan's fair and happy land," to which their eyes seem constantly turned.

A complaint might be made against these songs on the score of monotony. It is true there is a great deal of repetition of the music, but that is to accommodate the *leader*, who, if he be a good one, is always an improvisator. For instance, on one occasion, the name of each of our party who was present, was dexterously introduced.

As the same songs are sung at every sort of work, of course, the *tempo* is not always alike. On the water, the oars dip "Poor Rosy" to an even andante; a stout boy and girl at the hominy-mill will make the same "Poor Rosy" fly, to keep up with the whirling stone; and in the evening, after the day's work is done, "Heab'n shall-a be my home" peals up slowly and mournfully from the distant quarters. One woman,—a respectable house-servant, who had lost all but one of her twenty-two children, said to me:

"Pshaw! dont har to dese yer chil'en, misse. Dey just rattles it off,—dey dont know how for sing it. I likes 'Poor Rosy' better dan all de songs, but it cant be sung widout *a full heart and a troubled sperrit*!"

All the songs make good barcaroles. Whittier "builded better than he knew" when he wrote his "Song of the Negro Boatman." It seemed wonderfully applicable as we were being rowed across Hilton Head Harbor among United States gunboats,—the Wabash and the Vermont towering on either side. I thought the crew *must* strike up

> And massa tink it day ob doom,
> And we ob jubilee.

Perhaps the *grandest* singing we heard was at the Baptist Church on St. Helena Island, when a congregation of three hundred men and women joined in a hymn—

Roll, Jordan, roll, Jordan!
Roll, Jordan, roll!

It swelled forth like a triumphal anthem. That same hymn was sung by thousands of negroes on the 4th. of July last, when they marched in procession under the Stars and Stripes, cheering them for the first time as the "flag of *our* country." A friend writing from there, says that the chorus was indescribably grand,—"that the whole woods and world seemed joining in that rolling sound."

There is much more in this new and curious music, of which it is a temptation to write, but I must remember that it can speak for itself better than any one for it.

Very respectfully,
Lucy McKim.

1863

Under the Palmetto (excerpt)

by H. G. Spaulding

Continental Monthly, IV (New York, 1863), 188–203. (Pp. 195–200 reprinted here.)

*The part of Spaulding's article not reprinted describes some aspects of the life led by Sea Island Negroes in the early part of 1863. Too long for inclusion, but certainly worth the attention of anyone interested in the Sea Islanders, is Edward L. Pierce's "The Freedmen at Port Royal" (*Atlantic Monthly, *XII [September 1863], 291–315).*

The "shout" appears to have been one of the most vigorous African survivals among American Negroes. For extensive discussion, see Lydia Parrish, Slave Songs of the Georgia Sea Islands *(New York, 1942; reprinted Hatboro, Pa., 1965),* passim*; and Harold Courlander,* Negro Folk Music, U. S. A. *(New York, 1963), pp. 194–202.*

Spaulding's happy observation that the Negroes are learning some of the "best" songs in school might chill the folklorist's proverbial—if not anatomical—spine, for those well-meaning schoolmarms were doing their best to "do in" one of this country's most exciting musical traditions. His lament about the Negroes' donning blackface is not without current interest, for the influence of minstrelsy on tradition is still apparent. Roger D. Abrahams found "Amos 'n' Andy" not only popular but seriously imitated in a Negro neighborhood in Philadelphia as recently as 1959.

One wonders about Spaulding's comment regarding the paucity of secular songs on the Sea Islands. It does seem odd that this should be the only area where the former slaves directed all or most of their musical energy toward religious ends. Such may indeed have been the case, but many of the Negroes may have noticed that almost all the whites interested in songs were ministers or women, and there may have been some reluctance about revealing the entire repertory. His remarks about the great difference in effectiveness of Negro and white preachers suggest that the latter would have had considerable difficulty establishing a real rapport with the Negroes.

The religious condition of the South Carolina freedmen presents many peculiar and interesting features. Whether, like the negroes in the "old North State," they celebrated their new birth into freedom by services of praise and thanksgiving at the altar, I have been unable to learn; but certain it is, that the wonderful tranquillity of their sudden transition from bondage, and the good use which they have made of their liberty, are owing in great measure to their deep religious earnestness. This earnestness, it is evident, is not the result of conviction of enlightenment, so much as of the strong emotional nature of the blacks, intensified by sympathy, and kept alive to religious feeling by their frequent meetings for prayer and praise. Yet, to the careful observer, the blind and often superstitious worship of these people, which, as is now so plainly seen, was fostered by slavery, is one of the saddest results of the system. Those who are now permitted to watch over the religious progress of the freedmen, can bring new and abundant proof to the assertion of De Tocqueville, that "Christianity is a religion of *freemen*." The present opportunities for religious worship which the freedmen enjoy consist of their "praise meetings"—similar in most respects to our prayer meetings—which are held two or three times a week on the plantations, and the Sunday services at the various churches scattered about the islands. These services are usually conducted by white preachers, and are attended not only by the negroes, but also by the superintendents, teachers, and many casual visitors from the camps. At Beaufort and Hilton Head large and flourishing Sunday schools are in operation. Most of the freedmen belong either to the Baptist or Methodist denomination, and the fervor and zeal of the preachers of the latter persuasion always find a response in the excitable and impulsive nature of the blacks. It is not a little singular that, while Cochin can write concerning the freedmen in the French colonies that "the *Catholic* worship has incomparable attractions for the blacks," we find the negro in our own country everywhere attracted toward that sect of Protestants which has always been the most powerful antagonist to Romanism.

On Sunday, the 15th of March, in company with a party of superintendents and teachers, I attended a service held for the freedmen on St. Helena's Island. Our ride from the plantation took us through field and wood, till we reached the main road on which the church is situated. It is a simple, unpretending structure of brick, shaded on all sides by handsome live oaks. Near by is the small cemetery, and the drooping moss from the oaks hangs in sombre beauty over the graves. Under the trees is a group of superintendents discussing the news and the last order of General Hunter. As we ride up, a party of officers comes galloping in from camp, while from the other direction is seen approaching a venerable carryall, conveying a party of lady teachers from a distant plantation. The service has already begun, and the church is crowded with the dusky auditors, while here and there may be seen a pew filled with "white folks." The day is warm, so we can stand by the open window and take in the whole scene at a single glance. No danger to-day of any manifestations of overwrought feelings; no groans nor excited shoutings of "Amen." The preacher has taken his text from the first chapter of Genesis, and he is describing the wonders of the creation. His sermon might properly be entitled a "Disquisition upon the Universe." It is evident that his colored hearers fail to see the "beauty and mysterious order of the stellar world" which he is portraying, for most of them are already dozing, and the rest are nodding their heads as if in sleepy assent to the undoubted truth of the good man's words. He has overreached his mark, and hits neither the heads nor the hearts of his congregation. At length the discourse is ended, and all rise to join in the closing hymn, which is "deaconed off" by the minister, and responded to by the negroes in a monotonous "*yah, yah.*" They have not recovered from the soporific effect of the sermon, and, besides, can hardly be blamed for not catching the feebly uttered words. But their time is coming. No sooner is the benediction pronounced, than one of the negro elders strikes up a well known hymn, and, suddenly rousing from their stupor, the whole congregation join in singing in clear and ringing tones verse after verse of the jubilant song. Then follow other hymns and chants peculiar to the negro worship, the crude expressions of their deep emotional feeling. As we leave the church, we are convinced that the religious teachers of the newly freed blacks are sadly at fault in repeating so much the kind of preaching to which the negroes were accustomed under the old system, and in neglecting to pour into their perceptive souls both the light and warmth of the Gospel. As an officer remarked who had stood at our side listening to the services: "These people had enough of the Old Testament thrown at their heads under slavery. Now give them the glorious utterances and practical teachings of the Great Master."

At some of the meetings of the freedmen, they are addressed by negro preachers, who never fail to speak with great effect. In Alexandria, Va., I was told by the superintendent of freedmen of an old negro teacher and exhorter, the self-elected pastor of all the blacks there, going about from house to house to minister to the wants of the sick and afflicted, teaching the young, and speaking in all the meetings. "This old negro," said the superintendent, "has more influence over the blacks, and does more good among them, than all the missionaries and chaplains who have been sent here." To the same effect is the testimony of all who have listened to the colored preacher at Port Royal, and who know the great power which the chief elders of their churches possess over the rest of the negroes. A verbatim report of an exhortation given, just before the expedition to Jacksonville, Fla., to the soldiers of Colonel Higginson's 1st South Carolina Volunteers, by one of these negro preachers, would be worthy a place in "American Oratory." I remember only one striking passage, where, in his appeal to the troops to fight bravely, he urged them to seek always the post of danger, since heaven would be the immediate reward of all who should be killed in battle; for, said he, as if moved by an oracle: "What hab been, dat will be. He who is de fust man to get into de boat, and de fust to jump on shore, him, if he fall, will be de fust to get to heaben." Then, as if standing already in the midst of the fight, and with all the feelings of his nature roused against his enemies, he added: "An' when do battle comes—when you see de Kunn'l put his shoulder to de wheel, and hear de shot and shell flying all round like de rain drops, den remember dat ebery one ob dose shot is a bolt ob de Almightly God to send dem rebels to deir eberlasting damnation." Such fervent utterances are not uncommon among the negro preachers, and are well calculated to produce a powerful effect upon the susceptible natures of their hearers, "deep answering unto deep."

NEGRO "SHOUTS" AND SHOUT SONGS.

At the "praise meetings" on the plantations, one of the elders usually presides, and conducts the exercises with great solemnity. Passages of Scripture are quoted from memory, and the hymns, which constitute the principal features of the meeting, are deaconed off as at church. Sometimes the superintendent or one of the teachers attends these meetings, and is then expected to conduct the exercises and make an address. After the praise meeting is over, there usually follows the very singular and impressive performance of the "*Shout*," or religious dance of the negroes. Three or four, standing still, clapping their hands and beating time with their feet, commence singing in unison one of the peculiar shout melodies, while the others walk round in a ring, in single file, joining also in the song. Soon those in the ring leave off their singing, the others keeping it up the while with increased vigor, and strike into the shout step, observing most accurate time with the music. This step is something halfway between a shuffle and a dance, as difficult for an uninitiated person to describe as to imitate. At the end of each stanza of the song the dancers stop short with a slight stamp on the last note, and then, putting the other foot forward, proceed through the next verse. They will often dance to the same song for twenty or thirty minutes, once or twice, perhaps, varying the monotony of their movement by walking for a little while and joining in the singing. The physical exertion, which is really very great, as the dance calls into play nearly every muscle of the body, seems never to weary them in the least, and they frequently keep up a shout for hours, resting only for brief intervals between the different songs. Yet, in trying to imitate them, I was completely tired out in a very short time. The children are the best dancers, and are allowed by their parents to have a shout at any time, though, with the adults, the shout always follows a religious meeting, and none but church members are expected to join. It is to one of these shouts of the negro children that Mr. Russell alludes in his Diary when describing a visit which he paid to a plantation near Charleston in April, 1861. He speaks of the children as a set of "ragged, dirty, and shoeless urchins, who came in shyly, oftentimes running away till they were chased and captured, dressed into line with much difficulty, and, then, shuffling their flat feet, clapping their hands, and drawling out in a monotous sort of chant something about the 'River Jawdam.'" Such a sketch conveys no idea of the shout as it may be witnessed to-day on any of the plantations among the Sea Islands. You will find the children clean, and, in general, neatly dressed, coming into the room when asked by the superintendent, rendering their impressive and oftentimes pleasing melodies in a manner seldom surpassed in our schools at the North, while their "shouting" reveals a suppleness of limb and peculiar grace of motion beyond the power of our dancing masters to impart.

There are many features of the negro shout which amuse us from their strangeness; some, also, that strike the observer as wholly absurd. Yet, viewed as a religious exercise—and in this light it is always considered by the older negroes—I cannot help regarding it, in spite of many of its characteristics, as both a natural and a rational expression of devotional feeling. The negroes never indulge in it when, for any reason, they feel downhearted or sad at their meetings. The shout is a simple outburst and manifestation of religious fevor—a "rejoicing in the Lord"—making a "joyful noise unto the God of their salvation."

The words of the shout songs are a singular medley of things sacred and profane, and are the natural outgrowth of the imperfect and fragmentary knowledge of the Scriptures which the negroes have picked up. The substitution for these crude productions of appropriate hymns, would remove from the shout that which is now the chief objection to it in intelligent minds, and would make of the dance, to which the negroes are so much attached, a useful auxiliary in their religious culture. The tunes to which these songs are sung, are some of them weird and wild—"barbaric madrigals"—while others are sweet and impressive melodies. The most striking of their barbaric airs it would be impossible to write out, but many of their more common melodies are easily caught upon being heard a few times. This music of the negro shout opens a new and rich field of melody—a mine in which there is much rough quartz, but also many veins of sparkling ore.

What, for example, could be more animated, and at the same time more expressive of the thought conveyed in the verse than the following chorus?—the introduction to which is a sort of recitative or chant:

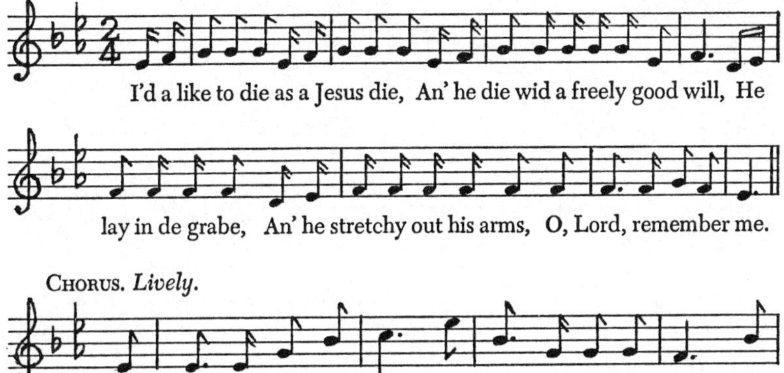

I'd a like to die as a Jesus die, An' he die wid a freely good will, He
lay in de grabe, An' he stretchy out his arms, O, Lord, remember me.
Chorus. Lively.
O, Lord, remember me, Do, Lord, remember me; Re-

member me when de year rolls round, O, Lord, remember me.

The words of the chant are evidently a very childlike expression of the wish to die with the same good will and spirit of forgiveness which were manifested in the Saviour's death.

Of a very different character is the following verse, sung to the same recitative:

O, Death he is a little man,
He goes from do' to do',

He kill some soul, an he wounded some,
An' he lef' some soul for to pray.

A most striking contrast between the recitative and chorus, is presented in the following:

RECITATIVE *(Sung to one note like a chant, with a cadence at the end)*:—

I wonder why Satan do follow me so?
Satan hab noting 't all for to do, long 'wid me.

CHORUS. Slowly and forcibly.
Hold your light, Hold your light, Hold your light on Canaan's shore.

The next song presents a greater variety in melody, as well as in the different verses, which seem to have no connection whatever with each other. The "Parson Fuller" referred to is the Rev. Dr. Fuller, of Baltimore, who owns a plantation on one of the islands:

Dar's a meetin' here to - night, Dar's a meetin' here to - night, Dar's a
meetin' here to - night, I hope to meet you dar.
1. Parson Fuller sittin' on de
2. Little children learn to
3. Let no angry word or
Tree of Life, An' he heary when Jordan roll.
fear de Lord, An' let your days be long.
spiteful boast Be heard up-on your tongue.
Roll, Jordan, roll, Jordan,
Roll, Jor-dan, roll, Roll, Jordan, roll, O roll, Jordan, roll, O my
soul will rise to heab'n above, An' heary when Jordan Roll.

The following has evidently been composed since the negroes became free, and expresses very forcibly their feelings toward "driber massa, and missus":

Done wid driber's dribin', Done wid driber's dribin,
Done wid driber's drib - in', Roll, Jordan, roll.

2. Done wid massa's hollerin',
Done wid massa's hollerin',
Done wid massa's hollerin',
Roll, Jordan, roll.

3. Done wid missus' scoldin',
Done wid missus' scoldin',
Done wid missus' scoldin',
Roll, Jordan, roll.

4. Sins so heaby dat I cannot get along,
Sins so heaby dat I cannot get along,
Sins so heaby dat I cannot get along,
Roll, Jordan, roll.

5. Cast my sins to de bottom ob de sea,
Cast my sins to de bottom ob de sea,
Cast my sins to de bottom ob de sea,
Roll, Jordan, roll.

Perhaps the best illustration of the Scriptural patchwork which characterizes many of the shout songs, is seen in the "Lonesome Valley," the music of which is very quaint and plaintive:

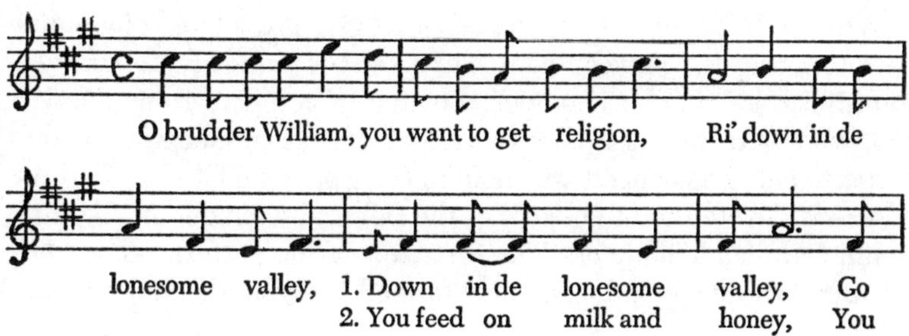
O brudder William, you want to get religion, Ri' down in de
lonesome valley, 1. Down in de lonesome valley, Go
2. You feed on milk and honey, You

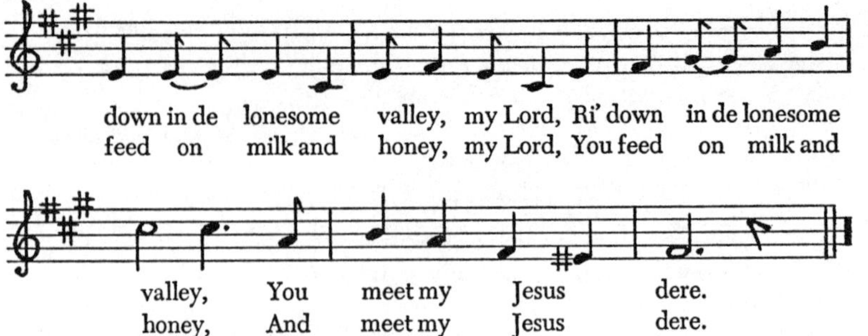
down in de lonesome valley, my Lord, Ri' down in de lonesome
feed on milk and honey, my Lord, You feed on milk and
valley, You meet my Jesus dere.
honey, And meet my Jesus dere.

The third and fourth stanzas are:

3. When Johnny brought a letter,
   When Johnny brought a letter, my Lord,
   When Johnny brought a letter,
         He meet my Jesus dere.

4. An' Mary and Marta read 'em,
   An' Mary and Marta read 'em, my Lord,
   An' Mary and Marta read 'em,
         Dey meet my Jesus dere.

The example above given will convey a good idea of the general character of the shout songs. Apart from these religious songs, there is no music among the South Carolina freedmen, except the simple airs which are sung by the boatmen, as they row on the rivers and creeks. A tinge of sadness pervades all their melodies, which bear as little resemblance to the popular Ethiopian melodies of the day as twilight to noonday. The joyous, merry strains which have been associated in the minds of many with the Southern negro, are never heard on the Sea Islands. Indeed, by most of the negroes, such songs as "Uncle Ned" and "O Susanna" are considered as highly improper. In the schools, many of the best songs which are sung in our Sunday and public schools have been introduced, and are opening new sources of pleasure to a race so musical by their very nature as are the negroes of the South.

While in Beaufort, I attended a concert given by a band of genuine "negro minstrels." The company had taken the name of the "Charleston Minstrels," and was composed mainly of refugees from Charleston, who were then servants to various officers in General Saxton's Department. The concert was held in the Episcopal Church, and the proceeds devoted to the benefit of the sick and wounded of the First South Carolina Volunteers. The first view of the performers, as they sat round the stage, a dozen finely formed and good-looking negroes caused the spectator to fancy himself in the presence of the famous band of Christy, or some other company of white Ethiopian serenaders. Soon, the opera glass revealed the amusing fact, that, although every minstrel was by nature as black as black could be, yet all the performers had given their faces a coating of burnt cork, in order that their resemblance to Yankee minstrels might be in every respect complete. There were excellent voices among the singers, and some of the players handled their instruments with surprising skill; but the presence of an audience composed entirely of white people, and including many of the highest officers in the Department, evidently caused great embarrassment to performers so unaccustomed to the stage. Not a single song which could be called comic was included in the programme; and, with the exception of a few patriotic airs, the songs were of the "Lily Dale," half-mournful sort. Between the pieces there was the customary telling of anecdotes and cracking of jokes, some of which were quite amusing, while others excited laughter from the manner in which they were told. As an imitation of our Northern minstrelsy given by a band of uneducated negro musicians, the performance was a wonderful success. Yet the general impression left upon the mind of the hearer was far from pleasing. One could not help feeling that a people, whose very natures are attuned to harmony, are capable of something better than even the most perfect imitation of those who have so grossly caricatured their race.

1865

The Negro Dialect

by Marcel [W. F. Allen]

Nation, I (New York, December 14, 1865), 744–745.

Although Lucy McKim and Charles Pickard Ware were listed as his co-editors of Slave Songs of the United States *(New York, 1867), it was W. F. Allen who wrote the long and extremely influential Introduction to the volume. That essay includes a detailed discussion of the dialect of the Sea Island Negroes (pp. xxiii–xxvi); it is considerably different from the* Nation *article and repays examination. Allen's hope that someone with a wider experience "would treat it with more fulness" was not realized until, seventy-four years later, Lorenzo D. Turner published his* Africanisms in the Gullah Dialect *(Chicago, 1949). Thanks to the later scholarship, we realize that many of the speech characteristics Allen ascribes to "Phonetic Decay" are instead African survivals. For more information regarding the song texts quoted, consult* Slave Songs of the United States, *Lydia Parrish's* Slave Songs of the Georgia Sea Islands *(New York, 1942; reprinted Hatboro, Pa., 1965), and Harold Courlander's* Negro Folk Music, U. S. A. *(New York, 1963).*

This article includes not only several interesting comments on speech patterns but also a number of excellent texts and a detailed description of the shouting procedure.

During a residence of some months upon one of the Sea Island plantations of Port Royal I gave considerable attention to the analysis of the negro dialect, and made some observations which I think possess interest and even philological value. I have hoped that some person with a wider experience than myself—for instance, Col. Higginson, who I know was interested in this subject—would treat it with more fulness than I can do. Fearing, however, that in the progress of civilization among these people these curious features will vanish, I wish to put them on record before they fade from my own memory.

Ordinarily negro-talk, such as we find in books, has very little resemblance to that of the negroes of Port Royal, who were so isolated that they seem to have formed a dialect of their own. Indeed, the different plantations have their own peculiarities, and adepts profess to be able to determine by the speech of a negro what part of an island he belongs to, or even, in some cases, his plantation. My observations were confined to a few plantations at the northern end of St. Helena Island.

With these people the process of "Phonetic Decay" appears to have gone as far, perhaps, as is possible, and with it the extremest simplification of etymology and syntax. The usual softening of *th* and *v* into *d* and *b* is observed among them; likewise a frequent interchange of *v* and *w:* as *veeds* and *vell* for *weeds* and *well;* "De wile' sinner may return" for *vilest*). This last illustrates also the habit of clipping syllables, which they do constantly: as *lee'* for *little; plänt'shun* for *plantation.* The lengthening of short vowels is illustrated in both these words—*a,* for instance, never has our short sound, but always the European sound. The following hymn illustrates these points:

Meet, O Lord, on de milk-white horse,
  An' de nineteen wile [voil] in his han',
Drop on, drop on de crown on my head,
  An' rolly in my Jesus' arm.
E'en [in] dat mornin' all day,
  When Jesus de Chris' bin born.

The same hymn, particularly the second verse,

Moon went into de poplar tree,
  An star went into blood.

(the figures evidently taken from the book of Revelations), is a fair specimen of the turn which Scriptural ideas and phraseology receive in their untutored minds. It should be observed, by the way, that the songs do not show the full extent of the debasement of the language. Being generally taken, in phrases, from Scripture, or from the hymns which they have heard sung by the whites, they retain words and grammatical forms which one rarely hears in conversation. The common speech, in its strange words and pronunciation, abbreviations, and rhythmical modulation, sounds to a stranger like a foreign language.

These strange words are, however, less numerous than one would imagine. There is *yedde* for *hear,* as in that sweetest of their songs:

O my sin is forgiben and my soul set free,
An' I yedde from heaben to-day.

There is *sh' um*, a corruption of *see 'em*, applied to all genders and both numbers. There is *huddy* (how-do?), pronounced "how-dy" by the purists among them. It is not irreverence, but affectionate devotion, that is expressed in the simple song:

In de mornin' when I rise,
Tell my Jesus huddy O,
Wash my han' in de mornin' glory, etc.

Studdy (steady) is used to denote any continued or customary action. "He studdy 'buse an' cuss me," complained one of the schoolchildren of another. This word *cuss*, by the way, is used by them with great latitude, to denote any offensive language. "He cuss me, 'git out,' " was the charge of one adult against another. "Ahvy [Abby: in this case the *b* had become *v*] do cuss me," was the serious-sounding but trifling accusation made by one little girl against her seatmate. *Both* they seldom use; generally "'all-two," or emphatically, "all-two boff togedder." *One* for alone. "Me one an' God," was the answer of an old man in Charleston when I asked him whether he escaped from his plantation. "Heaben 'nuff for me one" [*i.e.*, I suppose, "for my part"], says one of their songs. *Talk* is one of their most common words, where we should use *speak* or *mean*. "Talk me, sir?" asks a boy who is not sure whether you mean him or his comrade. "Talk lick, sir! nuffin but lick," was the answer to the question whether a particular master used to whip his slaves.

The letters *n* and *y* are often thrown in euphonically. I can only remember at this moment *n* before a long *u* as n'Europe, n'United States, no n'use; but I think it is used with other vowels. Of *y* also I can only recall one instance, which I will give presently. The most curious, however, of all their linguistic peculiarities is, I think, the following: It is well known that the negroes all through the South speak of their elders as "uncle" and "aunt"; from a feeling of politeness, I do not doubt—it seemed disrespectful to use the bare name, and from *Mr.* and *Mrs.* they were debarred. On the Sea Islands similar feeling has led to the use of *cousin* towards their equals. Abbreviating this after their fashion, they get co'n or co' (the vowel sound ŭ of *cousin*) as the common title when they spoke of one another. C' Abram, Co' Robin, Co'n Emma, C' Isaac, Co' Bob, are specimens of what one hears every day. I have heard Bro' (brother) used in the same way, but seldom; as in the song,

Bro' Bill, you ought to know my name,
My name is written in de book ob life.

I come now to the subject of grammar, upon which I might almost be entitled to repeat a very old joke, and say that there is no grammar; for there probably is no speech that has less inflection than that of these negroes. There is no distinction of case, number, tense, or voice—hardly of gender. Perhaps I am wrong in saying that there is no number, for this distinction is made in pronouns, and some of the most intelligent will, perhaps, occasionally make it in nouns. But "Sandy hat" would generally mean indifferently Sandy's hat or hats; "dem cow" is plural, "dat cow" singular; "nigger house" means the collection of negro houses, and is, I suppose, really plural. As to cases, I do not know that I ever heard a regular possessive, but they have begun to develop one of their own, which is a very curious illustration of the way inflectional forms have probably grown up in other languages. If they wish to make the fact of possession at all emphatic or distinct, they use the whole word "own." Thus, they will say "Mosey house"; but if asked whose house that is, the answer is "Mosey own." "Co' Molsy y'own," was the odd reply made by a little girl to the question whose child she was carrying; *Co'* is title; *y* euphonic.

Nearly all the pronouns exist. Perhaps *us* does not, *we* being generally in its place. *She* and *her* being rare, *him* is the usual pronoun of the third person singular, for all genders and cases. "Him lick we" was the complaint of some small children against a large girl. *Um* is still more common, as objective case, for all genders and numbers; as *Sh 'um (see 'em).*

It is too much to say that the verbs have no inflections; but it is true that these have nearly disappeared. Ask a boy where he is going, and the answer is "gwine crick for ketch crab,"—"going into the creek to catch crabs" (*for* being generally used instead of *to*, to denote purpose); ask another where the missing boy is, and the answer is the same, with *gone* instead of *gwine*. Present time is made definite by the auxiliary *do* or *da*, as in the refrains "Bell do ring," "Jericho da worry me." Past time is expressed by *done,* as in other parts of the South. The passive is rarely, if ever, indicated. "Ole man call John," is the answer when you ask who is such and such a person. "Him mix wid his own fät," was the description given of a paste made of bruised groundnuts—the oil of the nut furnishing moisture.

I have not by any means exhausted the subject, but have given the chief part of what I remember, and hope this may stimulate others to make a note of what I overlooked or have forgotten.

Many of my illustrations are taken from the songs of the colored people, and perhaps a few words upon this very interesting topic may not be out of place. The people of the Sea Islands have hardly any secular music. I heard, to be sure, one day, a verse beginning "Dog-flea da bite me"—profane enough one would say, but I think very likely it brought in the Jordan before the end. Even their boat msuic is chiefly religious; almost all the rowing tunes I recognized as having heard in the praise-meetings and "shouts." The only song that I am acquainted with which is purely a boat song, is the fine lyric:

Michael, row the boat ashore—Hallelujah,

and here I have no doubt that it is the archangel Michael that is alluded to.

For the rest, the songs may be divided into *hymns* and *shouts*; or, as they class them themselves, *sperituals* and *running sperituals*. The first class contains many sweet and touching tunes, and many which bear strongly the impress of their peculiar religious ideas. For instance, to "fin' dat ting" means to find religion; and I suppose this is referred to in the favorite song, some of the verses which are:

O where d' ye tink I fin' 'em?
I fin' 'em, Lord, in de grave-yard.
I fin' 'em in de boggy mire.

(For a verse is often only a single line, repeated with the refrain.) This last verse alludes also to their custom, when under religious excitement, of wandering through the woods and marshes, like the ancient Bacchantes. The following song, to a very beautiful tune, alludes to this still more distinctly:

I wait upon the Lord my God,
Who took away the sins of the world.
You want to be a Christian,—Go in the wilderness,
To wait upon the Lord.
Oh, come back, come back, etc.,
Oh, half-done Christian, etc.

The following will, perhaps, give as good a notion as any of the character of these hymns. It is often sung in the church in St. Helena Island:

De talles' tree in Paradise
De Christian call de tree ob life.
An' I hope dis trumpet blow me home
To de new Jerusalem.
Blow your trumpet, Gabriel,
Blow your trumpet, louder!
An' I hope, etc.

Paul an' Silas bound in jail
Sing God's praise both night and day,
    An' I hope, etc.

The greatest peculiarities are, however, found in the "shouting tunes," as, indeed, the "shout" is the most peculiar institution of these people. It is a kind of shuffling dance, accompanied by a measured movement of the arms and clapping of the hands, and a sort of ducking motion of the body at the turns of the tune, performed by a line of persons moving about in a circle. I am told that they sometimes move backward, but I do not think I ever saw this. The singing is usually done by a sort of choir of bystanders. One leading singer carries on the song, stringing verse after verse of the most absurd stuff, which he often makes up as he goes along. The others "base" him, as it is called; that is, sing the chorus or refrain. The "base" almost always overlaps the tune, striking in before the line is finished, when the singer at once stops without completing the line, taking up his part again in his time before the base is quite through. The whole is accompanied by clapping of hands. The tune is often preceded by an introduction, in chanting style, during which the "shouters" (that is, the dancers, not the singers) move quickly round in the circle, not beginning the "shout" proper until the turn in the tune. The following is a great favorite for "shouting" and is used also for rowing:

I know member, know Lord,
I know I yedde [hear] de bell da ring.
                    [*Repeated several times.*]
I want to go to meetin'—[Base] Bell da ring.
I want to go to 'ciety (lecter),
De heaven-bell a-heaven-bell,
De road so stormy (boggy),
Brudder, hain't you a member?

And so on to any extent. Every verse is repeated, and the refrain, "Bell da ring," repeated each time. The refrain in the "shouts" is usually some short phrase like the above, *e.g.*, "Hallelujah," "O Lord," "Yes, my Lord," "My army cross over," "Join the angel band." Sometimes it is a little longer, as "Turn, sinner turn O!" (the most beautiful and dramatic of all the shouts), "O Lord, de rock o' jubilee," and "Archangel open de door." Sometimes the whole tune is more elaborate, as in the following, perhaps the finest of all:

I can't stay behind my Lord,
I can't stay behind,
  There's room enough—[Base] Room enough,

Room enough in heaven for you (repeated),
I can't stay behind.
  I binny all aroun'—I binny all aroun',
  My fader call—An' I mus' go.
  O stoback member—stoback member.

"Stoback" is "shout backwards."

Most of the music of these people has a quite civilized sound, and much of it might no doubt be traced to tunes which they have heard from the whites, and transformed for their own use. They have so much native musical capacity that it is a real obstacle to their learning tunes by heart—as soon as they have one partly learned, they begin to sing it and soon change it into something quite different. At any rate, there is no doubt that their music as a whole has been influenced by their civilization, and is rather European than African in its character. It is probable, however, that the "shout" is the direct descendant of some African dance, as the Romaika is of the Pyrrhic; and I have thought that in a few tunes I observed a peculiar character that might point to an African origin. For instance, there is a strange, wild, minor "shout":

Jesus die—shall I die?
Die on de cross.
Jesus da comin',
Run for to meet him, etc.

Comparatively few of the tunes, however, are minor; some of them are even merry, and the prevailing character is that of sweetness and cheerfulness.

I append two of the most peculiar and characteristic of their "shouts":

Pray a little longer—[Base] O Lord—Yes, my Lord.
Pray, true believer.
Jericho da worry me,
Jericho—Jericho.
Went to de meetin',
Met brudder Haclers [Hercules].
Wha' d' ye tink 'e tell me?
Tell me for to turn back.
Patrol around me.
Tank God he no ketch me.

The two last lines point to the days of slavery. The other song has an incomprehensible introduction, followed by a very distinct allusion to the most prevalent form of illness—"pain in head an' feber!"

Way my brudder, better true belieb,
   Better true be long time got ober crosses;
Way my sister, better true belieb,
   An' 'e get up to heaben at las'.
My body rock 'long feber [Base] O, wid a pain in 'e head.
   I wish I bin to de kingdom,
To set along side o' my Lord.

1867

Negro Spirituals

[by Thomas Wentworth Higginson]

Atlantic Monthly, XIX (Boston, June 1867), 685–694.

Higginson's famous collection is still a useful source of texts. An intuitive idea of the validity of his collection may be obtained by comparing it with the perfectly proper and smoothed and grammatically improved lyrics that form so large a portion of collections like John W. Work's American Negro Songs and Spirituals *(New York, 1940). To be more scientific, one might compare Higginson's collection with volumes like* Slave Songs of the United States *(New York, 1867), in which we find field-collected variants of at least twenty of his thirty-seven songs (Higginson, I,* Slave Songs, *10; other parallels are II, 22–23; III, 6; IV, 45; V, 38; VI, 10–11; XII, 42; XIV, 72; XVIII, 19; XIX, 4; XXII, 12; XXIII, 44; XXIV, 14; XXV, 3; XVII, 47; XXVIII, 102; XXIX, 102; XXX, 102; XXXII, 97–98; XXXV, 48). Several appear in Newman White's* American Negro Folk-Songs *(Cambridge, Mass., 1928; reprinted Hatboro, Pa., 1965) (I, 76; V, 58; XX, 59–60; XXXVIII, 93–96; XXIX, 93–96; XXX, 93–96, etc.). Repetitions within these three collections would be considerably expanded if we were to consider the many floating verses that occur in varying contexts. "Hangman Johnny" is a well-known sea shanty found in both white and Negro tradition.*

The story of Higginson's First South Carolina Volunteers is splendidly told in his Army Life in a Black Regiment *(Boston, 1869; paperback reprint, Boston, 1962). His collection of spirituals was of considerable importance, for it was the first such collection available to a wide reading audience. He included the article in* Army Life *(as Chapter IX) and its influence extended still further. For a short sketch of Higginson's colorful and important career as minister, abolitionist, soldier, man of letters, and public servant, see John Hope Franklin's introduction to the reprint edition of* Army Life.

The war brought to some of us, besides its direct experiences, many a strange fulfilment of dreams of other days. For intance, the present writer had been a faithful student of the Scottish ballads, and had always envied Sir Walter the delight of tracing them out amid their own heather, and of writing them down piecemeal from the lips of aged crones. It was a strange enjoyment, therefore, to be suddenly brought into the midst of a kindred world of unwritten songs, as simple and indigenous as the Border Minstrelsy, more uniformly plaintive, almost always more quaint, and often as essentially poetic.

This interest was rather increased by the fact that I had for many years heard of this class of songs under the name of "Negro Spirituals," and had even heard some of them sung by friends from South Carolina. I could now gather on their own soil these strange plants, which I had before seen as in museums alone. True, the individual songs rarely coincided; there was a line here, a chorus there,—just enough to fix the class, but this was unmistakable. It was not strange that they differed, for the range seemed almost endless, and South Carolina, Georgia, and Florida seemed to have nothing but the generic character in common, until all were mingled in the united stock of camp-melodies.

Often in the starlit evening I have returned from some lonely ride by the swift river, or on the plover-haunted barrens, and, entering the camp, have silently approached some glimmering fire, round which the dusky figures moved in the rhythmical barbaric dance the negroes call a "shout," chanting, often harshly, but always in the most perfect time, some monotonous refrain. Writing down in the darkness, as I best could,—perhaps with my hand in the safe covert of my pocket,—the words of the song, I have afterwards carried it to my tent, like some captured bird or insect, and then, after examination, put it by. Or, summoning one of the men at some period of leisure,—Corporal Robert Sutton, for instance, whose iron memory held all the details of a song as if it were a ford or a forest,—I have completed the new specimen by supplying the absent parts. The music I could only retain by ear, and though the more common strains were repeated often enough to fix their impression, there were others that occurred only once or twice.

The words will be here given, as nearly as possible, in the original dialect; and if the spelling seems sometimes inconsistent, or the misspelling insufficient, it is because I could get no nearer. I wished to avoid what seems to me the only error of Lowell's "Biglow Papers" in respect to dialect,—the occasional use of an extreme misspelling, which merely confuses the eye, without taking us any closer to the peculiarity of sound.

The favorite song in camp was the following,—sung with no accompaniment but the measured clapping of hands and the clatter of many feet. It was sung perhaps twice as often as any other. This was partly due to the fact that it properly consisted of a chorus alone, with which the verses of other songs might be combined at random.

I. HOLD YOUR LIGHT

Hold your light, Brudder Robert,—
  Hold your light,
Hold your light on Canaan's shore.

What make ole Satan for follow me so?
Satan ain't got notin' for do wid me.
  Hold your light,
  Hold your light,
Hold your light on Canaan's shore.

This would be sung for half an hour at a time, perhaps, each person present being named in turn. It seemed the simplest primitive type of "spiritual." The next in popularity was almost as elementary, and, like this, named successively each one of the circle. It was, however, much more resounding and convivial in its music.

II. BOUND TO GO

Jordan River, I'm bound to go,
  Bound to go, bound to go,—
Jordan River, I'm bound to go,
  And bid 'em fare ye well.

My Brudder Robert, I'm bound to go,
  Bound to go, &c.

My Sister Lucy, I'm bound to go,
  Bound to go, &c.

Sometimes it was "tink 'em" (think them) "fare ye well." The *ye* was so detached, that I thought at first it was "very" or "vary well."

Another picturesque song, which seemed immensely popular, was at first very bewildering to me. I could not make out the first words of the chorus, and called it the "Romandàr," being reminded of some Romaic song which I had formerly heard. That association quite fell in with the Orientalism of the new tent-life.

III. ROOM IN THERE

O, my mudder is gone! my mudder is gone!
My mudder is gone into heaven, my Lord!
  I can't stay behind!

Dere's room in dar, room in dar,
Room in dar, in de heaven, my Lord!
  I can't stay behind,
Can't stay behind, my dear,
  I can't stay behind!

O, my fader is gone! &c.

O, de angels are gone! &c.

O, I'se been on de road! I'se been on de road:
I'se been on de road into heaven, my Lord!
  I can't stay behind!
O, room in dar, room in dar,
Room in dar, in de heaven, my Lord!
  I can't stay behind!

By this time every man within hearing, from oldest to youngest, would be wriggling and shuffling, as if through some magic piper's bewitchment; for even those who at first affected contemptuous indifference would be drawn into the vortex erelong.

Next to these in popularity ranked a class of songs belonging emphatically to the Church Militant, and available for camp purposes with very little strain upon their symbolism. This, for instance, had a true companion-in-arms heartiness about it, not impaired by the feminine invocation at the end.

IV. HAIL, MARY

One more valiant soldier here,
  One more valiant soldier here,
One more valiant soldier here,
  To help me bear de cross.
O hail, Mary, hail!
  Hail, Mary, hail!
Hail, Mary, hail!
  To help me bear de cross.

I fancied that the original reading might have been "soul," instead of "soldier,"—with some other syllable inserted, to fill out the metre, —and that the "Hail, Mary," might denote a Roman Catholic origin, as I had several men from St. Augustine who held in a dim way to that faith. It was a very ringing song, though not so grandly jubilant as the next, which was really impressive as the singers pealed it out, when marching or rowing or embarking:

V. MY ARMY CROSS OVER

My army cross over,
My army cross over.

O, Pharaoh's army drownded!
My army cross over.

We'll cross de mighty river,
  My army cross over;
We'll cross de river Jordan,
  My army cross over;
We'll cross de danger water,
  My army cross over;
We'll cross de mighty Myo,
  My army cross over. (*Thrice.*)
  O, Pharaoh's army drownded!
  My army cross over.

I could get no explanation of the "mighty Myo," except that one of the old men thought it meant the river of death. Perhaps it is an African word. In the Cameroon dialect, "Mawa" signifies "to die."

The next also has a military ring about it, and the first line is well matched by the music. The rest is conglomerate, and one or two lines show a more Northern origin. "Done" is a Virginia shibboleth, quite distinct from the "been" which replaces it in South Carolina. Yet one of their best choruses, without any fixed words, was, "De bell done ringing," for which, in proper South Carolina dialect, would have been substituted, "De bell been a-ring." This refrain may have gone South with our army:

VI. RIDE IN, KIND SAVIOUR

Ride in, kind Saviour!
  No man can hinder me.
O, Jesus is a mighty man!
  No man, &c.
We 're marching through Virginny fields.
  No man, &c.
O, Satan is a busy man,
  No man, &c.
And he has his sword and shield,
  No man, &c.
O, old Secesh done come and gone!
  No man can hinder me.

Sometimes they substituted "hinder *we*," which was more spicy to the ear, and more in keeping with the usual head-over-heels arrangement of their pronouns.

Almost all their songs were thoroughly religious in their tone, however quaint their expression, and were in a minor key, both as to words and music. The attitude is always the same, and, as a commentary on the life of the race, is infinitely pathetic. Nothing but patience for this life,—nothing but triumph in the next. Sometimes the present predominates, sometimes the future; but the combination is always implied. In the following, for instance, we hear simply the patience:

VII. THIS WORLD ALMOST DONE

Brudder, keep your lamp trimmin' and a-burnin',
Keep your lamp trimmin' and a-burnin',
Keep your lamp trimmin' and a-burnin',
  For dis world most done.
So keep your lamp, &c.
  Dis world most done.

But in the next, the final reward of patience is proclaimed as plaintively:

VIII. I WANT TO GO HOME

Dere's no rain to wet you,
  O, yes, I want to go home.
Dere's no sun to burn you,
  O, yes, I want to go home;
O, push along, believers,
  O, yes, &c.
Dere's no hard trials,
  O, yes, &c.
Dere's no whips a-crackin',
  O, yes, &c.
My brudder on de wayside,
  O yes, &c.
O, push along, my brudder,
  O, yes, &c.
Where dere's no stormy weather,
  O, yes, &c.
Dere's no tribulation,
  O, yes, &c.

This next was a boat-song, and timed well with the tug of the oar:

IX. THE COMING DAY

I want to go to Canaan,
I want to go to Canaan,
I want to go to Canaan,
  To meet 'em at de comin' day.
O, remember, let me go to Canaan, *(Thrice.)*
  To meet 'em, &c.

O brudder, let me go to Canaan, *(Thrice.)*
  To meet 'em, &c.
My brudder, you—oh!—remember *(Thrice.)*
  To meet 'em at de comin' day.

The following begins with a startling affirmation, yet the last line quite outdoes the first. This, too, was a capital boat-song.

X. ONE MORE RIVER

O, Jordan bank was a great old bank!
  Dere ain't but one more river to cross.
We have some valiant soldier here,
  Dere ain't, &c.
O, Jordan stream will never run dry,
  Dere ain't, &c.
Dere's a hill on my leff, and he catch on my right,
  Dere ain't but one more river to cross.

I could get no explanation of this last riddle, except, "Dat mean, if you go on de leff, go to 'struction, and if you go on de right, go to God, for sure."

In others, more of spiritual conflict is implied, as in this next:

XI. O THE DYING LAMB!

I want to go where Moses trod,
  O de dying Lamb!
For Moses gone to de promised land,
  O de dying Lamb!
To drink from springs dat never run dry,
  O, &c.
Cry O my Lord!
  O, &c.
Before I'll stay in hell one day,
  O, &c.
I'm in hopes to pray my sins away,
  O, &c.
Cry O my Lord!
  O, &c.
Brudder Moses promised for be dar too,
  O, &c.
To drink from streams dat never run dry,
  O de dying Lamb!

In the next, the conflict is at its height, and the lurid imagery of the Apocalypse is brought to bear. This book, with the books of Moses, constitute their Bible; all that lay between, even the narratives of the life of Jesus, they hardly cared to read or to hear:

XII. DOWN IN THE VALLEY

We'll run and never tire,
We'll run and never tire,
We'll run and never tire,
  Jesus set poor sinners free.
Way down in de valley,
  Who will rise and go with me?
You've heern talk of Jesus,
  Who set poor sinners free.

De lightnin' and de flashin',
De lightnin' and de flashin',
De lightnin' and de flashin',
  Jesus set poor sinners free.
I can't stand de fire. *(Thrice.)*
  Jesus set poor sinners free,
De green trees a-flamin'. *(Thrice.)*
  Jesus set poor sinners free,
    Way down in de valley,
      Who will rise and go with me?
    You've heern talk of Jesus
      Who set poor sinners free.

"De valley" and "de lonesome valley" were familiar words in their religious experience. To descend into that region implied the same process with the "anxious-seat" of the camp-meeting. When a young girl was supposed to enter it, she bound a handkerchief by a peculiar knot over her head, and made it a point of honor not to change a single garment till the day of her baptism, so that she was sure of being in physical readiness for the cleansing rite, whatever her spiritual mood might be. More than once, in noticing a damsel thus mystically kerchiefed, I have asked some dusky attendant its meaning, and have received the unfailing answer,—framed with thieir usual indifference to the genders of pronouns.—"He in de lonesome valley, sa."

The next gives the same dramatic conflict, while its detached and impersonal refrain gives it strikingly the character of the Scotch and Scandinavian ballads:

XIII. CRY HOLY

Cry holy, holy!
  Look at de people dat is born of God.
And I run down de valley, and I run down to pray,
  Says, look at de people dat is born of God.
When I get dar, Cappen Satan was dar,
  Says, look at, &c.

Says, young man, young man, dere's no use for pray.
  Says, look at, &c.
For Jesus is dead, and God gone away,
  Says, look at, &c.
And I made him out a liar and I went my way,
  Says, look at, &c.
    Sing holy, holy!

O, Mary was a woman, and he had a one Son,
  Says, look at, &c.
And de Jews and de Romans had him hung,
  Says, look at, &c.
    Cry holy, holy!

And I tell you, sinner, you had better had pray,
  Says, look at, &c.
For hell is a dark and dismal place,
  Says, look at, &c.
And I tell you, sinner, and I wouldn't go dar!
  Says, look at, &c.
    Cry holy, holy!

Here is an infinitely quaint description of the length of the heavenly road:

XIV. O'ER THE CROSSING

Yonder's my old mudder,
  Been a-waggin' at de hill so long.
It's about time she'll cross over;
  Get home bimeby.
Keep prayin', I do believe
  We're a long time waggin' o'er de crossin'.
Keep prayin', I do believe
  We'll get home to heaven bimeby.

Hear dat mournful thunder
  Roll from door to door,
Calling home God's children;
  Get home bimeby.
Little chil'en, I do believe
  We're a long time, &c.
Little chil'en, I do believe
  We'll get home, &c.

See dat forked lightnin'
  Flash from tree to tree,
Callin' home God's chil'en;
  Get home bimeby.
True believer, I do believe
  We're a long time, &c.

O brudders, I do believe,
  We'll get home to heaven bimeby.

One of the most singular pictures of future joys, and with a fine flavor of hospitality about it, was this:

XV. WALK 'EM EASY

O, walk 'em easy round de heaven,
Walk 'em easy round de heaven,
Walk 'em easy round de heaven,
  Dat all de people may join de band.
Walk 'em easy round de heaven. *(Thrice.)*
  O, shout glory till 'em join dat band!

The chorus was usually the greater part of the song, and often came in paradoxically, thus:

XVI. O YES, LORD

O, must I be like de foolish mans?
    O yes, Lord!
Will build de house on de sandy hill.
    O yes, Lord!
I'll build my house on Zion hill,
    O yes, Lord!
No wind nor rain can blow me down
    O yes, Lord!

The next is very graceful and lyrical, and with more variety of rhythm than usual:

XVII. BOW LOW, MARY

Bow low, Mary, bow low, Martha,
  For Jesus come and lock de door,
  And carry de keys away.
Sail, sail, over yonder,
And view de promised land.
  For Jesus come, &c.
Weep, O Mary, bow low, Martha,
  For Jesus come, &c.
Sail, sail, my true believer;
Sail, sail, over yonder;
Mary, bow low, Martha, bow low,
  For Jesus come and lock de door
  And carry de keys away.

But of all the "spirituals" that which surprised me the most, I think, —perhaps because it was that in which external nature furnished the images most directly,—was this. With all my experience of their ideal ways of speech, I was startled when first I came on such a flower of poetry in that dark soil:

XVIII. I KNOW MOON-RISE

I know moon-rise, I know star-rise,
  Lay dis body down.
I walk in de moonlight, I walk in de starlight,
  To lay dis body down.
I'll walk in de graveyard, I'll walk through de graveyard,
  To lay dis body down.
I'll lie in de grave and stretch out my arms;
  Lay dis body down.
I go to de judgment in de evenin' of de day,
  When I lay dis body down;
And my soul and your soul will meet in de day
  When I lay dis body down.

"I'll lie in de grave and stretch out my arms." Never, it seems to me, since man first lived and suffered, was his infinite longing for peace uttered more plaintively than in that line.

The next is one of the wildest and most striking of the whole series: there is a mystical effect and a passionate striving throughout the whole. The Scriptural struggle between Jacob and the angel, which is only dimly expressed in the words, seems all uttered in the music. I think it impressed my imagination more powerfully than in any other of these songs:

XIX. WRESTLING JACOB

O wrestlin' Jacob, Jacob, day's a-breakin';
  I will not let thee go!
O wrestlin' Jacob, Jacob, day's a-breakin';
  He will not let me go!
O, I hold my brudder wid a tremblin' hand;
  I would not let him go!
I hold my sister wid a tremblin' hand;
  I would not let her go!

O, Jacob do hang from a tremblin' limb,
  He would not let him go!
O, Jacob do hang from a tremblin' limb;
  De Lord will bless my soul.
  O wrestlin' Jacob, Jacob, &c.

Of "occasional hymns," properly so called, I noticed but one, a funeral hymn for an infant, which is sung plaintively over and over, without variety of words:

XX. THE BABY GONE HOME

De little baby gone home,
De little baby gone home,
De little baby gone along,
  For to climb up Jacob's ladder.
And I wish I'd been dar,
I wish I'd been dar,
I wish I'd been dar, my Lord,
  For to climb up Jacob's ladder.

Still simpler is this, which is yet quite sweet and touching:

XXI. JESUS WITH US

He have been wid us, Jesus,
  He still wid us, Jesus,
He will be wid us, Jesus,
  Be wid us to the end.

The next seemed to be a favorite about Christmas time, when meditations on "de rollin' year" were frequent among them:

XXII. LORD, REMEMBER ME!

O do, Lord, remember me!
  O do, Lord, remember me!
O, do remember me, until de year roll round!
  Do, Lord, remember me!

If you want to die like Jesus died,
  Lay in de grave.
You would fold your arms and close your eyes
  And die wid a free good will.

For Death is a simple ting,
  And he go from door to door,
And he knock down some, and he cripple up some,
  And he leave some here to pray.

O do, Lord, remember me!
  O do, Lord, remember me!
My old fader's gone till de year roll round;
  Do, Lord, remember me!

The next was sung in such an operatic and rollicking way that it was quite hard to fancy it a religious performance, which, however, it was. I heard it but once:

XXIII. EARLY IN THE MORNING

I meet little Rosa early in de mornin',
  O Jerusalem! early in de mornin';

And I ax her, How you do, my darter?
O Jerusalem! early in de mornin'.

I meet my mudder early in de mornin',
O Jerusalem! &c.
And I ax her, How you do, my mudder?
O Jerusalem! &c.

I meet Budder Robert early in de mornin',
O Jerusalem! &c.
And I ax him, How you do, my sonny?
O Jerusalem! &c.

I meet Tittawisa early in de mornin',
O Jerusalem! &c.
And I ax her, How you do, my darter?
O Jerusalem! &c.

"Tittawisa" means "Sister Louisa." In songs of this class the name of every person present successively appears.

Their best marching song, and one which was invaluable to lift their feet along, as they expressed it, was the following. There was a kind of spring and *lilt* to it, quite indescribable by words.

XXIV. GO IN THE WILDERNESS

Jesus call you. Go in de wilderness,
Go in de wilderness, go in de wilderness,
Jesus call you. Go in de wilderness
To wait upon de Lord.
Go wait upon de Lord,
Go wait upon de Lord,
Go wait upon de Lord, my God,
He take away de sins of de world.

Jesus a-waitin'. Go in de wilderness,
Go, &c.
All dem chil'en go in de wilderness
To wait upon de Lord.

The next was one of those which I had heard in boyish days, brought North from Charleston. But the chorus alone was identical; the words were mainly different, and those here given are quaint enough:

XXV. BLOW YOUR TRUMPET, GABRIEL

O, blow your trumpet, Gabriel,
Blow your trumpet louder;
And I want dat trumpet to blow me home
To my new Jerusalem.

De prettiest ting dat ever I done
Was to serve de Lord when I was young.
  So blow your trumpet, Gabriel, &c.

O, Satan is a liar, and he conjure too,
  And if you don't mind, he'll conjure you.
  So blow your trumpet, Gabriel, &c.

O, I was lost in de wilderness,
King Jesus hand me de candle down.
  So blow your trumpet, Gabriel, &c.

The following contains one of those odd transformations of proper names with which their Scriptural citations were often enriched. It rivals their text, "Paul may plant, and may polish wid water," which I have elsewhere quoted, and in which the sainted Apollos would hardly have recognized himself:

XXVI. IN THE MORNING

In de mornin',
In de mornin',
Chil'en? Yes, my Lord!
  Don't you hear de trumpet sound?
If I had a-died when I was young,
I never would had de race for run.
  Don't you hear de trumpet sound?

O Sam and Peter was fishin' in de sea,
And dey drop de net and follow my Lord.
  Don't you hear de trumpet sound?

Dere's a silver spade for to dig my grave
And a golden chain for to let me down.
  Don't you hear de trumpet sound?
In de mornin',
In de mornin',
Chil'en? Yes, my Lord!
  Don't you hear de trumpet sound?

These golden and silver fancies remind one of the King of Spain's daughter in "Mother Goose," and the golden apple, and the silver pear, which are doubtless themselves but the vestiges of some simple early composition like this. The next has a humbler and more domestic style of fancy:

XXVII. FARE YE WELL

My true believers, fare ye well,
Fare ye well, fare ye well,
Fare ye well, by de grace of God,
  For I'm going home.

Massa Jesus give me a little broom
For to sweep my heart clean,
And I will try, by de grace of God,
  To win my way home.

Among the songs not available for marching, but requiring the concentrated enthusiasm of the camp, was "The Ship of Zion," of which they had three wholly distinct versions, all quite exuberant and tumultuous:

XXVIII. THE SHIP OF ZION

Come along, come along,
  And let us go home,
  O, glory, hallelujah!
  Dis de ole ship o' Zion,
    Halleloo! Halleloo!
  Dis de old ship o' Zion,
    Hallelujah!

She has landed many a tousand,
She can land as many more.
  O, glory, hallelujah! &c.

Do you tink she will be able
For to take us all home?
  O, glory, hallelujah! &c.

You can tell 'em I'm a comin',
    Halleloo! Halleloo!
You can tell 'em I'm a comin',
    Hallelujah!
Come along, come along, &c.

XXIX. THE SHIP OF ZION *(Second version.)*

Dis de good ole ship o' Zion,
Dis de good ole ship o' Zion,
Dis de good ole ship o' Zion,
  And she's makin' for de Promise Land.
She hab angels for de sailors, *(Thrice.)*
  And she's, &c.
And how you know dey's angels? *(Thrice.)*
  And she's, &c.
Good Lord, shall I be de one? *(Thrice.)*
  And she's, &c.

Dat ship is out a-sailin', sailin', sailin',
  And she's, &c.
She's a-sailin' mighty steady, steady, steady,
  And she's, &c.

She'll neither reel nor totter, totter, totter,
And she's, &c.
She's a-sailin' away cold Jordan, Jordan, Jordan,
And she's, &c.
King Jesus is de captain, captain, captain,
And she's makin for de Promised Land.

XXX. THE SHIP OF ZION *(Third version.)*

De Gospel ship is sailin',
Hosann—sann.
O, Jesus is de captain,
Hosann—sann.
De angels are de sailors,
Hosann—sann.
O, is your bundle ready?
Hosann—sann.
O, have you got your ticket?
Hosann—sann.

This abbreviated chorus is given with unspeakable unction.

The three just given are modifications of an old camp-meeting melody; and the same may be true of the three following, although I cannot find them in the Methodist hymn-books. Each, however, has its characteristic modifications, which make it well worth giving. In the second verse of this next, for instance, "Saviour" evidently has become "soldier":

XXXI. SWEET MUSIC

Sweet music in heaven,
Just beginning for to roll.
Don't you love God?
Glory, hallelujah!

Yes, late I heard my soldier say,
Come, heavy soul, I am de way.
Don't you love God?
Glory, hallelujah!

I'll go and tell to sinners round
What a kind Saviour I have found.
Don't you love God?
Glory, hallelujah!

My grief my burden long has been,
Because I was not cease from sin.
Don't you love God?
Glory, hallelujah!

XXXII. GOOD NEWS

O, good news! O, good news!
De angels brought de tidings down,
  Just comin' from de trone.

As grief from out my soul shall fly,
  Just comin' from de trone;
I'll shout salvation when I die,
  Good news, O, good news!
  Just comin' from de trone.

Lord, I want to go to heaven when I die,
Good news, O, good news! &c.

De white folks call us a noisy crew,
  Good news, O, good news!
But dis I know, we are happy too,
  Just comin' from de trone.

XXXIII. THE HEAVENLY ROAD

You may talk of my name as much as you please,
  And carry my name abroad,
But I really do believe I'm a child of God
    As I walk in de heavenly road.
O, won't you go wid me? *(Thrice.)*
  For to keep our garments clean.

O, Satan is a mighty busy ole man,
  And roll rocks in my way;
But Jesus is my bosom friend,
  And roll 'em out of de way.
O, won't you go wid me? *(Thrice.)*

Come, my brudder, if you never did pray,
  I hope you may pray to-night;
For I really believe I'm a child of God
  As I walk in de heavenly road.
O, won't you, &c.

Some of the songs had played an historic part during the war. For singing the next, for instance, the negroes had been put in jail in Georgetown, S. C., at the outbreak of the Rebellion. "We'll soon be free," was too dangerous an assertion; and though the chant was an old one, it was no doubt sung with redoubled emphasis during the new events. "De Lord will call us home," was evidently thought to be a symbolical verse; for, as a little drummer-boy explained to me, showing all his white teeth as he sat in the moonlight by the door of my tent, "Dey tink *de Lord* mean for say *de Yankees.*"

XXXIV. WE'LL SOON BE FREE

We'll soon be free,
We'll soon be free,
We'll soon be free,
 When de Lord will call us home.
My brudder, how long,
My brudder, how long,
My brudder, how long,
'Fore we done sufferin' here?
It won't be long *(Thrice.)*
 'Fore de Lord will call us home.
We'll walk de miry road *(Thrice.)*
 Where pleasure never dies.
We'll walk de golden street *(Thrice.)*
 Where pleasure never dies.
My brudder, how long *(Thrice.)*
 'Fore we done sufferin' here?
We'll soon be free *(Thrice.)*
 When Jesus sets me free.
We'll fight for liberty *(Thrice.)*
 When de Lord will call us home.

The suspicion in this case was unfounded, but they had another song to which the Rebellion had actually given rise. This was composed by nobody knew whom,—though it was the most recent, doubtless, of all these "spirituals,"—and had been sung in secret to avoid detection. It is certainly plaintive enough. The peck of corn and pint of salt were slavery's rations.

XXXV. MANY THOUSAND GO

No more peck o' corn for me,
  No more, no more,—
No more peck o' corn for me,
  Many tousand go.

No more driver's lash for me, *(Twice.)*
  No more, &c.

No more pint o' salt for me, *(Twice.)*
  No more, &c.

No more hundred lash for me, *(Twice.)*
  No more, &c.

No more mistress' call for me,
  No more, no more,—
No more mistress' call for me,
  Many tousand go.

Even of this last composition, however, we have only the approximate date, and know nothing of the mode of composition. Allan Ramsay says of the Scotch songs, that, no matter who made them, they were soon attributed to the minister of the parish whence they sprang. And I always wondered, about these, whether they had always a conscious and definite origin in some leading mind, or whether they grew by gradual accretion, in an almost unconscious way. On this point I could get no information, though I asked many questions, until at last, one day when I was being rowed across from Beaufort to Ladies' Island, I found myself, with delight, on the actual trail of a song. One of the oarsmen, a brisk young fellow, not a soldier, on being asked for his theory of the matter, dropped out a coy confession. "Some good sperituals," he said, "are start jess out o' curiosity. I been a-raise a sing, myself, once."

My dream was fulfilled, and I had traced out, not the poem alone, but the poet. I implored him to proceed.

"Once we boys," he said, "went for tote some rice, and de nigger-driver, he keep a'callin' on us; and I say, 'O, de ole nigger-driver!' Den anudder said, 'Fust ting my mammy tole me was, notin' so bad as nigger-driver.' Den I made a sing, just puttin' a word, and den anudder word."

Then he began singing, and the men, after listening a moment, joined in the chorus as if it were an old acquaintance, though they evidently had never heard it before. I saw how easily a new "sing" took root among them:

XXXVI. THE DRIVER

O, de ole nigger-driver!
  O, gwine away!
Fust ting my mammy tell me,
  O, gwine away!
Tell me 'bout de nigger-driver,
  O, gwine away!
Nigger-driver second devil,
  O, gwine away!
Best ting for do he driver,
  O, gwine away!
Knock he down and spoil he labor,
  O, gwine away!

It will be observed that, although this song is quite secular in its character, its author yet called it a "spiritual." I heard but two songs among them, at any time, to which they would not, perhaps, have given this generic name. One of these consisted simply in the endless repetition—after the manner of certain college songs—of the mysterious line,

Rain fall and wet Becky Martin.

But who Becky Martin was, and why she should or should not be wet, and whether the dryness was a reward or a penalty, none could say. I got the impression that, in either case, the event was posthumous, and that there was some tradition of grass not growing over the grave of a sinner; but even this was vague, and all else vaguer.

The other song I heard but once, on a morning when a squad of men came in from picket duty, and chanted it in the most rousing way. It had been a stormy and comfortless night, and the picket station was very exposed. It still rained in the morning when I strolled to the edge of the camp, looking out for the men, and wondering how they had stood it. Presently they came striding along the road, at a great pace, with their shining rubber blankets worn as cloaks around them, the rain streaming from these and from their equally shining faces, which were almost all upon the broad grin, as they pealed out this remarkable ditty:—

XXXVII. HANGMAN JOHNNY

O, dey call me Hangman Johnny!
    O, ho! O, ho!
But I never hang nobody,
    O, hang, boys, hang!

O, dey call me Hangman Johnny!
    O, ho! O, ho!
But we'll all hang togedder,
    O, hang, boys, hang!

My presence apparently checked the performance of another verse, beginning, "De buckra 'list for money," apparently in reference to the controversy about the pay-question, then just beginning, and to the more mercenary aims they attributed to the white soldiers. But "Hangman Johnny" remained always a myth as inscrutable as "Becky Martin."

As they learned all their songs by ear, they often strayed into wholly new versions, which sometimes became popular, and entirely banished the others. This was amusingly the case, for instance, with one phrase in the popular camp-song of "Marching Along," which was entirely new to them until our quartermaster taught it to them, at my request. The words, "Gird on the armor," were to them a stumbling block, and no wonder, until some ingenious ear substituted, "Guide on de army," which was at once accepted, and became universal.

We'll guide on de army, and be marching along,

is now the established version on the Sea Islands.

These quaint religious songs were to the men more than a source of relaxation; they were a stimulus to courage and a tie to heaven. I never overheard in camp a profane or vulgar song. With the trifling exceptions given, all had a religious motive, while the most secular melody could not have been more exciting. A few youth from Savannah, who were comparatively men of the world, had learned some of the "Ethiopian Minstrel" ditties, imported from the North. These took no hold upon the mass; and, on the other hand, they sang reluctantly, even on Sunday, the long and short metres of the hymn-books, always gladly yielding to the more potent excitement of their own "spirituals." By these they could sing themselves, as had their fathers before them, out of the contemplation of their own low estate, into the sublime scenery of the Apocalypse. I remember that this minor-keyed pathos used to seem to me almost too sad to dwell upon, while slavery seemed destined to last for generations; but now that their patience has had its perfect work, history cannot afford to lose this portion of its record. There is no parallel instance of an oppressed race thus sustained by the religious sentiment alone. These songs are but the vocal expression of the simplicity of their faith and the sublimity of their long resignation.

1868

LITERATURE OF THE DAY: *Slave Songs of the United States* (review)

(Unsigned)

Lippincott's Magazine, I (Philadelphia, March 1868), 341–343.

The Negro did not have a "culture," for most white Americans, until the Emancipation Proclamation metamorphosed his status from chattel to person. For the first time many whites stopped thinking of the Negro as a device that worked, and began wondering about what made him tick. Slave Songs of the United States *was greeted with considerable interest. Most of the reviews were warm in praise of the editors and their material.*

One interesting review appeared in the Nation *(V [November 21, 1867]). That journal had been created for two reasons: to carry on the liberal traditions of William Lloyd Garrison's influential* Liberator, *and to give Wendell Phillips Garrison, William Lloyd's son, something useful to do. As the* Nation's *managing editor, Wendell quite likely had something to do with its review of* Slave Songs, *and we should note that his interest in the volume might have been more than coldly academic or warmly abolitionist: he was married to Lucy McKim, one of* Slave Songs' *three co-editors. This fact may qualify the context, but not the* Nation's *review, which was justifiably favorable.*

*But, as the hostile review reprinted here demonstrates, the enemy had not completely capitulated with the cessation of hostilities in 1865. A century later, Ralph Ellison would describe white men who could not see a Negro (*Invisible Man *[New York, 1952]), but the author of this review seems to be working very hard at not* hearing *him either. He offers us bastard biology in the harmonic extreme: "We think it can be proved that the negro requires the mixture of white blood to develop in him the musical qualities which, if they exist at all, in his native state, are, at least, dormant." Articles of this kind rarely appeared in the period, for the racists did not often comment in print on anything so inconsequential as folklore. Such attitudes con-*

tinued to qualify the atmosphere in which Negro song was studied, and it in part explains the reluctance of journals like Southern Workman *(see the article "Folk-Lore and Ethnology") to print anything concerning the Negro's Negro characteristics.*

It is possible that this reviewer's hostility was directed not so much toward the Negro as toward the music itself. In his discerning letter noted in the Introduction, Herbert Halpert wrote me, regarding this point: "His comment on the unmusical Africans was, and even still is, typical of the average European's reaction to any non-European music, not just to Negroes. It's typical of most city dwellers' reactions to genuine folk singing, unless it happens to be in a 'pop' norm. It is interesting as a precursor to G. P. Jackson's assertion that most Negro spiritual melodies are based on English folk tunes." Halpert's observation is of course borne out by the enthusiastic response given groups such as the Fisk Jubilee Singers as soon as they emasculated their traditional songs and made them sound almost European.

The object of this publication is clearly seen in the following paragraph, with which it commences:

> The musical capacity of the negro race has been recognized for so many years that it is hard to explain why no systematic effort has hitherto been made to collect and preserve these melodies. More than thirty years ago those plantation songs made their appearance which were so extraordinarily popular for a while; and if "Coal-black Rose," "Zip Coon" and "Old Virginny Nebber Tire" have been succeeded by spurious imitations, manufactured to suit the somewhat sentimental taste of our community, the fact that these were called "negro melodies" was itself a tribute to the musical genius of the race.

It has been a common idea for many years, accepted without examination or proof, that the negro was essentially musical in his nature. We now venture boldly to assert that the claim is unfounded in fact, and that, while the negro possesses a capacity for acquiring a certain degree of musical knowledge which he gets from his organ of imitativeness, he has in his *native* state (to which only we must look in examining the question) no idea whatever of music, so far as melody or harmony is an essential ingredient of such a quality.

Of the numerous travelers in Africa, none have reported anything but horribly discordant noises (both vocal and instrumental) when anything which represented music was introduced, even at the court of H. M. the King of Dahomey, who, being a very absolute sovereign, would doubtless have gathered into his band all the talent of his nation.

During a residence of several years in Brazil, we found much amusement in attending the *festas* which were held by a tribe of Africans in a lane back of our residence every Sunday afternoon. These were the real Simon Pures. Every one of them had been brought over from Africa within a few years of our visit, and were as nearly savage as they could be. Their faces were scarred with slashes of various shapes, given them in youth for ornament: their ears, and the noses of some of them, slit with the same object, and their teeth all filed like those of a saw. Their heads and bodies (nearly naked) were decorated with feathers and beads, and they held these *festas* as sacred rites, recalling their native land. They had a rude instrument, composed of several pieces of thick iron wire fastened on a block of wood,* which gave out clear, full sounds under vibration; and they had, also, some small, rudely-made drums.

To the sound of these instruments they howled in choice African, and danced(?) very much in the style of some of our Indian tribes. But nothing they played or sung approached, in the remotest degree, to anything which could be called music.

In Rio de Janeiro, until very recently, everything was carried through the streets on the heads of the negroes, who there occupied the place which carts, drays and furniture-wagons fill with us. In large gangs they moved through the streets, each with a bag of coffee or other load on his head, and all under the command of a leader, who ran before them with a large rattle resembling the mouthpiece of an immense watering-pot, or a child's huge rattle. The leader rattled and they all sang as they went along at a trot; but there was no music in their song, and seldom any words which had meaning. Generally, their song ran thus: "Ugh! ugh! ugh! ugh!" or "Eh! eh! eh! eh!" in every possible scale, and *ad infinitum*. Sometimes they got hold of a name, which they appropriated as a handle to their gruntings. When our distinguished townsman, Condy Raguet, was Chargé d'Affaires from the United States to Brazil, the negroes, in some inexplicable manner, got hold of his name, and were frequently heard grunting through the streets—

Condy Raguet, Condy Raguet,
Eh! eh! Condy Raguet!

The negroes in our Southern plantations have, for years, been within the influence of their masters' families, in which music has been universally cultivated, and often to a high degree of excellence; and although the field-hands may never have heard the music, the

* Called "*hoss-fiddle*" by the negroes of the Southern States.

house-servants have; and from them the airs have been readily transmitted (more or less correctly) to the others, who may, no doubt, have supposed that the tunes they were singing were made by themselves, while, in reality, they were but the growth from the seed dropped carelessly by others, which fell in a soil admirably fitted for its reception; for there is no doubt that the negro is a great lover of music, though he may not have the capacity to compose it.

And we do not credit the assertion that "Jim Crow," "Zip Coon" and others of that class of tunes, poor as they are, were composed by the Africans on the plantations. "Coal-black Rose" is only the old "Sicilian Hymn" put into allegro form, with the negro accent; and it is this very *accent*, in all negro singing, that makes it captivating to some ears and bearable to others. A writer in the *London Review*, for October 5, asserts as follows:

"Many negro melodies are of church origin, and, strange to say, the once popular 'Dandy Jim' is not a native of Carolina, but of Italy, where it has positively done service in High Mass."

Another writer in "Notes and Queries" for November 16, says that "the tune of 'Buffalo Gals' is said to be taken from an old air by Glück, and that of 'Old Joe' from an air in Rossini's Corradino."

It is scarcely a matter of question that nearly all the negro melodies (so called) which we have heard since the days of Jim Crow have been composed at the North by white men, because no such or similar melodies were to be found on the plantations of the South. If the "somewhat sentimental taste of our community" called for such songs, the sentiment was based distinctly upon sympathy with the slave, and would have been better pleased with the real article, had it existed, than with the imitation; but that community would never have endured the infliction of such "melodies" as this book introduces as proofs of "musical genius."

We do not believe that the negro, in his native state, knows what music is, if the term applies to melody or tune; and it is the native African alone whom we must consider when we are examining the claims of the negro race to musical genius. He loves music dearly, however, when he hears it, and readily appropriates a portion of it when he has been brought within its sphere. But does he ever reach excellence in it? Have not all the colored musicians we have known been of mixed blood? Is it not the musical genius of the white man grafted upon the African's love of music? Frank Johnson is well remembered by all middle-aged Philadelphians. Thirty years ago, his band, here and at the Springs, was the best to be had. But Frank, like the famous Bogle (Nicholas Biddle's "colorless colored man"), was a mulatto. By the way, Bogle's mantle has never descended upon any of his successors. Neither Morris, Dorsey, nor any of the helpers at our public and private entertainments, have ever taken his high position in society. Brown, the famous sexton of Grace Church, New York, must have caught the mantle when Bogle dropped it, for Brown fills, in Gotham, precisely the position which Bogle filled here, at balls, weddings, funerals, &c. But Brown, unfortunately, is a white man.

To return to our muttons: We think it can be proved that the negro requires the mixture of white blood to develop in him the musical qualities which, if they exist at all in his native state, are, at least, dormant.

A friend cites Blind Tom as opposed to this theory. But Tom is simply a prodigy—a *lusus naturae*—a phenomenon, whose case has defied the investigations of the most scientific musicians, here and in Europe, who have attempted to explain it. In fact, Tom is the exception which proves the general rule to be the opposite.

We doubt if this negro, with all his peculiar faculty for musical imitation, could compose a regular melody. Blind Tom is one of the best proofs that can be given of the wall of adamant (which seems only of gauze to some philanthropists) that is, and must be for ever, between the *genius* of the white and that of the negro; for in him we have the highest specimen that has been ever known of the negro coming near the white in delicate handling of the piano.

Such curiosities as Blind Tom, however, are phenomena of nervous impressibility and memory, united to a mysterious instinct for harmonious combinations, and a faculty of assimilation which assumes the character of divination; but the intellectual initiative is wanting in such beings, and therefore they come to nothing.

As regards the collection of tunes and words in the book under notice, we have played many of them on the piano, but have failed to discover melody in any of them, except where the *idea* of the tune was clearly traceable to some old hymn tune, to the composition of which no negro could lay claim. As to the words of the (so-called) hymns, they are generally so absurd and unmeaning, and often so absolutely profane (though not so intended), that it would be well for the teachers in the schools and meeting-houses where they are sung to commence, as speedily as possible, the destruction of the entire lot, in the interest, temporal and spiritual, of the wards in their care. The simple hymns which are taught our children would be as readily learned by the colored people, and would, in time, convey some idea to their minds, which this collection cannot.

It was hardly worth while to try to perpetuate this trash, vulgarity and profanity by putting it in print.

1868

SONGS OF THE SLAVE

by John Mason Brown

Lippincott's Magazine, II (Philadelphia, December 1868), 617–623.

*One can only regret that Brown found the worksongs "tiresomely similar" and chose to print but a few fragments; what he does publish is quite interesting. "Skewball," in various forms, describes the most durable horse in Anglo-American folksong. It derives from an Irish ballad, but seems to have become sufficiently acculturated for G. Malcom Laws, Jr., to categorize it as an unqualified American ballad (H 27 in his "Native American Balladry," PAFS I [rev. ed.; Philadelphia, 1964]). Dorothy Scarborough laments Brown's failures to print the rest of his verses and offers for comparison a London broadside published in 1822 (*On the Trail of Negro Folk-Songs *[Cambridge, Mass., 1925; reprinted Hatboro, Pa., 1963], pp. 61–65). The song is still current, especially among Negro convicts in the South, who use it as a worksong; Professor Harry Oster, of the State University of Iowa, and I have collected independently numerous versions in prisons in Louisiana, Texas, and elsewhere.*

Brown's text of "Oh, Su-zann!" is not the same song Stephen Foster copyrighted in 1848 and which subsequently appeared in numerous songsters, but it may be related (see Newman White, American Negro Folk-Songs *[Cambridge, Mass., 1928; reprinted Hatboro, Pa., 1965], p. 178). "Old Ship of Zion" has been collected through a wide area and is still quite healthy. Newman White says the earliest mention of the song he finds is 1853, when it seems to have been in use at white and Negro camp meetings; he finds songs about gospel ships in collections from whites as early as 1827 (pp. 93–96). Roger D. Abrahams has pointed out that "The Fifer's Son" is "obviously not what the author says but a ring game of the marriage type," and that "Weevily Wheat" is a play-party song. For an extensive discussion and several variant texts of the latter song, see B. A. Botkin,* The American Play-Party Song *([reprint ed.; New York, 1963], pp. 345–351).*

Brown's article is valuable not only for the fine texts and tunes, but also for his effective attack on stage minstrelsy and his detailed description of the steamboat songs. Herbert Halpert observed that the call and response pattern of the Negro worksong, such as Brown describes in this article and other authors in this volume note in connection with rowing songs, is exactly the same as the shantyman-chorus pattern of the "white" sea-shanty. The importance of the obvious bilateral influence demonstrated by these songs has yet to be adequately explored. Among the other songs in this volume found in white seafaring tradition are "Hangman Johnny" ([Higginson], "Negro Spirituals"); "Long time ago" and "Jenny get your hoecake done" ([J. K(innard)], "Who Are Our National Poets?"); "Gen'el Jackson" ([Nathanson], "Negro Minstrelsy"); and "Oh ho ho ho" and "Ho mer Riley" ([Barrow], "A Georgia Corn-Shucking").

The characteristics of the negro race in the United States are rapidly changing. The abolition of slavery, and the new privileges and responsibilities growing out of his changed condition, are speedily making of the freedman a being totally different from the slave of former years. Care and want and self-dependence are new ideas to the bulk of the negro population, but they are now ever present and demand recognition. As a consequence, the negro is daily becoming more reflective, more cautious and more shrewd. He grows taciturn as compared with his former habits, and keenly alive to the practical relations between labor and compensation. As might be expected, a new set of qualities are developing, which lay dormant in former years—useless to the slave, but indispensable to the freedman; and peculiarities, very marked under the old régime, are fast disappearing. A tendency to graver views of life and sobriety of thought is very observable.

In nothing has this mental change been more unmistakably shown than in the rapid disuse of a class of songs long popular with negro slaves, and in many instances exquisitely illustrative of their habits of thought. The round of sacred and secular song that for many years was so familiar to every ear throughout the Southern States, is now fading from use and remembrance. It is giving place to a totally different system of words and melody. It could not be perpetuated without perpetuating slavery as it existed, and with the fall of slavery its days were numbered.

A very erroneous idea has long prevailed which accepts "negro minstrelsy" as a mirror of the musical taste and feeling of the negro race in the United States. Nothing could be farther from truth. Beyond the external resemblance, due to burnt cork, there is in negro minstrelsy scarcely a feature of person, music, dialect or action that recalls, with any dramatic accuracy, the genuine negro slave of former years. True it is that Christy, Bryant and Newcomb have achieved great success as Ethiopian comedians, and are accepted as interpreters of the negro; but it is none the less true that their delineations are mere conventionalisms, and their Ethiopian music even farther from the truth than their very amusing but very inaccurate impersonations. No genuine negro song, composed by a negro slave, ever betrayed a straining after *vowel endings.* Such words as "Swanee," "Tennessee," "Ohio" (the final *o* lengthened *ad libitum*), are by no means as frequently used by the negro as minstrels would have us suppose. Triple time, too, it may be remarked, is such a rarity in negro music that but one instance now occurs to us, and *it* may be plausibly traced to an old Scotch air.

But it is not to the subject of negro minstrelsy that the present sketch will be devoted. It is proposed to offer a few specimens of genuine negro-slave song and music. If they be found neither touching in sentiment, graceful in expression nor well balanced in rhythm, they may, at least, possess interest as peculiarities of a system now no more for ever in this country.

Many eloquent writers have described the religious services of negro slaves and the thrilling effect of their hymns, sung to quaint and unusual tunes by congregations of impassioned and impressible worshipers. The effect can hardly be overstated. Their hymns, "lined out" by the preacher, are full of unpremeditated and irresistible dramatic power. We have seen negroes alternately agonized with fear and transported with a bliss almost frantic as they sang a revival hymn called "The Book of Seven Seals," replete with the imagery of the Apocalypse, picturing the golden streets of the New Jerusalem and the horrible pit of destruction. Such a chorus, sung with the energy of a people of simple and literal faith and strong and inflammable emotions, has often quickened the pulse and set aglow the heart of those whose social position or philosophy made them ashamed to acknowledge the effect.

The religious songs of the negro slave were composed and communicated without the aid of writing, and were unmistakably marked in their construction. As a general rule, but few hymns were borrowed from the collections used by white congregations. Of those that were adopted by the negroes, the favorites were always such as abounded in bold imagery or striking expressions, appealing to ardent hope or vivid fear. Hence the unction with which those well-known hymns, "Am I a Soldier of the Cross?" and "Hark, from the Tombs," were sung in negro churches.

But the religious songs composed by negro preachers or "exhorters" for the use of their congregations abounded to excess in metaphor of the most striking character. The saints were styled the "Army of the Lord," led by King Jesus, the "Captain" and "Conqueror." They were exhorted to listen to the summons of silver trumpets, marshaling the faithful to victory, and were described as sweeping down all the obstructions of evil, and marching forward, with measured tread, up the hill on which stands the city reserved for their habitation. The banners, trumpets, drums and other paraphernalia of an army were used without stint, and often with most graphic effect. Wherever a figure was attempted, it was fearlessly carried to its limit. There was current, not many years since, a hymn in which the Christian was likened to a traveler on a railway train. The conductor was the Lord Jesus, the brakemen were eminent servants of the Church, and stoppages were made at Gospel depôts to take up waiting converts or replenish the engine with the water of life or the fuel of holy zeal. The allegory was developed with as much accuracy and verisimilitude as though the author of the hymn had carefully studied the *Pilgrim's Progress*; yet it was imagined and composed by Oscar Buckner, an illiterate and ignorant negro slave.

It is doubtful if the authorship of that famous hymn, "The Old Ship of Zion," so popular among negroes everywhere, can be traced. It must have originated (judging from internal evidence) among the Maryland or Virginia negroes of the seaboard. As its name would indicate, the imagery of the hymn is exclusively nautical. A stanza or two will give an idea of many peculiarities of negro-slave religious song. This hymn is the original of very numerous imitations:

THE OLD SHIP OF ZION

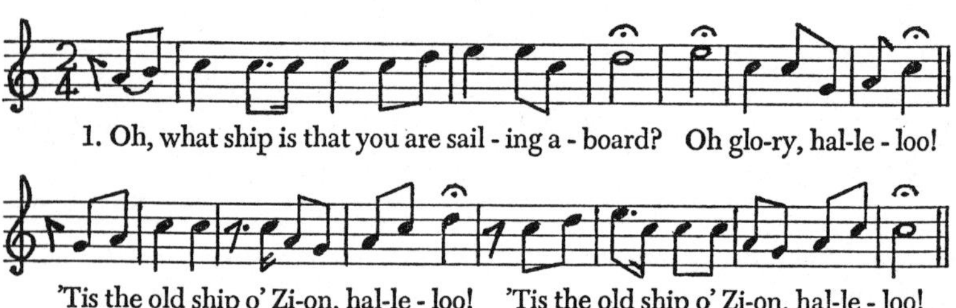

1. Oh, what ship is that you are sail - ing a - board? Oh glo-ry, hal-le - loo!
'Tis the old ship o' Zi-on, hal-le - loo! 'Tis the old ship o' Zi-on, hal-le - loo!

2. Oh what are the timbers for buildin' of the ship?
   Oh glory, halleloo!
   She is made o' gospel timbers, halleloo!
   She is made o' gospel timbers, halleloo!

3. Oh, what is the compass you've got aboard the ship?
   Oh, glory, halleloo!
   The Bible is our compass, halleloo!
   Oh, the Bible is our compass, halleloo!

As regards this hymn, it may be observed that the refrain of "glory, halleloo!" is not a singularity. It is found in many, perhaps most, negro songs of devotion. It serves to mark the time and keep the congregation well together in their singing, and also gives the leader time to recall the next verse. "The Old Ship of Zion" was a hymn of thirty to forty stanzas, each descriptive of some equipment, in a style similar to those already quoted.

A very popular hymn, still much sung, and evidently based upon the air of "The Old Ship of Zion," commences thus:

PRAY ON! PRAY ON!

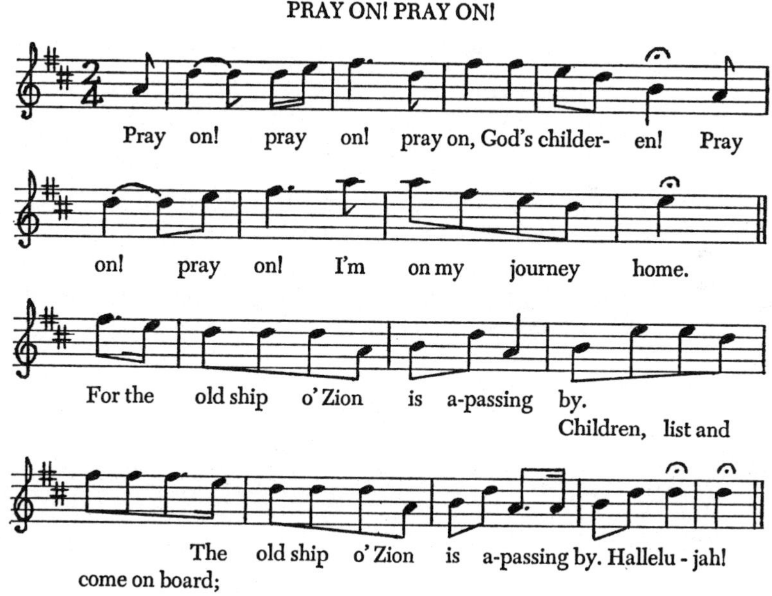
Pray on! pray on! pray on, God's childer- en! Pray
on! pray on! I'm on my journey home.
For the old ship o' Zion is a-passing by.
Children, list and
The old ship o' Zion is a-passing by. Hallelu - jah!
come on board;

Another quite popular but far inferior hymn runs thus:

OH WAKE THE NATIONS!

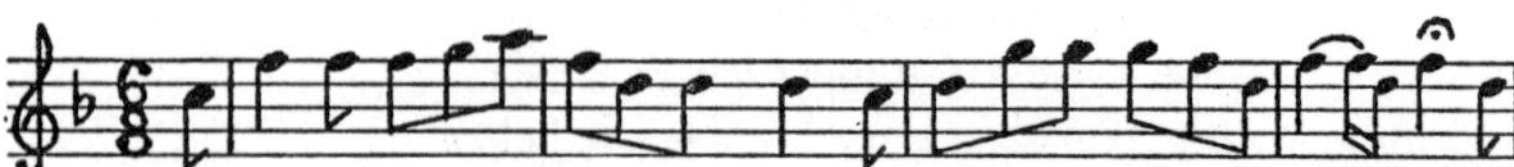

Oh wake the na-tions under the ground; oh hal - le, oh hal-le-a - lu - jah! Oh

wake the na-tions un-der the ground; oh hal - le, oh hal-le-a - lu - jah!

Did time and space allow, examples might be multiplied of a remarkably distinctive character of religious music; but there are other species of negro song which it is proposed to notice.

For many years the steamboats on Western and Southern rivers were, almost without exception, manned by crews of negro slaves. Even after white labor began to encroach upon the occupation of the "deck-hand" and "roustabout," the vocation of "fireman" was peculiarly the negro's. He basked in an atmosphere insupportable to whites, and delighted in the alternation of very hard labor and absolute idleness. It was not uncommon for large steamers to carry a crew of forty or fifty negro hands, and it was inevitable that these should soon have their songs and peculiar customs. Nine-tenths of the "river songs" (to give them a name) have the same refrain, and nearly all were constructed of single lines, separated by a barbarous and unmeaning chorus. The leader would mount the capstan as the steamer left or entered port, and affect to sing the *solo* part from a scrap of newspaper, "the full strength of the company" joining in the chorus. The effect was ludicrous, for no imagination was expended on the composition. Such songs were sung only for the howl that was their chief feature. A glance at the following will abundantly satisfy the reader with this department of negro music:

STEAMBOAT SONG

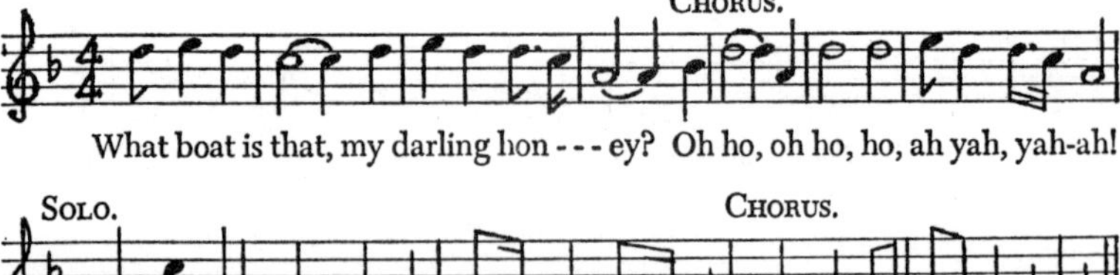

Chorus.
What boat is that, my darling hon - - - ey? Oh ho, oh ho, ho, ah yah, yah-ah!
Solo.
Chorus.
She is the "River Ruler;" Yes, my hon - - ey! Ah a - - a-a-a yah a - - ah!

Occasionally some stirring incident of steamboat achievement, as the great race between the "Shotwell" and the "Eclipse," would wake the Ethiopian muse and inspire special paeans. But as a general rule the steamboat songs were tiresomely similar to the one just given. In the department of farm or plantation songs there is much of singular music and poetry (?) to be found. Some of them are peculiar to the harvest-field, some belong exclusively to corn-shuckings (not huskings), and some are consecrated to fireside games. Long ago, when the mowing-machine and reaper were as yet unthought of, it was not uncommon to see, in a Kentucky harvest-field, fifteen or twenty "cradlers" swinging their brawny arms in unison as they cut the ripened grain, and moving with the regulated cadence of the leader's song. The scene repeated the poet's picture of ancient oarsmen and the chanter seated high above the rowers, keeping time with staff and voice, blending into one impulse the banks of the trireme.

For such a song strong emphasis of rhythm was, of course, more important than words. Each mower kept his stroke and measured his stride by musical intervals. A very favorite song for these harvesting occasions commenced thus:

RISE UP IN DUE TIME

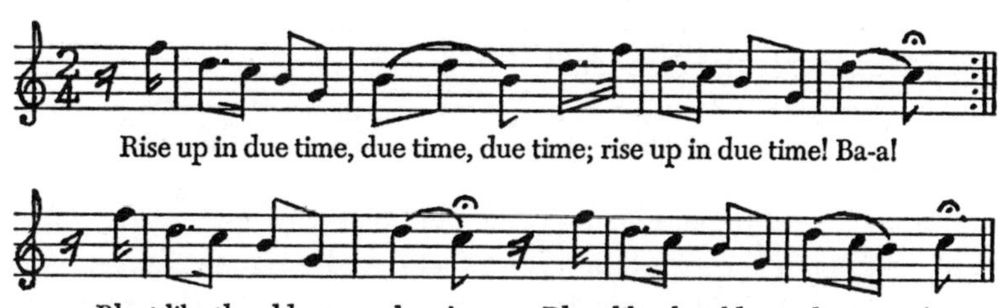
Rise up in due time, due time, due time; rise up in due time! Ba-a!
Bleat like the old ewe, ba-a! Bleat like the old ewe, ba-a-a - a!

To dignify such a specimen as the last with the name of a song may seem absurd, but in the practical life of the farmer its value was well known. A cheerful and musical leader in the harvest-field was fully appreciated and eagerly sought.

But the brisk melodies of the harvestfield and meadow were abandoned as the declining sun called the hands home to feed the "stock" and prepare for rest. Then the melancholy that tinges every negro's soul would begin to assert itself in dreamy, sad and plaintive airs, and in words that described the most sorrowful pictures of slave life—the parting of loved ones, the separation of mother and child or husband and wife, or the death of those whom the heart cherishes. As he drove his lumbering ox-cart homeward, sitting listlessly upon the heavy "tongue" behind the patient brutes, the creaking wheels and rough-hewn yokes exhibiting perhaps his own rude handiwork, the negro slave rarely failed to sing his song of longing. What if its words were rude and its music ill-constructed? Great poets like Schiller have essayed the same theme, and mighty musicians like Beethoven have striven to give it musical form. What their splendid genius failed adequately to express, the humble slave could scarce accomplish; yet they but wrought in the same direction as the poor negro, whose eyes unwittingly swam in tears, and whose heart, he scarce knew why, dissolved in tenderness, as he sang in a plaintive minor key some such song as this:

OH, SU-ZANN!
Very slow time.
Oh, Su - zann, Fare you well! And ain't you mighty sorry . . . To
think I married you just last night, And gwine away in the morning?
Refrain.
Oh, Su- zan- na, fare you well!

Within his cabin, and cheered by good company and a bright firelight, the negro slave resumed his gayety, and sang and danced and laughed as though life were but a long holiday. His day's work done and his appetite appeased, he cast off all care and abandoned himself to mirth and the old laugh renewed. Venerable songs were sung and time-honored jigs were fiddled. The origin and meaning of most of this class of songs have long been forgotten, and the jingle of rhyme and tune alone preserved.

We defy any one, however grave, to hear such a song as the following, sung in stentorian chorus by negroes, male and female, big and little, without laughing outright:

THE FIFER'S SON

Oh there was three young men a-fighting in the wars, And they all got

killed but the fif-er's son; They all got killed but the fif-er's son; And he
proved him- self a sol - dier. Oh take this cane - staff in your hand, And
choose that one that you wish to be; Choose that one that you
wish to be, And prove your- self a sol - - dier.

Or who could hear, without a responsive tapping of the foot and unbending of the wrinkled brow,

> I won't have none of your weevily wheat,
> I won't have none of your barley?

Who that has listened to the music of "Harry Cain," or "Send for the Barber," or "We'll knock around the Kitchen till the Cook comes in," will forget the merry cadence? And when the old patriarch of a plantation stood forth, before an admiring audience, to dance the famous "Turkey-buzzard Jig," was it not a scene ever to be remembered by the fortunate white who witnessed its performance?

Such events were peculiar to slavery, and disappeared with its extinction. The elements that produced them—compulsory labor and thoughtless relaxation—exist no longer. As the negro's hands are now his own property, so must his brain be used for other purposes than heretofore.

To close this sketch, already too long, a solitary instance of descriptive song may be given.

Many years ago there originated a negro ballad, founded on the incidents of a famous horse-race, on which large sums were staked. Its popularity among the negroes throughout the slaveholding States was very great, and it was their nearest approach to an epic. It was generally sung in chanting style, with marked emphasis and the prolongation of the concluding syllable of each line. The tenor of the narrative indicates that the "Gal-li-ant Gray Mar'" was imported from Virginia to Kentucky to beat the "Noble Skewball," and the bard is evidently a partisan of the latter. The commencement of the narrative is in approved invocatory style:

> Oh, ladies and gentlemen, come one and come all;
> Did you ever hear tell of the Noble Skewball?

and the author plunges at once *in medias res*, and presents to his auditors, regardless of rhyme, a view of the crowded race-course:

THE NOBLE SKEWBALL

The general reader will not probably feel interested in the preparation for the great race and the descriptions given of the horses, riders and owners, and the thread of the ballad may be given in short space. The owner of the "Noble Skewball" thus instructs his jockey:

> Stick close to your saddle, and don't be alarmed,
> For you shall not be jostled by the Noble Skewball!

and appeals confidently to the umpire—

> Squire Marvin, Squire Marvin, just judge my horse well,
> For all that I want is to see justice done.

At the signal—

> When the horses was saddled and the word was give, Go!
> Skewball shot like a arrow just out o' a bow;

and during the early part of the race the listener is assured,

> If you had a-been there at the first running round,
> You'd a-swore by your life that they never totch ground.

The excitement of the spectators, and the lavish betting of friends of the "Noble Skewball" and the "Gal-li-ant Gray Mar'," are minutely described, and the listener hurried by a current of incident to the grand climax—the triumph of the "Noble Skewball" and the payment of the stakes. The poetic fire is cooled down gradually through a dozen or more concluding couplets, the last of which proposes

> A health to Miss Bradley, that gal-li-ant Gray Mar',
> Likewise to the health of the Noble Skewball!

To convey a correct idea of negro pronunciation by ordinary rules of orthography is almost impossible. Combinations that would satisfy the ear would be grotesquely absurd to the eye. The habits of the negro in his pronunciation of English words are not such as minstrelsy would indicate. Just as the French and German characters in our comedies have passed into a conventional form of mispronunciation which the bulk of playgoers firmly believe to be lifelike and true, so have minstrels given permanency to very great mistakes in reproducing negro pronunciation. The use of "hab" for "have," of "lub" for "love," or 'massa" for "mäas," is by no means universal, nor nearly so.

In the preceding sample of slave songs no great care has been taken to convey an accurate idea of the pronunciation. We have rather aimed to put in permanent form a few random selections from a class of songs rapidly perishing, and soon to be entirely disused.

It only remains to be said that all slave songs seem best suited to barytone voices, and that no musical effect so delights the negro's ear as a well-executed swell on an emphatic word. It is in the chorus that the voices of negroes are heard to best advantage, and, though keenly appreciative of melody, it is very rare to hear among them any attempt at harmony. The remark may apply to serfs and very ignorant peasantry everywhere, but it is certainly almost without exception that the negro slaves in the United States never attempted even a rude bass in their singing, and that their most effective hymns were sung in unison.

1870

Sketches in Color: IV
[by Elizabeth Kilham]

Putnam's Monthly, XV (New York, March 1870), 304–311.

Miss Kilham's clear understanding of the only *correct approach to religious expression permits her to see the several defects in the Negroes' attitude; her conclusion reflects a position that was no doubt shared by many schoolteachers, white preachers, and well-meaning reformers. It does seem odd that she finds "Said He Wouldn't Die No Mo'" the "most meaningless of all that the negroes sing," for the song is obviously a straightforward estimate of the duration of the hereafter.*

Her reportage, however, more than compensates for her editorializing. The detail with which she describes the service is most valuable, particularly the audience's reactions to the various parts of the service. Also of interest is her observation that some songs are sung to a variety of tunes and some tunes are used for a variety of songs, and that this transference may occur in the course of a single evening; this is a fine example of the folk process in action.

The general, whose visit occasioned her excursion, was Oliver Otis Howard, commander of the Army of the Tennessee in Sherman's March to the Sea. Howard was also founder and first president of the university that bears his name.

The other three parts of Miss Kilham's article discuss a Negro maid's visit, a visiting former slave from the Dismal Swamp, schoolteaching, and a visit to "Slabtown" (see Putnam's Monthly, *XIV [December 1869], 741–746; XV [January 1870], 31–38; and XV [February 1870], 205–210).*

There came into our Sunday-school, one bright spring morning, a party of strangers; nothing very uncommon, for we had many visitors. But these interested us more than usual; for one wore a general's star upon his shoulder, and the sleeve that should have held the strong right arm hung empty by his side. Ah! those empty sleeves. What volumes of pathetic meaning speak from their mute helplessness. How they recall the days of darkness, the long struggle, the fears, the agonies, the bleeding hearts, the desolated homes, the final triumph,—purchased, how? By the pride and vigor of our country's manhood, offered up in blood and fire, for the cause of truth and freedom, on the altar of their country. Bow reverently before that empty sleeve. It belongs to a hero, and a martyr.

The school closed, and the visitors departed, our superintendent asked:

"Do you know who that was?"

"No. Who?"

"General Howard. He is on his way to Richmond, to organize the Freedmen's Bureau. He is going to address the colored people to-night at Old Billy's church; don't you want to go?"

Of course we did. So the evening found us struggling in the crowd around the door of the house where Old Billy dispensed instruction and exhortation to his flock. He was possessed of great natural abilities, and considerable shrewdness and originality, though totally uneducated, and was held in great honor among his people; so there was "gathering from near and from far," to the Sunday evening services, when he administered reproof, instruction, warning or encouragement, according to his judgment to the needs of his hearers, and in his own peculiar style.

We were too late for the opening services; General Howard was beginning his address as we entered. He spoke to the people for half an hour, as, I believe, they had never been spoken to before; of the privileges, the duties, and the possibilities of their new life. Simply, so that the youngest might understand; kindly, as friend to friend; frankly, as man to man; earnestly, as "one having authority" to those who so greatly needed counsel and instruction. Many of them, as yet, realized nothing of their freedom, save the right to go hither and thither as they would, and to wear the "same kind of clothes that white folks wear"; but I think the words of truth and soberness they heard that night, must have brought some, at least, to a truer understanding of the solemnity of life, and the dignity of self-help.

The address over, the congregation rose and sang the doxology, and General Howard and his party left the church. Then the exercises proceeded as usual. Billy announced his text. I have forgotten chapter and verse, but almost any thing would answer the purpose, being sure to fit some of the numerous subjects embraced in that discourse, which went entirely through the Bible, from the Creation to the last chapter of Revelation. In the course of his remarks, he stated some facts concerning the transgression, and consequent punishment, of Adam and Eve, which have not, I think, been brought to light by the researches of any commentator:

> Eve was jes' like all de women; dey's sich hard-headed creeturs, dat when dey gits dar minds sot, you can't nebber 'suade dem outen it. So when Eve done made up her mind to eat dat ar apple, she'd ha' ate it, ef de angel Gabr'el had ben a stan'in' right dar. But Adam wouldn't nebber ha' ate it 'tall ef Eve hadn't 'suaded him; an' jes' as he was swallerin' de fus' piece, he felt mighty sorry, an' he tried to spit it out; but it done gone too far down; an' Eve, she tole him not to make a fool ob hisself, but jes' eat de res'. So he done eat it up, an' yer knows, my bruddren, what come ter him den; how he got druv outen de garden, an' 'bleeged ter work for a libin'. De women oughter work; dat's so; fer ef it hadn't a ben for Eve, we wouldn't none on us ha' ben 'bleeged to work 'tall.

The sisters sat in "solemn silence all," under this portion of the discourse; but the brethren manifested their appreciation audibly.

The sermon was divided and subdivided, and extended to such a length that Old Billy's warmest admirers began to show signs of weariness before the close. There was considerable restlessness, and going out, among the young men near the door; and annoyed by it, Billy at last paused in his discourse, and addressed them:

> You folks in de back ob de church, stop dat ar goin' out and comin' in. It's jes' ondecent, 'sturbin' de meetin' dat ar way; ef yer wants ter go out, go out—an' stay out, too; but ef yer wants ter stay in, stay in, and 'have yerselves. 'Spose yer tinks dis yer 'scourse 's too long, too many heads ter it; but ef I'm a mind ter make forty chaws ob a grain ob rice, 'tain't none ob your business—an' some ob yer ain't got teeth 'nuff ter eat it den.

At last, with an exhortation to his hearers to join the multitude that were coming from "de Norf pole, an' from de Souf pole, an' from de Eas' pole, an' from de Wes' pole, an' shovin' right 'long inter de kingdom," the sermon closed. Then followed a prayer; the congregation kneeling, and repeating, as is their frequent custom, each sentence after the minister—a somewhat noisy exercise, and not calculated to promote devotional feelings. The colored people never generalize in their petitions; each person or class of persons for whom a blessing is desired, is mentioned by name. So now the prayer proceeded:

God bress de President.

And the congregation chanted in chorus:

God bress de President.
God bress de Congress.
Chorus—God bress de Congress.
God bress de Army.
Chorus—God bress de Army.
God bress de Major-Gen'als.
Chorus—God bress de Major-Gen'als.
God bress de Brig'dier-Gen'als.
Chorus—God bress de Brig'dier-Gen'als.

And so on, through every grade of the service; first and second lieutenants being mentioned separately, down to corporals. Then,

God bress Gen'al Howard.
Chorus—God bress Gen'al Howard.
An' do' he loss an arm,
Chorus—An' do' he loss an arm,
May he fin' it in Heaben.
Chorus—May he fin' it in Heaben.

The prayer threatened to be as long as the sermon, for Billy remembered everybody, calling them by name, until it seemed as if he must need a Directory to help him through. But it was finished at last, and he came down from the pulpit, and stood within the railing. Then began one of those scenes, which, when read of, seem the exaggerations of a disordered imagination; and when witnessed, leave an impression like the memory of some horrid nightmare—so wild is the torrent of excitement, that, sweeping away reason and sense, tosses men and women upon its waves, mingling the words of religion with the howlings of wild beasts, and the ravings of madmen.

The leader, on these occasions, usually starts a hymn, in which the congregation join. Sometimes all sing together; sometimes the leader and the congregation sing alternate lines; and again, he sings the verse throughout, the congregation only giving the chorus. In the pauses between the hymns, some brother or sister give their "experience," always talking in a scream, and as if crying; a natural tone of voice not being considered suitable for such occasions; while the others clap their hands, stamp, and shout, "yes, yes"; "dat's so"; "praise de Lord"; and the moment the speaker pauses, some voice starts a hymn, the leading sentiment of which harmonizes with what has just been said. Their quickness in finding hymns appropriate to the different phases of experience, and expressions of feeling is something wonderful.

Two or three hymns are usually sung, before they get warmed up to the talking. The first one was, as is almost invariably the case in negro meetings, "When I can read my title clear." This seems to be their chief favorite; I have heard it sung six times in the course of an evening, to different tunes. Simultaneously with the first note of the hymn, began a tapping of feet by the whole congregation, gradually increasing to a stamp as the exercises proceeded, until the noise was deafening; and as the excitement increased, one and another would spring from their seats, and jump up and down, uttering shriek after shriek; while from all parts of the house came cries of, "Hallelujah"; "Glory to God"; "Jes' now Lord, come jes' now"; "Amen"; and occasionally a prolonged, shrill whoop, like nothing earthly, unless it be some savage war-cry. At the close of the first hymn, without a moment's pause, they struck into another; a strange wild tune, the words of which we could not distinguish, except in the chorus:

Oh! I wants you to tote de young lambs in your bosom,
And carry de ole sheep along.

Then in strange contrast to this, came the most beautiful melody the negroes have—one of the most beautiful, I think, in the world—a chant, carried by full, deep bass voices; the liquid soprano of the melody wandering through and above it, now rising in triumphant swell, now falling in softened cadence, with the words,

John saw, John saw,
John saw de holy angels,
Sittin' by de golden altar.
Sittin' by de golden altar, chillens,
Sittin' by de golden altar, chillens.
John saw, John saw,
John saw de holy angels,
Sittin' by de golden altar.

At the close of this hymn there was a pause, and a woman rose and begun, "My dear bruddren and sisters, I feel, I feel, I feel,"—then, apparently unable to find words, she burst into a hymn, in which the others joined:

I'll tell you what de Lord done fer me;
  Lord come an' water Zion;
He tuk my feet from de miry clay;
  Lord come down.
Come down Lord an' water Zion,
  Come along down.

He sot my feet upon de rock;
  Lord come an' water Zion;

An' gib me David's golden harp;
  Lord come down.
Come down Lord an' water Zion,
  Come along down.

Another sister followed, who after a lengthy expression of her feelings, closed by saying:

I goes ter some churches, an' I sees all de folks settin' quiet an' still, like dey dunno know what de Holy Sperit am. But I fin's in my Bible, that when a man or a 'ooman gets full ob de Holy Sperit, ef dey should hol' dar peace, de stones would cry out; an' ef de power ob God can make de stones cry out, how can it help makin' us poor creeturs cry out, who feels ter praise Him fer His mercy. Not make a noise! Why we makes a noise 'bout ebery ting else; but dey tells us we mustn't make no noise ter praise de Lord. I don't want no sich 'ligion as dat ar. I wants ter go ter Heaben in de good ole way. An' my bruddren an' sisters, I wants yer all ter pray fer me, dat when I gits ter Heaben I wont nebber come back 'gain.

As she took her seat, the congregation, as by one impulse sang:

Oh! de way ter Heaben is a good ole way;
Oh! de way ter Heaben is a right ole way;
Oh de good ole way is de right ole way;
Oh! I wants ter go ter Heaben in de good ole way.

Several of the sisters spoke, all closing with the same words: "I hopes yer'll all pray fer me, dat when I gits to Heaben, I wont nebber come back." The women, by the way, go upon the principle of "early and often," in speaking, and frequently in these meetings monopolize the greater part of the time. It was some time before any of the brethren had a chance; at last, one seizing an opportunity, exhorted every one to

"Git on board de ship ob Zion, an' take yer anchor wid yer. Dar's two kin's ob anchors, my fren's, dar's a kedgin' anchor, an' dar's a bower anchor." (*A voice from the crowd,* "Yes, Lord, sen' down bofe on 'em.") "Take yer anchor, an' git on board de ship ob Zion. Git on board dat ole black steamer, for she's a sailin' on, an' she'll git safe froo de swellin's ob Jerdan, an' run jam up agin de walls ob Heaben, an' lan' us all safe; an' we'll march up de golden streets to de tree ob life, singin' Hallelujah Jerusalem."

Then from the hundreds of voices, rose the full, rich swell of, "Roll, Jordan, roll," or as they pronounce it,—"Jerdan."

King Jesus sittin' on de tree ob life,
  Roll, Jerdan, roll,

Gabr'el sittin' on de tree ob life,
Watchin' Jerdan, roll.
Moses sittin' on de tree ob life,
Roll, Jerdan, roll,
'Lijah sittin' on de tree ob life,
Watchin' Jerdan roll.

So on through Bible history, till prophets and apostles, in successive verses, are gathered on the "tree of Life." To this company, they join their own friends, living or dead, it matters not:

My fader sittin' on de tree ob life,
Roll, Jerdan, roll,
My mudder sittin' on de tree ob life,
Watchin' Jerdan, roll.
My sister sittin' on de tree ob life,
Roll, Jerdan, roll,
My brudder sittin' on de tree ob life,
Watchin' Jerdan, roll.

Then any others for whom they entertain special respect or affection, this part varying according to feelings and circumstances. Now they sang:

Abe Lincoln sittin' on de tree ob life,
Roll, Jerdan, roll;
Gen'l Howard sittin' on de tree ob life,
Watchin' Jerdan, roll.

They went through with most of the generals, and prominent men known as their friends; finally, having deposited Gen. Butler on the "tree of Life," to "Watch Jerdan roll,"—a somewhat novel position, I thought, for that versatile gentleman,—they came to a pause. Some one in the audience seized the opportunity to start a hymn. Apparently, this was out of order, for he had not got through a line, when old Billy interrupted him:

"What yer start dat ar fer? Dat ain't no way t'all. Don't yer start nuffin' on'y what I tells yer."

Then he proceeded to "*reform* de bruddren an' sistern, dat sis Sally Tolliver done 'ceasded" [they never say a person is dead, always she "done 'ceasded"], "dis ebenin at fo' 'clock, an' her funeral will be preach' in our place of wusshup on Chuseday (Tuesday) ebenin. Sis Sally, as you all know, war a good 'ooman, an' she hab gone whar sickness an' sorrer am no mo,' an' whar dey don't die no mo'. Sing now, all sing, 'Jesus said He wouldn't die no mo'.' "

Then we heard that hymn, the strangest, wildest, most meaningless of all that the negroes sing, and at the same time, the one which seemed to excite them the most powerfully, not so much I imagine, by the words, as the music, which is utterly indescribable, almost unearthly with its sudden changes, each one ushered in, by a long quavering shriek:

Jesus said He wouldn't die no mo',
Said He wouldn't die no mo',
So my dear Chillens don' yer fear,
Said He wouldn't die no mo'.

De Lord tole Moses what ter do,
Said He wouldn't die no mo',
Lead de chillen ob Isr'el froo',
Said He wouldn't die no mo'.
Chorus—Jesus said He wouldn't die no mo',
Said He wouldn't die no mo'.

Come 'long Moses, don' git los',
Said He wouldn't die no mo',
I'll keep yer from de heat an' fros',
Said He wouldn't die no mo'.
Chorus—Jesus said He wouldn't die no mo'.

Git 'long Moses, don't fear ter go,
Said He wouldn't die no mo',
De Lord'll guide yer heel an' toe,
Said He wouldn't die no mo'.
Chorus—Jesus said He wouldn't die no mo'.

What shoes are dose dat yer do wear?
Said He wouldn't die no mo',
So I can walk upon de air,
Said He wouldn't die no mo'.
Chorus—Jesus said He wouldn't die no mo'.

My shoes are washed in Jesus' blood,
Said He wouldn't die no mo',
An' I am trabbellin' home ter God,
Said He wouldn't die no mo'.
Chorus—Jesus said He wouldn't die no mo'.
Said He wouldn't die no mo',
So my dear chillens don' yer fear,
Said He wouldn't die no mo'.

During the singing of this hymn, the excitement, which had been gradually increasing with each change in the exercises, reached its height. Men stamped, groaned, shouted, clapped their hands; women shrieked and sobbed, two or three tore off their bonnets and threw them across the church, trampled their shawls under foot, and sprang into the air, it seemed almost to their own height, again and again, until they fell exhausted, and were carried to one side, where they lay stiff and rigid like the dead. No one paid them any farther attention, but wilder grew the excitement, louder the shrieks, more violent the stamping; while through and above it all,—over and over again,—each time faster and louder,—rose the refrain, "Jesus said He wouldn't die no mo'!"

A fog seemed to fill the church; the lights burned dimly, the air was close, almost to suffocation; an invisible power seemed to hold us in its iron grasp; the excitement was working upon us also, and sent the blood surging in wild torrents to the brain, that reeled in darkened terror under the shock. A few moments more, and I think we should have shrieked in unison with the crowd.

We worked our way through the struggling mass, sometimes pushed and beaten back, by those who, with set eye-balls and rigid faces,—dead, for the time, to things external,—were not conscious what they did. With the first breath of cool night air upon our faces, the excitement vanished; but the strain upon the nervous system had been too great, for it to recover at once its usual tone. More than one of the party leaned against the wall, and burst into hysterical tears; even strong men were shaken, and stood trembling and exhausted.

It has been much the custom to look upon the excitement of these meetings, and its effects, as an amusing, serio-comic exhibition; but there is more than comic or amusing, there is something of the terrible, in a power that makes itself, alike by impressionable ignorance, and,—though not so quickly as surely,—by the self-control and poise of character, the natural out-growth of enlightenment, education, and knowledge of the truth. It is a humiliating admission, that the physical in great measure dominates the mental, but it is true. Nerves of steel and iron, and an iron will, might pass through such scenes unmoved; I cannot believe it possible of any nature cast in the common mould of our humanity.

The distinctive features of negro hymnology, are gradually disappearing, and with another generation will probably be obliterated entirely. The cause for this, lies in the education of the younger people. With increasing knowledge, comes growing appreciation of fitness and propriety, in this, as in everything else; and already they have learned to ridicule the extravagant preaching, the meaningless hymns, and the noisy singing of their elders. Not perhaps as yet, to any great extent in the country; changes come always more slowly there, but in the cities, the young people have, in many cases, taken the matter into their own hands, formed choirs, adopted the hymns and tunes in use in the white churches, and strangers who go with the expectation of something novel and curious, are disappointed at having only ordinary church music.

A collection of negro hymns, will, a few years hence, be one of the "Curiosities of Literature." A fruitful question for the antiquarian will be, where and how did they originate? Were they composed as a whole, with deliberate arrangement and definite meaning, or are they fragments, caught here and there, and pieced into mosaic, haphazard as they come? Take, for instance, this:

> I looked inside ob Heaben,
> An' dar I saw King Jesus a comin',
> Wid a white a cater nappen tied 'roun' he wais,
> Moses an' chillen wid de Lamb.

Was this the original wording and arrangement? If so, what visions or ideas could they have been, that thus fitly phrased themselves? We questioned several of the colored people as to the meaning of "cater nappen," but received no further explanation than, "Why, dat's jes' in de hymn."

Some of the old familiar hymns, they alter in most ludicrous fashion. The lines

> Then while ye hear my heart-strings break,
> How sweet my moments roll,

they render,

> Then while ye hear my heart-strings break,
> *And see my eyeballs roll.*

Watts and Newton would never recognize their productions through the transformations they have undergone at the hands of their colored admirers.

A hymn that is a particular favorite, they will sing several times in the course of a service, each time to a different tune; and the same with tunes; they will sometimes sing three or four hymns in succession, to a tune that especially pleases them. It frequently happens in such cases, that the hymn and the tune will be in different metres; a long metre hymn will go stumbling over a short metre tune, or a hymn in short metre will be swallowed up by a tune twice as long as itself. In the latter case the words are stretched, and "drag their slow length along" over half a dozen notes, while in the former they rush along with a hop, skip and jump, that fairly takes one's breath away, and that constitutes one of the wonders of vocalism.

The colored people scarcely ever sing a hymn without a chorus, their favorite being, "Shall we know each other there?" This they sing with almost everything, sometimes in rather startling association, as,

> Plunged in a gulf of dark despair,—
> *Chorus*—Shall we know each other,
> Shall we know each other *there*?

Or,

> Hark from the tombs a doleful sound,—
> *Chorus*—Shall we know each other *there*?

Or this, which is one of the most popular:

> Hell is a dark an' a dreffnl affair,
> An' ef I war a sinner I wouldn't go dar,—
> *Chorus*—Shall we know each other *there*?

And they make almost all their hymns into this kind of patchwork, without apparently, the slightest perception of any incongruity in the sentiments thus joined together.

The question is frequently asked of teachers of freedmen,—that is, it is so far a question that it terminates in a mark of interrogation, but is really an affirmation with an upward inflexion, to which an asset is expected as a matter of course;—"You find them a universally religious people, do you not?" I know that the answer, according with the honest belief, is generally—"Yes," and I know that I shall place myself in a small and unpopular minority by answering, "No"; yet, in reviewing my observations and experience, that is the only answer I can truthfully give.

Before going among the freedmen, I held in common with others, the idea that they were naturally religious, and that there was both reality and depth in their religious life. "Perfect through suffering," "purified in the fires," were in our minds; and we judged that they who had so greatly suffered must needs be thereby greatly purified, and raised to a higher plane of religious life, than we had attained. It seemed that those over whose heads "all the waves and the billows" of sorrow had closed in over-whelming flood, must have laid firm hold upon the only anchor that could sustain them; that those whose very souls were scorched by the "fiery trial" that tried them, must have drank deep draughts of the "Water of Life," to soothe their agony; that they, who could call nothing on earth their own, must have laid up for themselves abundant treasures in Heaven. And so thinking, we forgot that faith is born of knowledge, and that this was withheld from them; we forgot that their inability to read made the truths and teachings of the Bible a dead letter to most of them; that the only instruction they received was from men, ignorant as themselves, who jumbled together words and phrases only half caught and not at all understood, in one mass of senseless jargon; and that all their ideas of religion were gathered in noisy meetings, where those who shouted the loudest and jumped the highest, were the best Christians.

Our sympathy overruled our judgment, and led us into a great mistake in our work. In everything else we strove to teach and elevate the freedmen; in this, most important of all, we sat humbly down to be learners instead of teachers. The managers of the societies had the same idea, and frequently, when teachers lamented the loss of church privileges, would say, "Why, you can go to the colored churches, can you not?" never, apparently, suspecting that there might be any lack of food, mental or spiritual. It was a mistake born of reverence and humility, but nevertheless a mistake, and one that cannot now be remedied; for the moulding stage of freedom, when these people were as wax in our hands, has passed. By our presence and silence we sanctioned their extravagances; and they stand now self-confident, proof against remonstrance and instruction.

The question, "Are the colored people truly and deeply religious?" resolves itself into several other questions, which considered separately, answer this, I think, conclusively.

Can an ignorant religion ever be a high type of religion? Many of these people are undoubtedly sincere; but the majority of them were ignorant as heathens of the objects and foundation of our faith. As one proof of this, I never met one of the freedmen, no matter what their life and character, who did not claim to be a Christian, hoping to "meet de face ob Heaben in peace." Other teachers, who have been much among them, have found it the same, and one of the most discouraging features in attempting to make any impression upon them. Opposition may in time be overcome; smiling acquiescence is almost hopeless. Easy assurance is the perfect fruit of utter ignorance, and one of its surest proofs.

"Is noisy excitement a proof of religious feeling?" Yet this is almost the only way in which the religion of the colored people manifests itself. It is very easy to stamp and groan, and shout glory; not so easy to learn understandingly what glory means, and the way to obtain a "good hope" of it. It is easy to call, "jes' now, Lord, come jes' now," without the slightest idea of how the Lord they call upon, does really come, and dwell in the believing heart. It is easy to do and say almost any thing in the excitement of a crowd, and what is so said and done, cannot be taken as the genuine feeling of the heart, nor as any proof of the life. The children in our schools would tell us sometimes: "Betty, or Milly, or Tom, done got 'ligion las' night";—that is, they were so worked upon by the excitement around them, that they screamed and stamped (having the "power" they call it), until worn out, they were carried home exhausted and fainting. But that was religion as they understood it, and these children had got it.

Is the habitual use of religious expressions, a proof of real religion? The colored people constantly use such expressions, and this, I think, more than any thing else, misled those who were unaccustomed to them. But it will be asked, Are not such expressions prompted by religious feeling? Generally, I think not. Why do they use them, then? From habit. A person may not be the least a hypocrite, and yet use such expressions without thought or meaning. I have heard children on their way to school say, "I ain't late dis mornin', bress de Lord"; or boys at play, "I didn't loss dat ar marble, tank de Lord fer dat." What prompts these expressions? They repeat what they hear their elders say, and these again, speak after the fashion of their people.

Is regular attendance at church, proof of religious feeling? Not generally among the colored people. It must be remembered that religious meetings were the only change their life in slavery afforded; in fact, their one amusement. What wonder that they flocked to them; and that the pent-up feelings and emotions, found here, the expression that was denied elsewhere. But they go to the evening meetings, stamp, shout, have the "power" and "get religion," and the next day fight, and swear and steal, as they did before, without apparently the slightest recollection of last night's excitement; and at the next evening meeting, they will go through the same exercise, with precisely the same results.

But, it is asked, are there no Christians among them? Undoubtedly. There are many who seem to have been directly taught of God, and who show the fruits of that teaching in their lives; but I have invariably found them among the quieter ones. Said an old woman, one of the "poor of this world, rich in faith":

Honey, I don't say dat ar ain't all right, but I can't feel ter do it. I used ter do it, an' I ra'lly b'liebed it was de Holy Sperit movin' me; but one day I war in a heap o' trouble, 'peared like nuffin' didn't gib me no comfort, an' I prayed to de Lord to comfort me hisself; an' peared like suffin' spoke right in my heart, soft an' quiet like, an' I 'membered how de Lord war not in de whirlwind, nor in de storm, but in de "still, small voice"; an' I knowed dat ef He spoke ter us wid a still voice, He want us ter speak ter Him de same

> way. So, honey, sence dat ar time I nebber feeled one bit like hollerin' or stampin'.

And so I have almost invariably found it with those who were Christians in heart and life, as well as in profession.

One strong argument against the idea of natural religious feeling in the colored people, is the fact, that as they become educated, it generally decreases. The reaction from excitement to indifference, is natural and sure, and as the circumstances of their lives change this feeling is weakened. Those who have been always or for many years free, manifest little of such disposition. It is a fact, painful but undeniable, that among the best educated of the colored people, there is a strong tendency to infidelity, which is, in a measure, forced on them by circumstances. A highly educated colored woman said, not long since, in answer to one who remonstrated with her on her neglect of religious services:

> I don't know whether I believe in anything or not. So far as I hear anything about religion, I don't see much to believe in. If I went to church, I might; but I am shut out from that. I won't go to the colored churches, for I'm only disgusted with bad grammar and worse pronunciation, and their horrible absurdities; I can't go to your churches, for if I am admitted at all, I am put away off in a dark corner, out of reach of everybody, as if I were some unclean thing, and I will not voluntarily place myself in such a position.

There are many in the same case, with the same bitter feelings, standing on the verge of infidelity.

Am I my brother's keeper?

Perhaps not. Nevertheless, the question may be asked one day, when shades of distinction are invisible in the light of eternity—by what right we shut out any human being, from participation in the knowledge of that truth, that was to be preached to "all men, everywhere."

1870

Negro Superstitions

by Thaddeus Norris

Lippincott's Magazine, VI (Philadelphia, July 1870), 90–95.

Though this article has some obvious defects, it does include much valuable information, particularly reports that are among the first in America of hag-riding and psychiatric exorcism among Negroes, and an excellent text of the Tar-Baby story. Aurelio Espinosa discusses the latter in considerable detail in several articles, and points out that the story was in circulation in this country long before it was brought to popular attention by Harris in 1881. Anyone interested in the story should begin study with Espinosa's "Notes on the Origin and History of the Tar-Baby Story," JAF, *43 (1930), 31–37.*

The hoodoo cures described by Norris were not uncommon. Few believers in the power of conjure managed to be as attuned to psychosomatic relativism as the informant who told Julien A. Hall, "You don't know; dey can't trick you 'cause you is white folks and don't believe in it, but de old conjure doctor kin kill us poor niggers" ("Negro Conjuring and Tricking," JAF, *10 [1897], 243). For further information on the material in Norris' article, see N. N. Puckett,* Folk Beliefs of the Southern Negro *(Chapel Hill, 1926);* Gumbo-Ya-Ya, *compiled by Lyle Saxon, Robert Tallant, and Edward Dreyer (Boston, 1945); Robert Tallant,* Voodoo in New Orleans *(New York, 1946); and* Drums and Shadows: Survival Studies among the Georgia Coastal Negroes, *Savannah Unit of the Georgia Writers' Project, WPA (Athens, Ga., 1940). A superb first-person account of a conjure doctor's training is found in Zora Neale Hurston,* Mules and Men *([Philadelphia and London, 1935], pp. 229–304).*

Last Sat'day night
De niggas went a huntin'.
De dogs dey run de coon,
De coon he run de wolver,
De wolver run de Stiff-leg,

De Stiff-leg run de Devil;
Dey run him up de hill,
But dey cotch him on the level.

Many a mythical story has originated in some such weird song as I have just quoted, and in time gained credence with the ignorant. I listened to this jargon for the first time in my early boyhood, as it was sung with banjo accompaniment by an old negro named Cato, who rejoiced in the euphonic surname of Escutcheons. On my way home from his cabin in the dim twilight, I drew, in my childish imagination, a picture, and half dreamed it over at night. Foremost came a bounding devil, with horns and tail erect, closely pursued by something half human, half animal (*i. e.*, the Stiffleg), which with rapid strides but halting gait had almost clutched his Sable Majesty. The Stiff-leg in turn was pursued by a wolf, the wolf by a raccoon of tremendous proportions, and the raccoon by a pack of yelping, barking dogs; while the negro huntsmen, with wild mirth, over fallen logs and through brambly brake, brought up the rear. I have thought since, if I had wealth at command, and could find an artist who could form a like conception of the wild chase, I would have it painted in fresco on the walls of some favorite room. If such an impression was made on the childish imagination of a white boy, the song no doubt impressed itself with a strong semblance of reality on the dark minds of some half dozen negro children who listened to Cato at the same time.

We find in our cities, even at the present day, amongst people of intelligence and culture, minds having a strong tendency to superstition; and if we could look over a record of the names of those who stealthily visit fortune-tellers, we might lose faith in the right-mindedness of some of our intimate acquaintances. Romance, though, even as history, is not without its uses, and the heroisms of either will still continue to incite boys and girls and men and women to deeds of daring and noble suffering. The perusal of the one, especially to the youthful mind, is no less absorbing than that of the other. The boy or girl does not ask whether the story be true or not; and he would be a hard-hearted parent who would rob the boy of his pleasure, as he pores over *Robinson Crusoe* or the *Arabian Nights*, or the story of Captain John Smith and Pocahontas, by telling him that what he reads is not true, or say to the little girl who weeps over the *Babes in the Woods* that it is all a fib.

Every era has had its peculiar myths. So also has every people. But there are superstitions which have been, and now are, common to different nations. Many of them have found place in the fabulous stories of newer nations, and most of them, whether ancient or modern, have originated in some trifling incident. We are told in books how the idea of the Centaur, the Dragon, the Unicorn, the Kraken, and even the Sea-serpent, originated; and I think I have shown how a wild legend might grow out of an imaginative, nonsensical song, the vagary of a woolly pate.

Although belief in witchcraft has almost faded away, it is not probable that a general diffusion of knowledge will ever entirely dissipate films of a like nature from the minds of the masses. Animal magnetism, the power of communicating through "mediums" with the spirits of the departed, et cetera, still find believers. It is human, and ever will be, to grope after the hidden, the ideal, and to hold them up as real.

The more refined a people, the more interesting its mythical legends. Those of the Caucasian race are attractive, while those of the negroes are repulsive, especially when connected with their heathenish religions. An extenuation for slavery put forth by many Southerners is, that the negro is modified, his nature softened, by association with the white man: I might add that his superstitions are humanized also. An illustrative argument in favor of this notion is to be found in a poem by a Mr. Randolph of Lower Virginia. There are some exceedingly fine passages in it for so unpretending a title, which is "A Fish Story," wherein an old negro fiddler, fishing one day, after waiting a long time in vain for a bite, ties his line to his ankle and commences playing his fiddle. The warm sunshine and the soothing music after a while cause him to fall asleep, when a huge drum-fish seizes his bait and pulls him with a sudden jerk from his canoe. The fish and fisherman both lose their lives, and, the one entangled in the line and the other hooked in the jaw, are cast ashore "by the heaving tide." The poet draws the contrast between Old Ned the fisherman and the wild African in the following lines:

Although philanthropists can see
The degrading effects of Slavery,
I cannot help thinking that this old creature
Was a great advance on his African nature,
And straighter of limb and thinner of lip
Than his grandsire who came in the Yankee ship.

Albeit bent with weary toil
Of sixty years on the slave-trodden soil,
Though thoughtless, and thriftless, and feeble of
mind,
His life was gentle, his heart was kind:

He lived in a house, and loved his wife,
And was higher far in hope and in life,
And a nobler man, with his hoe in his hand,
Than an African prince in his native land.

For perhaps the most odious thing upon earth
Is an African prince in the land of his birth,
With his negative calf and his convex shin,
Triangular teeth and pungent skin;
So bloated of body, so meagre of limb,
Of passions so fierce, of reason so dim;
So cruel in war, and so torpid in peace,
So strongly addicted to entrails and grease;
So partial to eating, by morning light,
The wife who had shared his repose over night;
In the blackest of black superstitions down-trod
In his horrible rites to his beastly god,
With all their loathsome and hideous mystery;—
But that has nothing to do with *the fish story*.

Nevertheless these lines, as we shall presently see, have some bearing on a certain mythological worship which still has existence in a limited way in Louisiana. I will first refer to a few of the negro superstitions of the Atlantic Southern States.

Of course there is the universal horseshoe branded on the door of negro cabins as a bar to witches and the devil. There are also the "conjuring gourd" and the frog-bones and pounded glass carefully hidden away by many an old negro man or woman, who by the dim light of a tallow candle or a pine-torch works imaginary spells on any one against whom he or she may have a grudge. There are also queer beliefs that are honestly maintained. One is, that the cat-bird carries sticks to the devil, and that by its peculiar note, "*Snake, snake,*" it can call snakes to its rescue and drive away those who would rob its nest. Another is, that every jay-bird carries a grain of sand to the infernal regions once a year, and that when the last grain of sand is so taken away from the earth the world will come to an end; all of which, of course, is at variance with Father Miller's calculations. Then there is a belief in a certain affinity and secret communication between themselves and wild and domestic animals. Many persons have observed a negro's way of talking to his dog or to a horse. "Aunt Bet" will say as she is milking, "Stan' aroun' now, you hussy, you. You want to git you foot in de piggin, do you?" and the cow with careful tread and stepping high will assume a more favorable position.

Amongst the mythical animals of the woods is the moonack. It is generally supposed to live in a cave or hollow tree. The negro who meets with it in his solitary rambles is doomed. His reason is impaired until he becomes a madman, or he is carried off by some lingering malady. The one who has the misfortune to encounter it never recovers from the blasting sight: he dares not speak of it, but old, knowing negroes will shake their heads despondingly and say, "He's gwine to die: he's seed de moonack."

Many of these superstitions, as the efficacy of the frog-bones and conjuring gourd, are no doubt handed down from their African ancestors. A few years back the rites of the "Hoodoo" were practiced and believed in in the city of New Orleans. From the description I have had from those who have witnessed the ceremony, it must have resembled the incantation scene in *Macbeth.*

It is well known in Louisiana that many a cargo of slaves from Africa was landed on the Gulf coast soon after that portion of our national domain was purchased from France, and that this traffic in human flesh was stealthily kept up for some years after the war of 1812. Labor was in demand, and this demand increased as the rich alluvial lands along the Mississippi and the lagoons and bayous to the west of New Orleans were opened to the culture of cotton and sugar. The planters, whether they were creoles of French or Spanish extraction or emigrants from the Atlantic States, were not disposed to quibble as to the legality of procuring slaves in this way; they were only too glad to get them; and the numerous lagoons running from the Gulf into the interior offered facilities for the landing of slaves. That the heathenish rites of the Hoodoo should exist in Louisiana even at the present day is therefore not wonderful.

But to return to the votaries of Hoodoo in New Orleans. There was the fire in the middle of the earthen floor, with the iron pot swung over it. What its contents were none but the official negroes knew; but as it boiled and bubbled, the negroes, with song of incantation, would join hands and dance around it until they were successively exhausted and fell on the floor. Amongst the votaries of the Hoodoo, it is said, could occasionally be found white women of wealth and respectability who had been influenced by their old Negro servants.

For some years before the war of the rebellion it was my fortune to be connected in a business with a firm in New Orleans. One of my partners, as an act of humanity and to secure his services as porter, bought a negro boy who we had been hiring for some years by the month. His name was Edwa, and at the time of buying him he was about eighteen years of age. When not employed in his regular duties, he improved the hours by learning to read and write. He was constitutionally and practically honest. His services were valuable, and he was a favorite with all. Still, his hereditary aptness for such things led him to join in the Hoodoo; and as a matter of course, he became bewitched, and, although a consistent professor of the Christian religion, he believed in this superstition. It was about three years after my partner became his owner that he was thus affected. All arguments against his foolish impressions were useless. He imagined that some one of his co-worshipers had put a spell on him; that his enemy had poured frog-spawn into some water which he had given him to drink, and that this spawn had hatched and entered into the circulation of his blood; that his veins were full of small tadpoles.

Dr. H——, a shrewd physician, became acquainted with Edwa's malady, and assured him that he was correct, and his master and friends unreasonable and entirely in the wrong, as to his complaint; and, to use an old saying, "to fight fire with fire" and restore his favorite servant, he put him under a course of medicine and made a final cure as follows: Procuring some hundreds of minute tadpoles from the ditches back of the city, he made an appointment with Edwa to be at his office at an hour of a certain day. Giving him a dose of some sickening and stupefying medicine, he then bled him copiously and shook the tadpoles from his coat sleeve into the basin of blood. His master and a few friends who were present acknowledged their error on seeing the tadpoles, and Edwa had ocular demonstration that he was delivered from these internal pests, and soon recovered his usual health and spirits.

Negroes are naturally suspicious of each other—that is, of some secret power or influence those of greater age have over them—and will entrust their money and health and well-being to white persons with perfect confidence, while they are distrustful of those of their own color. I cite the following as a case in point—its truthfulness I can vouch for: A gentleman in Alexandria, Virginia, had an old servant by the name of Friday, who filled the office of gardener and man-of-all-work about his premises. One summer, Friday, from some cause unknown to his master, was very "ailing." He lost his appetite, his garrulity, his loud-ringing laugh, became entirely incapable of attending to his duties, and appeared to be approaching his last end. On questioning him closely, he told his master, with some reluctance, that he was suffering from a spell that had been put upon him by Aunt Sina, the cook, who was some years older than himself. When pressed hard for some proof, he said that he had seen her, one moonlight night, raise one of the bricks in the pavement leading from the portico to the street, near the gate, and place something under it which he knew was a charm, for he had tried several times, without avail, to raise the brick; and that he could not even see that it had ever been moved. Further, that he had frequently heard Aunt Sina muttering something to herself which he could not understand, and on one occasion saw her hide something in her chest, which he was pretty sure was a conjuring gourd. All of this, he said, was a part of the spell; that all of the physic he had taken was of no avail; that he was troubled with a constant "misery in his head," and was certain he was going to die.

His master, knowing how useless it would be to endeavor to reason him out of such belief, and being a practical wag, determined to treat Friday's case with a like remedy. He accordingly enjoined strict secresy toward Aunt Sina as to any knowledge of his being bewitched, and put him on a course of bread-pills tinctured with asafoetida. He then searched the garret, and finding a pair of old boots with light morocco interlinings, he cut out and drew distinctly, on two similar pieces, a skull and crossbones encompassed by a circle. He further warned Friday of the evil effect that might ensue by passing over or near the brick under which Aunt Sina had deposited the charm, and promised to write a celebrated Indian doctor who lived some thousand miles away, and get his advice. Then he sent his old servant with a letter on some pretended business which would keep him away for a few days.

When Friday had departed, with considerable difficulty and much care his master raised a brick as near as possible to the place where the charm was supposed to have been hidden, and carefully laying down one of the cabalistic pieces of leather, as carefully replaced the brick.

In a few days Friday returned. Some heavy rain having fallen during his absence, all marks of disturbance in the pavement were effaced. Friday still continued to grow worse, and in a few days more his master produced a letter from a long envelope with a singular-looking postmark and mysterious characters on it, which he informed him was from the Indian doctor. The letter of this wise sachem, as his master read it to Friday, informed him that the conjuring gourd had no power of evil in his case, but that the person who had put the spell on him had hidden two charms; that if one of these could be found and certain conditions observed, the other could also; and if they were both alike the spell would be broken. The letter then went on to describe the place where one of them was hidden. It was in an old churchyard, but the doctor could not say where the church was: it might be in America or England or France. The description of the church, however, was so graphic that by the time his master had read it through the white of Friday's eyes had enlarged considerably, and he gaspingly exclaimed, "Fo' God, Maas Ant'ony! it's Christ Church, here in dis very town!" His master here laid aside the letter, and bringing his fist heavily down on the table, declared that it was: it had not occurred to him before. The charm, so said the doctor's letter, was under the topmost loose brick (which was covered with leaves) of a certain old tomb, the fourth one from the gate, on the left-hand side of the middle walk, going in. It was to be taken from under the brick, and by the bewitched, going out of the churchyard backward—all the time repeating the Lord's Prayer. He was to turn around when he reached the street and throw a handful of sulphur backward over the wall.

The day on which the letter was read to the patient, Aunt Sina was sent on an errand which would detain her all night; and when the moon was well up Friday complied with all the conditions, his master awaiting his return. Then a few bricks in the pavement were removed with much difficulty, and the other charm was found. They were compared by the light of a red wax candle in his master's office, and to Friday's joy one was an exact duplicate of the other. "Now, Friday, drink this," said Maas Anthony, handing him a large tumbler of whisky, into which he had stirred a teaspoonful of sulphur taken from the same paper as that he had thrown over the churchyard wall. "The spell is broken, and if you sleep well to-night, you will be all right in a day or two. Remember, though, if you hint to old Sina anything about breaking the spell she will bewitch you again. Now go to bed."

Of course Friday slept well. With his mind at ease, and under the influence of nearly a pint of whisky, why shouldn't he? He soon recovered his health, his garrulity and his loud laugh.

Every Southern boy has heard the story of the "Rabbit and the Tar Baby." It runs thus: An old negro, who cultivated a little truck-patch for his own private benefit, had his black-eyed peas stolen frequently, without being able to detect the thief. At length, as he crossed the branch near his patch one morning, he discovered rabbit tracks in the mud, and was convinced that Puss was the depredator. He knew from the size of the tracks that it was a very large and wary old rabbit which had haunted the neighborhood from time immemorial. His cunning was proof against all the snares, traps, deadfalls, gins and gums that were ever set for him. If he was captured, he managed by some device to get off and continue his thieving. After long consideration, and knowing the curiosity of wild animals, as well as the tenacity of tar, the old man concluded to make a "tar baby" or image, and set it where the rabbit was in the habit of crossing the branch. The rabbit, after feeding plentifully on the old man's peas through the night, was returning to his nest across the branch about daybreak one morning, and to his surprise saw a black baby standing bolt upright before him. After some hesitation he approached, and throwing himself on his haunches and nodding to the baby, bade it "Good-morning," but the baby gave no answer or sign of recognition. He then upbraided the baby for its impoliteness: still it gave no answer. He then abused it outright for its incivility, but the baby treated him with silent contempt. Infuriated at this insulting behavior, the rabbit gave the baby a terrible slap in the face with his right forepaw, when it stuck fast. "Let go my hand," said the rabbit: the baby maintained its silence, but held on to the paw. He then gave the baby a heavy left-hander, and that paw also stuck fast. Then he kicked the baby in the stomach with his left and then with his right hind foot, and they also were held. Losing all discretion in his rage, he gave the baby a vigorous butt in the face, when his head stuck, and he was irrevocably held fast—that cunning old rabbit—and outwitted by a *tar baby!*

The owner of the patch, going to his work about sunrise, discovered the arch old thief a victim to his curiosity and bad manners, and loosing him from the baby and holding him by the hind legs, rejoiced over his captive thus: "Ah ha, ole fellow! I got you at last, I is. You been thievin' dis long time, but now I got you, sartain. You good for roast, you good for bile, you good for fry, you good for potten-pie." But the rabbit, after remaining passive for some moments, suddenly thrust both of its tarry forepaws into the old man's eyes, so that he was compelled to let go the rabbit's legs to rub his aching orbs. Of course the rabbit escaped, and as he went bounding off, the old man exclaimed, "Go 'long, you big-eye, whopper-jaw, long-leg, cotton-tail! you ain't got nuff fat on you whole body for fry you hind leg."

When such stories were told, and I became inquisitive as to animals talking with human beings or with each other, I was generally told, "Dat was a long time ago, but dey don't do so any mo'." In my childhood I firmly believed in witches, and it was with some dread that I went out of doors or through a room when it was dark, and frequently dreamed of them after hearing some of the stories told by the servants on long winter evenings. An old houseservant of my father was as chock full of these witch stories as Sancho Panza was of proverbs. According to his teachings, wizards ("conjerors," he called them) and witches made a bargain with the devil that they were to possess extraordinary powers over their fellow-mortals in this life, and in exchange their souls belonged to him. There were some restrictions, however, which the devil could not free them from. For instance, they had no power over a child who not arrived at the age of discretion, could work no evil to a person who had a Bible in the room at night, and could not utter the Lord's name. Stanton, the man referred to, said that a witch could creep out of her skin and leave it in bed, so that her absence could not be noted; that it was not uncommon for one witch, when she had enmity against another, and knew when she made a nocturnal excursion, to get her skin, and, turning it wrong side out, to salt and pepper it well; and then, turning it with the fleshy part side in again, to replace it in bed. One of Stanton's stories was as follows. I will narrate it, as nearly as I can, in the language in which he used to tell it:

Once der was a ole man dat was a conjeror, an' his wife was a witch; an' dey had a son, an' dey larnt him to be a conjeror too; an' every night dey use to git out of deir skins an' go ride deir neighbors. Well, one night de conjeror tetch his son wid his staff an' say, "Horum sacrum" (dat mean, "It's pas' de hour o' midnight"). "Come, git up; let's go ride de overseer an' his oldes' son: I had a spite 'gin 'em dis long time." So dey goes to de overseer's house, an' give de sign an' slip t'rough de keyhole. Den dey unbar de door on de inside an' take out de overseer an' his son, widout deir knowin' it; an' de conjeror tetch de overseer wid his switch an' he turns to a bull, an' tetch de overseer's son an' he turns to a bull-yerlin'. Den de conjeror mounts de bull, an' de boy he mounts de bull-yerlin', an' sets off a long way over de creek to blight a man's wheat what de conjeror had a spite agin. Well, dey rode a long time to git dar, an' when dey was cummin' back dey see de mornin' star shinin' mighty bright, an' de conjeror say to his son, "S'pose we run a race? Whoever git to de ole gallus cross de creek fust will live de longes'." So off dey goes, nip and tuck—sometimes de bull ahead, and sometimes de yerlin' ahead. But de bull, he gets to de creek fust, an' stops to drink, de yerlin' little ways behind; an' when *he* gits to de creek de boy gin him a cut, an' he would ha' gone clean over, but de boy as he went over hollered out, "God, daddy! dat's a good jump for bull-yerlin'." An' dat same minit dey was bofe standin' in de water forty miles from home. De bull wasn't dar. An' de same minit de overseer was asleep in his bed at home, an' his son was in *his* bed. An' in de mornin' dey feel very tired, an' know dat de witches been ridin' 'em, but dey never find out what witches it was.

1877

Folklore of the Southern Negroes

by William Owens

Lippincott's Magazine, XX (Philadelphia, December 1877), 748–755.

Considering how little was known about Negro folklore at the time this article was written, one can hardly blame Owens for his error about the state of superstition and witchcraft—these facts of Negro life were by no means so moribund in 1877 as he suggests. The article's importance rests in the nine stories and miscellaneous comments that follow his introductory pages. Joel Chandler Harris said that this was the article that inspired him to begin gathering and publishing his Uncle Remus tales (see Harris, "An Accidental Author"), and for that reason Owens had an influence ranging far beyond his actual contribution. Harris set a fashion in Negro folktale collection and, with rare exceptions, it was not until well along in this century that collectors began to study in depth nonanimal tales.

One could spend a considerable amount of time attempting to annotate the nine stories. The story of the Rabbit riding the Wolf, for example, has been collected frequently in Africa and the New World. For a simplified version from Sierra Leone, see Florence M. Cronise and Henry W. Ward, Cunie Rabbit, Mr. Spider and the other Beef *([New York, 1930], pp. 70–76); see also Joel Chandler Harris,* Uncle Remus: His Songs and Sayings *([rev. ed.; New York, 1908], pp. 24–29), and Charles C. Jones, Jr.,* Negro Myths from the Georgia Coast *([Columbia, S.C., 1925], pp. 29–33). Elsie Clews Parsons offers several Bahaman texts of the story, and notes several other published versions in her "Folk-Tales of Andros Island, Bahamas,"* MAFS, *13 (New York, 1918). She published a comprehensive note on the story in her "'Folk-Lore of the Antilles, French and English,"* MAFS, *26, Pt. III (1943), 73–76. The story of the pigs and the fox has far broader distribution than is indicated by Owens' identification of it as an "Anglo-Saxon story." T. F. Crane, in his excellent review of Harris' book reprinted in this volume offers further comments on Owens' article.*

All tribes and peoples have their folk-lore, whether embodied in tales of daring adventure, as in our own doughty Jack the Giant-killer, or in stories of genii and magic, as in the *Arabian Nights*, or in legends of wraiths, witches, bogles and apparitions, as among the Scotch peasantry; and these fables are so strongly tinged with the peculiarities—or rather the idiosyncrasies—of the race among whom they originate as to furnish a fair index of its mental and moral characteristics, not only at the time of their origin, but so long as the people continue to narrate them or listen to them.

The folk-lore of Africo-Americans, as appearing in our Southern States, is a medley of fables, songs, sayings, incantations, charms and superstitious traditions brought from various tribes along the West African coast, and so far condensed into one mass in their American homes that often part of a story or tradition belonging to one tribe is grafted, without much regard to consistency, upon a part belonging to another people, while they are still further complicated by the frequent infusion into them of ideas evidently derived from communication with the white race.

Any one who will take the trouble to analyze the predominant traits of negro character, and to collate them with the predominant traits of African folk-lore, will discern the fitness of each to each. On every side he will discover evidences of a passion for music and dancing, for visiting and chatting, for fishing and snaring, indeed for any pleasure requiring little exertion of either mind or body; evidences also of a gentle, pliable and easy temper—of a quick and sincere sympathy with suffering wheresoever seen—of a very low standard of morals, combined with remarkable dexterity in satisfying themselves that it is right to do as they wish. Another trait, strong enough and universal enough to atone for many a dark one, is that, as a rule, there is nothing of the fierce and cruel in their nature, and it is scarcely possible for anything of this kind to be grafted permanently upon them.

Of their American-born superstitions, by far the greater part are interwoven with so-called religious beliefs, and go far to show their native faith in dreams and visions, which they are not slow to narrate, to embellish, and even to fabricate extemporaneously, to suit the ears of a credulous listener; also showing their natural tendency to rely upon outward observances, as if possessed of some *fetish*-like virtue, and in certain cases a horrible debasement of some of the highest and noblest doctrines of the Christian faith. These superstitions must of course be considered apart from the real character of those who are sincerely pious, and upon which they are so many blemishes. They are, in fact, the rank and morbid outgrowth of the peculiarities of religious denominations grafted upon the prolific soil of their native character.

Of the few which may be mentioned without fear of offence, since they belong to the negro rather than to his denomination, the following are examples: Tools to be used in digging a grave must never be carried through a house which any one inhabits, else they will soon be used for digging the grave of the dweller. Tools already used for such a purpose must not be carried directly home. This would bring the family too closely for safety into contact with the dead. They must be laid reverently beside the grave, and allowed to remain there all night. A superstition in respect to posture is by some very rigorously observed. It is, that religious people must never sit with their legs crossed. The only reason given—though we cannot help suspecting that there must be another kept in concealment—is, that *crossing the legs is the same as dancing, and dancing is a sin.*

These are fair samples of Americanized superstitions—puerile, it is true, but harmless. It is only when we come into contact with negroes of pure African descent that we discover evidences of a once prevalent and not wholly discarded demonolatry. The native religion of the West African, except where elevated by the influence of Mohammedanism, was not—and, travellers tell us, is not yet—a worship of God as such, nor even an attempt to know and honor Him, but a constant effort at self-protection. The true God, they say, calls for no worship; for, being good in and of himself, He will do all the good He can without being asked. But there are multitudes of malignant spirits whose delight is to mislead and to destroy. These must be propitiated by gifts and acts of worship, or rendered powerless by charms and incantations.

No one knows, or has the means of ascertaining, to what extent real devil-worship is practised in America, because it is always conducted in secret; but we have reason to believe that it has almost entirely ceased, being shamed out of existence by the loveliness of a purer and better faith, and a belief in the agency of evil spirits, and consequent dread of their malign powers, although still more or less dominant with the negroes, has also greatly declined.* To give a sample of this last: The time was—but it has nearly passed away, or else the writer has not been for many years in the way of hearing of

* Of the terrible forms of superstition prevalent under the names of Obi, Voodooism, Evil-eye or Tricking, in which a trick-doctor or witch-doctor works against another person's life or health or plans, or seeks to neutralize the influence of another doctor, our subject leads us to say nothing.

it, as in the days of childhood—when one of the objects of greatest dread among our seaboard negroes was the "Jack-muh-lantern." This terrible creature—who on dark, damp nights would wander with his lantern through woods and marshes, seeking to mislead people to their destruction—was described by a negro who seemed perfectly familiar with his subject as a hideous little being, somewhat human in form, though covered with hair like a dog. It had great goggle eyes, and thick, sausage-like lips that opened from ear to ear. In height it seldom exceeded four or five feet, and it was quite slender in form, but such was its power of locomotion that no one on the swiftest horse could overtake it or escape from it, for it could leap like a grasshopper to almost any distance, and its strength was beyond all human resistance. No one ever heard of its victims being bitten or torn: they were only compelled to go with it into bogs and swamps and marshes, and there left to sink and die. There was only one mode of escape for those who were so unfortunate as to be met by one of these mischievous night-walkers, and that was by a charm; but that charm was easy and within everybody's reach. Whether met by marsh or roadside, the person had only to take off his coat or outer garment and put it on again inside out, and the foul fiend was instantly deprived of all power to harm.

Multifarious, however, as are the forms and aspects of folk-lore among this remarkable and in some respects highly interesting people, the chief bulk of it lies stored away among their fables, which are as purely African as are their faces or their own plaintive melodies. Travellers and missionaries tell us that the same sweet airs which are so often heard in religious meetings in America, set to Christian hymns, are to be recognized in the boats and palm-roofed houses of Africa, set to heathen words, and that the same wild stories of Buh Rabbit, Buh Wolf, and other *Buhs* that are so charming to the ears of American children, are to be heard to this day in Africa, differing only in the drapery necessary to the change of scene.

Almost without exception the actors in these fables are brute animals endowed with speech and reason, in whom mingle strangely, and with ludicrous incongruity, the human and brute characteristics. The *dramatis personae* are always honored with the title of *Buh,* which is generally supposed to be an abbreviation of the word "brother" (the *br* being sounded without the whir of the *r*), but it probably is a title of respect equivalent to our Mr. The animals which figure in the stories are chiefly Buh Rabbit, Buh Lion, Buh Wolf and Buh Deer, though sometimes we hear of Buh Elephant, Buh Fox, Buh Cooter and Buh Goose. As a rule each Buh sustains in every fable the same general character. Buh Deer is always a simpleton; Buh Wolf always rapacious and tricky; Buh Rabbit foppish, vain, quick-witted, though at times a great fool; Buh Elephant quiet, sensible and dignified.

Of the Buh fables, that which is by all odds the greatest favorite, and which appears in the greatest variety of forms, is the "Story of Buh Rabbit and the Tar Baby." Each variation preserves the great landmarks, particularly the closing scene. According to the most thoroughly African version, it runs thus: Buh Rabbit and Buh Wolf are neighbors. In a conversation one day Buh Wolf proposes that they two shall dig a well for their joint benefit, instead of depending upon chance rainfalls or going to distant pools or branches, as they often have to do, to quench their thirst. To this Buh Rabbit, who has no fondness for labor, though willing enough to enjoy its fruits, offers various objections, and finally gives a flat refusal.

"Well," says Buh Wolf, who perfectly understands his neighbor, "if you no help to dig well, you mustn't use de water."

"What for I gwine use de water?" responds Buh Rabbit with affected disdain. "What use I got for well? In de mornin' I drink de dew, an' in middle o' day I drink from de cow-tracks."

The well is dug by Buh Wolf alone, who after a while perceives that some one besides himself draws from it. He watches, and soon identifies the intruder as Buh Rabbit, who makes his visits by night. "Ebery mornin' he see Buh Rabbit tracks—every mornin' Buh Rabbit tracks." Indignant at the intrusion, he resolves to set a trap for his thievish neighbor and to put him to death. Knowing Buh Rabbit's buckish love for the ladies, he fits up a *tar baby,* made to look like a beautiful girl, and sets it near the well. By what magical process this manufacture of an attractive-looking young lady out of treacherous adhesive tar is accomplished we are not informed. But listeners to stories must not be inquisitive about the mysterious parts: they must be content to hear.

Buh Rabbit, emboldened by long impunity, goes to the well as usual after dark, sees this beautiful creature standing there motionless, peeps at it time and again suspiciously; but being satisfied it is really a young lady, he makes a polite bow and addresses her in gallant language. The young lady makes no reply. This encourages him to ask if he may not come to take a kiss. Still no reply. He sets his water-bucket on the ground, marches up boldly and obtains the kiss, but finds to his surprise that he cannot get away: his lips are held fast by the tar. He struggles and tries to persuade her to let him go. How is he able to speak with his lips sticking fast is another unexplained mystery; but no matter: he does speak, and most eloquently, yet in vain. He now changes his tone, and threatens her with a slap. Still no answer. He administers the slap, and his hand sticks fast. One after the other, both hands and both feet, as well as his mouth, are thus caught, and poor Buh Rabbit remains a prisoner until Buh Wolf comes the next morning to draw water.

"Eh! eh! Buh Rabbit, wah de matter?" exclaims Buh Wolf, affecting the greatest surprise at his neighbor's woeful plight.

Buh Rabbit, who has as little regard for truth as for honesty, replies, attempting to throw all the blame upon the deceitful maiden by whom he has been entrapped, not even suspecting yet—so we are to infer—that she is made of tar instead of living flesh. He declares with all the earnestness of injured innocence that he was passing by, in the sweet, honest moonlight, in pursuit of his lawful business, when this girl *hailed* him, and decoyed him into giving her a kiss, and was now holding him in unlawful durance.

The listener ironically commiserates his captive neighbor, and proposes to set him free; when, suddenly noticing the water-bucket and the tracks by the well, he charges Buh Rabbit with his repeated robberies by night, and concludes by declaring his intention to put him to immediate death.

The case has now become pretty serious, and Buh Rabbit is of course woefully troubled at the near approach of the great catastrophe; still, even in this dire extremity, his wits do not cease to cheer him with some hope of escape. Seeing that his captor is preparing to hang him—for the cord is already around his neck and he is being dragged toward an overhanging limb—he expresses the greatest joy by capering, dancing and clapping his hands—so much that the other curiously inquires, "What for you so glad, Buh Rabbit?"

"Oh," replies the sly hypocrite, "because you gwine hang me and not trow me in de briar-bush."

"What for I mustn't trow you in de brier-bush?" inquires Mr. Simpleton Wolf.

"Oh," prays Buh Rabbit with a doleful whimper, "please hang me: please trow me in de water or trow me in de fire, where I die at once. But don't—oh don't—trow me in de brief-bush to tear my poor flesh from off my bones."

"I gwine to do 'zactly wah you ax me not to do," returns Wolf in savage tone. Then, going to a neighboring patch of thick, strong briers, he pitches Buh Rabbit headlong in the midst, and says, "Now, let's see de flesh come off de bones."

No sooner, however, does the struggling and protesting Buh Rabbit find himself among the briers than he slides gently to the ground, and peeping at his would-be torturer from a safe place behind the stems, he says, "Tankee, Buh Wolf—a tousand tankee—for *bring me home!* De brier-bush *de berry place where I been born.*"

Another favorite story is that of the "Foot-Race." Buh Rabbit and Buh Frog are admirers of the beautiful Miss Dinah, and try their best to win her. The lady likes them both, but not being permitted to marry both, she resolves to make her choice depend upon the result of a foot-race. The distance is to be ten miles—that is, five miles out and five miles in—along a level road densely bordered with bushes. The day arrives. Miss Dinah, seated at the starting-point, is to give the word to the rivals, who stand one on either side, and the goal for the winner is to be a place *in her lap*. By agreement, Buh Rabbit to take the open road, and Buh Frog, who prefers it, is allowed to leap through the bushes, and both are to halloo to each other at the end of every mile. Buh Rabbit, however, with all his cunning, has this time met his match; for Buh Frog has engaged five of his kinsmen, so nearly like himself in appearance that they cannot be distinguished from him, and has stationed one in concealment near each mile-post, with instructions how to act, while he has provided for himself a nice hiding-place in the bushes near Miss Dinah's seat. At the word Go! the rivals start, Buh Frog leaping into the bushes, where he disappears, and Buh Rabbit capering along the road and flaunting his white tail merrily at the thought of distancing the other so far that he shall never see or hear of him again till after Miss Dinah has been won. At the end of the first mile Buh Rabbit turns his head back and tauntingly halloos, "I here, Buh Frog! How you git 'long?"

To his dismay, however, he hears the voice of the other in the bushes ahead of him singing out, "Boo-noo! I here too! I beat you here, I'll beat you there: I'll beat you back to Miss Dinah's lap!"

On hearing this boast repeated ahead of him in the bushes at each mile-post, Buh Rabbit becomes frantic, and rushes through the last mile as he had never run before. But all in vain. Just as he comes within easy view of the coveted goal he sees Buh Frog leap from the bushes plump into Miss Dinah's lap, and hears him sing, with as good breath as though he had not run a mile,

> Boo-noo! Before you!
> I beat you there, I beat you here:
> I've beat you back to Miss Dinah's lap!

Another version makes the competitors Buh Deer and Buh Cooter (the negro name for terrapin or land-tortoise), in which Buh Cooter wins the day by collusion with some of his closely-resembling kin. Substantially the same story is to be heard from the natives of each of the four continents, but whether the African gained his idea of it from Europe or Asia, or whether the European or Asian gained it from Africa, is perhaps past determining. The writer can testify that the story as above narrated, or rather the substance of it, was told him in childhood by negroes supposed to have obtained it direct from Africa.

Some of these stories are mere laudations of Buh Rabbit's shrewdness and common sense. Buh Wolf has long had a watering of the mouth for rabbit-flesh, but has never been able to gratify it. He finally hits upon the following expedient: He causes a report to be spread that he has suddenly died, and all his neighbors, especially Buh Rabbit, are invited to his funeral. He has no doubt that his plump, short-tailed neighbor, being once enclosed within the walls of his house, will fall an easy prey to himself and his attending cousins. Buh Rabbit, however, is not to be easily ensnared. He goes demurely to the house of mourning, but does not enter. He seats himself on the steps by the side of Buh Cat, who is enjoying the sunshine in the doorway.

"Is Buh Wolf dead, for true and true?" he inquires.

"I suppose so. Eberybody say he dead," answers Buh Cat.

"How did he die, and when?" he continues to inquire.

Buh Cat gives the particulars as reported to him, and Buh Rabbit pretends to receive them with all faith, expressing great sorrow for the loss experienced by the neighborhood. But after a little musing, he seems to be struck with a new idea, and turning to Buh Cat he inquires in hopeful tone, "But did he *grin* or *whistle* before he died? People who die *must* do one or t'other; and some, who die hard, do both. I'm a doctor, you know."

This is said in the doorway, near the stiff-looking corpse, and in a whisper loud enough to be heard all through the room. Very soon Buh Wolf is heard to whistle, and then his lips settle into a grin so broad as to show his teeth.

"Buh Cat," says Buh Rabbit, putting his hand on his stomach and screwing up his face as if seized with mortal sickness, "I mus' hurry home and take some yarb tea, or mebbe I'll have to grin and whistle like our poor neighbor. Goodbye, Buh Cat. Come to me, please, after Buh Wolf done berry and tell me all about it. Good-bye."

To the surprise of all who are not in the secret, the corpse gives a loud sneeze, then leaps from the table, throws off his "berryin' clothes," and joins his friends in eating heartily of his own funeral dinner.

His hankering, however, for rabbit-mutton still continues, and he resolves, notwithstanding his recent inglorious defeat, to attempt again to gratify it. With this end in view he makes frequent visits to his neighbor and talks with him across the fence, but is never invited beyond. One day, in the course of conversation, he informs him that there is a fine pear tree on the other side of a neighboring field, loaded with luscious fruit just in condition to be gathered.

"I will go get some."

"When?"

"To-morrow, when the sun is about halfway up the sky."

"Go: I will join you there."

Buh Rabbit rises very early, goes to the tree soon after daybreak, finds the pears uncommonly good, and is laughing to himself to think how he has outwitted his enemy, when he hears a voice under the tree: "Ho, Mr. Rabbit! in the tree a'ready?"

"Yes," replies Buh Rabbit, trembling at the sight of his dreaded foe: "I wait for you, and tink you nebber gwine come. I tell you w'at," smacking his lips, "dem here pear too good."

"Can't you trow me down some?" inquires Buh Wolf, so strongly impressed by the sound of that eloquent smack that he longs to get a taste of the fruit.

Buh Rabbit selects some of the finest, which he throws far off in the soft grass, in order, he says, to avoid bruising, and while Buh Wolf is engaged in eating them, with his head buried in the grass, Buh Rabbit slides quietly from the tree and hurries home.

A few days thereafter Buh Wolf makes still another attempt. He pays a visit as before, and speaks of a great fair to be held next day in a neighboring town. "I am going," says the rash Buh Rabbit; and he does go, although we might suppose that he would have sense enough to keep out of harm's way. On returning home, late in the day, he sees Buh Wolf sitting on a log by the roadside, at the bottom of a hill, waiting for him. His preparations for escape have already been made in the purchase of a quantity of hollow tinware. Slipping quietly into the bushes, without being seen by the waylayer, he puts a big tin mug on his head and a tin cup on each hand and foot, and, hanging various tin articles around his body, he comes rolling down the hill toward Buh Wolf, who is so frightened at the unearthly noise that he runs off with his tail between his legs, and never troubles Buh Rabbit again.

The struggle between them, however, does not cease even with this triumph of the weaker party. There is a contest now of love and stratagem. They both pay their addresses to the same young lady, making their visits to her on alternate evenings. In the progress of the courtship Buh Rabbit learns that his rival has spoken of him contemptuously, saying that he is very dressy and foppish, it is true, but that he has no manliness; adding that he (Buh Wolf) could eat him up at a mouthful. To this Buh Rabbit retorts the next evening by assuring Miss Dinah that Buh Wolf was nothing but his grandfather's old *riding horse*; adding, "I ride him, and whip him too, whenever I choose, and he obeys me like a dog." The next afternoon Buh Rabbit tempts his unsuspecting rival to join him in the play of riding horse, which consists in each in turn mounting the other's back and riding for a while. Buh Rabbit, who has thought out the whole case beforehand, offers to give the first ride, and so times it that the ride ends at his own door about the time for the usual visit to Miss Dinah. He runs into the house and puts on his dandy clothes, pleading that he cannot enjoy a ride unless he is in full dress; and pleading, moreover, that he cannot ride without saddle and bridle and all that belongs to a horseman, he persuades Mr. Fool Wolf to allow a strong, rough bit to be put into his mouth and a close-fitting saddle to be girded to his back, upon which Buh Rabbit mounts, holding in his hand a terrible whip and having his heels armed with a pair of long sharp spurs. Thus accoutred, he prevails upon Buh Wolf to take the road toward Miss Dinah's house, on approaching which he so vigorously applies both whip and spur as to compel his resisting steed to trot up to the door, where Buh Rabbit bows politely to his lady-love, saying, "I told you so: now you see for yourself." Of course he wins the bride.

There is a class of stories approaching somewhat in character those related of our own Jack the Giant-killer, leaving out the giants. The one given below seems to have a common origin with the Anglo-Saxon story of the "Three Blue Pigs." This is entitled "Tiny Pig."

A family of seven pigs leave home to seek their fortunes, and settle in a neighborhood harassed by a mischievous fox. Each of these pigs builds himself a house of dirt, except Tiny Pig, who, though the runt of the litter, is a sensible little fellow and the hero of the tale. He builds his house of stone, with good strong doors and a substantial chimney. In due course of time, Fox, being hungry, comes to the house of one of the brothers, and asks to be admitted, but is refused. The request and refusal, as told by the negroes, is couched in language which is intended to be poetical, and is certainly not without some pretension to the picturesque. Fox's request in each case is—

> Mr. Pig, Mr. Pig, oh let me in:
> I'll go away soon, and not touch a thing.

And the refusal is—

No, no, Mr. Fox, by the beard on my chin!
You may say what you will, but I'll not let you in.

On being refused, Fox threatens to *blow down* the house and eat up the occupant. Pig continuing to refuse—as what pig would not?—the house is blown down and the owner eaten up. This sad fate befalls in turn each of the six who had been so foolish or so lazy as to build their houses of dirt. Fox, having finished all six, and becoming again hungry, comes at last to the stone house, where he makes the same hypocritical request, and meets the same heroic refusal. He now threatens to blow down the house. "Blow away and welcome!" retorts the little hero. Fox blows "until his wind gives out," but cannot move the first stone. He then tries scratching and tearing with his paws, but only succeeds in tearing off two of his own toe-nails. "I will come down your chimney," he threatens, leaping as he says so to the roof of the house. "Come soon as you please," sturdily replies Tiny Pig, standing before his fireplace with a big armful of dry straw ready to be thrown upon the fire. As soon as Fox has entered the chimney, and come down too far to return quickly, Tiny Pig throws the dry straw upon the fire, which creates such a blaze that Fox is scorched and smoked to death, and Tiny Pig lives the rest of his life in peace, the hero of his neighborhood.

This story certainly furnishes foundation for a moral which we will leave the reader to construct for himself, remarking as we pass that, so far as we know, no moral has ever been drawn. Several other stories may be regarded as inculcating, though feebly, some moral precept.

One of these bears some features of American negro life, grafted probably upon African stock: The denizens of a certain farmyard—ducks, geese, turkeys, pea-fowls, guinea-fowls, hens, roosters and all—were invited by those of another farmyard to a supper and a dance. They all went as a matter of course, headed by the big farmyard rooster, who strutted and crowed as he marched. They were a merry set, and such an amount of quacking, cackling and gabbling as they made was seldom heard. After a few rounds of dancing, just to give them a better appetite for supper and fit them for a longer dance afterward, they were introduced to the supper-room. There they saw on the table a pyramid of eatables high as the old gobbler's head when stretched to its utmost; but, alas! it was, or seemed to be, a pyramid of *corn bread* only—pones upon pones of it, yet nothing but corn bread.

On seeing this the rooster becomes very indignant, and struts out of the house, declaring that he will have nothing to do with so mean a supper, for he can get corn bread enough at home. As he is angrily going off, however, the others, who are too hungry to disdain even the plainest fare, fall to work; and no sooner has the outer layer of corn loaves been removed—for it is only the outer layer—than they find within a huge pile of bacon and greens, and at the bottom of the pile, covered and protected by large dishes, any amount of pies and tarts and cakes and other good things.

Poor Rooster looks wistfully back, and is sorry that he had made that rash speech. But it is too late now, for his word is out, and no one ever knew Rooster take back his word if he had to die for it. He learned, however, a valuable lesson that night, for from that time to this it has been observed that Rooster always *scratches* with his feet the place where he finds, or expects to find, anything to eat, and that he never leaves off scratching until he has searched to the bottom.

Our last story is more purely African, at least in its *dramatis personae.* Buh Elephant and Buh Lion were one day chatting upon various subjects, when the elephant took occasion to say that he was afraid of no being on earth except man. On seeing the big boastful eyes of the lion stretching wider and his mane bristling, as if in disdain, he added, "You know, Buh Lion, that, although you are held as the most dreaded of all beasts, I am not afraid of any of your tribe, for if any of them should attack me I could receive him on my tusk, or strike him dead with my trunk, or even shake him off from my body and then trample him to death under my feet. But man—who can kill us from a distance with his guns and arrows, who can set traps for us of which we have no suspicion, who can fight us from the backs of horses so swift that we can neither overtake him nor escape from him—I do fear, for neither strength nor courage can avail against his wisdom."

Buh Lion, on hearing this, shook himself, and said that he was no more afraid of man that he was of any other creature which he was in the habit of eating; and added that the only beings on earth he was afraid of were *partridges.*

"Patridges!" exclaims Buh Elephant in wonder. "What do you mean?"

"Why this," says Buh Lion, "that when I am walking softly through the woods I sometimes rouse a covey of partridges, and then they rise all around me with such a whir as to make me start. I am afraid of nothing but partridges."

Not long afterward Buh Elephant heard a gun fired near a neighboring village, followed by a loud, prolonged roar. Going there to learn what was the matter, he saw Buh Lion lying dead by the roadside with a great hole in his body made by a musket-ball. "Ah, my poor friend," said he, "partridges could never have treated you in this way."

1881

Plantation Folk-Lore (review)

by T. F. Crane

Popular Science Monthly, XVIII (New York, 1881), 824–833.

Thomas Frederick Crane was, from 1868 to 1913, professor of Romance languages at Cornell; he was also a folklore scholar of extraordinary scope, as the range of reading and depth of understanding in this critical review clearly indicate. His translation and compilation of Italian folktales and his researches on medieval exempla are still valuable works.

*Immediately upon publication, Joel Chandler Harris' book—*Uncle Remus. His Songs and his Sayings. The Folk-lore of the Old Plantation *(New York, 1881)—was widely and favorably reviewed, and Crane's review is probably the most important of them all. With it, the study of Negro folklore became academically respectable. Crane treats the stories as part of the rich humanistic heritage to which he is so obviously devoted, not as mere entertaining bits of narrative or expressions of that vague cliché "the Negro Character."*

The fact that his approach is literary may explain his incorrect comments about the paucity of local legends and superstitions among white Americans. He seems to mean that no such material had been published and identified as folklore, and was therefore not available to a writer who might want to incorporate it in his fiction. It would be some time before folklore collectors in any significant number turned seriously to the study of native American traditions.

The Riverside Magazine *articles to which he refers were "Negro Fables," II (November 1868), 505–507, and III (March 1869), 116–118. That journal published for children, and the stories, unfortunately, were mangled accordingly.*

In a passage in his recent essay on Hawthorne, which was received with some disfavor by his countrymen, Mr. James enumerated the "items of high civilization which are absent from the texture of

American life." To these might be added an item of low civilization, but what, for the purpose of the imaginative writer, is of greater utility than the court or Epsom—folk-lore. With the exception of a few legends of the Hudson due to the Dutch, and an occasional Indian legend (generally manufactured by the white man), there are no local legends from one end of the land to the other. In minor matters, such as superstitions, the case is no better; aside from the aversion to Friday, and sitting thirteen at table, we know of no general superstition. There are, however, two classes of native Americans which must be exempted from the application of the above rule—the Indians and the Southern negroes. The superstitions of the latter, chiefly religious, have been darkly hinted at from time to time, and have occasionally afforded slight contributions to fiction; a few, the reader will remember, are to be found in Mark Twain's amusing book, "Tom Sawyer."

It was not suspected that the negroes possessed a large fund of one of the most entertaining classes of popular tales—animal stories—until a number were published in the "Riverside Magazine" (November, 1868; March, 1869), "taken down from the lips of an old negro in the vicinity of Charleston," variants of which appeared in the New York "Independent" (September 2, 1875), and from time to time in other papers. The first attempt at anything like a full or complete collection of these tales is in the book before us, which is not only a most entertaining and novel work but a valuable contribution to comparative folklore. The volume is divided into "Legends of the Old Plantation" and "Uncle Remus's Songs and Sayings." In addition to these there are some proverbs and "A Story of the War." The true value of the book, however, is in the thirty-four inimitable "Legends of the Old Plantation," which are related night after night by an old negro to the little grandson of his former owner. Too much praise can not be bestowed upon Mr. Harris for the manner in which he has executed his task: not only is the representation of the dialect better than anything that has heretofore been given, but he has shown himself a master in the difficult art of collecting popular tales. A glance at the variants of these stories published elsewhere will show the vast superiority of Mr. Harris's. It is not, however, in their literary character, interesting as it is, that we intend to examine briefly these fables, but simply in their relations to the similar tales of other countries.

Mr. Harris does not state the precise locality where he collected his fables. To cite the words of a competent critic ("The Nation," December 2, 1880): "Presumably his stories are all of Georgia origin, though he cites a variant from Flroida; and he gives us proof that 'they have become a part of the domestic history of every Southern family.' However widely they may have been spread through our domestic slave-trade, we regard it as highly probable that the Sea-Isl[ands] and neighborhood from South Carolina to Florida was, as in the case of the slave-songs, the focus of the animal fables—an hypothesis which finds its support in the reference of both to an African and heathen origin." We have at present but scanty information as to the extent of the diffusion of these stories—variants have been found in South Carolina and Florida; no locality is mentioned for those given in the interesting article on "Folk-Lore of the Southern Negroes," by William Owens, in "Lippincott's Magazine," December, 1877, pp. 748–755.*

These stories narrate the contests of wit between the rabbit, the terrapin, the bear, the wolf, and the fox. The first two, who are the embodiments of weakness and harmlessness, are always victorious; as Mr. Harris says, "It is not virtue that triumphs, but helplessness; it is not malice, but mischievousness." The animals are all dignified with the title *Brer,* or *Buh,* as represented by Mr. Owens, who says, "It is generally supposed to be an abbreviation of the word 'brother' " (the *br* being sounded without the whir of the *r*), "but it probably is a title of respect equivalent to our Mr." The manners and customs of human beings are, after the usual fashion of fables, transferred to the animals in a way that excites the wonder of Uncle Remus' youthful auditor, and a mysterious Miss Meadows and "de gals" are introduced, with whom the animals are on terms of intimacy, and at whose house some of the most amusing incidents take place. A glance at the contents of these fables will at once reveal many familiar episodes, a few of which we shall note for a specific purpose.

In No. XVI, "Old Mr. Rabbit he's a Good Fisherman," Brer Rabbit, while the Fox, Coon, and Bear are clearing up "a new groun' fer ter plant a roas'n' year patch," slips away and hunts for a cool place to rest in. He finally came across a well with a bucket hanging in it and looking so cool that Brer Rabbit climbed in, and of course the bucket began to descend; "but Brer Rabbit he keep mighty still, kaze he dunner w'at minnit gwineter be de nex'. He des lay dar en shuck en shiver." The Fox saw the Rabbit slip away and followed him, and

* There are four stories in this article which have no parallels in "Uncle Remus": "Buh Rabbit, Buh Wolf, and the Pears"; "Bub Rabbit frightens Buh Wolf"; "The Rooster and the Cornbread"; and "Buh Elephant and Buh Lion," which last has a distant resemblance to a story in Koelle's "African Native Literature," London, 1854, p. 177.

his amazement can be imagined when he saw the Rabbit disappear down the well. The Rabbit on being asked, "Who you wizzitin' down dar?" answered that he was fishing, and invited the Fox to get into the other bucket and come down and help him. This the Fox did, and as he went down up went Brer Rabbit. The Fox is afterward pulled up by the owner of the well and escapes. This fable will be recognized at once from the familiar version in La Fontaine (XI, 6, "'Le Loup et le Renard"), which he took from the "Roman de Renart." A much older version is found in the "Disciplina Clericalis," a collection of Oriental stories made in the first years of the twelfth century.

No. XVII, "Mr. Rabbit gobbles up the Butter," relates how Brer Rabbit, Brer Fox, and Brer Possum laid up their provisions together in the same shanty, and put the butter that Brer Fox brought into the spring-house to keep it cool. Brer Rabbit, however, under the pretense of going to see his family, leaves his companions at their work and takes a nibble at the butter. This goes on until the butter disappears, and, while the others are sleeping, Brer Rabbit smears Brer Possum's mouth with the butter on his paws. Brer Possum on waking up was naturally indignant, and demanded an ordeal by fire to prove his innocence, but, as ordeals among men even must sometimes have failed, the innocent Possum is burned up, greatly to the indignation of Uncle Remus's listener. With this story may be compared Grimm, No. 2, "The Cat and the Mouse in Partnership." A closer parallel is found in W. H. I. Bleek's "Reynard the Fox in South Africa; or Hottentot Fables and Tales" (London, Trübner, 1864, p. 18), "Which was the Thief?"

"A Jackal and a Hyena went and hired themselves to a man to be his servants. In the middle of the night the Jackal rose and smeared the Hyena's tail with some fat, and then ate all the rest of it which was in the house. In the morning the man missed his fat, and he immediately accused the Jackal of having eaten it. 'Look at the Hyena's tail,' said the rogue, 'and you will see who is the thief.' The man did so, and then thrashed the Hyena till she was nearly dead."

In No. XXV, "How Mr. Rabbit lost his Fine Bushy Tail," the Rabbit is victimized by the Fox, who persuades him to fish, one cold night, by dropping his long, bushy tail (rabbits formerly had such) into the water. It freezes fast, of course, and the poor Rabbit to get away is obliged to leave his tail in the ice. This is one of the familiar episodes in the "Roman de Renart."

Some of the stories contain incidents which are common to European popular tales, as in No. XX, "How Mr. Rabbit saved his Meat."

Brer Wolf suspected Brer Rabbit of stealing some of his fish, and killed Brer Rabbit's best cow. The latter frightened the Wolf away by telling him that the "patter-rollers" (patrol, policemen) were coming, and proceeded to skin the cow and salt down the hide and stow away the carcass in the smoke-house. The end of the cow's tail he stuck in the ground, and called Brer Wolf. "Run yer, Brer Wolf, run yer! Yo' cow gwine in de groun' !" When Brer Wolf arrived, he found Brer Rabbit holding the tail with all his might to keep the cow from going into the ground. Brer Wolf caught hold, and off came the tail. The Wolf was not going to give the matter up so, and got a spade, a pick-axe, and a shovel, and began to dig for his cow, while Brer Rabbit sat on his front-porch smoking his cigar and watching him. This episode is found in a Basque story (Webster's "Basque Legends," p. 10) and in an Italian tale ("Jahrbuch für roman. und eng. Lit." VIII, 252), and in many others that we have not space to mention.

No. XIII, "The Awful Fate of Mr. Wolf," relates how the Wolf persecuted Brer Rabbit, and carried off some of his family. To protect those left, "Brer Rabbit b'ilt 'im a straw house, en hit wuz tored down; den he made a house outen pine-tops, en dat went de same way; den he made 'im a bark house, en dat wuz raided on; en eve'y time he los' a house, he los' wunner his chilluns." Finally, he built a plank house with rock foundations, and then could live in peace. One day the Wolf, pursued by dogs, took refuge in Brer Rabbit's house, and begged him to hide him from the dogs. The Rabbit told him to get into a chest, and, the Wolf once secure, the Rabbit bored holes in the top of the chest, and poured boiling water in and scalded the Wolf to death. A similar story, except that seven Pigs and a Fox take the place of the Rabbits and Wolf, is told by Mr. Owens ("Lippincott," December, 1877, page 753), who cites as a parallel the Anglo-Saxon story of "The Three Blue Pigs." Another parallel may be found in a Venetian story (Bernoni, "Tradizioni Popolari Venezaine," p. 69, "El Galo").

One of the incidents in No. XX, "A Story about the Little Rabbits," is also familiar, and seems like a curious metamorphosis of a well-known trait of fairy tales. The Fox goes to Brer Rabbit's house, and the sight of the fat little Rabbits makes his mouth water, and he endeavors to invent some excuse for killing them. He finally sets them difficult tasks to do, intending to devour them if they fail; but a little Bird on top of the house sings the solution of all the difficulties, which are: to break off a piece of sugar-cane; to bring water in a sieve; and to put a big log on the fire. The second task is the one found in European folk-lore, an example occurring in another Venetian story (Bastanielo, Bernoni, "Fiabe," No. 6).

One of the most amusing stories in "Uncle Remus" is No. II, "The Wonderful Tar-Baby Story" (versions also in "Riverside Magazine," 1868, p. 505, and "Lippincott," December, 1877, p. 750), in which the Fox made "a contrapshun wat he call a Tar-Baby," out of tar and turpentine, and put it in the way of the Rabbit, who got stuck to it, and thus fell into the Fox's clutches. In the "South-African Folk-Lore Journal," I, p. 69, there is a curious parallel to the above story. A number of animals build a dam to hold water, and the jackal comes and muddies the water. A baboon is set to guard the dam, but the jackal easily outwits him. Then the tortoise offers to capture the jackal and proposes "that a thick coating of 'bijenwerk' (a kind of sticky, black substance found on beehives) should be spread all over him, and that he should go and stand at the entrance of the dam, on the water-level, so that the jackal might tread on him, and stick fast." The jackal is caught, but, with his customary craft, escapes.

In the last of Uncle Remus's stories, No. XXXIV, "The Sad Fate of Mr. Fox," the Fox and the Rabbit jump down the mouth of a cow and help themselves to meat, the Fox warning the Rabbit not "to cut 'roun' de haslett." The Rabbit disobeys the injunction, and the cow falls dead. The owner cuts her open to see what was the matter, and the Rabbit betrays the Fox, who was hiding in the "maul," and who is thereupon killed. In Bleek, p. 27, the Elephant and the Tortoise have a dispute, and the former determined to kill the latter, and asked him, "Little Tortoise, shall I chew you or swallow you down?" The little Tortoise said, "Swallow me, if you please!" and the Elephant swallowed it whole. After the Elephant had swallowed the little Tortoise, and it had entered his body, it tore off his liver, heart, and kidneys. The Elephant said, "Little Tortoise, you kill me." So the Elephant died; but the little Tortoise came out of his dead body and went wherever he liked.*

More remarkable, however, than the above casual points of resem-

* Mr. Harris includes among the animal fables a story which properly does not belong there, and which is nothing but a well-known European tale which Uncle Remus must have heard from the whites, although Mr. Harris, p. 136, note, says, "This story is popular on the coast and among the rice-plantations, and since the publication of some of the animal-myths in the newspapers, I have received a version of it from a planter in southwest Georgia." The story in question is No. XXXII, "Jacky-my-Lantern," and is nothing but a version of the French story of "Bonhomme Misère," which is of Italian origin. (See Pitrè, "Fiabe," Nos. 124, 125; De Gubernatis, "Novelline di Sto. Stefano," No. 32, etc.)

blance is the substantial identity of these stories with those of a tribe of South American Indians. In 1870 Professor C. F. Hartt heard, at Santarem on the Amazons, from his guide in the *lingua geral,* a story, "The Tortoise that outran the Deer," a version of which he afterward published in the "Cornell Era" (January 20, 1871), and which attracted the attention of a writer in "The Nation" (February 23, 1871), who gave a variant of the same myth, as found among the negroes of South Carolina (the same story occurring in "Uncle Remus," p. 80). This singular resemblance does not seem to have been noticed again until Mr. Herbert Smith, in his "Brazil, the Amazons, and the Coast" (New York, Charles Scribner's Sons, 1879), in a chapter devoted to "The Myths of the Amazonian Indians," gave a number of animal fables, but, owing to his insufficient acquaintance with comparative folk-lore, he was unable to throw any light on the subject, merely noticing the resemblances which had already attracted the attention of Professor Hartt and others. The proof-sheets of this chapter were sent to Mr. Harris, who at once saw that the similarity extended to almost every story quoted by Mr. Smith, and some are so nearly identical as to point unmistakably to a common origin; but when and where? Mr. Harris asks, "When did the negro or the North American Indian come into contact with the tribes of South America?"

Before examining this question, it may be well to compare hastily the stories in Hartt's "Amazonian Tortoise Myths" (Rio de Janeiro, 1875) and Smith's "Brazil" with their parallels in "Uncle Remus" and elsewhere. First, let us examine the stories common to Hartt, Smith, and Uncle Remus:

I. "How the Tortoise outran the Deer" (Hartt, p. 7; Smith, p. 543, gives the version in Hartt, saying: "I quote Professor Hartt's words for this story, as being better than the version, substantially the same, that I find in my note-book. The story is very common all over the Amazons."—"Riverside Magazine," November, 1868, p. 507; "Cornell Era," January 20, 1871; "Nation," February 23, 1871, p. 127; and "Lippincott's Magazine," December, 1877, p. 751). The Tortoise declares that it can outrun the Deer, and the latter challenges it to a race. The Tortoise secretly posts members of its family along the course, who answer for him when the Deer asks if he is ahead. The race begins, and the Deer is so bewildered at hearing the Tortoise's voice always ahead of him, that he runs against a tree and falls down dead. In "Uncle Remus" the Rabbit takes the place of the Deer, and the story ends with the Terrapin's victory without the death of his rival. In "Lippincott's" the actors are Buh Rabbit and Buh Frog; but the writer remarks that another version makes the competitors Buh

Deer and Buh Cooter (the Negro name for terrapin, or land-tortoise). A German version of this story is given in the "Riverside Magazine," September, 1868, and a version from Siam may be found in the "Orient und Occident," III, 497. A more important and significant parallel, however, is to be found in Bleek, No. 16, p. 32, "The Tortoises hunting the Ostriches": "One day, it is said, the Tortoises held a council how they might hunt Ostriches, and they said: 'Let us, on both sides, stand in rows near each other, and let one go to hunt the Ostriches, so that they must flee along through the midst of us.' They did so, and, as they were many, the Ostriches were obliged to run along through the midst of them. During this they did not move, but, remaining always in the same places, called each to the other, 'Are you there?' and each one answered, 'I am here.' The Ostriches, hearing this, ran so tremendously that they quite exhausted their strength, and fell down. Then the Tortoises assembled at the place where the Ostriches had fallen, and devoured them."

II. "How the Tortoise provoked a Contest of Strength between the Tapir and the Whale" (Hartt, p. 20; Smith, p. 545; "Uncle Remus," p. 111). In Hartt, a Tortoise went down to the sea to drink, and a Whale made sport of him, but the former said he was stronger than the latter, and could pull him on shore. The Whale laughed, but the Tortoise went into the forest to get a long root, and, while, looking for it, met a Tapir, who asked him what he was doing. The Tortoise replied that he was looking for a root to pull the Tapir into the sea with. The Tortoise found his root, and tied one end to the Tapir and the other end to the Whale (of course, both remaining in ignorance of the performance); the two then tugged against each other, and finally gave up the struggle from sheer exhaustion. In another version (p. 23) the *cobra grande,* or mythical great serpent, and the jaguar are made to pull against each other in the same way. Smith mentions a version he himself heard, and then gives Professor Hartt's. In "Uncle Remus" Brer Terrapin brags that he can out-pull Brer Bear, and, borrowing Miss Meadows's bed-cord, he gives one end to the Bear, and, diving down into the water, fastens his own end to a big root, and the Bear soon gives up pulling against Brer Terrapin.

III. In a version of another story, "How a Tortoise killed a Jaguar" (Hartt, p. 29; Smith, p. 542; "Uncle Remus," p. 60), the Jaguar is represented as reaching down into the burrow and catching hold of the Tortoise, who, resisting, calls out, "Oh, you foolish fellow! you think you have caught me, when it is only the root of a tree you have secured." In "Uncle Remus," the Fox, in revenge for what will be told in the following story, determines to kill Brer Terrapin. The latter begs piteously not to be drowned, and the Fox, taken in by this, souses him into the water, still holding on to him, when the Terrapin "begin fer ter holler, 'Tu'n loose dat stump, en ketch holt er me.' Brer Fox he holler back, 'I ain't got holt er no stump, en I is got holt er you.'" But at last he was deceived by the Terrapin's cry that he was drowning, and let go of him.

IV. In the last-mentioned story, "How a Tortoise killed a Jaguar" (Hartt, p. 26; Smith, p. 541; for one incident only, "Uncle Remus," p. 52), a Monkey carried a Tortoise up into a palm-tree to eat the fruit. When his hunger was satisfied, the Tortoise had to remain there until a Jaguar came along and asked him why he didn't come down. The Tortoise said he was afraid, but the Jaguar said: "Don't be afraid! Jump! I will catch you!" Then the Tortoise jumped down and struck the Jaguar on the head and killed him. In Mr. Smith's version, collected at the same place (Santarem), the Tortoise, after throwing the Jaguar down some fruit, slips off the tree, and, falling on the Jaguar's head, kills him. In "Uncle Remus," while the Rabbit and Terrapin are calling at Miss Meadows's, the Fox comes in on them unawares, and the Terrapin, who has been put up on a shelf, rolls off in his agitation, falls on the head of the Fox, and stuns him a moment, so that Brer Rabbit escapes.

These are all the stories in Hartt which have full or partial parallels in "Uncle Remus"; there are, however, several additional ones in Smith that belong here.

V. "Story of the Jaguar who wanted to marry the Deer's Daughter, but was cut out by the Cotia" (Smith, p. 547; "Riverside Magazine," 1868, p. 505; "Lippincott's," 1877, p. 753; and "Uncle Remus," p. 34). The Cotia brags that he can ride the Jaguar, and the Deer promises to give him his daughter if he does. The Cotia pretends to be ill, and the Jaguar charitably takes him on his back, and even ties him on with a root, and gives him a switch. When the Cotia finds himself master of the situation, he whips the Jaguar unmercifully, and rides him by the Deer's house. In "Lippincott's" the Rabbit and Wolf, in the other versions the Rabbit and Fox, are the parties concerned.

VI. In the conclusion of Smith's version, p. 549, the Cotia slipped off the Jaguar's back, and hid in a hole before the latter could catch him. The Jaguar set an Owl to watch the hole, but the Cotia peeped out and threw a handful of sand in the Owl's face and ran away. A somewhat similar incident is found in "Uncle Remus," p. 39 ("Riverside Magazine," 1868, p. 506, III, at end), but, instead of throwing sand in the Buzzard's eyes, the Rabbit makes him believe that there is a squirrel in the tree in which the Rabbit is imprisoned, and, when the Buzzard rushes around to catch it, the Rabbit escapes.

VII. "Story of the Cotia who played Tricks on the Jaguar and outwitted him" (Smith, p. 549, at end). The Jaguar, enraged at the tricks played upon him by the Cotia, caught the latter and tied him to a tree, intending to drown him in the morning. The Cotia expressed his joy at this determination, and remarked that he would be very sad if he was going to be thrown into a brier-bush. The Jaguar, of course, changed his mind and threw his enemy into a brier-bush; whereat the Cotia ran away laughing. The same incident precisely occurs in "Uncle Remus," p. 29 ("Riverside Magazine," 1868, p. 505, I), with the Fox and the Rabbit, who begs, "fer de Lord's sake, don't fling me in dat brier-patch!" The Fox is again deceived, and the Rabbit, as he escapes unhurt, cries out, "Bred en bawn in a brier-patch, Brer Fox!"

VIII. A variant of the last story (Smith, pp. 552, 554) relates that, to be avenged on the Cotia, the Lion and Jaguar guarded a spring, so that the Cotia could get nothing to drink. After a time the Cotia became very thirsty, and, seeing a man pass with a jar on his head, said to himself, "I will see if I can get some water from that jar." So he ran ahead of the man and lay down in the path. The man thought it was a dead Cotia, and shoved it aside with his foot and went on. This the Cotia repeated four times, and at last the man said: "Here's another dead Cotia! Now, I will go back and get the others, and carry all four home." He put down the jar and went to look for the other Cotias. Then the Cotia jumped up and thrust his head into the jar, which contained molasses instead of water. In "Uncle Remus," p. 70, the Rabbit, by a similar stratagem, steals Brer Fox's game. Mr. Smith, p. 558, note, mentions a parallel to this story from Egypt (Khunzinger, "Upper Egypt, its People and its Products," p. 401). I do not recall any parallel in which animals are the actors; but a similar trick is found in many versions of the story of "The Master Thief," for instance, in Asbjörnsen and Moe's "Norske Folke-Eventyr," No. 34, "Mestertyven."

We are prepared now to consider briefly the origin of these stories, which are substantially the same in Brazil and in the Southern States. That the negroes of the United States obtained these stories from the South American Indians is an hypothesis no one would think of maintaining; but that the Indians heard these stories from the African slaves in Brazil, and that the latter, as well as those who were formerly slaves in the United States, brought these stories with them from Africa is, we think, beyond a doubt, the explanation of the resemblances we have noted. Owing to a scarcity of materials, we have not been able to show very clearly the African origin of these stories, but what we have cited makes it at least probable. Whether the African stories of "Reynard the Fox" are original with Hottentots, or have been communicated to them by the Dutch, is a point we can not decide, in the absence of more ample material for comparison.

The most interesting point in the present investigation, and one that connects it with the recent discussions on the subject of folk-lore, is that, if our explanation be true, it shows that popular tales are more readily diffused than has heretofore been supposed. Professor Hartt ("Amazonian Tortoise Myths," p. 5) says: "The question has arisen, whether many of the stories I have given, that bear so close a resemblance to Old World fables, may not have been introduced by the negroes? But I see no reason for entertaining this suspicion, for they are too widely spread, their form is too thoroughly Brazilian, they are most numerous in just those regions where negroes are not and have not been abundant, and, moreover, they occur, not in Portuguese but in the *lingua geral.*" The first objection would simply show the extent of the diffusion, the second what would naturally take place on the introduction of stories from a country with a different fauna, and the final objections were overthrown, we believe, by Professor Hartt's hearing these same stories from the negroes in Rio. He gave up the hypothesis of an Indian origin, and did not continue his collection. Mr. Smith (p. 548) makes about the same objections, which are invalidated by the writer's own admissions: "They are repeated in remote provinces, among half-wild tribes who *hardly* (the italics are ours) ever see the negroes. . . . Many of the tortoise myths are told by the Mundurucú Indians, the *majority* of whom can not speak Portuguese." Mr. Smith also confirms, what has been said above, that these stories are told in Rio by the negroes, and a very suspicious circumstance is the introduction of a lion into one of the stories (p. 551), which, as Mr. Smith remarks, "shows that the narrator had heard of lions, probably from the slaves."

In taking leave of this interesting subject we must reiterate our praise of Mr. Harris's charming volume, and we trust that its scientific side may not be overlooked, but awaken an interest in negro folk-lore which will result in other works as entertaining and valuable as "Uncle Remus."

1882

A Georgia Corn-Shucking

by David C. Barrow, Jr.

Century Magazine, XXIV, (New York, 1882), 873–878.

Barrow's article is valuable not only for its detailed and vivid description of the corn-shucking ceremony and its fine collection of secular songs but also for what may be the first published account of the tradition of "beating straws." Kenneth S. Goldstein and Judith McCulloh, who have been collecting data on the tradition, find that it is rare among Negroes today, but quite widespread among whites. "Interestingly enough," Professor Goldstein writes (private communication), "the two best published reports of 'beating straws' describe the tradition in use by Negroes in the 19th century." One of these reports is Barrow's; the other is found in W. C. Handy's Father of the Blues: An Autobiography, *edited by Arna Bontemps ([London, 1957], pp. 5–7). Handy's account differs from most others in that his beaters use knitting needles rather than straws, but the practice is otherwise the same: "A boy would stand behind the fiddler with a pair of knitting needles in his hands. From this position the youngster would reach around the fiddler's left shoulder and beat on the strings in the manner of a snare drummer" (p. 5). An example may be heard on Library of Congress Recording AAFS L9,* Play and Dance Songs and Tunes, *edited by B. A. Botkin; the song "Pore Little Mary Settin' in the Corner" was recorded in 1939 in Magee, Mississippi, by Herbert Halpert.*

The first work toward gathering the corn crop in Georgia is to strip the stalks of their blades, *i.e.*, "pull the fodder," which is done in August or September. This work is done by hand, the laborer stripping the blades from stalk after stalk until he gets his hands full, and then tying them together with a few blades of the same; and this constitutes a "hand." These hands are hung on the stalks of corn a day or two until they are "cured," after which they are tied up, three or four together, in bundles, and these bundles are stacked in the fields, or hauled up to the stables and thrown into the fodder-loft. The corn is thus left on the naked stalk until some time in October or November, by which time it will have become hard and dry. If Georgians, like the Western farmers, had nothing to gather in the fall but the corn, we might spend the whole fall gathering it; but, on any farm where cotton is cultivated to any considerable extent, most of this season of the year must be devoted to gathering and preparing it for market. King Cotton is a great tyrant, and unless you are a willing and ready subject, he will make you suffer.

It will appear, then, that the corn must be disposed of in the quickest possible manner. Now, if the corn were thrown in the crib with the shuck on it, it would probably be eaten by vermin; and, besides, the farmer would be deprived of the use of his shucks, which form the chief item of food for his cattle during the winter. If we had large barns, we might throw the corn in them and shuck it at our leisure; but we have no barns—at least, very few—in Georgia.

Out of these conditions has sprung the corn-shucking; and it has grown into importance, even more as a social than as an economic feature among our farming people. It is peculiarly suited to negro genius. Among no other people could it flourish and reach the perfection which it here attains.

The farmer who proposes to give a corn-shucking selects a level spot in his lot, conveniently near the crib, rakes away all trash, and sweeps the place clean with a brush broom. The corn is then pulled off the stalks, thrown into wagons, hauled to the lot, and thrown out on the spot selected, all in one pile. If it has been previously "norated" through the neighborhood that there is to be plenty to eat and drink at the corn-shucking, and if the night is auspicious, there will certainly be a crowd. Soon after dark the negroes begin to come in, and before long the place will be alive with them,—men, women, and children. After the crowd has gathered and been moderately warmed up, two "gin'r'ls" are chosen from among the most famous corn-shuckers on the ground, and these proceed to divide the shuckers into two parties, later comers reporting alternately to one side or the other, so as to keep the forces equally divided. The next step, which is one of great importance, is to divide the corn-pile. This is done by laying a fence-rail across the top of the corn-pile, so that the vertical plane, passing through the rail, will divide the pile into two equal portions. Laying the rail is of great importance, since upon this depends the accuracy of the division; it is accompanied with much argument, not to say wrangling. The position of the rail being determined the two generals mount the corn-pile, and the work begins. The necessity for the "gin'r'ls" to occupy the most conspicuous position accessible, from which to cheer their followers, is one reason why they get up on top of the corn; but there is another, equally important, which is to keep the rail from being moved, it being no uncommon thing for one side to change the position of the rail, and thus throw an undue portion of the work upon their adversaries. The position of "gin'r'l" in a corn-shucker differs from that of the soldier in that the former is in greater danger than any of his followers; for the chances are that, should his side seem to be gaining, one of their opponents will knock the leader off the corn-pile, and thus cause a momentary panic, which is eagerly taken advantage of. This proceeding, however, is considered fair only in extreme cases, and not unfrequently leads to a general row. If it is possible, imagine a negro man standing up on a pile of corn, holding in his hand an ear of corn and shouting the words printed below, and you will have pictured the "corn gin'r'l." It is a prime requisite that he should be ready in his improvisations and have a good voice, so that he may lead in the corn-song. The corn-song is almost always a song with a chorus, or, to use the language of corn-shuckers, the "gin'r'ls give out," and the shuckers "drone." These songs are kept up continuously during the entire time the work is going on, and though extremely simple, yet, when sung by fifty pairs of lusty lungs, there are few things more stirring.

The most common form is for the generals to improvise words, which they half sing, half recite, all joining in the chorus. As a specimen of this style of corn-song, the following will answer:

First Gen.: Here is yer corn-shucker.
All Hands: Oh ho ho ho ho.
Second Gen.: Here is yer nigger ruler.
All Hands: Oh ho ho ho ho.
Both Gens.: Oh ho ho ho ho.
All Hands: Oh ho ho ho ho.
First Gen.: Don't yer hyer me holler?
All Hands: Oh ho ho ho ho.
Second Gen.: Don't yer hyer me lumber?
All Hands: Oh ho ho ho ho, etc.

In this the generals frequently recount their adventures, travels and experiences. The writer knew of a negro who went down to the seacoast, and when he returned, carried by storm a corn-shucking of which he was general, with the words: "I've bin ter de ilund."

Of course "Brer Rabbit" must come in for his share of the honor, as he does in the following song, which is illustrative of the negro's appreciation of rabbit cunning. It is sung just as the other was, the generals and shuckers alternating:

Gen.: Rabbit in de gyordin.
Cho.: Rabbit hi oh.
Gen.: Dog can't ketch um.
Cho.: Rabbit hi oh.
Gen.: Gun can't shoot um.
Cho.: Rabbit hi oh.
Gen.: Mon can't skin um.
Cho.: Rabbit hi oh.
Gen.: Cook can't cook um.
Cho.: Rabbit hi oh.
Gen.: Folks can't eat um.
Cho.: Rabbit hi oh, etc.

Any reader who has followed so far, may by courtesy be called a corn general, and is therefore at liberty to add indefinitely to the verses, or repeat them as he pleases. Any words at all may be taken and twisted into a chorus, as is illustrated in the following:

Gen.: Slip shuck corn little while.
Cho.: Little while, little while.
Gen.: Slip shuck corn little while.
Cho.: Little while, I say.
Gen.: I'm gwine home in little while, etc.

The finest corn-song of them all is one in which the chorus is, "Ho mer Riley ho." The words here given were some of them picked up in South-west Georgia, and some in other portions of the State. Competent judges say there is really music in this song, and for this reason, as well as to give readers who have never heard the corn-song an idea of the tunes to which they are sung, the notes of this song are given below. No full knowledge of the way in which the song is rendered can be conveyed by notes, but it is believed that the tune is properly reported.

Lit-tle Bil-ly Woodcock lived o'er de mount-in, Ho mer Ri - ley, ho!
In er mighty build-in' lived Bil - ly Woodcock, Ho mer Ri - ley, ho!

Little Billy Woodcock got er mighty long bill.
Ho mer Riley ho.
He stuck it through de mountin and clinch it on tother side.
Ho mer Riley ho.

'Possum up de gum stump, Raccoon in de holler.
Ho mer Riley ho.
Rabbit in de ole feel fat ez he kin waller.
Ho mer Riley ho.

Nigger in de wood-pile can't count seb'n.
Ho mer Riley ho.
Put him in de fedder bed he thought he wuz in Heb'n.
Ho mer Riley ho.

Did yer ever see er gin sling made outer bramdy?
Ho mer Riley ho.
Did you ever see er yaller gal lick 'lasses candy?
Ho mer Riley ho.

There is one more very short song which is sung by all hands. The work of finishing the shucking of the last few ears is called "rounding up" the corn-pile, and is almost invariably in the following words:

Round up, dub - ble up, round up corn; Round up, nub-bins up, round up corn.

These words are repeated, over and over, until the last of the corn is shucked, and the work finished.

An amount of work which would astonish the shuckers themselves, and which, if demanded of them in the day-time would be declared impossible, is accomplished under the excitement of the corn-song. They shuck the corn by hand, sometimes using a sharp stick to split open the shuck, but most commonly tearing them open with the fingers. As the feeling of rivalry grows more and more intense, they work faster and faster, stripping the shuck from the ears so fast that they seem to fly almost constantly from their hands.

A staid New-England farmer and his friends, gathered in a comfortable, well-lighted barn, quietly doing the laborious part of his "husking-bee" would think they had been transferred to pandemonium if they could be conveyed to a Georgia corn-shucking and see how our colored farmers do the same work; and I imagine the social gathering which follows the husking-bee, and the frolic which is the after-piece of the corn-shucking, resemble each other as little as do their methods of work.

It is no rare occurrence for a corn-shucking to terminate in a row instead of a frolic. If one side is badly beaten, there is almost sure to be some charge of fraud; either that the rail has been moved, or part of the corn of the successful party thrown over on the other side "unbeknownst" to them, or some such charge. These offenses are common occurrences, and are aided by the dimness of the light. If any of these charges can be proved, a first-class row ensues, in which ears of corn fly thick and fast, and sometimes more dangerous weapons are used. The owner of the premises can always stop them, and does do so. Negroes have great respect for proprietorship, and yield whenever it is asserted. It is most often the case, however, that the race has been about an equal one, and that good humor prevails amid the great excitement.

The first thing in order is to express thanks for the entertainment, which is done by taking the host, putting him on the shoulders of two strong men, and then marching around, while all hands split their throats to a tune, the chorus of which is "Walk away, walk away!" This honor, though of questionable comfort, or rather most unquestionable discomfort, must be undergone, for a refusal is considered most churlish, and a retreat gives too much license to the guests. The general feeling that most handsome behavior has been shown toward the host, raises the opinion the guests entertain for themselves, and they are prepared to begin in earnest the sports of the occasion. The fun usually begins by some one who is a famous wrestler (pronounced "rasler") offering to throw down anybody on the ground, accompanying the boast by throwing aside his coat and swaggering round, sometimes making a ring and inviting "eny gemman ez warnts ter git his picter tuk on de groun'," to come in. The challenge is promptly accepted, and the spectators gather around, forming a ring, so that they may be in a position to watch, and, at the same time, encourage and advise their friends. They keep up a continual stream of talk during the whole time, and not unfrequently come to blows over the merits of the wrestlers.

The "rasler's" account of his performance is as much unlike his real conduct as can well be imagined. The fellow who swaggers around boastfully at the shucking will make himself out the most modest person in the world, in recounting his adventures next day. There is a famous corn-shucker and wrestler who is a tenant of the writer, named Nathan Mitchell, more commonly known in the neighborhood as "An' Fran's Nath." He loves to go over his adventures generally in about these words:

Mars Dave, yer know dis hyer Ike Jones whar live down Mr. Brittels'? Well, sir, I went down ter Miss Marfy Moore's night efore las'. Dey had er little corn-shuckin' down dar, en arter we got done wid de shuckin', Ike he kerminced cuttin' up his shines, 'lowed he cud fling down enything ter his inches on de ground, en ef dey didn't b'lieve it, all dey had ter do wuz ter toe de mark. De boys dey all wanted me fer ter try 'im, but I wudn't do it, kase I knowed p'intedly ef I tuk holt er dat nigger he wuz bound ter git hurt. When he seed me sorter hol'in' back, he got wusser en wusser, twell finerly I sed: "Beenst how yer so manish, I'll take one fall wid yer, jest ter give yer sattifacshun." Wal, sir, I flung dat nigger so hard I got oneasy 'bout him; I wuz nattally feared I had kilt him, and I aint here if he didn't get up en swor it wuz er dog-fall* Gemini! den I got mer blood up. I sed, I did: "Jest buckle round me." En no sooner en he tuk his holt, en gin de word ter cut mer patchin, den I tuk him up wid de ole h'ist, en flung him clean over mer shoulder, right squar on top of his hed. De wust uv it wuz, arter dat he wanted to go fite An' Kalline's little Jim, kase he sed: "Dat jarred de gemman." I tole him ef he toch dat chile, I gim de wust whippin, ever he toted. I don't like dat nigger, nohow.

I happened to hear this same man telling one of his companions about some corn-"gin'r'l," who "got up on de corn-pile en kep' singin' en gwine on twell I got tired, en took him behine de year wid er year er corn en axed him down"; from which I inferred he had been guilty of misconduct of throwing at the generals, which has already been mentioned, and which he was sufficiently ashamed of to try and hide from me.

A corn-shucking which is to be considered in the light of a finished performance should end with a dance. Of late years, colored farmers who are "members" frequently give corn-shuckings where no dancing is allowed, but it is common for the party to have a dance before they disperse. These dances take place either in one of the houses, or else out of doors on the ground. The dance of late years is a modification of the cotillon, the old-time jig having given place to this, just as in the cities the German and the others have ousted the old-time dances. There is a great deal of jig-dancing in these cotillons, and the man who cannot "cut the pigeon-wing" is considered a sorry dancer indeed; but still it purports to be a cotillon. Endurance is a strong point in the list of accomplishments of the dancer, and, other things being equal, that dancer who can hold out the longest is considered the best. The music is commonly made by a fiddler and a straw-beater,

* *I.e.*, a drawn battle, both striking the ground at the same moment.

the fiddle being far more common than the banjo, in spite of tradition to the contrary. The fiddler is the man of most importance on the ground. He always comes late, must have an extra share of whisky, is the best-dressed man in the crowd, and unless every honor is shown him he will not play. He will play you a dozen different pieces, which are carefully distinguished by names, but not by tunes. The most skilled judge of music will be unable to detect any difference between "Run, Nigger, Run," "Arkansaw Traveler," "Forky Deer," and any other tune. He is never offended at a mistake which you may make as to what piece he is playing; he only feels a trifle contemptuous toward you as a person utterly devoid of musical knowledge. The straw-beater is a musician, the description of whose performances the writer has never "read or heard repeated." No preliminary training is necessary in this branch of music; any one can succeed, with proper caution, the first time he tries. The performer provides himself with a pair of straws about eighteen inches in length, and stout enough to stand a good smart blow. An experienced straw-beater will be very careful in selecting his straws, which he does from the sedge-broom; this gives him an importance he could not otherwise have, on account of the commonness of his accomplishment. These straws are used after the manner of drum-sticks, that portion of the fiddle-strings between the fiddler's bow and his left hand serving as a drum. One of the first sounds which you hear on approaching the dancing party is the *tum tee tum* of the straws, and after the dance begins, when the shuffling of feet destroys the other sounds of the fiddle, this noise can still be heard.

With the cotillon a new and very important office, that of "caller-out," has become a necessity. The "caller-out," though of less importance than the fiddler, is second to no other. He not only calls out the figures, but explains them at length to the ignorant, sometimes accompanying them through the performance. He is never at a loss, "Gemmen to de right!" being a sufficient refuge in case of embarrassment, since this always calls forth a full display of the dancers' agility, and gives much time.

The corn-shucking is one of the institutions of the old plantations which has flourished and expanded since the negroes were freed. With the larger liberty they enjoy there has come increased social intercourse, and this has tended to encourage social gatherings of all kinds. Then, too, the great number of small farmers who have sprung up in the South since the war necessitates mutual aid in larger undertakings, so that at this time the corn-shucking, as an institution, is most flourishing. No doubt with improved culture its features will be changed, and, in time, destroyed. Indeed, already it is becoming modified, and the great improvement which the negro race is continually manifesting indicates that in time their simple songs and rough sports must yield to higher demands.

1883

Plantation Music

by Joel Chandler Harris

The Critic, III:95 (New York, December 15, 1883), 505–506.

In this article Harris sought to controvert the widespread belief that the banjo furnished the usual accompaniment for Negro singing. His demotion of this instrument did not go unchallenged. Hannah Street, "a colored woman, born and raised in Georgia," sent the editors of Critic *a letter (III:96 [December 22, 1883], 523) in which she told of banjo playing on plantations in Wayne County, where she was born. In the issue of the following week there were two more letters (III:97 [December 29, 1883], 534–535)—one from J. A. Harrison, attesting the use of the banjo in Virginia and New Orleans, and one from E. Brainerd, who had worked with Harris on the Atlanta* Constitution, *testifying for the popularity of the instrument in Virginia, middle Georgia, and on the street in front of the* Constitution's *office.*

Although Harris may have erred about the popularity of the banjo, the point of his article was indeed well taken, for the image of the Negro and his music so popular in the cities was nothing more than a well-paying lie, "a silly trick of the clowns to give him over to burlesque; for his life, though abounding in humor, was concerned with all that the imagination of man has made pathetic."

Quite recently one of The Critic's metropolitan contemporaries—*The World*, if I am not mistaken—made a statement to the effect that the negroes of the South would doubtless be proud to hear that their favorite instrument—the banjo—was making its way in fashionable circles at the North. Commenting upon this somewhat lightly and flippantly, a Georgian newspaper—*The Atlanta Constitution*—reminded *The World* that the negroes of the South know little about the banjo and care a great deal less. This comment has evidently been copied into some of the Northern exchanges of *The Constitution*, for I have before me a number of letters from friends and correspondents in New York, Massachusetts and elsewhere, making inquiries as to the authenticity of the statement which the Atlanta newspaper makes by inference concerning the relations between the hilarious plink-plank-plunk of the banjo and the musical accomplishments of the negro. These inquiries are all very pointed and eager. For instance, a young lady who dates her letter from Brookline, Massachusetts, declares: "I see a paragraph in the evening paper that really distresses me." After giving the substance of the paragraph, she continues: "I should be shocked to learn that the negroes of the South know nothing of the banjo. Somehow it has been a great comfort to me to associate them with that instrument."

It is not difficult to understand the feelings of the young lady. All her life, in common with the people of the whole country, including a large majority of the people of the South, she has been accustomed to associate the negro with the banjo, the bones, and the tambourine. Especially with the banjo. Here sentiment, and romance, and probability join hands and sing "ring around the roses"; and they make a tough team when the partnership, as in this instance, receives the approval of custom. Romance may become a little frayed around the edges, but sentiment is a very stubborn thing. It is sometimes stronger than facts; and the ideal and impossible negro will continue to exist in the public mind as a banjoist only less expert than Dobson or French, or the inimitable and unapproachable Sweeny.

What more natural? In the negro minstrel show, which is supposed to present to us the negro as he was and is and hopes to be, an entire scene is devoted to the happy-go-lucky darkey with his banjo. The stage is cleared away; the pleasant and persuasive bass voice of Mr. Hawkins, the "interlocutor," is hushed; there is silence in the pit and gallery until a gurgling ripple of laughter, running merrily through the audience, announces the appearance of Mr. Edward McClurg, in his justly celebrated banjo act. Mr. McClurg, disguised by burnt cork, is black, and sleek, and saucy. He wears a plug hat, enormous shoes, and carries his banjo on his shoulder. He seats himself, crosses his legs, waves an enormous shoe, and looks at the audience as much as to say, "Here is where the laugh comes in." Mr. McClurg is garrulous. As he tunes his banjo (inlaid with silver and costing seventy-five dollars) he tells several stories that were in last year's newspapers, and makes various allusions that savor strongly of the plantations through which the back streets of New York City run. Passing his nimble fingers lightly over the strings, he gives "Home, Sweet Home" and "The Mocking-Bird" with variations, just as they were played on the plantations that exist on the stage. To audiences in nearly every part of the country this scene is real and representative, because it falls in with their ideas of the plantation negro. Only the other day the editor of the Philadelphia *Times* remarked that "it is doubtful if the real negro can be got very clearly into literature except by the way of minstrel shows and the comic drama." This statement, ridiculous as it may seem to those who have the opportunity to compare the real negro with the stage negro, suggests the truth. It is not only difficult, but impossible, to displace the stage negro in literature with the real negro. The stage negro is ground into the public mind, and he cannot be ground out. It is so at the North, and, in a great measure, it is so at the South. The first song the writer ever learned was a string of nonsense with this chorus:

> Oh, Susanna! don't you cry for me,
> I'm gwine to Alabama, wid my banjo on my knee!

There was another in which the refrain advised everybody to hang up his banjo on the wall, and there was still another in which a negro, who was supposed to have lost his Nelly Gray, declared that he would "take his banjo down and sing a little song." Nelly, in the mean time, was down in Georgia "a-toiling in the cotton and the cane." These songs, and hundreds of similar ones, were written by white men who knew even less about the negro than they did about metre; but the ditties were sung all over the country, and there was nobody in the South willing to laugh good-humoredly at the idea of a negro girl (or man) toiling in the cane in Georgia. If the cane had been insisted on in negro stage literature as strenuously as the banjo has been, there would be few persons willing to laugh at it today.

Now, I am not going to laugh at the banjo any more than I laughed at the idea of the negro girl toiling in the Georgian cane. The banjo may be the typical instrument of the plantation negroes, but I have never seen a plantation negro play it. I have heard them make sweet music with the quills—Pan's pipes; I have heard them play passably well on the fiddle, the fife, and the flute; and I have heard them blow a tin-trumpet with surprising skill; but I have never seen a banjo, or a tambourine, or a pair of bones in the hands of a plantation negro. This statement, however, should not be misunderstood. It covers an experience which was limited to plantations in the counties of Putnam, Jasper, Morgan, Greene, Hancock and Jones in Middle Georgia. The banjo may have been greatly in vogue on other plantations and in other parts of the South; but, if on other plantations, why not in Middle Georgia? In the counties I have named there were hundreds of Virginian negroes—negroes of every stripe and kind. If the banjo had been a favorite instrument among the negroes of any part of the country, surely it would have been in vogue in Middle Georgia; surely it would have been played on some of the Putnam plantations on the Oconee.

I have seen the negro at work and I have seen him at play; I have attended his corn-shuckings, his dances, and his frolics; I have heard him give the wonderful melody of his songs to the winds; I have heard him fit barbaric airs to the quills; I have seen him scrape jubilantly on the fiddle; have seen him blow wildly upon the bugle, and beat enthusiastically on the triangle; but I have never heard him play on the banjo. A year or more ago, a band of negro serenaders made its appearance upon the streets of Atlanta. The leader of this band carried a banjo, upon which he strummed while singing. His voice drowned out the banjo, but a close observer could see that he was thumping the strings aimlessly. I have heard of another negro since the war who could play the banjo, and there may be dozens who have acquired the art. But I think it is not wide of the truth to say that the genuine plantation negro left the banjo and banjo-playing to nimbler fingers.

But the old traditions will remain. What the negro did not care to do, the sentiment which has grown up around the stage negro has done for him, and he will go down to history accompanied by his banjo. A representation of negro life and character has never been put upon the stage, nor anything remotely resembling it; but, to all who have any knowledge of the negro, the plantation darkey, as he was, is a very attractive figure. It is a silly trick of the clowns to give him over to burlesque; for his life, though abounding in humor, was concerned with all that the imagination of man has made pathetic.

1884

Banjo and Bones
(Unsigned article)

Saturday Review of Politics, Literature, Science and Art, LVII (London, June 7, 1884), 739–740.

Two quite artificial representations of Negro song enjoyed wide popularity during the last part of the nineteenth century. One was promulgated by Negroes themselves, who smoothed the tunes and corrected the grammar of the spirituals, then performed in America and England to full houses and enthusiastic critics. One group involved in this commercialization was the Fisk Jubilee Singers, who toured with great sucess from 1871 to 1878. In his lengthy letter commenting on the contents of this book, Herbert Halpert said that "the Fisk singers made Negro singers good conventional art singers, and cut the folk guts out of spirituals just as badly as any of today's 'folk singers' do for secular songs." Even though the Fisk singers translated, for better or worse, traditional materials into concert-hall terms, their influence was not sufficient to undo the incredible stereotype maintained by such heirs of Dan Emmet as "Mr. Haverly's American and European Mastodon Minstrels." Like plastic in the years immediately following the Second World War, minstrelsy was an American export that grew more successful as its forms became more grotesque. Harris' Critic *article, which had appeared six months earlier, described how unfortunate was minstrelsy's effect upon the image of the Negro held by many white Americans; this article indicates that Europe was only partially immune to the stereotype.*

We should note that whites were not the only ones influenced by the image: there was considerable feedback to the Negro community, in which it outlasted the whites' stereotype. Professor Roger D. Abrahams told me recently of a trumpet player acquaintance who played the blackface circuit not very long ago. He noted that "it is one of the many ways in which the Negro has accepted and adapted the white stereotype of himself—just as Amos 'n' Andy were still the most popular entertainers among the Negro in Camingerly [a Philadelphia neighborhood] in 1959!"

"I have a reasonable good ear in music," remarks that typical amateur actor, Bottom the Weaver; "let's have the tongs and the bones" The tongs, though not obsolete, are now something archaic, but masters of the noisy art and mystery of bone-playing are still to be found disguised in black and set over against masters of the more dulcet tambourine, at the opposite ends of the semi-circle of sable performers known to the world at large as negro minstrels. It is, perhaps, more accurate to confess at once that the negro minstrel is practically known and loved only in those parts of the world where the English language is spoken. The burnt-cork opera of the Christy Minstrel is appreciated only in Great Britain, in Greater Britain, and in the United States of America—where, in fact, it had its rise some two score years ago. Where the English language is not spoken, the grotesque verbal dislocations of Brudder Bones somehow fail of their reward. Indeed nothing can be more humorously pathetic than the dignified and reserved attitude of the audience in a Parisian *café chantant*—the Alcazar or the Ambassadeurs in summer or the Eldorado in winter—when a pair of blacked-up and hopelessly *h*-less Cockneys are attempting an exact imitation of the sayings and doings of the American plantation negro, studied by them at secondhand from some Irish-American performer who had probably never in his life seen a cotton-field or a sugar-house. And the estate of the Germans is yet less gracious than that of the Frenchman; there is even a legend in circulation setting forth the absolute failure of an enterprising American manager's attempt to invade Germany with a resolute band of negro minstrels, in consequence of the perspicacity of the German critics in detecting the fraud of trying to pass off as negroes white men artificially blackened! Obviously, the imitation darkey of the negro-minstrel stage did not coincide with the genuine darkey as evolved from the Teutonic inner consciousness. Probably the German critics would have objected even to the conscientious display of misplaced zeal which it was our good fortune once to behold in America. At the huge summer hotels which make Saratoga one of the brightest and gayest of American watering-places, the attendants in the dining-rooms are generally negroes, varying in hue from the ebony of the full-blooded black to the tawny ivory of the octoroon. The waiters of one of these hotels sometimes obtain permission to give "a minstrel show" in the dining-room, to which the amused "guests" of the hotel are admitted for a price. It was one of these minstrel shows, given at a Saratoga hotel three summers ago by genuine darkeys, that we were privileged to attend; and when the curtains were drawn aside, discovering the row of sable performers, it was perceived to the great and abiding joy of the spectators that the musicians were all of a uniform darkness of hue, and that they, genuine negroes as they were, had "blacked up" the more closely to resemble the professional negro minstrels.

This personal experience is valuable in so far as it may show how firm is the rule of convention in theatrical circles, and how the accepted type comes in time to seem preferable to the real thing. It is useful also in suggesting that the negro minstrel is getting to be a law unto himself, and ceasing to be an imitator of the exact facts of plantation life. In the beginning of negro minstrelsy, when the first band of "Ethiopian Serenaders," as they were then called, came into existence, its sole excuse for being was that it endeavoured to reproduce the life of the plantation darkey. The songs sung by the early Ethiopian Serenaders, before the original E. P. Christy or his nephew, the late George Christy, came into prominence, were reminiscences of songs heard where the negro was at work, on the river steamboat, in the sugar-field, or at the camp-meeting—the hardest kind of labour to a negro was religion. These songs retained the flavour of slave life, with all its pathos, its yearning, its hopelessness, its mournfulness. To this period belongs Stephen C. Foster, who remains to this day the most truly American of all American composers. As the slave songs are the only indigenous tunes which America has produced, Foster availed himself of hints from them, and he borrowed from wandering negroes both the themes and the method of some of his best songs. The typical song of this period is "The Old Folks at Home," with its wailing refrain and its suggestion of unutterable longing. The actual melodies of the plantation slave have been made known to European critics by the various wandering bands of Jubilee Singers, who have travelled the world over singing their rude and effective hymns. Some of their songs have been borrowed by Mr. Sankey, and others, as we have said, have been taken by the negro minstrels. Their full beauty will not be recognized generally until America shall bring forth a composer with imagination enough and with skill enough to do for these rich themes what has already been done so brilliantly and so effectively for the folk-songs of Hungary and of Scandinavia.

The first negro-minstrel company was organized in 1843, and it consisted of four performers, who had each appeared singly as impersonators of the plantation negro. One of the original four, D. D. Emmett, who still survives, was the composer of "Dixie," which afterwards became the battle-song of the Southern Confederacy. In the beginning these performers gave their concert as an interlude between two plays in a regular theatre. The popularity of the new entertainment led to its expansion, until it could fill the bill of an entire evening's amusement. It was at a very early stage in its career that the programme of a negro-minstrel performance fell into three divisions—the "first part," the "olio," and the after-piece. The "first part" retains its name to the present day; it is the portion of the entertainment provided by a single row of negro minstrels seated on chairs, with the grave "Interlocutor" in the centre, while at the ends are Bones and Tambo, the "end-men," who are known in England, oddly enough, as the "corner-men." This row of negro minstrels consisted at first of four, but it gradually expanded to twenty, until the great Mr. Haverly suddenly declared that he had "forty—count them—forty." In the performances now given at Drury Lane Theatre by Mr. Haverly's Mastodon Minstrels—and the name is not ill chosen, for some of the merry jests retailed by Mr. Haverly's comedians are surely as old as the mastodon and the mammoth—there are nearly sixty performers visible, line upon line, rising in tiers nearly to the flies. On the wings of this sable array are a score of end-men with tambourines and with bones; while the star end-men, the chief comedians, are so many and so important that they appear in relays, one replacing the other. This, of course, is a doing of things on a large scale, and certainly it succeeds in breaking up the monotony of a single line of performers quite as effectually as did the New York minstrel manager who scattered the actors in his "first part" through a handsomely furnished drawing-room in a vain effort to make the entertainment appear in the semblance of an evening party. The second part of a minstrel show is the "olio"—and this is only a variety entertainment, of banjo-playing, clog-dancing, and the like, by imitation negroes. Occasionally one of the sketches now and again performed really recalls the actual negro, notably the little charcoal outline of the "Watermelon Man" as presented by Mr. McAndrews. But in general the "olio" is as far away from the actual facts of plantation life as the first part; and when we say that two of Mr. Haverly's Mastodon Minstrels are sufficiently conscience-less to sing Irish comic songs, the full extent of this decadence is made visible. And, in like manner, the after-piece, which once attempted to reproduce dramatically the mingled simplicity and cunning of the negro, is now a parody of a popular play, a burlesque opera, or any other comic drama as far removed as possible from the ken of the dwellers on the old plantation. Nowadays any kind of a farce may be performed as an afterpiece. We have seen, with much amusement, a broadly comic play called the *Great Sheep Case,* in which we recognized a blackened perversion of the *Village Lawyer,* a farce of Garrick's day; and we happened to know that the *Village Lawyer* was a free rendering of *L'Avocat Pathelin* of Brueys and Palaprat, which in turn was a modernization of *Pathelin,* one of the oldest surviving farces of the French stage.

The entertainment now offered at Drury Lane Theatre by Mr. Haverly's American and European Mastodon Minstrels is emphatically a Big Thing after the most approved fashion of American Big Things. Mr. Haverly is, plainly enough, a manager with Napoleonic conceptions, worthy of comparison with those of the mysterious and mighty Mr. Barnum, whose Own and Only Greatest Show on Earth is hardly more astounding or more kaleidoscopic than this sable exhibition of Mr. Haverly's. We incline to think that Mr. Barnum's show is scarcely more unlike the primitive circus than Mr. Haverly's Minstrels are unlike the original Ethiopian Serenaders. And Mr. Haverly has a full share of the sublime self-confidence and of the marvellous knowledge of effect which combine to make Mr. Barnum what he is—one of the wonders of the world, far more remarkable and better worth the full price of admission than any of the Living Curiosities gathered into his Ethnological Congress. From the first part of Mr. Haverly's programme to the last part everything is done on a grand scale; there are six eminent end-men appearing in pairs in relays; there are eighteen other exponents of the bones and the tambourine; there are about sixty performers on the stage at once; there are sand-dances by a sextet of agile and ebony operators, and clog-dances by a score of glittering and airy apparitions, who appear in shiny mail to go through a Silver Combat Clog-Dance—which, indeed, must be seen to be appreciated. Above all, there is Mr. Frank E. McNish, one of the most quaintly humorous performers it has ever been our good fortune to see. Mr. McNish is primarily an acrobat, and he is an acrobat of very unusual skill and of a most delightful felicity and certainty of execution. But what gives zest to the merit of his performance is his odd dramatic assumption that he is in danger of interruption from some unseen bully of an overseer. Mr. McNish's extraordinary performance, as extraordinary in its humour as in its novelty, is beyond all question a thing to be seen. Among the other performers, Mr. William Emerson and Mr. William Sweetman are the most amusing, and Messrs. Sanford and Wilson are the most true to the negro character. In general, as we have said, there is but a bare pretence of the imitation of plantation life in any modern minstrel performance; and perhaps Haverly's Mastodon Minstrels are no worse in this respect than any other. But the sentimental ballads of the first part—not as many nor as delicately shaded as other minstrel companies have accustomed us to—have no trace of the real negro song, which is to be detected, however, in one or two of the comic ditties, notably in Mr. Morton's "I'm high-minded." In general, the comic songs of Mr. Haverly's performers are better than the sentimental; they are sung, too, with better assistance from the chorus; and some of them are rendered with a certainty of effect, and indeed a multiplicity of effects, most amusing. In fact, of the entire programme of Mr. Haverly's Mastodon Minstrels—despite the melancholy fact that that programme is unduly long—we may say, with Abraham Lincoln, that "those who like that sort of thing will find this just the sort of thing they like."

The instruments of the four performers in the original band of Ethiopian Serenaders were the banjo and the bones, the violin and the tambourine—and for a long while the place of the stately Interlocutor (who sits in the entre of the semicircle and allows the humorous end-men to extract unlimited fun from the extremely complicated relations of the Interlocutor's numerous fathers and brothers and sisters) was filled by the banjoist, who repeated the conundrum propounded by Brudder Bones or Brudder Tambo, so that there might be no misunderstanding of its conditions, making the point clear to the dullest comprehension, much in the manner of the catechizing Sunday-school visitor. Of these four instruments most persons would at once pick out the banjo as most characteristic of the negro race, recognizing the Elizabethan existence of the bones, the Basque origin of the tambourine, and the wholly un-Ethiopian genesis of the violin. Mr. Joel Chandler Harris, however, the creator of the always delightful *Uncle Remus,* and a very close student of the actual facts of negro life, wrote a paper last winter in which he declared that the banjo was not a negro instrument at all, and that the preference of the darkey was wholly for the violin. Mr. Harris, whose opportunities for observation, especially in Georgia, have been as well utilized as they have been ample, declared that "the banjo may be the typical instrument of the plantation-negroes, but I have never seen a plantation-negro play it. I have heard them make sweet music with the quills—Pan's pipes; I have heard them play passably well on the fiddle, the fife, and the flute; but I have never seen a banjo, or a tambourine, or a pair of bones, in the hands of a plantation-negro." And, after specifying that his experience extends only to Middle Georgia, where, however, there were negroes from Virginia and from other parts of the South, Mr. Harris adds:—"I have seen the negro at work, and I have seen him at play; I have attended his corn-shuckings, his dances, and his frolics; I have heard him give the wonderful melody of his songs to the winds; I have heard him fit barbaric airs to the quills; I have seen him scrape jubilantly on the fiddle; I have seen him blow wildly on the bugle, and beat enthusiastically on the triangle; but I have never heard him play on the banjo." This iconoclastic shattering of tradition and convention was most intolerable and not to be endured; and the succeeding numbers of *The Critic* (in which Mr. Harris's pungent paper was published) contained letters from many correspondents, all of whom bore witness to the fact that the plantation-negro did sometimes play on the banjo. No attempt was made to show that the negro knew anything at all about the bones or the tambourine. But the use of the banjo by plantation-negroes in Virginia was established beyond all cavil. One correspondent aptly quoted a foot-note from the rare first edition of Jefferson's *Notes on Virginia* (1784) which supplemented an assertion in the text that the negroes have an accurate ear for music with the declaration that "the instrument proper to them is the Banjar, which they brought hither from Africa, and which is the origin of the guitar, its chords being precisely the four lower chords of the guitar." Mr. George W. Cable, the author of the fresh and subtle sketches of life in New Orleans, *Old Creole Days,* has had occasion to observe the negro in Louisiana as carefully as Mr. Harris has observed him in Georgia; and Mr. Cable has found a hundred times as many fiddles on a plantation as banjos. Mr. Cable agrees with Mr. Harris in asserting that the banjo is not a very common instrument on the plantation; but he asserts that he has often spent half the night listening to negroes "picking" the banjo in monotonous accompaniment to their songs. Mr. Cable quoted a little Creole song, in which the slave seems to take his banjo into his confidence as he describes a passing dandy:—

Voyez ce mulet-là, Musieu Bainjo,
Comme il est insolent;
Chapeau sur côté, Musieu Bainjo,
La canne à la main, Musieu Bainjo,
Botte qui fait crin, crin, Musieu Bainjo.

Mr. Cable, however, disagrees absolutely with Mr. Harris in the main issue. He says that the banjo is just as much a negro instrument as the barrel with the jawbone drumsticks which the negroes use in their dances. And all truly conservative lovers of tradition will rejoice that Mr. Harris has been overthrown. It is bad enough to deprive the negro of his tambourine and his bones; to rob him of his banjo is brutal.

1886

The Dance in Place Congo

by George Washington Cable

Century Magazine, XXXI (New York, February 1886), 517–532.

Cable was born in New Orleans (1844), served in the Confederate Army, and lived in the South until his writings created hostilities so uncomfortable he decided to resettle in Massachusetts (1885). He is best known for his fiction, much of which details Creole life in New Orleans. Two of his most important books are Creole Days *(1879), a collection of short stories, and* The Grandissimes *(1880), a novel. Though his portraits of Creole life are vivid, there is some question about their validity; the case against him is argued in Grace King's* Memories of a Southern Woman of Letters *(New York, 1932). His two articles on Creole Negro folklore not only are full of valuable textual information, but also are so rich in background material one cannot help but sense the excitement he describes.*

Cable was fortunate to have many of the musical transcriptions done by H. E. Krehbiel, author of Afro-American Folksongs *(New York, 1914) and for many years music critic on the New York* Tribune.

The largest collection of New Orleans material is Gumbo Ya-Ya, *compiled by Lyle Saxon, Edward Dreyer, and Robert Tallant (Boston, 1945). Tallant's* Voodoo in New Orleans *may be of collateral interest. There were seven Louisiana songs in* Slave Songs of the United States*—"Belle Layotte," "Rémon," "Aurore Bradaire," "Caroline," "Calinda," "Lolotte," and "Musieu Bainjo"—all of which "were obtained from a lady who heard them sung, before the war, on the 'Good Hope' plantation, St. Charles Parish, Louisiana" (pp. 109–113).*

We should note that the folklore found among the Creole Negroes was very different from the Negro folklore found elsewhere in the United States—the fusion was with French rather than Anglo-Irish traditions—and many of the items Cable reports seem unrelated to the folklore recorded in the other articles in this anthology. But the Creole tradition is an important one—in many aspects it still survives—and we would lack an important point of reference if we did not have Cable's two articles.

I. CONGO SQUARE

Whoever has been to New Orleans with eyes not totally abandoned to buying and selling will, of course, remember St. Louis Cathedral, looking south-eastward—riverward—across quaint Jackson Square, the old Place d'Armes. And if he has any feeling for flowers, he has not forgotten the little garden behind the cathedral, so antique and unexpected, named for the beloved old priest Père Antoine.

The old Rue Royale lies across the sleeping garden's foot. On the street's farther side another street lets away at right angles, north-westward, straight, and imperceptibly downward from the cathedral and garden toward the rear of the city. It is lined mostly with humble ground-floor-and-garret houses of stuccoed brick, their wooden door-steps on the brick sidewalks. This is Orleans street, so named when the city was founded.

Its rugged round-stone pavement is at times nearly as sunny and silent as the landward side of a coral reef. Thus for about half a mile; and then Rampart street, where the palisade wall of the town used to run in Spanish days, crosses it, and a public square just beyond draws a grateful canopy of oak and sycamore boughs. That is the place. One may shut his buff umbrella there, wipe the beading sweat from the brow, and fan himself with his hat. Many's the bull-fight has taken place on that spot Sunday afternoons of the old time. That is Congo Square.

The trees are modern. So are the buildings about the four sides, for all their aged looks. So are all the grounds' adornments. Tremé market, off, beyond, toward the swamp, is not so very old, and the scowling, ill-smelling prison on the right, so Spanish-looking and dilapidated, is not a third the age it seems; not fifty-five. In that climate every year of a building's age counts for ten. Before any of these M. Cayetano's circus and menagerie were here. Cayetane the negroes called him. He was the Barnum of that region and day.

> Miché Cayetane, qui sortie l' Havane,
> Avec so chouals et somacaques.

That is, "who came from Havana with his horses and baboons."

Up at the other end of Orleans street, hid only by the old padre's garden and the cathedral, glistens the ancient Place d'Armes. In the early days it stood for all that was best; the place for political rallying, the retail quarter of all fine goods and wares, and at sunset and by moonlight the promenade of good society and the haunt of true lovers; not only in the military, but also in the most unwarlike sense, the place of arms, and of hearts and hands and of words tender as well as words noble.

The Place Congo, at the opposite end of the street, was at the opposite end of everything. One was on the highest ground; the other on the lowest. The one was the rendezvous of the rich man, the master, the military officer—of all that went to make up the ruling class; the other of the butcher and baker, the raftsman, the sailor, the quadroon, the painted girl, and the negro slave. No meaner name could be given the spot. The negro was the most despised of human creatures and the Congo the plebeian among negroes. The white man's plaza had the army and navy on its right and left, the court-house, the council-hall and the church at its back, and the world before it. The black man's was outside the rear gate, the poisonous wilderness on three sides and the proud man's contumely on its front.

Before the city overgrew its flimsy palisade walls, and closing in about this old stamping-ground gave it set bounds, it was known as Congo Plains. There was wide room for much field sport, and the Indian villagers of the town's outskirts and the lower class of white Creoles made it the ground of their wild ball game of *raquette.* Sunday afternoons were the time for it. Hence, beside these diversions there was, notably, another.

The hour was the slave's term of momentary liberty, and his simple, savage, musical and superstitious nature dedicated it to amatory song and dance tinctured with his rude notions of supernatural influences.

II. GRAND ORCHESTRA

The booming of African drums and blast of huge wooden horns called to the gathering. It was these notes of invitation, reaching beyond those of other outlandish instruments, that caught the Ethiopian ear, put alacrity into the dark foot, and brought their owners, male and female, trooping from all quarters. The drums were very long, hollowed, often from a single piece of wood, open at one end and having a sheep or goat skin stretched across the other. One was large, the other much smaller. The tight skin heads were not held up to be struck; the drums were laid along on the turf and the drummers bestrode them, and beat them on the head madly with fingers, fists, and feet,—with slow vehemence on the great drum, and fiercely and rapidly on the small one. Sometimes an extra performer sat on the ground behind the larger drum, at its open end, and "beat upon the wooden sides of it with two sticks." The smaller drum was often made from a joint or two of very large bamboo, in the West Indies where such could be got, and this is said to be the origin of its name; for it was called the *Bamboula.*

In stolen hours of night or the basking-hour of noon the black man contrived to fashion these rude instruments and others. The drummers, I say, bestrode the drums; the other musicians sat about them in an arc, cross-legged on the ground. One important instrument was a gourd partly filled with pebbles or grains of corn, flourished violently at the end of a stout staff with one hand and beaten upon the palm of the other. Other performers rang triangles, and others twanged from jew's-harps an astonishing amount of sound. Another instrument was the jawbone of some ox, horse, or mule, and a key rattled rhythmically along its weather-beaten teeth. At times the drums were reënforced by one or more empty barrels or casks beaten on the head with the shank-bones of cattle.

A queer thing that went with these when the affair was pretentious —full dress, as it were—at least it was so in the West Indies, whence Congo Plains drew all inspirations—was the Marimba brett, a union of reed and string principles. A single strand of wire ran lengthwise of a bit of wooden board, sometimes a shallow box of thin wood, some eight inches long by four or five in width, across which, under the wire, were several joints of reed about a quarter of an inch in diameter and of graduated lengths. The performer, sitting cross-legged, held the board in both hands and plucked the ends of the reeds with his thumb-nails. The result was called—music.

But the grand instrument at last, the first violin, as one might say, was the banjo. It had but four strings, not six: beware of the dictionary. It is not the "favorite musical instrument of the negroes of the Southern States of America." Uncle Remus says truly that that is the fiddle; but for the true African dance, a dance not so much of legs and feet as of the upper half of the body, a sensual, devilish thing tolerated only by Latin-American masters, there was wanted the dark inspiration of African drums and the banjo's thrump and strum.

And then there was that long-drawn human cry of tremendous volume, richness, and resound, to which no instrument within their reach could make the faintest approach:

Eh! pou' la belle Layotte ma mourri 'nocent,
Oui 'nocent ma mourri!

all the instruments silent while it rises and swells with mighty energy and dies away distantly, "Yea-a-a-a-a!"—then the crash of savage drums, horns, and rattles—

For the fair Layotte I must crazy die!
Yes, crazy I must die!

Eh-h-h! pou' la belle La - yotte ma mour-ri 'no -cent, Oui, 'no - cent ma mour - ri!
Yea! For the fair La - yotte I must cra - zy die, Yes, cra - zy I must die.

To all this there was sometimes added a Pan's-pipe of but three reeds, made from single joints of the common brake cane, and called by English-speaking negroes "the quills." One may even at this day hear the black lad, sauntering home at sunset behind a few cows that he has found near the edge of the cane-brake whence he has also cut his three quills, blowing and hooting, over and over,—

But to show how far the art of playing the "quills" could be carried, if we are not going too much aside, see this "quill tune" given me by Mr. Krehbiel, musical critic of the "New York Tribune," and got by him from a gentleman who heard it in Alabama:

QUILL TUNE

Such was the full band. All the values of contrast that discord can furnish must have been present, with whatever there is of ecstasy in maddening repetition, for of this the African can never have too much.

And yet there was entertaining variety. Where? In the dance! There was constant, exhilarating novelty—endless invention— in the turning, bowing, arm-swinging, posturing and leaping of the dancers.

Moreover, the music of Congo Plains was not tamed to mere monotone. Monotone became subordinate to many striking qualities. The strain was wild. Its contact with French taste gave it often great tenderness of sentiment. It grew in fervor, and rose and sank, and rose again, with the play of emotion in the singers and dancers.

III. THE GATHERING

It was a weird one. The negro of colonial Louisiana was a most grotesque figure. He was nearly naked. Often his neck and arms, thighs, shanks, and splay feet were shrunken, tough, sinewy like a monkey's. Sometimes it was scant diet and cruel labor that had made them so. Even the requirement of law was only that he should have not less than a barrel of corn—nothing else,—a month, nor get more than thirty lashes to the twenty-four hours. The whole world was crueler those times than now; we must not judge them by our own.

Often the slave's attire was only a cotton shirt, or a pair of pantaloons hanging in indecent tatters to his naked waist. The bond-woman was well clad who had on as much as a coarse chemise and petticoat. To add a *tignon*—a Madras handkerchief twisted into a turban—was high gentility, and the number of kerchiefs beyond that one was the measure of absolute wealth. Some were rich in *tignons*; especially those who served within the house, and pleased the mistress, or even the master—there were Hagars in those days. However, Congo Plains did not gather the house-servants so much as the "field-hands."

These came in troops. See them; wilder than gypsies; wilder than the Moors and Arabs whose strong blood and features one sees at a glance in so many of them; gangs—as they were called—gangs and gangs of them, from this and that and yonder direction; tall, well-knit Senegalese from Cape Verde, black as ebony, with intelligent, kindly eyes and long, straight, shapely noses; Mandingoes, from the Gambia River, lighter of color, of cruder form, and a cunning that shows in the countenance; whose enslavement seems specially a shame, their nation the "merchants of Africa," dwelling in towns, industrious, thrifty, skilled in commerce and husbandry, and expert in the working of metals, even to silver and gold; and Foulahs, playfully miscalled "*Poulards*,"—fat chickens,—of goodly stature, and with a perceptible rose tint in the cheeks; and Sosos, famous warriors, dexterous with the African targe; and in contrast to these, with small ears, thick eyebrows, bright eyes, flat, upturned noses, shining skin, wide mouths and white teeth, the negroes of Guinea, true and unmixed, from the Gold Coast, the Slave Coast, and the Cape of Palms—not from the

Grain Coast; the English had that trade. See them come! Popoes, Cotocolies, Fidas, Socoes, Agwas, short, copper-colored Mines—what havoc the slavers did make!—and from interior Africa others equally proud and warlike: fierce Nagoes and Fonds; tawny Awassas; Iboes, so light-colored that one could not tell them from mulattoes but for their national tattooing; and the half-civilized and quick-witted but ferocious Arada, the original Voudou worshiper. And how many more! For here come, also, men and women from all that great Congo coast,—Angola, Malimbe, Ambrice, etc.,—small, good-natured, sprightly "boys," and gay, garrulous "gals," thick-lipped but not tattooed; chattering, chaffering, singing, and guffawing as they come: these are they for whom the dance and the place are named, the most numerous sort of negro in the colonies, the Congoes and Franc-Congoes, and though serpent worshipers, yet the gentlest: and kindliest natures that came from Africa. Such was the company. Among these *bossals*—that is, native Africans—there was, of course, an ever-growing number of negroes who proudly called themselves Creole negroes, that is, born in America;* and at the present time there is only here and there an old native African to be met with, vain of his singularity and trembling on his staff.

IV. THE BAMBOULA

The gathering throng closed in around, leaving unoccupied the circle indicated by the crescent of musicians. The short, harsh turf was the dancing-floor. The crowd stood. Fancy the picture. The pack of dark, tattered figures touched off every here and there with the bright colors of a Madras *tignon.* The squatting, cross-legged musicians. The low-roofed, embowered town off in front, with here and there a spire lifting a finger of feeble remonstrance; the flat, grassy plain stretching around and behind, dotted with black stumps; in the distance the pale-green willow undergrowth, behind it the *cyprière* —the cypress swamp—and in the pale, seven-times-heated sky the sun, only a little declined to south and westward, pouring down its beams.

With what particular musical movements the occasion began does not now appear. May be with very slow and measured ones; they had such that were strange and typical. I have heard the negroes sing one—though it was not of the dance-ground but of the cane-field—

* This broader use of the term is very common. The Creole "dialect" is the broken English *of the Creoles,* while the Creole *patois* is the corrupt French, not of the Creoles, but rather of the former slave race in the country of the Creoles. So of Creole negroes and Creole dances and songs.

that showed the emphatic barbarism of five bars to the line, and was confined to four notes of the open horn:

An -no - qué, An - no - bia, Bia - ta - ia, Que - re - qué, Nal - lé - oua.
Au - mon - dé, Au - tap - o - té, Au - pé - to - té, Au - qué - ré - qué, Bo.

But I can only say that with some such slow and quiet strain the dance may have been preluded. It suits the Ethiopian fancy for a beginning to be dull and repetitious; the bottom of the ladder must be on the ground.

The singers almost at the first note are many. At the end of the first line every voice is lifted up. The strain is given the second time with growing spirit. Yonder glistening black Hercules, who plants one foot forward, lifts his head and bare, shining chest, and rolls out the song from a mouth and throat like a cavern, is a *candio*, a chief, or was before he was overthrown in battle and dragged away, his village burning behind him, from the mountains of High Soudan. That is an African amulet that hangs about his neck— a *greegree*. He is of the Bambaras, as you may know by his solemn visage and the long tattoo streaks running down from the temples of the neck, broadest in the middle, like knife gashes. See his play of restrained enthusiasm catch from one bystander to another. They swing and bow to right and left, in slow time to the piercing treble of the Congo women. Some are responsive; others are competitive. Hear that bare foot slap the ground! one sudden stroke only, as it were the foot of a stag. The musicians warm up at the sound. A smiting of breasts with open hands begins very softly and becomes vigorous. The women's voices rise to a tremulous intensity. Among the chorus of Franc-Congo singing-girls is one of extra good voice, who thrusts in, now and again, an improvisation. This girl here, so tall and straight, is a Yaloff. You see it in her almost Hindoo features, and hear it in the plaintive melody of her voice. Now the chorus is more piercing than ever. The women clap their hands in time, or standing with arms akimbo receive with faint courtesies and head-liftings the low bows of the men, who deliver them swinging this way and that.

See! Yonder brisk and sinewy fellow has taken one short, nervy step into the ring, chanting with rising energy. Now he takes another, and stands and sings and looks here and there, rising upon his broad toes and sinking and rising again, with what wonderful lightness! How tall and lithe he is. Notice his brawn shining through his rags. He too, is a *candio*, and by the three long rays of tattooing on each side of his face, a Kiamba. The music has got into his feet. He moves off to the farther edge of the circle, still singing, takes the prompt hand of an unsmiling Congo girl, leads her into the ring, and leaving the chant to the throng, stands her before him for the dance.

Will they dance to that measure? Wait! A sudden frenzy seizes the musicians. The measure quickens, the swaying, attitudinizing crowd starts into extra activity, the female voices grow sharp and staccato, and suddenly the dance is the furious Bamboula.

THE BAMBOULA

ARR. BY MISS M. L. BARTLETT.
Quand pa-tate la cuite na va man - gé li, Na va man - gé, Na va man - gé.
Quand pa-tate la cuite na va man -gé, Na va man -gé li.

Now for the frantic leaps! Now for frenzy! Another pair are in the ring! The man wears a belt of little bells, or, as a substitute, little tin vials of shot, "bram-bram sonnette!" And still another couple enter the circle. What wild—what terrible delight! The ecstasy rises to madness; one—two—three of the dancers fall—*bloucoutoum! boum!*—with foam on their lips and are dragged out by arms and legs from under the tumultuous feet of crowding new-comers. The musicians know no fatigue; still the dance rages on:

Quand patate la cuite na va mangé li!

And all to that one nonsense line meaning only,

When that 'tater's cooked don't you eat it up!

It was a frightful triumph of body over mind, even in those early days when the slave was still a genuine pagan; but as his moral education gave him some hint of its enormity, and it became a forbidden fruit monopolized by those of reprobate will, it grew everywhere more and more gross. No wonder the police stopped it in Congo Square. Only the music deserved to survive, and does survive—coin snatched out of the mire. The one just given, Gottschalk first drew from oblivion. I have never heard another to know it as a bamboula; but Mr. Charles P. Ware, in "Slave Songs of the United States," has printed one got from Louisiana, whose characteristics resemble the bamboula reclaimed by Gottschalk in so many points that here is the best place for it:

Arr. by H. E. Krehbiel.

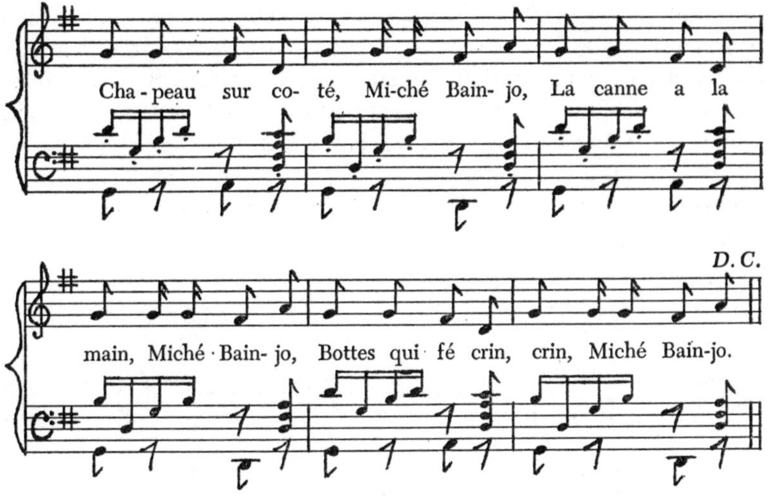

As much as to say, in English, "Look at that darky,"—we have to lose the saucy double meaning between *mulet* (mule) and *mulâtre* (mulatto)—

Look at that darky there, Mr. Banjo,
　Doesn't he put on airs!
Hat cocked on one side, Mr. Banjo,
Walking-stick in hand, Mr. Banjo,
Boots that go "crank, crank," Mr. Banjo,—
Look at that darky there, Mr. Banjo,
　Doesn't he put on airs!

It is odd that such fantastical comicality of words should have been mated to such fierce and frantic dancing, but so it was. The reeking faces of the dancers, moreover, always solemnly grave. So we must picture it now if we still fancy ourselves spectators on Congo Plains. The bamboula still roars and rattles, twangs, contorts, and tumbles in terrible earnest, while we stand and talk. So, on and on. Will they dance nothing else? Ah!—the music changes. The rhythm stretches out heathenish and ragged. The quick contagion is caught by a few in the crowd, who take it up with the spirited smitings of the bare sole upon the ground, and of open hands upon the thighs. From a spot near the musicians a single male voice, heavy and sonorous, rises in improvisation,—the Mandingoes brought that art from Africa,—and in a moment many others have joined in refrain, male voices in rolling, bellowing resonance, female responding in high, piercing unison. Partners are stepping into the ring. How strangely the French language is corrupted on the thick negro tongue, as with waving arms they suit gesture to word and chant (the translation is free, but so is the singing and posturing):

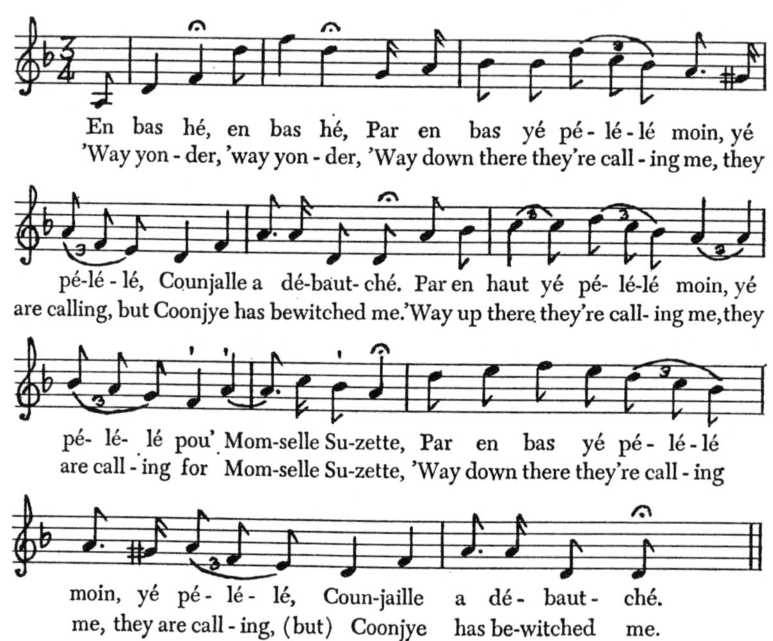

En bas hé, en bas hé, Par en bas yé pé-lé-lé moin, yé
'Way yon-der, 'way yon-der, 'Way down there they're call-ing me, they
pé-lé-lé, Counjalle a dé-baut-ché. Par en haut yé pé-lé-lé moin, yé
are calling, but Coonjye has bewitched me.'Way up there they're call-ing me, they
pé-lé-lé pou' Mom-selle Su-zette, Par en bas yé pé-lé-lé
are call-ing for Mom-selle Su-zette, 'Way down there they're call-ing
moin, yé pé-lé-lé, Coun-jaille a dé-baut-ché.
me, they are call-ing, (but) Coonjye has be-witched me.

V. THE COUNJAILLE.

Suddenly the song changes. The rhythm sweeps away long and smooth like a river escaped from its rapids, and in new spirit, with louder drum-beat and more jocund rattle, the voices roll up into the sky and the dancers are at it. Aye, ya, yi!

Inne, dé, trois, Caroline, Qui ci ça yé comme ça ma chère?
Inne, dé, trois, Caroline,
Mo l'aimé toé, to conné ça, Si -
Quo fère t'apé crïé ma chère?
yé to zi-é et vien bo moin; Mo l'aimé toé, to con-né ça, Si-yé to zié et vien bo moin.

I could give four verses, but let one suffice; it is from a manuscript copy of the words, probably a hundred years old, that fell into my hands through the courtesy of a Creole lady some two years ago. It is one of the best known of all the old Counjaille songs. The four verses would not complete it. The Counjaille was never complete, and found its end, for the time being, only in the caprice of the improvisator, whose rich, stentorian voice sounded alone between the refrains.

But while we discourse other couples have stepped into the grassy arena, the instrumental din has risen to a fresh height of inspiration, the posing and thigh-beating and breast-patting and chanting and swinging and writhing has risen with it, and the song is changed:

RÉMON, RÉMON

ARR. BY JOHN A. BROEKHOVEN.
Mo parlé Ré-mon, Rémon, Li parlé Si-mon, Si-mon, Li par-lé Ti-tine, Ti-
tine li tombé dans chagrin. O femme Romolus, O-o! Belle femme Romolus,
O-o! O femme Romolus, O-o! Belle femme, qui ça volez mo fé.

But the dance is not changed, and love is still the theme. Sweat streams from the black brows, down the shining black necks and throats, upon the men's bared chests, and into dark, unstayed bosoms. Time wears, shadows lengthen; but the movement is brisker than ever, and the big feet and bent shanks are as light as thistles on the air. Let one flag, another has his place, and a new song gives new vehemence, new inventions in steps, turns, and attitudes.

BELLE LAYOTTE

Arr. by John A. Broekhoven.
Mo de - ja rou - lé tout la côte, Pancore 'oir pa - reil belle La - yotte,
Mo de - ja rou - lé tout la côte, Pancore 'oir pa - reil belle Layotte.
Mo rou-lé tout la co - lo - nie, Di - pi cé Mi - ché Pierre So - niat,

Pancore 'oir in grif-fonne comme ça, Com-pa - rabe a mò belle La - yotte.

More stanzas could be added in the original *patois*, but here is a translation into African English as spoken by the Creole negro:

CHORUS: I done been 'roun' to evvy spot
Don't foun' nair match fo' sweet
Layotte. } *Bis.*

SOLO: I done hunt all dis settle*ment*
All de way 'roun' fum Pierre Soniat';
Never see yalla gal w'at kin
'Gin to lay 'longside sweet Layotte.
I done been, etc.

SOLO: I yeh dey 'talk 'bout 'Loïse gal—
Loïse, w'at b'long to Pierre Soniat';
I see her, but she can't biggin
Stan' up 'longside my sweet Layotte.
I done been, etc.

SOLO: I been meet up wid John Bayou,
Say to him, "John Bayou, my son,
Yalla gal nevva meet yo' view
Got a face lak dat chahmin' one!"
I done been, etc.

The fair Layotte appears not only in other versions of this *counjaille* but in other songs:

MA MOURRI
ARR. BY H. E. KREHBIEL.
Mo connin, zins zens, ma mourri, Oui, 'nocent, ma mourri;
Mo connin, zins zens, ma mourri 'nocent, Oui, 'nocent, ma mour-ri.
Eh-h! pou' la belle La-yotte ma mour-ri 'nocent, Oui, 'no-cent, ma mourri.

Mo connin, zins zens, ma mourri, Oui, 'nocent, ma mourri.
Mo connin, zins zens, ma mourri 'nocent, Ma mourri pou' la belle Layotte.

Or in English:

Well I know, young men, I must die,
  Yes, crazy, I must die.
Well I know, young men, I must crazy die,
  Yes, crazy, I must die. Eh-h-h-h!
For the fair Layotte, I must crazy die,—Yes, etc.
Well I know, young men, I must die,—Yes, etc.
Well I know, young men, I must crazy die,
  I must die for the fair Layotte.

VI. THE CALINDA.

There were other dances. Only a few years ago I was honored with an invitation, which I had to decline, to see danced the Babouille, the Cata (or Chacta), the Counjaille, and the Calinda. Then there were the Voudou, and the Congo, to describe which would not be pleasant. The latter, called Congo also in Cayenne, Chica in San Domingo, and in the Windward Islands confused under one name with the Calinda, was a kind of Fandango, they say, in which the Madras kerchief held by its tip-ends played a graceful part.

The true Calinda was bad enough. In Louisiana, at least, its song was always a grossly personal satirical ballad, and it was the favorite dance all the way from there to Trinidad. To dance it publicly is not allowed this side the West Indies. All this Congo Square business was suppressed at one time; 1843, says tradition.

The Calinda was a dance of multitude, a sort of vehement cotillion. The contortions of the encircling crowd were strange and terrible, the din was hideous. One Calinda is still familiar to all Creole ears; it has long been a vehicle for the white Creole's satire; for generations the man of municipal politics was fortunate who escaped entirely a lampooning set to its air.

In my childhood I used, at one time, to hear, every morning, a certain black *marchande des calas*—peddler-woman selling rice croquettes—chanting the song as she moved from street to street at the sunrise hour with her broad, shallow, laden basket balanced on her head.

Mi- chié Pre- val li don- né youn bal, Li fé naig payé trois pi- ass pou ren- tré.

Dan- cé Ca- lin- da, Bon- djoum! Bon- djoum!
Dan- cé Ca- lin- da, Bon- djoum! Bon- djoum!

In other words, a certain Judge Preval gave a ball—not an outdoor Congo dance—and made such Cuffees as could pay three dollars a ticket. It doesn't rhyme, but it was probably true. "Dance, dance the Calindá! Boujoum! Boujoum!"

The number of stanzas has never been counted; here are a few of them.

Dans l'equirie la 'y' avé grand gala;
Mo cré choual la yé t b'en étonné.

Miché Preval, li té capitaine bal;
So cocher Louis, té maite cérémonie.

Y avé des négresses belle passé maitresses,
Qui volé bel-bel dans l'ormoire momselle.

. . . .

Ala maite la geôle li trouvé si drôle,
Li dit, "moin aussi, mo fé bal ici."

Ouatchman la yé yé tombé la dans;
Yé fé gran' déga dans léguirie la. etc.

"It was in a stable that they had this gala night," says the song; "the horses there were greatly astonished. Preval was captain; his coachman, Louis, was master of ceremonies. There were negresses made prettier than their mistresses by adornments stolen from the ladies' wardrobes (*armoires*). But the jailer found it all so funny that he proposed to himself to take an unexpected part; the watchmen came down"——

No official exaltation bought immunity from the jeer of the Calinda. Preval was a magistrate. Stephen Mazureau, in his attorney-general's office, the song likened to a bull-frog in a bucket of water. A page might be covered by the roll of victims. The masters winked at these gross but harmless liberties and, as often as any others, added stanzas of their own invention.

The Calinda ended these dissipations of the summer Sabbath afternoons. They could not run far into the night, for all the fascinations of all the dances could not excuse the slave's tarrying in public places after a certain other *bou-djoum!* (that was not of the Calinda, but of the regular nine-o'clock evening gun) had rolled down Orleans street from the Place d'Armes; and the black man or woman who wanted to keep a whole skin on the back had to keep out of the Calaboose. Times have changed, and there is nothing to be regretted in the change that has come over Congo Square. Still a glamour hangs over its dark past. There is the pathos of slavery, the poetry of the weak oppressed by the strong, and of limbs that danced after toil, and of barbaric love-making. The rags and semi-nakedness, the bamboula drum, the dance, and almost the banjo, are gone; but the *bizarre* melodies and dark lovers' apostrophes live on; and among them the old Counjaille song of Aurore Pradère:

ARR. BY H. E. KREHBIEL.
Au - rore Pra - dère, belle 'ti' fille, Au - rore Pra - dère, belle 'ti' fille, Au -

Fine.
rore Pra - dère, belle 'ti' fille, C'est le mo ou - lé, C'est li ma prend.
1. Ya moun qui dit le trop zo - lie; Ya moun qui dit li pas po-lie; Tout
2. Ya moun qui dit li gagne la geole; Ya moun qui dit so m'man te folle; etc.
3. Li pas man-dé robe mous-se - line, Li pas man-dé des bas brodée; Li
D. C.
ça ye dit Sia! Mo bin fou bin, C'est li mo ou-lé, c'est li ma prend.
. . .
pas man-dé sou-liers prinelle, C'est li, etc.

Cho.: || Aurore, Pradère, pretty maid, || *(ter)*
She's just what I want and her I'll have.
Solo: Some folks say she's too pretty, quite;
Some folks they say she's not polite;

All this they say—Psha-a-ah!
More fool am I!
For she's what I want and her I'll have.

Cho.: || Aurore Pradère, pretty maid, || *(ter)*
She's just what I want and her I'll have.

Solo: Some say she's going to the bad;
Some say that her mamma went mad;
All this they say—Psha-a-ah!
More fool am I!
For she's what I want and her I'll have.

Mr. Ware and his associate compilers have neither of these stanzas, but one very pretty one; the third in the music as printed here, and which we translate as follows:

Solo: A muslin gown she doesn't choose,
She doesn't ask for broidered hose,
She doesn't want prunella shoes,
O she's what I want and her I'll have.

Cho.: Aurore Pradère, etc.

This article and another on a kindred theme were originally projected as the joint work of Mr. H. E. Krehbiel, musical editor of the "New York Tribune," author of "The History of Choral Music in New York City," etc.; and the present writer. But under the many prior claims of the journalist's profession, Mr. Krehbiel withdrew from the work, though not until he had finished a number of instrumental accompaniments, as well as the "Quill Song" credited to him, and much valuable coöperation.

As may in part be seen by the names attached to the musical scores, the writer is indebted to a number of friends: Mr. Krehbiel; Miss Mary L. Bartlett, of Hartford, Conn.; Madame Louis Lejeune, of New Orleans; Dr. Blodgett, of Smith College, Northampton, Mass.; Mr. C. G. Ware, of Brookline, in the same State; Madame Clara Gottschalk Petersen, of Philadelphia; and in his earlier steps—for the work of collection has been slow—to that skillful French translator and natural adept in research, Mr. Lafcadio Hearn of New Orleans; the late Isaac N. Philips, Mr. Louis Powers, Miss Clara Cooper Hallaran, the late Professor Alexander Dimitry, all of the same city; Madame Sidonie de la Houssaye, of Franklin, La.; and through the editors of THE CENTURY, to Mr. W. Macrum, of Pittsburg.—G. W. C.

1886

Creole Slave Songs

by George Washington Cable

Century Magazine, XXXI (New York, April 1886), 807–828.

"Creole Slave Songs," was the lead article in Century's *April 1886 issue—some indication of how high was public interest in slave material at the time. With the honest curiosity about the Negro, there was no doubt mixed a considerable portion of the Old South Syndrome; Cable was sufficiently accomplished as writer and observer to satisfy both interests.*

For further information on the voodoo described in Part IV, see the texts suggested in my Preface to Cable's preceding article and the several articles on the topic appearing a few years later in JAF*'s early volumes (see Appendix II of this anthology). One's perspective on both of Cable's articles profits from a reading of Harold Courlander's excellent study of Haitian folk life,* The Drum and the Hoe *(Berkeley and Los Angeles, 1960). See also the second part of Zora Neale Hurston's* Mules and Men *(Philadelphia and London, 1935), and N. N. Puckett's* Folk Beliefs of the Southern Negro *(Chapel Hill, 1926).*

I. THE QUADROONS

The patois in which these songs are found is common, with broad local variations, wherever the black man and the French language are met in the mainland or island regions that border the Gulf and the Caribbean Sea. It approaches probably nearer to good French in Louisiana than anywhere in the Antilles. Yet it is not merely bad or broken French; it is the natural result from the effort of a savage people to take up the language of an old and highly refined civilization, and is much more than a jargon. The humble condition and great numbers of the slave-caste promoted this evolution of an African-Creole dialect. The facile character of the French master-caste, made more so by the languorous climate of the Gulf, easily tolerated and often condescended to use the new tongue. It chimed well with the fierce notions of caste to have one language for the master and another for the slave, and at the same time it was convenient that the servile speech should belong to and draw its existence chiefly from the master's. Its growth entirely by ear where there were so many more African ears than French tongues, and when those tongues had so many Gallic archaisms which they were glad to give away and get rid of, resulted in a broad grotesqueness all its own.

We had better not go aside to study it here. Books have been written on the subject. They may be thin, but they stand for years of labor. A Creole lady writes me almost as I write this, "It takes a whole life to speak such a language in form." Mr. Thomas of Trinidad has given a complete grammar of it as spoken there. M. Marbot has versified some fifty of La Fontaine's fables in the tongue. Père Gaux has made a catechism in, and M. Turiault a complete grammatical work on, the Martinique variety. Dr. Armand Mercier, a Louisiana Creole, and Professor James A. Harrison, an Anglo-Louisianian, have written valuable papers on the dialect as spoken in the Mississippi delta. Mr. John Bigelow has done the same for the tongue as heard in Hayti. It is an amusing study. Certain tribes of Africa had no knowledge of the *v* and *z* sounds. The sprightly Franc-Congos, for all their chatter, could hardly master even this African-Creole dialect so as to make their wants intelligible. The Louisiana negro's *r*'s were ever being lost or mislaid. He changed *dormir* to *dromi'*. His master's children called the little fiddler-crab *Tourlourou*; he simplified the articulations to *Troolooloo.* Wherever the *r* added to a syllable's quantity, he either shifted it or dropped it overboard. *Po'té ça? Non!* not if he could avoid it. It was the same with many other sounds. For example, final *le*; a thing so needless—he couldn't be burdened with it; *li pas capab'!* He found himself profitably understood when he called his master *aimab' et nob'*, and thought it not well to be *trop sensib'* about a trifling *l* or two. The French *u* was vinegar to his teeth. He substituted *i* or *ei* before a consonant and *oo* before a vowel, or dropped it altogether; for *une*, he said *eine*; for *puis, p'is; absolument* he made *assoliment; tu* was nearly always *to;* a *mulâtresse* was a *milatraisse.* In the West Indies he changed *s* into *ch* or *tch*, making *songer chongé*, and *suite tchooite*; while in Louisiana he reversed the process and turned *ch* into *ç—c'erc'é* for *cherchez* or *chercher.*

He misconstrued the liaisons of correct French, and omitted limiting adjectives where he conveniently could, or retained only their final sound carried over and prefixed to the noun: *nhomme—zanimaux—zherbes—zaffaires.* He made odd substitutions of one word for another. For the verb to go he oftener than otherwise used a word that better signified his slavish pretense of alacrity, the verb to run: *mo courri,—mo* always, never *je,—mo courri, to courri, li courri*; always seizing whatever form of a verb was handiest and holding to it without change; *no courri, vo courri, yé courri.* Sometimes the plural was *no zôtt*—we others—*courri, vo zôtt courri, yé zôtt courri; no zôtt courri dans bois*—we are going to the woods. His auxiliary verb in imperfect and pluperfect tenses was not to have, but to be in the past participial form *été,* but shortened to one syllable. I have gone, thou hadst gone: *mo'té courri, to'té courri.*

There is an affluence of bitter meaning hidden under these apparently nonsensical lines:

Mi - la - traisse cour - ri dans bal, Co - co - drie po' - té fa - nal, Trou-lou-

lou! C'est pas zaf - faire à tou, C'est pas zaf - faire à tou, Trou-lou-lou!

It mocks the helpless lot of three types of human life in old Louisiana whose fate was truly deplorable. *Milatraisse* was, in Creole song, the generic term for all that class, famous wherever New Orleans was famous in those days when all foot-passengers by night picked their way through the mud by the rays of a hand-lantern—the freed or free-born quadroon or mulatto woman. *Cocodrie* (Spanish, *cocodrilla,* the crocodile or alligator) was the nickname for the unmixed black man; while *trouloulou* was applied to the free male quadroon, who could find admittance to the quadroon balls only in the capacity, in those days distinctly menial, of musician—fiddler. Now sing it!

Yellow girl goes to the ball;
Nigger lights her to the hall.
          Fiddler man!
Now, what is that to you?
Say, what is that to you,
          Fiddler man?

It was much to him; but it might as well have been little. What could he do? As they say, "*Ravette zamein tini raison divant poule*" ("Cockroach can never justify himself to the hungry chicken"). He could only let his black half-brother celebrate on Congo Plains the mingled humor and outrage of it in satirical songs of double meaning. They readily passed unchallenged among the numerous nonsense rhymes—that often rhymed lamely or not at all—which beguiled the hours afield or the moonlight gatherings in the "quarters," as well as served to fit the wild chants of some of their dances. Here is one whose characteristics tempt us to suppose it a calinda, and whose humor consists only in a childish play on words:

QUAND MO 'TE
ARR. BY MISS M. L. BARTLETT.
1st and 2d time.
3d time.
Quand mo 'te dans grand chi-min Mo con-tré nion vie pa - pa.
Mo 'man-de quel heure li yé, Li dit moin mi - di pas-sé.
Mo 'man-de mou - choi' ta - bac, Li don moin mou- [OMIT . . . . .] choi Ma-dras.
1st time.
2d time.
Prize to - bac jam - bette à cou - teau, Taí - fia doux pas - sé si - rop. sé si - rop.

There is another nonsense song that may or may not have been a dance. Its movement has the true wriggle. The dances were many; there were some popular in the West Indies that seem to have remained comparatively unknown in Louisiana: the *belair, bèlè*, or *béla*; the *cosaque*; the *biguine*. The *guiouba* was probably the famed *juba* of Georgia and the Carolinas:

NEG' PAS CAPA' MARCHE

Allegro.
Arr. by Miss M. L. Bartlett.
1. Neg pas ca - pa' mar-ché sans ma-is dans poche, c'est pou vo-lé
2. Millate pas ca-pa' mar-ché sans la corde dans poche, d'est pou volé
3. Blanc pas ca - pa' mar-ché sans la'zent dans poche, c'est pou vo-lé
poule.
choual.
filles.
After last verse.

II. THE LOVE-SONG

Among the songs which seem to have been sung for their own sake, and not for the dance, are certain sentimental ones of slow movement, tinged with that faint and gentle melancholy that every one of Southern experience has noticed in the glance of the African slave's eye; a sentiment ready to be turned, at any instant that may demand the change, into a droll, self-abasing humor. They have thus a special charm that has kept for them a place even in the regard of the Creole of to-day. How many ten thousands of black or tawny nurse "mammies," with heads wrapped in stiffly starched Madras kerchief turbans, and holding *'tit mait'e* or *'tit maitresse* to their bosoms, have made the infants' lullabies these gently sad strains of disappointed love or regretted youth, will never be known. Now and then the song would find its way through some master's growing child of musical ear, into the drawing-room; and it is from a Creole drawing-room in the Rue Esplanade that we draw the following, so familiar to all Creole ears and rendered with many variations of text and measure:

AH! SUZETTE
ARR. BY MADAME L. LEJEUNE.
Ah! Su-zette, Su-zette to vé pas chère. Ah! Su-zette, chère a - mie,
Fine.
to pas lai - mein moin. 1. M'al - lé haut mon-tagne za-mie, M'al - lé cou-pé
2. Mo Cour-ri dans bois, za-mie, Pou' tou - é zo-
canne za - mie, M'al - lé fé l'a'-zent, chère a - mie, Pou' po' - té donne toi.
zo, za-mie, Pou' . . . fé L'a'-zent, chère a - mie, Pou' mo baille Su - zette.
D. C.

One may very safely suppose this song to have sprung from the poetic invention of some free black far away in the Gulf. A Louisiana slave would hardly have thought it possible to earn money for himself in the sugar-cane fields. The mention of mountains points back to St. Domingo.

It is strange to note in all this African-Creole lyric product how rarely its producers seem to have recognized the myriad charms of nature. The landscape, the seasons, the sun, moon, stars, the clouds, the storm, the peace that follows, the forest's solemn depths, the vast prairie, birds, insects, the breeze, the flowers—they are passed in silence. Was it because of the soul-destroying weight of bondage? Did the slave feel so painfully that the beauties of the natural earth were not for him? Was it because the overseer's eye was on him that his was not lifted upon them? It may have been—in part. But another truth goes with these. His songs were not often contemplative. They voiced not outward nature, but the inner emotions and passions of a nearly naked serpent-worshiper, and these looked not to the surrounding scene for sympathy; the surrounding scene belonged to his master. But love was his, and toil, and anger, and superstition, and malady. Sleep was his balm, food his reënforcement, the dance his pleasure, rum his longed-for nepenthe, and death the road back to Africa. These were his themes, and furnished the few scant figures of his verse.

The moment we meet the offspring of his contemplative thought, as we do in his apothegms and riddles, we find a change, and any or every object in sight, great or trivial, comely or homely, is wrought into the web of his traditional wit and wisdom. "Vo mié, savon, passé godron," he says, to teach a lesson of gentle forbearance ("Soap is worth more than tar"). And then, to point the opposite truth,—"Pas marré so chien avé saucisse" ("Don't chain your dog with links of sausage"). "Qui zamein 'tendé souris fé so nid dan zoré ç'at?" ("Who ever heard of mouse making nest in cat's ear?") And so, too, when love was his theme, apart from the madness of the dance—when his note fell to soft cooings the verse became pastoral. So it was in the song last quoted. And so, too, in this very African bit, whose air I have not:

Si to té tit zozo,
Et mo-même, mo té fizi,
Mo sré tchoué toé—boum

Ah! tchère bizou
D'acazou,
Mo laimein ou
Comme cochon laimein la bou!

Shall we translate literally?

If you were a little bird
And myself, I were a gun,
I would shoot you–boum!
Ah! dear jewel
Of mahogony,
I love you
As the hog loves mud.

One of the best of these Creole love-songs—one that the famed Gottschalk, himself a New Orleans Creole of pure blood, made use of—is the tender lament of one who sees the girl of his heart's choice the victim of chagrin in beholding a female rival wearing those vestments of extra quality that could only be the favors which both women had coveted from the hand of some one in the proud master-caste whence alone such favors could come. "Calalou," says the song, "has an embroidered petticoat, and Lolotee, or Zizi," as it is often sung, "has a—heartache." Calalou, here, I take to be a derisive nickname. Originally it is the term for a West Indian dish, a noted ragout. It must be intended to apply here to the quadroon women who swarmed into New Orleans in 1809 as refugees from Cuba, Guadeloupe, and other islands where the war against Napoleon exposed them to Spanish and British aggression. It was with this great influx of persons neither savage nor enlightened, neither white nor black, neither slave nor truly free, that the famous quadroon caste arose and flourished. If Calalou, in the verse, was one of these quadroon fair ones, the song is its own explanation:

POV' PITI MOMZEL ZIZI

ARR. BY MME. L. LEJEUNE.

dim.
kèr à li.
1. Cal-a - lon po té ma-drasse
Li po-té ji - pon gar -
2. D'amour quand poté la chaine,
Adieu, cour-ri tout bon -
dim.
pp
f
dim.
D. S.
ni;
Cal - a - lon po - té ma - drasse
Li po - té ji - pon gar - ni!
hèr;
D'amour quand po-té la chaine,
A-dieu, cour-ri tout bon - hèr!
dim.
pp
* Ending of Refrain after the Closing Stanza.
dim.
-bo li gag-nin bo-bo, bo-bo , . . . bo-bo , . . . Li gagnin bo-bo , . . . dans kèr à li.
mf
dim.

"Poor little Miss Zizi!" is what it means—"She has pain, pain in her little heart." "A li" is simply the Creole possessive form; "corps à moin" would signify simply *myself*. Calalou is wearing a Madras turban; she has on an embroidered petticoat; [they tell their story and] Zizi has achings in her heart. And the second stanza moralizes: "When you wear the chain of love"—maybe we can make it rhyme:

> When love's chains upon thee lie
> Bid all happiness good-bye.

Poor little Zizi! say we also. Triumphant Calalou! We see that even her sort of freedom had its tawdry victories at the expense of the slave. A poor freedom it was, indeed: To have f. m. c. or f. w. c. tacked in small letters upon one's name perforce and by law, that all might know that the bearer was not a real freeman or freewoman, but only a free man (or woman) of color,—a title that could not be indicated by capital initials; to be the unlawful mates of luxurious bachelors and take their pay in muslins, embroideries, prunella, and good living, taking with them the loathing of honest women and the salacious derision of the blackamoor; to be the sister, mother, father, or brother of Calalou; to fall heir to property by sufferance, not by law; to be taxed for public education and not allowed to give that education to one's own children; to be shut out of all occupations that the master class could reconcile with the vague title of gentleman; to live in the knowledge that the law pronounced "death or imprisonment at hard labor for life" against whoever should be guilty of "writing, printing, publishing, or distributing anything having a tendency to create discontent among the free colored population": that it threatened death against whosoever should utter such things in private conversation; and it decreed expulsion from the State to Calalou and all her kin of any age or condition if only they had come in across its bounds since 1807. In the enjoyment of such ghastly freedom as this the flesh-pots of Egypt sometimes made the mouth water and provoked the tongue to sing its regrets for a past that seemed better than the present.

BON D'JE

H. E. Krehbiel.
1. Dans tan mo té zène Mo zamein zonglé, bon Djé! A ç'tair m'a-pé vi - ni
2. Dans tan mo té nesclavé Mo servis mo maite, bon Djé! A ç'tair mo be-soin re -
vié, M'a - pé zonglé, bon Djé! M'apé zon-glé bon tan qui pas-
pos, Mo sers ton moune, bon Djé! M'apé zon-glé, etc.
sé, M'apé zonglé bon tan qui pas-sé, M'a-pé zon-glé bon tan que pas-sé.

Word for word we should have to render it,—"In times when I was young I never pondered—indulged in reverie, took on care," an archaic French word, *zongler*, still in use among the Acadians also in Louisiana; "mo zamein zonglé, bon D'jé"—"good Lord!" "*Açtair*" is "à cette heure"—"at this hour," that is, "now—these days." "These days I am getting old—I am pondering, good Lord!" etc. Some time in the future, it may be, some Creole will give us translations of these things, worthy to be called so. Meantime suffer this:

In the days of my youth not a dream had I, good
  Lord!
These times I am growing old, full of dreams am I,
  good Lord!
I have dreams of those good time gone by! *(ter)*

When I was a slave, one boss had I, good Lord!
These times when I'm needing rest all hands serve I,
  good Lord!
I have dreams, etc.

III. THE LAY AND THE DIRGE

There were other strains of misery, the cry or the vagabond laugh and song of the friendless orphan for whom no asylum door would open, but who found harbor and food in the fields and wildwood and the forbidden places of the wicked town. When that Creole whom we hope for does come with his good translations, correcting the hundred and one errors that may be in these pages, we must ask him if he knows the air to this:

Pitis sans popa, pitis sans moman,
Qui ça 'ou' zaut' fé pou' gagnein l'a'zanc,[1]
  No courri l'aut' bord pou' cercé patt ç'at'[2]
  No tournein bayou pou' péç'é patassa;[3]
  Et v'là comm ça no té fe nou' l'a'zan.

Pitis sans popa, pitis sans moman,
Qui ça 'ou' zaut' fé, etc.
  No courri dans bois fouillé latanié,[4]
  No vend' so racin' pou' fou'bi' planç'é;
Et v'là comm' ça, etc.

[1] L'argent—money.

[2] "We go to the other side" [of the river] "to get cats' paws," a delicious little blue swamp berry.

[3] The perch. That little sunfish or "pumpkin seed," miscalled through the southwest.

[4] Dwarf palmetto, whose root is used by the Creoles as a scrubbing-brush.

Pitis sans popa, etc.
  Pou' fé di thé n'a fouillé sassaf'as,
  Pou' fé di l'enc' no po'té grain' sougras;[5]
  Et v'là ,etc.

Pitis sans popa, etc.
  No courri dans bois ramassé cancos;[6]
  Avé' nou' la caze no trappé zozos;[7]
  Et v'là, etc.

Pitis sans popa, etc.
  No courri à soir c'ez Mom'selle Maroto,
  Dans la rie St. Ann ou no té zoué loto;
  Et v'là," etc.

Little ones without father, little ones without mother,
What do you to keep soul and body together?
  The river we cross for wild berries to search;
  We follow the bayou a-fishing for perch;
  And that's how we keep soul and body togther.

Little ones without, etc.
  Palmetto we dig from the swamp's bristling stores
  And sell its stout roots for scrubbing the floors;
  And that's how, etc.

Little ones, etc.
  The sassafras root we dig up; it makes tea;
  For ink the ripe pokeberry clusters bring we;
  And that's how, etc.

Little ones, etc.
  We go to the woods *cancos* berries to fetch,
  And in our trap cages the nonpareils[8] catch;
  And that's how, etc.

Little ones, etc.
  At evening we visit Mom'selle Maroto,
  In St. Ann's street, to gamble awhile at keno;
  And that's how we keep soul and body together.

[5] Pokeberries.

[6] *Cancos*, Indian name for a wild purple berry.

[7] Oiseaux, birds.

[8] The nonpareil, pape, or painted bunting, is the favorite victim of the youthful bird-trappers.

Here was companionship with nature—the companionship of the vagabond. We need not doubt that these little orphan vagrants could have sung for us the song, from which in an earlier article we have already quoted a line or two, of Cayetano's circus, probably the most welcome intruder that ever shared with the man Friday and his song-dancing fellows and sweethearts the green, tough sod of Congo Square.

C'est Miché Cayétane,
Qui sorti la Havane
Avec so chouals[9] et so macacs.[10]
Li gagnein ein nhomme qui dancé dans sac;
Li gagnein qui dancé si yé la main;
Li gagnein zaut' à choual, qui boir' di vin;
Li gagnein oussi ein zein, zoli mom'selle,
Qui monté choual sans bride et sans selle!
Pou' di tou' ça mo pas capab';
Mé mo souvien ein sui 'valé sab'!
Yé n'en oussi tou' sort' bétail.
Yé pas montré pou la négrail';
Gniapas là dotchians dos-brilé,[11]
Pou' fé tapaze et pou' hirlé;
Cé gros madame et gros miché,
Qui ménein là tous pitits yé,
'Oir Miché Cayétane,
Qui 'rivé la Havane
Avec so chouals et so macacs.

Should the Louisiana Creole negro undertake to render his song to us in English, it would not be exactly the African-English of any other State in the Union. Much less would it resemble the gross dialects of the English-torturing negroes of Jamaica, or Barbadoes, or the Sea Islands of Carolina. If we may venture—

[9] Chevals—chevaux.
[10] Macaques.
[11] "Gniapas là dotchians dos-brilé."
"Il n'y a pas là des *dotchians* avec les dos brulés."
The *dotchian dos-brile* is the white trash with sunburnt back, the result of working in the fields. It is an expression of supreme contempt for the *pitits blancs*—low whites—to contrast them with the *gros madames et gros michies.*

Dass Cap'm Cayetano,
W'at comin' fum Havano,*
Wid 'is monkey' an' 'is nag!
An' one man w'at dance in bag,
An' mans dance on dey han'—cut shine'
An' gallop hoss sem time drink wine!
An' b'u'ful young missy dah beside,
Ridin' 'dout air sadd' aw brid'e;[12]
To tell h-all dat—he cann' be tole.
Man teck a sword an' swall' 'im whole!
Beas'es?[13] ev'y sawt o' figgah!
Dat show ain't fo' no common niggah!
Dey don' got deh no po' white cuss'—
Sunbu'nt back!—to holla an' fuss.
Dass ladies fine, and gennymuns gran',
Fetchin' dey chilluns dah—all han'!
Fo' see Cayetano,
W'at come fum Havano
Wid 'is monkey' an' 'is nag'!

A remarkable peculiarity of these African Creole songs of every sort is that almost without exception they appear to have originated in the masculine mind, and to be the expression of the masculine heart. Untrained as birds, their males made the songs. We come now, however, to the only exception I have any knowledge of, a song expressive of feminine sentiment, the capitulation of some belle Layotte to the tender enticement of a Creole-born chief or *candjo*. The pleading tone of the singer's defense against those who laugh at her pretty chagrin is—it seems to me—touching:

* To turn final *a* into *o* for the purpose of rhyme is the special delight of the singing negro. I used to hear as part of a moonlight game,—

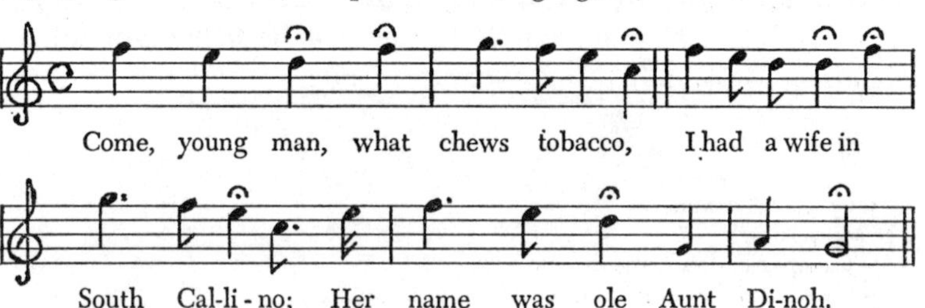
Come, young man, what chews tobacco, I had a wife in
South Cal-li-no; Her name was ole Aunt Di-noh.

[12] Riding without e'er a saddle or bridle.
[13] Beasts—wild animals.

CRIOLE CANDJO

3. Mais li té tant cicané moi,
   Pou' li té quitté moin youn fois
   Mo té 'blizé pou li dire,
   Oui, miché, mo oulé rire.
      Oui miché, etc.

4. Zaut tous qui'ap'es rire moin là bas,
   Si zaut té conné Candjo là,
   Qui belle façon li pou' rire,
   Djé pini moin! zaut s'ré dire,
      "Oui, miché," etc.

One day one young Creole candio,
Mo' fineh dan sho nuf white beau,
   Kip all de time meckin' free—
   "Swithawt, meck merrie wid me."
"Naw, sah, I dawn't want meck merrie me.
Naw, sah, I dawn't want meck merrie."

I go teck walk in wood close by;
But Creole tek' sem road, and try
   All time, all time, to meck free—
   "Swithawt, meck merrie wid me."
"Naw, sah, I dawn't want meck merrie, me.
Naw, sah, I dawn't want meck merrie."

But him slide roun' an' roun' dis chile,
Tell, jis' fo' sheck 'im off lill while,
   Me, I was bleedze fo' say, "Shoo!
   If I'll meck merrie wid you?
O, yass, I ziss leave meck merrie, me;
Yass, seh, I ziss leave meck merrie."

You-alls w'at laugh at me so well,
I wish you'd knowed dat Creole swell,
Wid all 'is swit, smilin' trick'.
'Pon my soul! you'd done say, quick,
"O, yass, I ziss leave meck merrie, me;
Yass, seh, I ziss leave meck merrie."

But we began this chapter in order to speak of songs that bear more distinctly than anything yet quoted the features of the true lay or historical narrative song, commemorating pointedly and in detail some important episode in the history of the community.

It is interesting to contrast the solemnity with which these events are treated when their heroes were black, and the broad buffoonery of the song when the affair it celebrates was one that mainly concerned the masters. Hear, for example, through all the savage simplicity for the following rhymeless lines, the melancholy note that rises and falls but never intermits. The song is said to be very old, dating from the last century. It is still sung, but the Creole gentleman who procured it for me from a former slave was not able to transcribe or remember the air:

LUBIN

Tremblant-terr'[14] vini 'branlé moulin;
Tonnerr' chiel[15] tombé bourlé [16] moulin;
Tou' moun [17] dans houlin là péri.
Temoins vini qui vend'[18] Libin.
Yé dit Libinametté di fé.
Yé hissé saffaud[19] pou' so la tête.[20]

Saïda! m'allé mourri, Saïda!
Mo zamis di comm' ça: "Libin,
Faut to donn' Zilié to bitin[21]."
Cofaire[22] mo sré donnein Zilié?

[14] Tremblement de terre—earthquake.
[15] Ciel.
[16] Brulée.
[17] Tout le monde.
[18] Vendaient—sold, betrayed.
[19] Echafaud.
[20] So la tête: Creole possessive form for *his head*.
[21] Butin: literally *plunder*, but used, as the word *plunder* is by the negro, for personal property.
[22] Pourquoi faire.

Pou' moin Zilié zamein lavé;[23]
Zilié zamein 'passé[24] pou moin.
Saïda! m'allé mourri, Saïda!

An earthquake came and shook the mill;
The heavens' thunders fell and burned it;
Every soul in the mill perished.
Witnesses came who betrayed Lubin.
They said he set the mill on fire.
They raised a scaffold to take off his head.
Saïda! I am going to die!
My friends speak in this way: "Lubin,
You ought to give Julia your plunder."
Why should I give it to Julia?
For me Julia never washed clothes;
Julia never ironed for me.
Saïda! I am going to die!

Or notice again the stately tone of lamentation over the fate of a famous negro insurrectionist, as sung by old Madeleine of St. Bernard parish to the same Creole friend already mentioned, who kindly wrote down the lines on the spot for this collection. They are fragmentary, extorted by littles from the shattered memory of the ancient crone. Their allusion to the Cabildo places their origin in the days when the old colonial council administered Spanish rule over the province:

OUARRÂ ST. MALO

Aïe! zein zens, vini fé ouarrâ
Pou' pôv' St. Malo dans l'embas!
Yé ç'assé li avec yé chien,
Yé tiré li ein coup d'fizi,
. . . .
Yé halé li la cyprier,
So bras yé 'tassé[25] par derrier,
Yé 'tassé so la main divant;
Yé marré[26] li apé queue choual,
Yé trainein li zouqu'à la ville.
Divant michés là dans Cabil'e
Yé quisé[27] li li fé complot

[23] Washed (clothes).
[24] Ironed.
[25] Attachée.
[26] Amarré, an archaism, common to negroes and Acadians: moored, for fastened.
[27] Accusée.

Pou' coupé cou à tout ye blancs.
Yé 'mandé li qui so compères;
Pôv' St. Malo pas di' a-rien!
Zize[28] là li lir' so la sentence,
Et pis[29] li fé dressé potence.
Yé halé choual—ç'arette parti—
Pôv St. Malo resté pendi!
Eine hèr soleil deza levée
Quand yé pend li si la levée.
Yé laissé so corps balancé
Pou' carancro gagnein manzé.

THE DIRGE OF ST. MALO

Alas! young men, come, make lament
For poor St. Malo in distress!
They chased, they hunted him with dogs,
They fired at him with a gun,
. . . .
They hauled him from the cypress swamp.
His arms they tied behind his back,
They tied his hands in front of him;
They tied him to a horse's tail,
They dragged him up into the town.
Before those grand Cabildo men
They charged that he had made a plot
To cut the throats of all the whites.
They asked him who his comrades were;
Poor St. Malo said not a word!
The judge his sentence read to him,
And then they raised the gallows-tree.
They drew the horse—the cart moved off—
And left St. Malo hanging there.
The sun was up an hour high
When on the Levee he was hung;
They left his body swinging there,
For carrion crows to feed upon.

It would be curious, did the limits of these pages allow, to turn from such an outcry of wild mourning as this, and contrast with it the clownish flippancy with which the great events are sung, upon whose issue from time to time the fate of the whole land—society, government, the fireside, the lives of thousands—hung in agonies of suspense. At the same time it could not escape notice how completely

[28] Juge.
[29] Puis.

in each case, while how differently in the two, the African has smitten his image into every line: in the one sort, the white, uprolled eyes and low wail of the savage captive, who dares not lift the cry of mourning high enough for the jealous ear of the master; in the other, the antic form, the grimacing face, the brazen laugh, and self-abasing confessions of the buffoon, almost within the whisk of the public jailer's lash. I have before me two songs of dates almost fifty years apart. The one celebrates the invasion of Louisiana by the British under Admiral Cochrane and General Pakenham in 1814; the other, the capture and occupation of New Orleans by Commodore Farragut and General Butler in 1862.

It was on the morning of the twenty-third of December, 1814, that the British columns, landing from a fleet of barges and hurrying along the narrow bank of a small canal in a swamp forest, gained a position in the open plain on the banks of the Mississippi only six miles below New Orleans, and with no defenses to oppose them between their vantage-ground and the city. The surprise was so complete that, though they issued from the woods an hour before noon, it was nearly three hours before the news reached the town. But at nightfall General Jackson fell upon them and fought in the dark the engagement which the song commemorates, the indecisive battle of Chalmette.

The singer ends thus:

Fizi z'Anglé yé fé bim! bim!
Carabin Kaintock yé fé zim! zim!
Mo di' moin, suavé to la peau!
Mo zété corps au bord do l'eau;
Quand mo rivé li té fé clair.
Madam' li prend' ein coup d'colère;
Li fé donn' moin ein quat' piquié,
Passequé mo pas sivi mouchié;
Mais moin, mo vo mié quat' piquié
Passé ein coup d'fizi z'Anglé!

The English muskets went bim! bim!
Kentucky rifles went zim! zim!
I said to myself, save your skin!
I scampered along the water's edge;
When I got back it was day-break.
Mistress flew into a passion;
She had me whipped at the "four stakes,"

Because I didn't stay with master;
But the "four stakes" for me is better than
A musket shot from an Englishman.

The story of Farragut's victory and Butler's advent in April, 1862, is sung with the still lighter heart of one in whose day the "quatre piquets" was no longer a feature of the calaboose. Its refrain is:

An-hé!
Qui ça qui rivé?
C'est Ferraguitt et p'i Botlair,
Qui rivé.

The story is long and silly, much in the humor of

Hark! hark!
The dogs do bark.

We will lay it on the table.

IV. THE VOODOOS

The dance and song entered into the negro worship. That worship was as dark and horrid as bestialized savagery could make the adoration of serpents. So revolting was it, and so morally hideous, that even in the West Indian French possessions a hundred years ago, with the slave-trade in full blast and the West Indian planter and slave what they were, the orgies of the Voodoos were forbidden. Yet both there and in Louisiana they were practiced.

The Aradas, St. Méry tells us, introduced them. They brought them from their homes beyond the Slave Coast, one of the most dreadfully benighted regions of all Africa. He makes the word Vaudaux. In Louisiana it is written Voudou and Voodoo, and is often changed on the negro's lips to Hoodoo. It is the name of an imaginary being of vast supernatural powers residing in the form of a harmless snake. This spiritual influence or potentate is the recognized antagonist and opposite of Obi, the great African manitou or deity, or him whom the Congoes vaguely generalize as Zombi. In Louisiana, as I have been told by that learned Creole scholar the late Alexander Dimitry, Voodoo bore as a title of greater solemnity the additional name of Maignan, and that even in the Calinda dance, which he had witnessed innumerable times, was sometimes heard, at the height of its frenzy, the invocation—

Aïe! Aïe!
Voodoo Magnan!

The worship of Voodoo is paid to a snake kept in a box. The worshipers are not merely a sect, but in some rude, savage way also an order. A man and woman chosen from their own number to be the oracles of the serpent deity are called the king and queen. The queen is the more important of the two, and even in the present dilapidated state of the worship in Louisiana, where the king's office has almost or quite disappeared, the queen is still a person of great note.

She reigns as long as she continutes to live. She comes to power not by inheritance, but by election or its barbarous equivalent. Chosen for such qualities as would give her a natural supremacy, personal attractions among the rest, and ruling over superstitious fears and desires of every fierce and ignoble sort, she wields no trivial influence. I once saw, in her extreme old age, the famed Marie Laveau. Her dwelling was in the quadroon quarter of New Orleans, but a step or two from Congo Square, a small adobe cabin just off the sidewalk, scarcely higher than its close board fence, whose batten gate yielded to the touch and revealed the crazy doors and windows spread wide to the warm air, and one or two tawny faces within, whose expression was divided between a pretense of contemptuous inattention and a frowning resentment of the intrusion. In the center of a small room whose ancient cypress floor was worn with scrubbing and sprinkled with crumbs of soft brick—a Creole affectation of superior cleanliness—sat, quaking with feebleness in an ill-looking old rocking-chair, her body bowed, and her wild, gray witch's tresses hanging about her shriveled, yellow neck, the queen of the Voodoos. Three generations of her children were within the faint beckon of her helpless, waggling wrist and fingers. They said she was over a hundred years old, and there was nothing to cast doubt upon the statement. She had shrunken away from her skin; it was like a turtle's. Yet withal one could hardly help but see that the face, now so withered, had once been handsome and commanding. There was still a faint shadow of departed beauty on the forehead, the spark of an old fire in the sunken, glistening eyes, and a vestige of imperiousness in the fine, slightly aquiline nose, and even about her silent, woe-begone mouth. Her grandson stood by, an uninteresting quadroon between forty and fifty years old, looking strong, empty-minded, and trivial enough; but his mother, her daughter, was also present, a woman of some seventy years, and a most striking and majestic figure. In features, stature, and bearing she was regal. One had but to look on her, impute her brilliancies—too untamable and severe to be called charms or graces—to her mother, and remember what New Orleans was long years ago, to understand how the name of Marie Laveau should have driven itself inextricably into the traditions of the town and the times. Had this visit been postponed a few months it would have been too late. Marie Laveau is dead; Malvina Latour is queen. As she appeared presiding over a Voodoo ceremony on the night of the 23d of June, 1884, she is described as a bright mulattress of about forty-eight, of "extremely handsome figure," dignified bearing, and a face indicative of a comparatively high order of intelligence. She wore a neat blue, white-dotted calico gown, and a "brilliant *tignon* (turban) gracefully tied."

It is pleasant to say that this worship, in Louisiana, at least, and in comparison with what it once was, has grown to be a rather trivial affair. The practice of its midnight forest rites seemed to sink into inanition along with Marie Laveau. It long ago diminished in frequency to once a year, the chosen night always being the Eve of St. John. For several years past even these annual celebrations have been suspended; but in the summer of 1884 they were—let it be hoped, only for the once—resumed.

When the queen decides that such a celebration shall take place, she appoints a night for the gathering, and some remote, secluded spot in the forest for the rendezvous. Thither all the worshipers are summoned. St. Méry, careless of the power of the scene, draws in practical, unimaginative lines in the picture of such a gathering in St. Domingo, in the times when the "*véritable Vaudaux*" had lost but little of the primitive African character. The worshipers are met, decked with kerchiefs more or less numerous, red being everywhere the predominating color. The king, abundantly adorned with them, wears one of pure red about his forehead as a diadem. A blue ornamental cord completes his insignia. The queen, in simple dress and wearing a red cord and a heavily decorated belt, is beside him near a rude altar. The silence of midnight is overhead, the gigantic forms and shadows and still, dank airs of the tropical forest close in around, and on the altar, in a small box ornamented with little tinkling bells, lies unseen, the living serpent. The worshipers have begun their devotions to it by presenting themselves before it in a body, and uttering professions of their fidelity and belief in its power. They cease, and now the royal pair, in tones of parental authority and protection, are extolling the great privilege of being a devotee, and inviting the faithful to consult the oracle. The crowd makes room, and a single petitioner draws near. He is the senior member of the order. His prayer is made. The king becomes deeply agitated by the presence within him of the spirit invoked. Suddenly he takes the box from the altar and sets it upon the ground. The queen steps upon it and with convulsive movements utters the answers of the deity beneath her feet. Another and another suppliant, approaching in the order of seniority, present, singly, their petitions, and humbly or exultingly, according to the nature of the responses, which hangs on the fierce caprice of the priestess, accept these utterances and make way for the next, with his prayer of fear or covetousness, love, jealousy, petty spite or deadly malice. At length the last petitioner is answered. Now a circle is formed, the caged snake is restored to the altar, and the humble and multifarious oblations of the worshipers are received, to be devoted not only to the trivial expenses of this worship, but also to the relief of members of the order whose distresses call for such aid. Again the royal ones are speaking, issuing orders for execution in the future, orders that have not always in view, mildly says St. Méry, good order and public tranquillity. Presently the ceremonies become more forbidding. They are taking a horrid oath, smearing their lips with the blood of some slaughtered animal, and swearing to suffer death rather than disclose any secret of the order, and to inflict death on any who may commit such treason. Now a new applicant for membership steps into their circle, there are a few trivial formalities, and the Voodoo dance begins. The postulant dances frantically in the middle of the ring, only pausing from time to time to receive heavy alcoholic draughts in great haste and return more wildly to his leapings and writhings until he falls in convulsions. He is lifted, restored, and presently conducted to the altar, takes his oath, and by a ceremonial stroke from one of the sovereigns is admitted a full participant in the privileges and obligations of the devilish freemasonry. But the dance goes on about the snake. The contortions of the upper part of the body, especially of the neck and shoulders, are such as threaten to dislocate them. The queen shakes the box and tinkles its bells, the rum-bottle gurgles, the chant alternates between king and chorus—

Eh! eh! Bomba, honc! honc!*
Canga bafio tay,
Canga moon day lay,
Canga do keelach,
Canga li——

There are swooning and ravings, nervous tremblings beyond con-

* "Hen: hen:" in St. Méry's spelling of it for French pronunciation. As he further describes the sound in a foot-note, it must have been a horrid grunt.

trol, incessant writhings and turnings, tearing of garments, even biting of the flesh—every imaginable invention of the devil.

St. Méry tells us of another dance invented in the West Indies by a negro, analogous to the Voodoo dance, but more rapid, and in which dancers had been known to fall dead. This was the "Dance of Don Pedro." The best efforts of police had, in his day, only partially suppressed it. Did it ever reach Louisiana? Let us, at a venture, say no.

To what extent the Voodoo worship still obtains here would be difficult to say with certainty. The affair of June, 1884, as described by Messrs. Augustin and Whitney, eye-witnesses, was an orgy already grown horrid enough when they turned their backs upon it. It took place at a wild and lonely spot where the dismal cypress swamp behind New Orleans meets the waters of Lake Pontchartrain in a wilderness of cypress stumps and rushes. It would be hard to find in nature a more painfully desolate region. Here in a fisherman's cabin sat the Voodoo worshipers cross-legged on the floor about an Indian basket of herbs and some beans, some bits of bone, some oddly wrought bunches of feathers, and some saucers of small cakes. The queen presided, sitting on the only chair in the room. There was no king, no snake—at least none visible to the onlookers. Two drummers beat with their thumbs on gourds covered with sheepskin, and a white-wooled old man scraped that hideous combination of banjo and violin, whose head is covered with rattlesnake skin, and of which the Chinese are the makers and masters. There was singing—"*M'allé couri dans déser*" ("I am going into the wilderness"), a chant and refrain not worth the room they would take—and there was frenzy and a circling march, wild shouts, delirious gesticulations and posturing, drinking, and amongst other frightful nonsense the old trick of making fire blaze from the mouth by spraying alcohol from it upon the flame of a candle.

But whatever may be the quantity of the Voodoo *worship* left in Louisiana, its superstitions are many and are everywhere. Its charms are resorted to by the malicious, the jealous, the revengeful, or the avaricious, or held in terror, not by the timorous only, but by the strong, the courageous, the desperate. To find under his mattress an acorn hollowed out, stuffed with the hair of some dead person, pierced with four holes on four sides, and two small chicken feathers drawn through them so as to cross inside the acorn; or to discover on his door-sill at daybreak a little box containing a dough or waxen heart stuck full of pins; or to hear that his avowed foe or rival has been pouring cheap champagne in the four corners of Congo Square at midnight, when there was no moon, will strike more abject fear into the heart of many a stalwart negro or melancholy quadroon than to face a leveled revolver. And it is not only the colored man that holds to these practices and fears. Many a white Creole gives them full credence. What wonder, when African Creoles were the nurses of so nearly all of them? Many shrewd men and women, generally colored persons, drive a trade in these charms and in oracular directions for their use or evasion; many a Creole—white as well as other tints—female, too, as well as male—will pay a Voodoo "*monteure*" to "make a work," *i.e.*, to weave a spell, for the prospering of some scheme or wish too ignoble to be prayed for at any shrine inside the church. These milder incantations are performed within the witch's or wizard's own house, and are made up, for the most part, of a little pound cake, some lighted candle ends, a little syrup of sugar-cane, pins, knitting needles, and a trifle of anisette. But fear naught; an Obi charm will enable you to smile defiance against all such mischief; or if you will but consent to be a magician, it is they, the Voodoos, one and all, who will hold you in absolute terror. Or, easier, a frizzly chicken! If you have on your premises a frizzly chicken, you can lie down and laugh—it is a checkmate!

A planter once found a Voodoo charm, or *ouanga* (wongah); this time it was a bit of cotton cloth folded about three cow-peas and some breast feathers of a barn-yard fowl, and covered with a tight wrapping of thread. When he proposed to take it to New Orleans his slaves were full of consternation. "Marse Ed, ef ye go on d'boat wid dat-ah, de boat'll sink wi' ye. Fore d'Lord, it will!" For some reason it did not. Here is a genuine Voodoo song, given me by Lafcadio Hearn, though what the words mean none could be more ignorant of than the present writer. They are rendered phonetically in French:

Hé-ron man - dé, Hé - ron man - dé Ti - gui li pa- pa, Hé - ron man - dé, Ti - gui
D. C.
li pa - pa, Hé - ron man - dé, Hé - ron man-dé, Hé - ron man-dé, Do sé dan go - do.

And another phrase: "Ah tingouai yé, Ah tingouai yé, Ah ouai ya, Ah ouai ya, Ah tingouai yé, Do sé dan go-do, Ah tingouai yé," etc.

A last page to the songs of the chase and of the boat. The circumstances that produced them have disappeared. There was a time, not so long ago, when traveling in Louisiana was done almost wholly by means of the paddle, the oar, or the "sweep." Every plantation had its river or bayou front, and every planter his boat and skilled crew of black oarsmen. The throb of their song measured the sweep of the oars, and as their bare or turbaned heads and shining bodies, naked to the waist, bowed forward and straightened back in ceaseless alternation, their strong voices chanted the praise of the silent, broad-hatted master who sat in the stern. Now and then a line was interjected in manly boast to their own brawn, and often the praise of the master softened off into tender laudations of the charms of some black or tawny Zilié, 'Zabette, or Zalli. From the treasures of the old chest already mentioned comes to my hand, from the last century most likely, on a ragged yellow sheet of paper, written with a green ink, one of these old songs. It would take up much room; I have made a close translation of its stanzas:

ROWERS' SONG

Sing, lads; our master bids us sing.
For master cry out loud and strong.
The water with the long oar strike.
Sing, lads, and let us haste along.

'Tis for our master we will sing.
We'll sing for our young mistresses.
And sweethearts we must not forget—
Zoé, Mérente, Zabelle, Louise.

Sing, fellows, for our own true loves.
My lottery prize! Zoé, my belle!
She's like a wild young doe, she knows
The way to jump and dance so well!

Black diamonds are her bright, black eyes,
Her teeth and lilies are alike.
Sing, fellows, for my true love, and
The water with the long oar strike.

See! see! the town! Hurrah! hurrah!
Master returns in pleasant mood.
He's going to treat his boys all 'round.
Hurrah! hurrah for master good!

From the same treasury comes a hunting song. Each stanza begins and ends with the loud refrain: "*Bomboula! bomboula!*" Some one who has studied African tongues may be able to say whether this word is one with Bamboula, the name of the dance and of the drum that dominates it. *Oula* seems to be an infinitive termination of many Congo verbs, and *boula,* De Lanzières says, means to beat. However, the dark hunters of a hundred years ago knew, and between their outcries of the loud, rumbling word sang, in this song, their mutual exhortation to rise, take guns, fill powder-horns, load up, call dogs, make haste and be off to the woods to find game for master's table and their own grosser *cuisine;* for the one, deer, squirrels, rabbits, birds; for the other, *chat oués* (raccoons), that make "*si bon gomba*" (such good gumbo!). "Don't fail to kill them, boys,—and the tiger-cats that eat men; and if we meet a bear, we'll vanquish him! Bomboula! bomboula!" The lines have a fine African ring in them, but—one mustn't print everything.

Another song, of wood and water both, though only the water is mentioned, I have direct from former Creole negro slaves. It is a runaway's song of defiance addressed to the high sheriff Fleuriau (Charles Jean Baptiste Fleuriau, Alguazil mayor), a Creole of the Cabildo a hundred and fifteen years ago. At least one can think so, for the name is not to be found elsewhere.

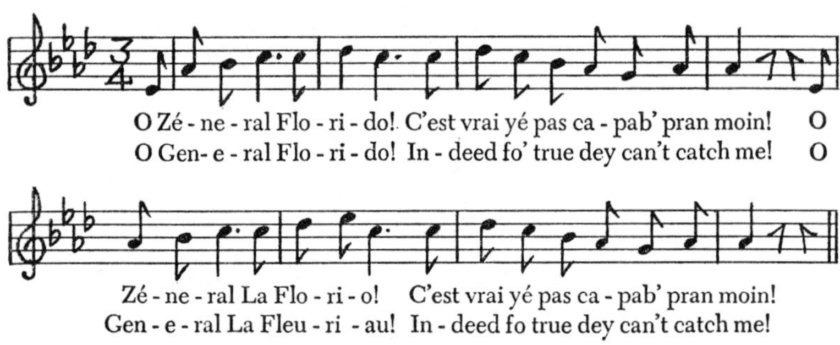

O Zé - ne - ral Flo - ri - do!. C'est vrai yé pas ca - pab' pran moin! O
O Gen- e - ral Flo - ri - do! In - deed fo' true dey can't catch me! O
Zé - ne - ral La Flo - ri - o! C'est vrai yé pas ca - pab' pran moin!
Gen - e - ral La Fleu - ri - au! In - deed fo true dey can't catch me!

2. Yen a ein counan si la mer
C'est vrai, etc. } *Bis.*

2. Dey got* one schooner out at sea
Indeed fo' true, etc. } *Bis.*

Sometimes the black man found it more convenient not to run away himself, but to make other articles of property seem to escape from custody. He ventured to forage on his own account, retaining

* "Dey got" is a vulgarism of Louisiana Creoles, white and colored, for "There is." It is a transfer into English of the French idiom *Il y a.*

his cabin as a base of operations, and seeking his adventures not so far from the hen-coop and pig-pens as rigid principles would have dictated. Now that he is free, he is willing to reveal these little pleasantries—as one of the bygones—to the eager historian. Much nocturnal prowling was done on the waters of the deep, forest-darkened bayous, in *pirogues* (dug-outs). For secret signals to accomplices on shore they resorted to singing. What is so innocent as music! The words were in some African tongue. We have one of the songs from the negroes themselves, with their own translation and their own assurance that the translation is correct. The words have a very Congo-ish sound. The Congo tongue knows no *r;* but the fact is familiar that in America the negro interchanges the sounds or *r* and *l* as readily as does the Chinaman. We will use both an English and a French spelling:

DÉ ZAB

ARR. BY MISS M. L. BARTLETT.
mf
Day zab, day zab day koo - noo wi wi, Day zab, day zab, day
Dé zab, dé zab, dé kou - nou ouaïe, ouaïe, Dé zab, dé zab, dé
koo-noo wi wi, Koo-noo wi wi wi wi, Koo-noo
kou-nou ouaïe, ouaïe, Kou-nou ouaïe, ouaïe, ouaïe, ouaïe, Kounou

wi wi wi wi, Koo-noo wi wi wi mom - zah...... Mom-
ouaïe, ouaïe, ouaïe, ouaïe. Kounou ouaïe, ouaïe, ouaïe, mom-za...... Mom-
mf dim. mf p
zah, mom-zah, mom - zah, mom-zah, Ro - zah, ro - zah, ro - zah a-a mom -zah.
za, mom - za, mom - za, mom - za, Ro - za, ro -za, ro - za et mom - za.

The whole chant consists of but six words besides a single conjunction. It means, its singers avowed, "Out from under the trees our boat moves into the open water—bring us large game and small game!" *Dé zab* sounds like *des arbs,* and they call it French, but the rest they claimed as good "Affykin." We cannot say. We are sappers and miners in this quest, not philologists. When they come on behind, if they ever think it worth their while to do so, the interpretation of this strange song may not be more difficult than that of the famous inscription discovered by Mr. Pickwick. But, as well as the present writer can know, all that have been given here are genuine antiques.

1886

An Accidental Author

by Joel Chandler Harris

Lippincott's Magazine, XXXVII (Philadelphia, April 1886), 417–420.

*Harris, in this article and others, claimed that he was no more than a journeyman journalist (ink and grit under fingernails, sweat on brow, etc.), and we take that claim with the same seriousness we take the claims of Faulkner and Horace when they represent themselves as farmers. Although Harris was indeed a respectable journalist (and Faulkner and Horace did own homes in rural territories), we must note that his definition and our definition of a "literary man" are no doubt quite different. Even without his influential collections of Uncle Remus stories—which stimulated interest in Negro folktales but at the same time created a fallacious conception of the form those stories should take and the themes they should cover that was not corrected until some time after Elsie Clews Parsons began to publish her fine collections—Harris is an important figure in nineteenth-century American literature. His fiction anthologies—*Mingo and Other Sketches in Black and White *(1884),* Free Joe *(1887), and others—would have obtained for him a place of respect in accounts of American literary history; one hears little about them only because of the immense success of his adaptations of Negro folktales. He may choose to discount his literary activities, but from our point of view he was a skillful and sensitive creator and our literature would have been much the poorer had he not taken time from his newspaper work to write his fiction and his recreations of Negro folktales.*

It is interesting to read his account of his aural introduction to literature; apparently the ability to listen well stayed with him throughout his life. The article in Lippincott's *to which he refers is William Owens' "Folklore of the Southern Negroes."*

As this paper is to be part of an experience meeting, I may as well begin it by relating how I have been pursued by a scientific lunatic who formerly hailed from Florida. In 1870, while associate editor of the Savannah *Morning News*, I was introduced by a prominent gentleman of that city to a preacher from Florida. I do not know to what religious denomination this preacher belonged, but he appeared, at first sight, to be a very serious person, full of grace and fervor. He was a fluent talker, and after I had known him a day or two he imparted to me certain information which he declared was of the utmost importance to the country and to myself. He said he had discovered that the earth, instead of being round, was shaped like an egg, and that, instead of revolving around the sun, it was itself the centre around which the sun revolved; that the seasons, the periods of heat and cold, were the results of the endosmose and exosmose processes; and so on and so forth. My friend proved to be a great bore. He not only had his theory, but he had composed a poem to describe and substantiate it,—a tremendous poem as to length,—and this he left with me, stating that he expected me to be the medium or the means of bringing his extraordinary theory and his remarkable poem to the attention of the public. I was a young man then,—younger in experience than in years,—and a spirit of mischief, almost inconceivable in its stupidity, led me to write a satirical paragraph or two about this preacher's theory. He sent for the manuscript of his remarkable poem, and made his way Northward, probably to Chicago, and has busied himself with my biography from that day to this. There is nothing malicious in his inventions, and I have no doubt they are worth something in the shape of advertisements, but their wild improbability has given them a place in the current newspaper literature of the day.

For instance, few readers of this magazine have failed to see the announcement in the daily papers that "the author of 'Uncle Remus' is a native of Africa, having been born at Joel, on the northeast coast, of missionary parents." This is only one of many inventions which have been put forth by my Florida friend. He never fails to send me a marked copy of the paper in which his inventions first appear, attaching his initials, as if to remind me of the penalty of satirizing his poem. But, as I have said, he is not malicious. He merely insists that I was born in Africa, and that my hair is snowy white as the result of a "strangely romantic career." He is determined that I shall figure as a myth. I desire to say here that I have reconsidered my youthful views in regard to his poem; moreover, I am willing to give his theory of the exosmose and endosmose processes a complete, if not a cordial, endorsement. When one's dearest enemy has access to the columns of a Chicago newspaper it is time to suggest a truce. I gladly hoist the white flag.

I was born in the little village of Eatonton, Putnam county, Georgia, December 9, 1848, in the humblest sort of circumstances. My desire to write—to give expression to my thoughts—grew out of hearing my mother read "The Vicar of Wakefield." I was too young to appreciate the story, but there was something in the style or something in the humor of that remarkable little book that struck my fancy, and I straightway fell to composing little tales in which the principal character—whether hero or heroine—astonished and silenced the other characters by crying *Fudge!* at every possible opportunity. None of these little tales have been preserved, but I am convinced that, since their keynote was *Fudge!* they must have been very close to human nature.

In 1862 I saw an advertisement in a little weekly paper, *The Countryman*, calling for an apprentice to learn the printing-business. This advertisement I responded to, and it was not many days before I was installed in the office of the only genuine country newspaper ever printed in this country. *The Countryman* was edited by Mr. Joseph A. Turner, and was published on his plantation, nine or ten miles from any post-office. In truth, *The Countryman* was published in the country. A partridge built her nest within five paces of the window where I learned to set type, and hatched her brood undisturbed. The cat-squirrels frolicked on the roof, and a gray fox, whose range was in the neighborhood, used to flit across the orchard-path in full view. *The Countryman* was published on a plantation, and it was on this and neighboring plantations that I became familiar with the curious myths and animal stories that form the basis of the volumes credited to Uncle Remus. I absorbed the stories, songs, and myths that I heard, but had no idea of their literary value until, some time in the seventies, *Lippincott's Magazine* printed an article on the subject of negro folklore, containing rough outlines of some of the stories. This article gave me my cue, and the legends told by Uncle Remus are the result.

While setting type for *The Countryman* I contributed surreptitiously to the columns of that paper, setting my articles from the "case" instead of committing them to paper, and thus leaving no evidence of authorship. I supposed that this was a huge joke; but, as Mr. Turner read the proof of every line that went into his paper, it is probable that he understood the situation and abetted it. At any rate, he began to lend me books from his library, which comprised a collection of literature both large and choice. The books forming this library have since been dispersed, but there were at least five hundred volumes in the collection that modern book-lovers would pay high prices for.

This was the accidental beginning of a career that has been accidental throughout. It was an accident that I went to *The Countryman,* an accident that I wrote "Uncle Remus," and an accident that the stories put forth under that name struck the popular fancy. In some respects these accidents are pleasing, but in others they are embarrassing. For instance, people persist in considering me a literary man, when I am a journalist and nothing else. I have no literary training, and know nothing at all of what is termed literary art. I have had no opportunity to nourish any serious literary ambition, and the probability is that if such an opportunity had presented itself I would have refused to take advantage of it.

1888

Superstitions of the Negro

by Eli Shepard

Cosmopolitan, V (New York, March 1888), 47–50.

Credence in many of the items included in Shepard's collection is shared by whites, but it is nevertheless a valuable contribution to our knowledge of Negro folklore. It includes more than eighty examples of beliefs, superstitions, and signs, and we can only regret that the author did not think to tell us just where in the South the collection was made. For an extensive discussion of the kinds of folk concepts illustrated here, see N. N. Puckett, Folk Beliefs of the Southern Negro *(Chapel Hill, 1926).*

Professor Herbert Halpert has suggested to me that there might be some connection between the author of this article and the E. Shepperd listed as the author of Plantation Songs for My Lady's Banjo, and other Negro Lyrics and Monologues *(New York, 1901). Newman I. White says "E. Shepperd" was the pseudonym of Martha Young (*American Negro Folk-Songs *[Cambridge, Mass., 1928; reprinted Hatboro, Pa., 1965], p. 480).*

"And what is death?" I asked an old negro woman. She had come from several miles out in the hill-country to sell to the townspeople a basket of late "roasting-ears." She was such a queer specimen of humanity, and ideas and fancies from her weird world of ignorance flew so rapidly to her tongue, that one was enticed into desire to hear more of her jargon.

"And what is death?" I asked her. "Do you know it?"

"Ey! I know it," she answered. "I ha' done seen it in times er sorrer, in times er sickness. Hit's er shader en er darkness; hit's like er spider's web, 'cept 'ez hit's black, black ez de long hours er night—dee legs uv it, dar whar hit hangs o'er de wool' by, dee air—long—long—long. Dee reach, one ter de eas', one ter de wes', one ter de north, en one ter de south: right fum its middle hangs er reap-hoop. En dat shadder en darkness hit comes drappin' down on yer, creepin' up on yer; hit gits hol 'er yo' feet. Den hit slips up ter yer knees, den hit slips up, up, up, twel hit gits ter yo' breas'. Dat reap-hook hit gi's er wrench ter de breaf er yo' mouf, en dar! yer gone—caze yer breaf hit's yer soul!"

Among those of the race that live far from white people, their teaching and their influence, there is a barbarous belief that, whereas God is indeed Creator of the dominant white race, they, poor blacks, are the handiwork of Satan. This making a man contra to the commands of our Creator was the sin for which the devil, once an angel of high degree, was flung from heaven: "Flung into hell," declared my informant, the corn-vender, "en dar he be now tied ter de wheel er de chariot er fire! Chained ter de turnin' wheel er fire; en dar he gwine stay twel de great Risin' Day."

Finishing the uncouth legend: The devil, succeeding only in forming the shape of a man without the soul, became, as it were, a creator of death. "He blew en he blew, but dar come no life, dar come no breaf!" said the woman, excitedly. "But de Lo'd he feel s'sorry for de dead man dat he gin him er breaf en er soul same ez er white man."

The larger amount of their superstitions, however, affect not such primal beliefs, but bear upon little daily events which their ignorant minds translate into signs and wonders. Their folk-lore is rife with signs of coming death—"death-warnin's." If apple-trees put on twice in one year their rosy covering of blossoms, death's cold feet are sure to walk that way. More still do the white blooms of the pear, coming at undue season, portend a shroud for some person passing beneath those white flowers, expected only to show their kindly sweetness at early spring. When a dog comes to the yard in front of a house-door, there lying on his back with legs pawing the air, making a motion to and fro as if rubbing his back, know that he measures a grave for some member of the household. Or, if death be very near, the dog will bark and whine at unseemly hours. If a person sneeze once while eating, it is his death-sign. Should a rooster come to a house-door and crow lustily *into* the house, the death-spirit will be the unwelcome guest who will soon enter that door. If, on a sunny morning, a brood of chickens lie flatly on the ground all in a row, with wings spread wide, sunning themselves, they are measuring a grave; if the row of extended wings cover a long space, a long grave shall be needed; if a short space be measured by the wings, a child will pass over the dark river.

Three lamps burning at once in a room is portent for either the eldest or youngest person occupying the apartment to quit life for death ere a full year passes.

Screech-owls, with their quivering, harrowing cries, portend death; but they are very sensitive little creatures to all counter-charms put upon them from within the house over which they croon their dolorous monologue. Just "jam de shevel into de fire, en time hit git red hot dee'll hesh dere shiverin' !" or sprinkle salt on the blaze, or turn a pair of shoes up on the floor with soles against the walls; perhaps this faint semblance to a laid-out corpse will pacify the hungry spirit; the charm certainly (according to negro belief) will silence its harsh-voiced emissary.

To hear cows lowing late in the night—"down deep in de night"—is as sure a warning of approaching death to a near and a dear one "ez ef some pusson were a' ready laid on de coolin' board."

When shy forest-birds come to flutter about a dwelling as if they were frightened; when they seek entrance, and, agitated by unwonted signs of civilization, beat their wings wildly for exit, so some soul will flutteringly seek its exit from that house. And a black butterfly, woesome one of a lightsome breed, will bear into a home dreadful portent.

Woe to that careless individual who strides through a happy home bearing on his shoulder a hoe, or an ax, or shovel, or spade; that looks as if he were bound for the place of graves; and the ever-watchful, too-eager spirit of death will follow through that house with swift gait to choose his own.

Never dig a grave until the day of the burial; for, if left open over night, the gaping mouth will call, and call, and call for a whole family to follow that way. Neither must the burying of the dead be after sundown, for doing the deed on the wane of the day will place a direful spell upon all the dead one's family and friends to follow soon to the last rest. One must never step over graves; neither must one count graves, nor ever point at a grave. A house must never be swept out after sunset: there is some woeful portent attached to the act; nor must a broom, used with cleanly intent, touch the floor while a corpse lies cold within the house. When a grave is filled, the tools used thereabout should be laid on either side of it and left until other use absolutely requires them; if taken straight from the new grave, the anxious spirit will seek them. Nor should an old grave be freshened and remounded when a new one is dug.

Very meaningless are most of the negro superstitions, yet in some way all seem to point to the vast insatiability of death. He must be invited by no weird circumstances; by no careless freak, such as carrying sharp, heavy implements through a house; by no undue delay in the performance of offices for the dead, or any undue haste to leave the lost to hurry back to life; by the greedy carrying away of the last things needed by the dead—the shovel and the hoe—to have on hand to begin straightway the making of bread to fill living mouths.

Even to the simple act of poultry raising queer superstitions are attached. For instance, a successful poultry raiser will always take the shells just cracked and left by the downy brood and place them above the nest; the higher the broken shells are placed the more rapid and satisfactory will be the growth of the brood. And here is an infallible rule by which one can "raise turkeys," those least hardy of yard fowls: "Ef yer want ter raise turkeys, en raise'em certain en sure, des ee you take dem shells whar de small turkeys ha' des busted, en string 'em all on er yaller-homespun stringer yarn, en hang 'em up 'ginst de lef' side er de jam er de chimney; den you gi' dem young turkeys pepper-grass ter eat, en gi' hit ter 'em soon!"

When a nestful of fluffy little chickens are taking their first peep at the world from under the mother-hen's wings, the careful poulterer on the watch for such welcome event will run hastily to the nest with an empty sifter. This she will shake over the brood; the empty sifter lets through nothing, nor does it catch anything, but shaken thus over the "hatching nest" will be an efficacious charm against all hawks or other birds of prey: "Dem sifter-shuck chickens 'll be too spry ter be cotch!"

Now if a person be so lucky as to find a nestful of wild turkeys, just hatched, he can secure and tame the whole brood if he sprinkle over them nestling in the grasses a handful of black pepper.

To make fruit trees, or indeed any species of tree, grow rapidly, hang an old horseshoe on one of its limbs. To find a horseshoe will invariably bring good luck to its finder; and a horseshoe hung in front of a house will keep off witches and insure to the inmates of the house sound, healthful slumber. To find a knife, or needle, or pin, or pair of scissors—indeed anything at the same time *sharp* and *useful* —in the "big road" will insure the finder good fortune. If the point of the thing found be turned to the finder, the luck will be especially fitted to the man or woman who picks it up.

A rabbit-foot kept in the vest pocket, or worn as a charm about the neck, will ward off evil, and will also bestow great strength upon its keeper. A black cat's foot will insure its wearer against the bite of any dog, however vicious the dog may be, or however roguish may be the wearer's intent and appearance. A certain crook of the arm, too, will defend one from any attack of the watch-dog; but this bit of *sleight of arm* is known only to a few, and those mostly (we learn) who are of very roguish disposition. To have about a house some place of deposit for old shoes, and therein to keep all the worn-out leather of the household, will bring good luck to the family. To lace or button one shoe ere putting on the other is bad luck, probably because the stepping of the feet would be as uneven as was the attiring of the same. Hair should never be cut from the human head if excess of good fortune be craved.

Whereas it is a deathful portent for woodbirds to flutter in and about a house, it is a very excellent omen for gentle, fearless little birds to nest about a dwelling.

By dreams this race, as well as all other races in the infancy of their civilization, make augury of coming events. To dream of eating fruit out of its season is fatefully ominous. And to dream of finding a hen's nest full of eggs, none broken, is a sign of coming evil. If a person dream of finding a purse full of money then let him begin to make locks fast, for thievish hands are reaching for the dreamer's goods. But if the purse found in dreams be empty, there will be a fortune left to its finder. To dream of a death signifies that a marriage is near at hand; if of a marriage, a death will soon follow the dream: all of which seem but to heap proof of truth upon the adage, "Dreams go by contraries." If there is laughter before breakfast, there will be tears before night; if singing before breakfast, crying will fill the singing mouth before sunset. To burn sassafras-wood will make a breach and direful feuds among the most loving of friends and families.

A housekeeper watchful for "signs" will ever be ready for whatever guest may come. She will know that if a dishcloth be dropped, a hungry guest will be coming. If a spider drops half-way on his web from the ceiling, and then turns back and clambers up to the ceiling again, the expected guests have started to your house, but untoward circumstances (the "breakdown" of the vehicle, perhaps) have detained them; they may not be expected that day. But if the insect comes all the way to the floor, begin to cook a good dinner; the house will be filled with company.

The rooster, too, keeps a long lookout for coming guests. If he crow toward the front door, or the back door, you can form some idea of the high or low degree of the newcomer.

Young girls sitting meditatively before the wood-fire of an evening may form some idea as to who will bear them company; if a long log should roll down from the blazing heap, a tall man will be the visitor; if a short log roll down, a "short statured" man will call. And if a girl can make up a pretty bed—an accomplishment that Ruskin says every woman should possess—she will be rewarded, inasmuch as she will be sure to marry a man with a well-shaped nose. If, on the contrary, her bed-making is not approvable, the man of her choice will have a most ungainly nose. If a girl should spill a handful of salt, she will not marry during that year; or, if she carelessly knock over a chair, she will not in a year wear a bridal veil.

To twirl a chair about in the hands will bring bad luck. To step over a broom will call misfortunes upon one. To move a cat from house to house is bad luck, or to move a broom. But never, in leaving a house, leave it uncleanly; yet the woman must not herself scour the floors, for that will (in some inexplicable way) be moving herself out of the house into which she is going. A neighbor must be called in to do the necessary scouring. But the mover may herself sweep the house and yard, then pass out of the gate, leaving the broom with handle toward the street (or more properly, road or path, for this is plantation lore), ready to the hand of the next housekeeper who takes possession here. This careful sweeping and leaving of the broom will both leave good luck behind and carry good luck along with the prudent housekeeper.

In making a journey, if a rabbit or any four-footed beast run across the path, it portends evil to the traveler. Whether he be riding or walking he must get down to the ground, and make a cross there ere he dare move on. Turn back on any journey you are making if a screech-owl cries above you! However, an "old hooting-owl" may foretell either good or bad fortune according as its three hoots are given on the right or left hand. This is an unfailing sign (to its faithful believers) if one goes at night either 'coon or 'possum hunting. Three hoots to the left will send any hunter home hopeless from the chase, while three hoots on the right will bring him success. Starting to visit a neighbor, if the right foot trip while walking, know that the visit is expected with pleasure; but if the left foot trip, turn back or be an unwelcome guest. But before turning back, sit flat on the ground; no prudent person will turn square back on his tracks without taking this precaution. And in taking a stroll, never turn until you have reached a turn of the road or the corner of a fence.

The good farmer or gardener will do his planting or sowing according to the waxing or waning of the moon. He will sow his watermelons, or peas, or beans, or corn—indeed any vegetable that bears its product above ground—on the increase of the moon. But potatoes, turnips, all "root crops," must be planted on the decrease of the moon to insure a full garnering. Nor will the careful householder kill his supply of meat on the moon's wane, for meat killed and cured on the wane will dry up in the cooking, whereas that made ready for storage on the wax of the moon will swell in the pot.

When at early spring the fields are brown and sweet with upturned earth; when all the woods are rich with penetrating odor of wild grape blossoms, and mellow with perfume of crab-apple thickets blushing with weight of most fragrant flowers; when streams are loosed from the cold clamping hand of winter, note the groups of laborers at their task of corn-shelling. They are gathered about the smoldering fires in the humble cabins scattered over our wide-stretching plantation: how careful they are that no cob from which the planting-corn is shelled shall fall among the coals! The prudent wife, when the shelling is over, will gather into her apron all the cobs, taking care not to leave even one to be burned, or to be thrown perhaps where wandering stock might set foot on it. She will carry them to some running stream, and beneath its bed, under the light of the growing moon, she will bury deep the cobs, that the coming fields of corn may be molested neither by prowling stock, nor thievish hands, nor drouth, nor "firing up" of fields. May her efforts and her faith insure to the laborers a full crop!

1891

Word Shadows
(in "Contributors' Club")

Atlantic Monthly, LXVII (Boston, January 1891), 143–144.

Point of view is all. Linguistic chauvinism of the kind manifested in this article deafens the anonymous author to some trenchant folk metaphor. He has, however, fortunately given us a good, small collection of apparently authentic material so that we can reach our own conclusions. Other articles, later in the decade, discussed Negro slang in literature. William Cecil Elam, in "Lingo in Literature" (Lippincott's Magazine, *LV [February 1895], 286–288) claims that the Negro speaks a dialect much closer to the white man's than one would realize by reading the literature of the day; he also demonstrates that many of the grammatical irregularities have Shakespearian parallels, though it is not clear whether he means to suggest some influence from that source. His article is notable for its last line, which may still be of some use: "Above all things, let the lingoist emulate the wisdom of the oyster, which knows so well when to shut its mouth." Another slight-of-content-high-on-altruism piece is W. S. Scarborough's "Negro Folk-Lore and Dialect"* (Arena, *XVIII [January 1897], 186–192). One sentence should illustrate his problem: "The primitive negro is on intimate terms with the wild animals and birds, with the flora and fauna of the wild stretches of pine woods among which for generations his habitation has been pitched" (p. 188). This floral rhetoric, though well-intentioned, is pretty much devoid of folklore content, though it does talk around the subject at some length and with some passion.*

If shadows of material objects are grotesque, even more so are the shadows cast by words from fairly educated lips into the minds of almost totally ignorant people. Display in utterance of these quaint word-shadows, if one may so call them, makes dialect.

This grotesquerie, this quaint transformation of something well known, real, and admirable into something queer, fanciful, and awkward, yet bearing resemblance to the fair formation it shadows, gives to dialect writing and to dialect speech that piquant flavor that all the world favors. Especially is this true of that lately full fashionable style of literary production, song and story, in negro dialect. The words of our language that enter the mind of the old-time negro have indeed found their way into a dusky realm. Here is with us a race which has wholly forgotten its own language, or whatever methods of communication it made use of in its African home. The language of an utterly diverse race it must perforce employ, since it has lost the tongue of its own people. Into the minds of the individuals of this race, a people hardly a century out of barbarism, the light of civilization shines with dazzling effect. The language they must use is the growth of centuries of civilization, its roots reaching to even older civilizations, its branches grafted with luxuriant word-growths of almost every nation on earth. It is little wonder that this language of ours assumes in these startled brains most fanciful shapes. To take down some of these shadowy effects, with our language for cause, would be to make a dialect dictionary, a glossary of plantation *patois*, a work for which, happily, there is now no need. But an effort to show a few of these vague, dusky shapes that our words take on may not be wholly uninteresting.

See, for instance, how our simple word "fertilizer" becomes on the tongue of an old darky gardener "pudlie." A giant is dubbed a "high-jinted man." A maid who will prove obedient to orders is described as an "orderly gal." A piece of ground that shows a bad yield of cotton or corn is called "failery lan'." Farming in the mouth of a negro laborer is "crapping." The favorite food of the cotton-field hand, the food he cannot live without, the strengthening bread made from corn meal, has its expressive name, "John Constant." Wheaten bread, a rare treat to the field hand, is "Billy Seldom." Bacon has its name, "Ole Ned." The best field laborer is the "lead hoe hand." To quit work for the day is to "lay by." To rise early to go to the field is "ter be in patch by hour by sun." An early breakfast is "a soon brekkus." Our word "accuse"—alas! one the negro often has occasion to use—is "'scuse." There are too few of the race who have not been, at some time or other, "'scuse of a pig," "'scuse of a cow," "'scuse of cotton-pickin' by night," "'scuse of a pa'r shoes," and so on down a long list of material and tempting articles.

The quaint technical phrases that the negroes make use of in their business talk are innumerable. To be ready to hire for a cook is to be "des on han' ter jump in de cook-pot." In ironing, to leave a cluster of wrinkles on the garment in hand is to put "cat-faces" on it. To wash only for visitors to a town or village is to "des only take in trans' washin'." To take day boarders is to take "transoms." To say that one is obliged to turn a hand to anything is to say, "Ever' little drug dere is, I hatter wag it."

A half-starved calf is a "calf dat's been whipped wid de churn-dasher." A good ploughman is a "noble plough han'." Rich land is "strong ground." To keep down grass is to "fight wid Gen'al Green."

To leave the technicalities for generalities, we find that any matter that is but ill adjusted is a matter "squowow"; ill adjusted in a lesser degree is "weewow." A well-arranged matter is pronounced all "commojious,"—a shadow of our word "commodious." A matter well accomplished is "essentially done"; as, for instance, "When she cooks, she des essentially cooks good." A person fit to adorn wealth is a "high-minded person," or "big-minded," or "great-minded." A wealthy person is one "stout in worldly goods." A proud person is an "umptious somebody." One who is only proud enough is "proud to de ikle." One who is slightly petted by good Dame Fortune is "des pettish." To be in trouble or distress is to "walk on de wearried line." To live easily and happily is to live "jobly and wid pleadjure." To be ill is to "have a misery." To be quite well is to be "des sorter tollerble." Entertaining conversation becomes in that shadow-language "mockin'-bird talk." A girl who loves to stay at home, what the poets would call "a home-keeping heart," becomes a "homely gal"; keeping for the word its English meaning, not its American perversion.

A queer gamut of color they run in their descriptions of their race: "a dark man," "a bright man," "a light gal," "a mustee 'oman," "a gingerbread boy," a "honey-colored lady."

Entering the mystic world, we find that a ghost is "a hant." Magic, black art, becomes "conjure"; the accent on the first syllable. Entering the world of song, we find that all lively lyrics are "sinner-songs," or "reels," or "corn-hollers," "jump-up-songs," or "chunes dat skip wid de banjo." Religious songs are "member-songs" or "hymn-chunes." Long chants are "spirituelles."

The dweller in the realm of negro religious beliefs and forms of worship endows our language with meanings entirely new to our experience. Not to be a church member is to be "settin' on de sinner-seat," "still in de open fiel'," "drinkin' de cup er damnation," and many other such phrases. To enter the church is to "jine de band," to "take up de cup er salvation," to "git a seat wid de members," to "be gethered in," to "put on a shine-line gyarment," and so on *ad infinitum.*

1891

Certain Beliefs and Superstitions of the Negro

(in "Contributors' Club")

Atlantic Monthly, LXVIII (Boston, August 1891), 286–288.

With an appallingly deliberate insensitivity that on one hand suggests the anonymous author of "Word Shadows" and on the other makes one wonder whether the attitude isn't feigned, the author of this article asks stupid questions and gets for answers some of the most striking examples of folk metaphor on record. In his letter commenting on this anthology Herbert Halpert described this article as "one of the best collections of brief cosmological myths and dites *and origin legends to be reported from the U. S." The article also has several interesting "experience" stories which suggest that the image of the Promised Land was, for some informants, by no means abstract or vague. In our thermonuclear day, the Negro speaker's description of boiling sea and melting rocks on Judgment Day does not seem at all strange, and the answer to "Of what are the stars made?" is not incorrect.*

The negroes on our Southern plantations have apparently adopted with marvelous rapidity the customs, language, and religion of the race that brought them into slavery a mere century ago. Yet, though they seem so readily to have accepted the forms of worship of the dominant race, one finds, on looking closely into the matter, that they cling to some very barbarous beliefs and superstitions, and oftentimes these strange fancies are wrapped about with the garb of religion.

The negro has his church. His church has its bell that peals forth cheerily on Sunday morning. He has his Sunday-schcol, his marching with banners, and his reading of essays on Children's Day. He learns, and he sings wondrously well, many gospel hymns; and we trust, in truth believe, that many of the great lessons of Christianity fix themselves in his heart and exhibit themselves in his life. Knowing all this, and seeing how he reaches toward the light, reaching out of the darkness of an ignorance near akin to barbarism, it is strange to note how he retards his progress toward the acquisition of clear light by clinging to purposeless and very curious superstitions.

For instance, it is surprising to learn that negroes of honesty and sobriety, who profess a desire to live better lives, are sometimes excluded from membership in these same churches because "the candiduct," as he is called, has not had "a 'sperience" of "bein' shuck over hell." Such strange beliefs the negro treasures down deep in his heart; beliefs of which his advancement in religion, education, and civilization—adopted all from the white man—takes no cognizance.

It is not often that we can lift a corner of that dusky brain curtain to catch a glimpse into that cloudy adytum where the moon shows herself a lump of ice, and the sun is considered to exhibit itself as a woman singing, singing, forever singing.

A few questions put at various times to the people of the dark race have brought to me answers which serve in some sort as glimpses into that repository of quaint fancies.

I shall endeavor to transcribe a few of these replies as nearly as possible as the negro himself would give them.

"What," I once asked a negro, "is your idea of this world we live in?" "Dee tell me," was the answer, "dat dis worl' is a gre't star; but hit 'pear ter me ter be a gre't big flower."

Again I asked, "What is thunder?"

To this came divers replies. One negro said that thunder was a round ball not larger than a boy's toy marble. "It do make s' much noise rollin' 'caze hit 's let loose fum de hand of God."

Another thought thunder was "de movin' of God's feet on de sky, and de lightenin' is de winklein' of his eye."

"What is wind?" I asked.

"Hit's a blaze," was the reply; "hit's red like fire, but hit's cold. How does I know hit's red? 'Caze dem folks what can see wind is done tole me dat red is de color of hit. Some folks can see wind, and t'o'her folks can't. Hogs can always see wind; dee des run and grunt when dee see hits whirlin' redness. If any pusson will suck a sow, dat pusson will git power in his eyes to see wind. And whenever a wind rises, hit is risin' en dyin' breaf. Breaf of de dyin' folks in de worril fills de wind's wings and makes 'em strong."

To the question, "What is air?" came the answer, "Hit's des low wind." To the interrogation, "Where does snow come from?" came the reply, "It is blowed off de tops de highest mountains."

"What are clouds made of?"

"Made of all de smoke blowed up from de worril since de worril was made."

"Of what are the stars made?"

"Dee is des balls of fire hung up in de sky."

"How long will the stars hang in the sky?"

"Dee will hang twel de Great Day of Jedgement. On dat day John will take a shinin' broom in his hand, and he will sweep de sky clean of stars; sweep de sky clean of stars like a woman sweeps a floor clear of dust. De stars will fall from his broom, and will bust wid blazes and great noise des 'fo' dee touch de earth."

"You say the moon is a lump of ice; now what will become of that at the Last Great Day?" I have sometimes asked.

"Hit will drip away in blood."

The queer recitation of ignorance continued somewhat after this manner:—

"What will become of the rocks?"

"Dee will des melt. De rocks? Dee des growed. Dee'll des agin melt away. De ocean? Hit'll only des bile away. De sun? Well, you know de sun is a 'oman; hit got face, hit got eyes, hit can see all you do. She sings,—she do sing all day long. As she rises she sings low, but when she gits such a distance up she sings loud! All 'cross de high sky she sings loud, but when she gits sech a distance down she sings low agin. Dat's de reason noises can't carry far in de middle of de day; de sounds air des deadened by de sun's singin'. Nobody can edzactly hear what air de words of de song she sings, but ev'ybody is deefened by her hummin', 'caze hearin' her dee can't hear no other noise to speak of."

"What," I asked one wise in the doctrines of ignorance, "are those stars with long lights streaming from them?"

"Macomet stars. Dee come fer signs of wars. And often is de times dat us see strange lights and quare shadows all over de worril in spots. I don't know what dem be, but I does know dat de worril sometimes puts on mournin'. She puts on mournin'-close same like a widow 'oman. Is you notice dat dark shadow in de moon? Dat's a man, dat is. He put dar fer workin' on a Sunday. Dat little shadder by him is his little dog. De little dog didn't do no harm; he des follered de man. When you see a rainbow," continued my informant, "you'll des know den dat de moon is done got des behime de sun, and is lookin' over her shoulder."

I discover that there are various superstitions concerning the origin of the appearance of the rainbow. One old negro tells me that rainbows are kept in the bottom of brooks until such times as they are needed to "pen de sky." He tells me that he has seen a rainbow in the very act of rising from its watery bed.

"How did the world look when it was new?" I once asked.

"Mighty strange,—mighty strange. De jay-bird brung de first grit of dirt ever was brung ter dis earth. I don't know how come he done dat, but I do know dat de jay-bird is 'bleeged ter go down ter de devil ev'y Friday des at one o'clock and carry a grit of dirt in his bill. Also, I can tell how dar was no water in de worril twel de mournin'-dove dug de fust spring; she dug hit wid her bill. Also, I can tell how, when de white dove flew out of de Noray's Ark, she planted de first grain of corn [maize] dat ever had been planted on de earth. I can tell you, too, how de mockin'-bird stole dat first grain of corn. I know, I do, dat de robin did plant de first cedar-tree ever was in dis worril. De first fire was brung to de worril from de devil; hit's long been quench fer ourns usin', but dat left wid de devil, hit ain't never done been quench, and never is ter be."

I asked what sort of people were in the world when the world was new.

The reply came as follows: "Many of de animals you see now was oncet folks, old-time folks; dese big rattlesnakes, dee was one time bad folks. In de old days dee was changed ter snakes, and dee air des essentially dat way twel yit. Monkeys use ter be old-time folks also; dee ac' like folks yit. De squinch-owls, dem what shiver roun' de house when a pusson gwine die, dee was all ole women when de worril was young. Dese moles dat you see burrowin' undergroun', dee was old-time folks; dee was too proud to walk on de groun', and so dee was put under de groun'. Cats was oncet witches,—witcher-men and witcher-women. De swamp-owls, dee was ole women also. Dee one time 'fuse ter give de Lord a piece of bread, as he walk here on de earth, so dee was indain ter be owls. All de ole folks tell me," continued my informant, "dat dar use ter be three houses clost tog'er wherever you go, and dem three houses belong ter de Injun man, de fox, and de rabbit. De white man done drive off de Injun, done mos' drive off de fox, but Brer Rabbit, he say he gwine stay."

Besides these queer fancies of the causes of natural phenomena and of the world's earliest history, they of the dark race have a strange, unwritten law concerning religious belief, custom, and expression with which every professor of religion must be familiar. To the unconverted they apply phrases like these: "still in de open fiel'," "settin' on de sinner seat," and many more of like nature. To the converted they apply phrases like these: "He done been shuck over hell"; "He's done spilt de cup of damnation"; "He's done broke de bonds"; "He's tryin' on de gole waistband"; "He's waggin' wid de cross"; "He's shuck out de shine line gyarment, and he's ready ter put hit on"; "He's a shoutin' member"; "She's a rockin' Christian"; "He's on prayin' groun' and pleadin' terms"; "She's done des come th'oo"; "He's done been led a far way"; "She's sippin' de cup of salvation"; "He's tuck a seat wid de member-men"; "He's gethered in"; "She's done told her 'sperience and she's done profess."

The "experiences" that must be told before gaining admission to the church are sometimes marvelous, yet to one who has heard a repetition of many of these "experiences" there is observable in all an accord with certain unwritten laws.

Few sensations more startling to a fairly educated mind can be imagined than those that assail one after the hearing of several of these marvelous recitations of soul journeyings and soul experiences. The negroes who go through these soul ordeals are called "seekers." One must be a "seeker" ere he can become a "member." Many of the negroes, during the time for "seekin' 'ligion," tie a cloth about the head, and all who "seek" are expected to drop all work and look very woe-begone. The seeker must be carried in spirit to heaven and hell, and he must give in church an account of these spirit-journeys.

Though many of these recitations of spiritual experiences are strangely absurd, some are really striking and poetic.

One negro who applied for church membership said that he had passed much of his time for seeking in spiritual wanderings through the lower regions. He was surprised to find the dwellers of that land apparently far less unhappy than he had been taught to believe them to be: so he asked his guide through this realm of darkness: "Brother, whar's de fire? Brother, dis ain't nigh as bad as folks up yonder tell us it is, for dee tell us dis place is full of fire. Brother, whar's de fire?" For reply his guide stopped, turned to his questioner, opened up his heart, —"same as a cook-'oman opens a stove door,"—and all within his bared breast the horror-stricken seeker beheld a rolling, whirling sea of flame. "For, oh, my brother," cried the guide, "hit's widin,—de fire is widin!"

The negroes' descriptions of the beauty of heaven rarely, if ever, touch on any note of the sublime. I have heard from them only accounts of passing through many doors, of houses of many rooms, of drinking from golden vessels, of walking over glittering bridges, of offering to gain admission to those great gates that they love to describe, "a new heart." The most absurd " 'sperience" I ever heard was that of a very old negro, who professed to have been granted a glimpse into the great gates of what constitutes their poor ignorant ideal of a happy beyond. He saw there, he said, an old "fellow-servant," one who had died but a short time before. He described the happy state of his old friend as follows: "I seen him sittin' high in heaven. I seen him wid de eye of faith. He was sittin' right sider dat pool er molasses. He had a seat right under de fritter-tree dat grows by dat sweet pool, and des whenever he is so minded he do reach up his hand, and he do grab off a handful of dem good fritters dat hang thick on dat tree, and he do des reach over and dip dem fritters in dat pool, and eat des as commodious!"

It is in their hymns, unwritten by themselves save on their hearts, as one generation sings unto another, that the negroes preserve their best inspiration, their most fervid fancies. These hymns are rarely to be heard now, for they grow shyer day by day of singing those grand chants, those unique hymns, loved and sung often by them in their days of slavery. The younger generation, the negroes born "since surrender," though ambitious to learn the cheery and attractive songs taught in their "free schools," are willing enough to let those marvelous melodies of their people drift into oblivion.

1895

Music in America

by Antonin Dvorak

Harper's New Monthly Magazine, 90 (New York, February 1895), 428–434.

It would be difficult to overestimate Dvorak's influence on the attitudes of Americans toward their own music. In an article in the New York Herald *in the spring of 1893 he described some of the benefits he thought might result from the utilization of folk materials, then later in the same year demonstrated his point when his* Symphony No. 5 in E Minor, *Op. 95 ("From the New World") was premiered in New York. The article reprinted here was published seven years after the founding of the American Folklore Society—a time when folklore was in many quarters a suspect discipline still, and many folklorists had yet to discover the importance of native American material. His articles and composition stimulated composers (such as Ernest Kroeger, George Chadwick, Henry Hadley, Henry Gilbert, John Powell, Rubin Goldmark, and others) and musicologists (such as Henry Edward Krehbiel, whose* Afro-American Folksongs: A Study in Racial and National Music *[New York, 1914] seems to have received most of its impetus from "Music in America"). "As much as or more than the Fisk singers," wrote Professor Herbert Halpert, "it ['Music in America'] made 'plantation music' respectable, so that musicians and universities were forced to stop sneering about folk music. Of course he was wrong about there being nothing besides Indian and Negro music in America, but he certainly affected American (and world) opinion."*

It is a difficult task at best for a foreigner to give a correct verdict of the affairs of another country. With the United States of America this is more than usually difficult, because they cover such a vast area of land that it would take many years to become properly acquainted with the various localities, separated by great distances, that would have to be considered when rendering a judgment concerning them all. It would ill become me, therefore, to express my views on so general and all-embracing a subject as music in America, were I not pressed to do so, for I have neither travelled extensively, nor have I been here long enough to gain an intimate knowledge of American affairs. I can only judge of it from what I have observed during my limited experience as a musician and teacher in America, and from what those whom I know here tell me about their own country. Many of my impressions therefore are those of a foreigner who has not been here long enough to overcome the feeling of strangeness and bewildered astonishment which must fill all European visitors upon their first arrival.

The two American traits which most impress the foreign observer, I find, are the unbounded patriotism and capacity for enthusiasm of most Americans. Unlike the more diffident inhabitants of other countries, who do not "wear their hearts upon their sleeves," the citizens of America are always patriotic, and no occasion seems to be too serious or too slight for them to give expression to this feeling. Thus nothing better pleases the average American, especially the American youth, than to be able to say that this or that building, this or that new patent appliance is the finest or grandest in the world. This, of course, is due to that other trait—enthusiasm. The enthusiasm of most Americans for all things new is apparently without limit. It is the essence of what is called "push"—American push. Every day I meet with this quality in my pupils. They are unwilling to stop at anything. In the matters relating to their art they are inquisitive to a degree that they want to go to the bottom of all things at once. It is as if a boy wished to dive before he could swim.

At first, when my American pupils were new to me, this trait annoyed me, and I wished them to give more attention to the one matter in hand rather than to everything at once. But now I like it; for I have come to the conclusion that this youthful enthusiasm and eagerness to take up everything is the best promise for music in America. The same opinion, I remember, was expressed by the director of the new conservatory in Berlin, who, from his experience with American students of music, predicted that America within twenty or thirty years would become the first musical country.

Only when the people in general, however, begin to take as lively an interest in music and art as they now take in more material matters will the arts come into their own. Let the enthusiasm of the people once be excited, and patriotic gifts and bequests must surely follow.

It is a matter of surprise to me that all this has not come long ago. When I see how much is done in every other field by public-spirited men in America—how schools, universities, libraries, museums, hospitals, and parks spring up out of the ground and are maintained by generous gifts—I can only marvel that so little has been done for music. After two hundred years of almost unbroken prosperity and expansion, the net results for music are a number of public concert-halls of most recent growth; several musical societies with orchestras of noted excellence, such as the Philharmonic Society in New York, the orchestras of Mr. Thomas and Mr. Seidl, and the superb orchestra supported by a public spirited citizen of Boston; one opera company, which only the upper classes can hear or understand; and a national conservatory which owes its existence to the generous forethought of one indefatigable woman.

It is true that music is the youngest of the arts, and must therefore be expected to be treated as Cinderella, but is it not time that she were lifted from the ashes and given a seat among the equally youthful sister arts in this land of youth, until the coming of the fairy godmother and the prince of the crystal slipper?

Art, of course, must always go a-begging, but why should this country alone, which is so justly famed for the generosity and public spirit of its citizens, close its door to the poor beggar? In the Old World this is not so. Since the days of Palestrina, the three-hundredth anniversary of whose death was celebrated in Rome a few weeks ago, princes and prelates have vied with each other in extending a generous hand to music. Since the days of Pope Gregory the Church has made music one of her own chosen arts. In Germany and Austria princes like Esterhazy, Lobkowitz, and Harrach, who supported Haydn and Beethoven, or the late King of Bavaria, who did so much for Wagner, with many others, have helped to create a demand for good music, which has since become universal, while in France all governments, be they monarchies, empires, or republics, have done their best to carry on the noble work that was begun by Louis the Fourteenth. Even the little republic of Switzerland annually sets aside a budget for the furtherance of literature, music, and the arts.

A few months ago only we saw how such a question of art as whether the operas sung in Hungary's capital should be of a national or foreign character could provoke a ministerial crisis. Such is the interest in music and art taken by the governments and people of other countries.

The great American republic alone, in its national government as well as in the several governments of the States, suffers art and music to go without encouragement. Trades and commerce are protected, funds are voted away for the unemployed, schools and colleges are endowed, but music must go unaided, and be content if she can get the support of a few private individuals like Mrs. Jeannette M. Thurber and Mr. H. L. Higginson.

Not long ago a young man came to me and showed me his compositions. His talent seemed so promising that I at once offered him a scholarship in our school; but he sorrowfully confessed that he could not afford to become my pupil, because he had to earn his living by keeping books in Brooklyn. Even if he came on but two afternoons in the week, or on Saturday afternoon only, he said, he would lose his employment, on which he and others had to depend. I urged him to arrange the matter with his employer, but he only received the answer: "If you want to play, you can't keep books. You will have to drop one or the other." He dropped his music.

In any other country the state would have made provision for such a deserving scholar, so that he could have pursued his natural calling without having to starve. With us in Bohemia the Diet each year votes a special sum of money for just such purposes, and the imperial government in Vienna on occasion furnishes other funds for talented artists. Had it not been for such support I should not have been able to pursue my studies when I was a young man. Owing to the fact that upon the kind recommendation of such men as Brahms, Hanslick, and Herbeck, the Minister of Public Education in Vienna on five successive years sent me sums ranging from four to six hundred florins, I was able to pursue my work and to get my compositions published, so that at the end of that time I was able to stand on my own feet. This has filled me with lasting gratitude towards my country.

Such an attitude of the state towards deserving artists is not only a kind but a wise one. For it cannot be emphasized too strongly that art, as such, does not "pay," to use an American expression—at least, not in the beginning—and that the art that has to pay its own way is apt to become vitiated and cheap.

It is one of the anomalies of this country that the principle of protection is upheld for all enterprises but art. By protection I do not mean the exclusion of foreign art. That, of course, is absurd. But just as the State here provides for its poor industrial scholars and university student, so should it help the would-be students of music and art. As it is now, the poor musician not only cannot get his necessary instruction, in the first place, but if by any chance he has acquired it, he has small prospects of making his chosen calling support him in the end. Why is this? Simply because the orchestras in which first-class players could find a place in this country can be counted on one hand; while of opera companies where native singers can be heard, and where the English tongue is sung, there are none at all. Another thing which discourages the student of music is the unwillingness of publishers to take anything but light and trashy music. European publishers are bad enough in that respect, but the American publishers are worse. Thus, when one of my pupils last year produced a very creditable work, and a thoroughly American composition at that, he could not get it published in America, but had to send it to Germany, where it was at once accepted. The same is true of my own compositions on American subjects, each of which hitherto has had to be published abroad.

No wonder American composers and musicians grow discouraged, and regard the more promising conditions of music in other countries with envy! Such a state of affairs should be a source of mortification to all truly patriotic Americans. Yet it can be easily remedied. What was the situation in England but a short while ago? Then they had to procure all their players from abroad, while their own musicians went to the Continent to study. Now that they have two standard academies of music in London, like those of Berlin, Paris, and other cities, the national feeling for music seems to have been awakened, and the majority of orchestras are composed of native Englishmen, who play as well as the others did before. A single institution can make such a change, just as a single genius can bestow an art upon his country that before was lying in unheeded slumber.

Our musical conservatory in Prague was founded but three generations ago, when a few nobles and patrons of music subscribed five thousand florins, which was then the annual cost of maintaining the school. Yet that little school flourished and grew, so that now more than sixfold that amount is annually expended. Only lately a school for organ music has been added to the conservatory, so that the organists of our churches can learn to play their instruments at home, without having to go to other cities. Thus a school benefits the community in which it is. The citizens of Prague in return have shown their appreciation of the fact by building the "Rudolfinum" as a magnificent home for all the arts. It is jointly occupied by the conservatory and the Academy of Arts, and besides that contains large and small concert-halls and rooms for picture-galleries. In the proper maintenance of this building the whole community takes an interest. It is supported, as it was founded, by the stockholders of the Bohemian Bank of Deposit, and yearly gifts and bequests are made to the institution by private citizens.

If a school of art can grow so in a country of but six million inhabitants, what much brighter prospects should it not have in a land of seventy millions? The important thing is to make a beginning, and in this the State should set an example.

They tell me that this cannot be done. I ask, why can't it be done? If the old commonwealths of Greece and Italy, and the modern republics of France and Switzerland, have been able to do this, why cannot America follow their example? The money certainly is not lacking. Constantly we see great sums of money spent for the material pleasures of the few, which, if devoted to the purposes of art, might give pleasure to thousands. If schools, art museums, and libraries can be maintained at the public expense, why should not musical conservatories and playhouses? The function of the drama, with or without music, is not only to amuse, but to elevate and instruct while giving pleasure. Is it not in the interest of the State that this should be done in the most approved manner, so as to benefit all of its citizens? Let the owners of private playhouses give their performances for diversion only, let those who may, import singers who sing in foreign tongues, but let there be at least one intelligent power that will see to it that the people can hear and see what is best, and what can be understood by them, not matter how small the demand.

That such a system of performing classic plays and operas pleases the people was shown by the attitude of the populace in Prague. There the people collected money and raised subscriptions for over fifty years to build a national playhouse. In 1880 they at last had a sufficient amount, and the "National Theatre" was accordingly built. It had scarcely been built when it was burned to the ground. But the people were not to be discouraged. Everybody helped, and before a fortnight was over more than a million had been collected, and the house was at once built up again, more magnificent than it was before.

In answer to such arguments I am told that there is no popular demand for good music in America. That is not so. Every concert in New York, Boston, Philadelphia, Chicago, or Washington, and most other cities, no doubt, disproves such a statement. American concert-halls are as well filled as those of Europe, and, as a rule, the listeners—to judge them by their attentive conduct and subsequent expression of pleasure—are not a whit less appreciative. How it would be with opera I cannot judge, since American opera audiences, as the opera is conducted at present, are in no sense representative of the people at large. I have no doubt, however, that if the Americans had a chance to hear grand opera sung in their own language they would enjoy it as well and appreciate it as highly as the opera-goers of Vienna, Paris, or Munich enjoy theirs. The change from Italian and French to English will scarcely have an injurious effect on the present good voices of the singers while it may have the effect of improving the voices of American singers, bringing out more clearly the beauty and strength of the *timbre*, while giving an intelligent conception of the work that enables singers to use a pure diction, which cannot be obtained in a foreign tongue.

The American voice, so far as I can judge, is a good one. When I first arrived in this country I was startled by the strength and the depth of the voices in the boys who sell papers on the street, and I am still constantly amazed at its penetrating quality.

In a sense, of course, it is true that there is less of a demand for music in America than in certain other countries. Our common folk in Bohemia know this. When they come here they leave their fiddles and other instruments at home, and none of the itinerant musicians with whom our country abounds would ever think of trying their luck over here. Occasionally when I have met one of my countrymen whom I knew to be musical in this city of New York or in the West, and have asked him why he did not become a professional musician, I have usually received the answer, "Oh, music is not wanted in this land." This I can scarcely believe. Music is wanted wherever good people are, as the German poet has sung. It only rests with the leaders of the people to make a right beginning.

When this beginning is made, and when those who have musical talent find it worth their while to stay in America, and to study and exercise their art as the business of their life, the music of America will soon become more national in its character. This my conviction I know is not shared by many who can justly claim to know this country better than I do. Because the population of the United States is composed of many different races, in which the Teutonic element predominates, and because, owing to the improved methods of transmission of the present day, the music of all the world is quickly absorbed by this country, they argue that nothing specially original or national can come forth. According to that view, all other countries which are but the results of a conglomeration of peoples and races, as, for instance, Italy, could not have produced a national literature or a national music.

A while ago I suggested that inspiration for truly national music might be derived from the negro melodies or Indian chants. I was led to take this view partly by the fact that the so-called plantation songs are indeed the most striking and appealing melodies that have yet been found on this side of the water, but largely by the observation that this seems to be recognized, though often unconsciously, by most

Americans. All races have their distinctively national songs, which they at once recognize as their own, even if they have never heard them before. When a Tsech, a Pole, or a Magyar in this country suddenly hears one of his folk-songs or dances, no matter if it is for the first time in his life, his eye lights up at once, and his heart within him responds, and claims that music as its own. So it is with those of Teutonic or Celtic blood, or any other men, indeed, whose first lullaby mayhap was a song wrung from the heart of the people.

It is a proper question to ask, what songs, then, belong to the American and appeal more strongly to him than any others? What melody could stop him on the street if he were in a strange land and make the home feeling well up within him, no matter how hardened he might be or how wretchedly the tune were played? Their number, to be sure, seems to be limited. The most potent as well as the most beautiful among them, according to my estimation, are certain of the so-called plantation melodies and slave songs, all of which are distinguished by unusual and subtle harmonies, the like of which I have found in no other songs but those of old Scotland and Ireland. The point has been urged that many of those touching songs like those of Foster, have not been composed by the negroes themselves, but are the work of white men, while others did not originate on the plantation, but were imported from Africa. It seems to me that this matters little. One might as well condemn the Hungarian Rhapsody because Liszt could not speak Hungarian. The important thing is that the inspiration for such music should come from the right source, and that the music itself should be a true expression of the people's real feelings. To read the right meaning the composer need not necessarily be of the same blood, though that, of course, makes it easier for him. Schubert was a thorough German, but when he wrote Hungarian music, as in the second movement of the C-Major Symphony, or in some of his piano pieces, like the Hungarian Divertissement, he struck the true Magyar note, to which all Magyar hearts, and with them our own, must forever respond. This is not a *tour de force*, but only an instance of how much can be comprehended by a sympathetic genius. The white composers who wrote the touching negro songs which dimmed Thackeray's spectacles so that he exclaimed, "Behold, a vagabond with a corked face and a banjo sings a little song, strikes a wild note, which sets the whole heart thrilling with happy pity!" had a similarly sympathetic comprehension of the deep pathos of slave life. If, as I have been informed they were, these songs were adopted by the negroes on the plantations, they thus became true negro songs. Whether the original songs which must have inspired the composers came from Africa or originated on the plantations matters as little as whether Shakespeare invented his own plots or borrowed them from others. The thing to rejoice over is that such lovely songs exist and are sung at the present day. I, for one, am delighted by them. Just so it matters little whether the inspiration for the coming folk-songs of America is derived from the negro melodies, the songs of the creoles, the red man's chant, or the plaintive ditties of the homesick German or Norwegian. Undoubtedly the germs for the best of music lie hidden among all the races that are commingled in this great country. The music of the people is like a rare and lovely flower growing amidst encroaching weeds. Thousands pass it, while others trample it under foot, and thus the chances are that it will perish before it is seen by the one discriminating spirit who will prize it above all else. The fact that no one has as yet arisen to make the most of it does not prove that nothing is there.

Not so many years ago Slavic music was not known to the men of other races. A few men like Chopin, Glinka, Moniuszko, Smetana, Rubinstein, and Tschaikovsky, with a few others, were able to create a Slavic school of music. Chopin alone caused the music of Poland to be known and prized by all lovers of music. Smetana did the same for us Bohemians. Such national music, I repeat, is not created out of nothing. It is discovered and clothed in new beauty, just as the myths and the legends of a people are brought to light and crystallized in undying verse by the master poets. All that is needed is a delicate ear, a retentive memory, and the power to weld the fragments of former ages together in one harmonious whole. Only the other day I read in a newspaper that Brahms himself admitted that he had taken existing folk-songs for the themes of his new book of songs, and had arranged them for piano music. I have not heard nor seen the songs, and do not know if this be so; but if it were, it would in no wise reflect discredit upon the composer. Liszt in his rhapsodies and Berlioz in his *Faust* did the same thing with existing Hungarian strains, as, for instance, the Racokzy March; and Schumann and Wagner made a similar use of the Marseillaise for their songs of the "Two Grenadiers." Thus, also, Balfe, the Irishman, used one of our most national airs, a Hussite song, in his opera, the *Bohemian Girl*, though how he came by it nobody has as yet explained. So the music of the people, sooner or later, will command attention and creep into the books of composers.

An American reporter once told me that the most valuable talent a journalist could possess was a "nose for news." Just so the musician must prick his ear for music. Nothing must be too low or too insignificant for the musician. When he walks he should listen to every whistling boy, every street singer or blind organ-grinder. I myself am often so fascinated by these people that I can scarcely tear myself away, for every now and then I catch a strain or hear the fragments of a recurring melodic theme that sound like the voice of the people. These things are worth preserving, and no one should be above making a lavish use of all such suggestions. It is a sign of barrenness, indeed, when such characteristic bits of music exist and are not heeded by the learned musicians of the age.

I know that it is still an open question whether the inspiration derived from a few scattering melodies and folk-songs can be sufficient to give a national character to higher forms of music, just as it is an open question whether national music, as such, is preferable. I myself, as I have always declared, believe firmly that the music that is most characteristic of the nation whence it springs is entitled to the highest consideration. The part of Beethoven's Ninth Symphony that appeals most strongly to all is the melody of the last movement, and that is also the most German. Weber's best opera, according to the popular estimate, is *Der Freischütz.* Why? Because it is the most German. His inspiration there clearly came from the thoroughly German scenes and situations of the story, and hence his music assumed that distinctly national character which has endeared it to the German nation as a whole. Yet he himself spent far more pains on his opera *Euryanthe*, and persisted to the end in regarding it as his best work. But the people, we see, claim their own; and, after all, it is for the people that we strive.

An interesting essay could be written on the subject how much the external frame-work of an opera—that is, the words, the characters of the personages, and the general *mise en scène*—contributes towards the inspiration of the composer. If Weber was inspired to produce his masterpiece by so congenial a theme as the story of *Der Freischütz*, Rossini was undoubtedly similarly inspired by the Swiss surroundings of William Tell. Thus one might almost suspect that some of the charming melodies of that opera are more the product and property of Switzerland than of the Italian composer. It is to be noticed that all of Wagner's operas, with the exception of his earliest work, *Rienzi*, are inspired by German subjects. The most German of them all is that of *Die Meistersinger*, that opera of operas, which should be an example to all who distrust the potency of their own national topics.

Of course, as I have indicated before, it is possible for certain composers to project their spirit into that of another race and country. Verdi partially succeeded in striking Oriental chords in his *Aïda*, while Bizet was able to produce so thoroughly Spanish strains and measures as those of *Carmen.* Thus inspiration can be drawn from the depths as well as from the heights, although that is not my conception of the true mission of music. Our mission should be to give pure pleasure, and to uphold the ideals of our race. Our mission as teachers is to show the right way to those who come after us.

My own duty as a teacher, I conceive, is not so much to interpret Beethoven, Wagner, or other masters of the past, but to give what encouragement I can to the young musicians of America. I must give full expression to my firm conviction, and to the hope that just as this nation has already surpassed so many others in marvellous inventions and feats of engineering and commerce, and has made an honorable place for itself in literature in one short century, so it must assert itself in the other arts, and especially in the art of music. Already there are enough public-spirited lovers of music striving for the advancement of this their chosen art to give rise to the hope that the United States of America will soon emulate the older countries in smoothing the thorny path of the artist and musician. When that beginning has been made, when no large city is without its public opera-house and concert-hall, and without its school of music and endowed orchestra, where native musicians can be heard and judged, then those who hitherto have had no opportunity to reveal their talent will come forth and compete with one another, till a real genius emerges from their number, who will be as thoroughly representative of his country as Wagner and Weber are of Germany, or Chopin of Poland.

To bring about this result we must trust to the ever-youthful enthusiasm and patriotism of this country. When it is accomplished, and when music has been established as one of the reigning arts of the land, another wreath of fame and glory will be added to the country which earned its name, the "Land of Freedom," by unshackling her slaves at the price of her own blood.

NOTE.—The author acknowledges the co-operation of Mr. Edwin Emerson, Jr., in the preparation of this article.

1895

Folk-Lore and Ethnology
(by the Editors)

Southtrn Workman, 24:8 (Hampton, Va., September 1895), 154–156.

The Hampton Institute, a Virginia college for Indians and Negroes, was founded in 1868 by the American Missionary Association. The administration and students watched the high-minded ideals promulgated during and immediately after the war dissolve in the frenetic days of Reconstruction and its terrible sequelae. *Over President Johnson's veto the Fourteenth Amendment had been passed in 1866 and immediately there were race riots throughout the South and hundreds of Negroes were killed. The Reconstruction Acts were passed, then were steadily negated. Mississippi had its Black Codes, in 1872 the Freedmen's Bureau was dissolved, and after the 1876 election military protection was no longer available in the South. The optimistic days were over and the old regime returned with a vengeance.*

In this atmosphere, Hampton, Fisk, Emerson, Leland, and the many other colleges for nonwhites had the problem of not only attempting to give their students a decent education, but at the same time trying to fit them with skills with which they could survive economically in a white world. This had to be accomplished in the middle of the enemy's territory. Obviously the administrators had to walk a taut line.

Beginning in 1871, Hampton published a monthly magazine, the Southern Workman. *For many years the journal was a hodgepodge of moral tales, letters to teachers, exemplary biographies, sermons, hints to teachers and students and composition writers, reports from and about Indian tribes, and travel accounts, all of this peppered with advertisements for printing presses, a resort hotel, Lydia Pinkham's Vegetable Compound, Webster's International, and other products and services of varying utility. One issue presented the Lord's Prayer in Arabic, Bulgarian, and Hawaiian (5:7 [July 1876], 53).*

There were many etchings—family scenes, Hawaiians, Indians—but not until 1881 did there appear an etching of a Negro, and it was a dilly. The caption read, "Possum fats and simmon Beer. Krismus come but once a year" (10:12 [December 1881], 118). The problem was not simple: the magazine had to help educate the Negro readers, show the Yankee contributors that the college's money was being well spent, and offend no one in the North or South. Such a multiplicity of reader perspectives made the editor's job a nightmare.

For several years, beginning in 1875, the editors mailed a free copy of Cabin and Plantation Songs, as Sung by the Hampton Students to anyone taking out a one-year subscription. This offer was, in all likelihood, mainly an attempt to increase the white readership; it was probably based on the enthusiastic reception accorded the Fisk Jubilee Singers and their successors and emulators. In the early 1880's there were several articles about Indian customs and folklore, but it was not until November 1893 that the editor acknowledged for the first time that the Negro also had folklore. Two important stimuli prompted that acknowledgment—Dvorak's public praise of the Negro songs and the steady recognition of Negro folklore by the Journal of American Folklore, then in its fifth year of publication. The first step in that November issue was a groping one, almost comic in retrospect. It published a letter that Hampton's musical director had sent the editor of the New York Herald. The letter tells us, grimly, that the students are carefully taught to sing spirituals, but the more contact they have with elocution, English, and music teachers, the deader the songs seem to sound. The old former slaves do not think the concerts sound right, "even when slight alterations of adding simple harmonies here and there are made." The director says he often hears, after concerts, "Dose are de same ole tunes, but some way dey don' sound right" (13:11, 174).

As soon as Hampton realized that the uncorrected folklore had a value recognized even by a white composer from another continent, it set out in a direction quite different from the one that had been taken by the music director. In the December 1893 issue of Southern Workman, the editors urged in an open letter to all readers the immediate collection of Negro folklore. After perceptively noting that white men could not do the job, the writer asked for folk tales (mentioning Brer Rabbit and Brer Fox specifically), customs, "traditions of ancestry in Africa, or of transportation to America," "African words surviving in speech or song," ceremonies and superstitions, proverbs and sayings, and songs (22:12, 180–181). A new department, "Folk-Lore and Ethnology," made its first appearance in the next *issue; it reported on the first monthly meeting of the newly founded Hampton Folk-Lore Society (23:1 [January 1894], 15–16).*

For the next six years the column was filled with almost everything that had been requested. Some of the folklore was prettified, but most appeared intact; all but a few of the columns are straightforward presentations of texts or descriptions of customs. Some idea of the richness of Hampton's collections can be gathered by examining the list of these articles appearing in Appendix II of this volume. Even though collectors ranged from barely literate field hands to professors, the collection is one of the most important we have. Only a few folklorists have made reference to the Workman *series—Richard M. Dorson, N. N. Puckett, and Newman I. White among them—and only rarely are the articles mentioned in reading lists or bibliographies.*

The first of the two articles reprinted here includes a reprinting of the original request for information and several sample texts. As can be seen, the range of material, both in genre and style, is wide. If the original files still survive, some folklorists might consider taking steps to publish and preserve the invaluable contents.

Since November, 1893, the SOUTHERN WORKMAN has been trying, through graduates of the School and other colored students in different parts of the South, to make a careful collection and study of Negro Folk-Lore. The work has excited much interest among students of folk-lore, and the collection already made comprises much that is new and valuable. The plan of work was first mapped out and printed in the WORKMAN of November, 1893, in an article which was afterwards printed in circular form for distribution over as wide an area as possible. Copies of this circular may be obtained by application to Miss A. M. Bacon, SOUTHERN WORKMAN Office, Hampton, Va.

The topics outlined for study and inquiry are as follows:—

1. Folk-tales, animal stories, legends, hero stories, fairy tales, etc.
2. Customs, especially in connection with birth, marriage, and death.
3. Traditions of ancestry in Africa or of transportation to America.
4. African words surviving in speech or song.
5. Ceremonies and superstitions, whether in connection with every day happenings, voudoo charms, or Christian worship.
6. Proverbs and sayings.
7. Songs—words or music, or both.

It would be possible for any educated colored man or woman

living in a community of less cultivated persons of his own race to collect a great deal of material along these lines which would be of great scientific value, not only to students of folk-lore, but to the future historians of the Negro race in America. The Hampton graduates resident at the School have formed a Folk-Lore Society, meeting once a month, by means of which the interest in the work has been kept up here. A subject is assigned a month in advance. One member of the society brings in a paper. All prepare themselves by one means or another to add to the information that the paper contains. The meeting is of the most informal character; there is no chairman, the society's secretaries take notes and ask questions on points not made quite clear. If there is formal business to be transacted by vote, the president of the society takes the chair, calls the meeting to order, takes the vote, puts the business through, and then the society drops its forms and becomes a mere social meeting once more.

By means of this society and the interest of non-resident graduates who have read of the Folk-Lore movement month by month in the SOUTHERN WORKMAN, the society has now a good-sized collection of material to be used in some future publication. But there is still a vast amount of material that might be gathered up and brought in that would much enhance the scientific value of the work. Early in our research our attention was attracted to the great number of gruesome hag and witch stories that were to be obtained. In the course of a few months we learned much about the weird beliefs in hags that ride at night and give rise to frightful night-mares, of their changes of form, of the spells by which they may be delayed even when most intent upon their wicked errands, and of the tests by which a neighbor who has night-riding tendencies may be identified. But though we have learned a good deal, we want to learn more. We would like a little more detail in regard to how the hag obtains her fearful power. We would like to know whether hags and witches are the same. We should like reports on the hag and witch belief, and stories about hags and witches from a great many parts of the South, that by a careful study of data drawn from many sources we may try to make out how much of this belief is a survival from Africa and how much is European, which has been held and preserved by the Negroes, after the whites from whom it was originally obtained have forgotten it.

Closely allied to the hag and witch beliefs are the beliefs and practises connected with "conjuration," or voudoo. We should like to hear from observers in localities where these beliefs are still in full force, and to obtain every possible detail in regard to conjurors, their medicines, their spells, their formulas, particular cures wrought or persons "fixed" by their enchantments. We should like to know from what source their powers are believed to be derived, and as much as can be gathered of the history of particular "conjure doctors." Comparison of their beliefs with those of Europe, Africa and Spanish America will afford information in regard to their derivation that will be of value to ethnologists.

Two lines of research which promise interesting results have been opened up during the past year. A paper by Mr. F. D. Banks, Vice-president of the Hampton Folk-Lore Society, delivered before that society, and subsequently printed both in the *American Folk-Lore Journal* and in the SOUTHERN WORKMAN, called attention to the curious riddles and dark sayings used in courtship on the plantations. It resulted in bringing in to us considerable testimony both as to the universality and the variety of such forms of speech among the colored people of the South. It is desired to enlarge our collection of "courtship questions and answers," and all who are interested in this work are earnestly invited to send in matter bearing on this subject.

We have also made an effort to study, as carefully as may be, the forms and ceremonies used in the Negro churches. We have secured, verbatim, some of the sermons and prayers used in these churches, and have endeavored to express, as correctly as possible, the rude rhythmic versification of these religious utterances, showing how the responses of the audience are but the chorus or burden of the song which comes from the preacher's mouth. The fact that many of these prayers and sermons are used over and over by their authors and are handed down from older to younger preachers, increases their resemblance to poetic rather than merely prose utterances, and renders it the more important that they be collected and preserved. They are not so much the work of individuals as they are the composition of a race in its childhood, and are a part of the folk-lore of that race. Every effort should be made to note down and preserve all sermons, prayers, and religious songs that can be obtained, for through these means much of the emotion that was repressed by the system of slavery found its noblest utterance. We give a few specimens of matter collected along different lines, showing how wide is the field that we wish to cover, and we earnestly entreat all who read this article with interest to write at once to the WORKMAN for copies of our circular and other matter relating to the work.

If a rat gnaw your clothes it is a sign you are going to move. Never mend the clothes yourself, it will bring bad luck if you do.

If you kill the first snake you meet in the spring, you will prevail over your enemy during the year.

Stir soap with a sassafras stick, especially the roots. It will make it come.

WEATHER SIGNS

In case of drought, kill a snake and turn its belly toward the sun, and it will soon rain.

If you see a whirlwind go toward the branch or any water, it is a sign of rain.

A circle around the moon containing more than five stars promises cold weather.

To hear a kildeer crying in the morning or evening means cold weather. A hog running around with straw in his mouth is another sign.

When turkeys go to roost with their heads all turned in the same direction, it indicates stormy weather.

MOON LORE

Cut your hair on the full moon and it will get dry and brittle. Cut it on the new moon and it will grow with the moon.

If you kill pork on the decrease of the moon, it shrinks in the pot.

FOLK MEDICINE

Take grave-yard dirt and tie on a dog-bite. It will cure the wound and every tooth will drop out of the dog's head.

Put hog's teeth around a child's neck to make its teeth come easily.

If a baby is bow-legged, sweep down his legs with a broom-sedge broom.

OMENS FROM DREAMS

To dream of the dead is a sign of rain.

If you dream of eggs it's a sign of a quarrel.

To dream of a mud-turtle is a sign of wealth.

Dream of muddy water, a sign of death.

To shake a table cloth out of the door after sunset is a sign of death.

If two people sit back to back, the younger will die.

If you sneeze at table, it is a sign you will hear of a death.

If a peach or apple tree blooms twice in the season, it is a sign of death.

LOVE CHARMS, DIVINATIONS, ETC.

Take an egg, put it in front of the fire place and put a straw on it. Call your lover's name, and if your lover loves you the straw will turn on the egg.

MISCELLANEOUS SUPERSTITIONS

Never sleep "crosswise of the world."

Never lift an umbrella in the house, or carry a hoe into the house on your shoulder.

It is bad luck to put fire to fire.

Bad luck to turn a chunk in the fire without spitting on the end.

If anyone do you a wrong, get a rooster and turn a wash-pot over it, and make all the people that you suspect go up and make a cross on the pot. When the one who has wronged you makes the mark the rooster will crow.

If a man has been murdered and the murderer can not be discovered, take a bone of the murdered man and make it into some household article. If, at any time in the future, the murderer should touch that bone it will bleed, no matter how white and dry it may have become.

In Courtship Questions we can hardly do better than reproduce the little dialogue given in Mr. Banks' article as a sample of the kind of material we wish.

HE: My dear kin' miss, has you any objections to me drawing my cher to yer side, and revolvin' de wheel of my conversation around de axle of your understandin'?

SHE: I has no objection to a gentleman addressin' me in a proper manner, kin' sir.

HE: My dear miss, de worl' is a howlin' wilderness full of devourin' animals, and you has got to walk through hit. Has you made up yer min' to walk through hit by yerself, or wid some bold wahyer?

SHE: Yer 'terrigation, kin' sir, shall be answered in a ladylike manner, ef you will prove to me dat it is not for er form and er fashion dat you puts de question.

HE: Dear miss, I would not so impose on a lady like you as to as' her a question for a form an' a fashion. B'lieve me, kin' miss, dat I has a pertickler objick in ingagin' yer in conversation dis afternoon.

SHE: Dear kin' sir, I has known many a gentleman to talk wid wise words and flatterin' looks, and at de same time he may have a deceivin' heart. May I as' yer, kin' gentleman, ef you has de full right to address a lady in a pertickler manner?

HE: I has, kin' miss. I has seen many sweet ladies, but I has never up to dis day an' time lef' de highway of a single gentleman to foller dese beacon lights. But now, kin' miss, as I looks in yer dark eyes, and sees yer hones' face, and hears yer kind voice, I mus' confess, dear lady, dat I would be joyous to come to yer beck and call in any time of danger.

SHE: Den, kin' sir, I will reply in answer to your 'terrigation in de fus' place, sense I think you is a hones' gentleman, dat I feels dat a lady needs de pertection of a bol' wahyer in dis worl' where dere's many wil' animals and plenty of danger.

HE: Den, kin' honored miss, will you condescen' to encourage me to hope dat I might, some glorious day in de future, walk by yer side as a perteckter?

SHE: Kin' sir, ef you think you is a bol' wahyer I will condescend to let you pass under my obervation from dis day on, an' ef you proves wuthy of a confidin' lady's trus', some lady might be glad to axcept yer pertection—and dat lady might be me.

Under the head of Religious Customs we have made note of the process of conversion—how the seeker finds a sign, how he is received and baptized, and the phraseology and forms of words that are used in connection with his different states of mind at different stages in his religious growth. We have noted, too the shouts or spirituals which belong to the ceremony of baptism and reception in the churches.

We have learned of a ceremony called a "footwash," which is practised in some of the Negro churches in Virginia. We would like to know whether the custom is universal and whether the order of exercises varies in different churches, or whether it is substantially the same wherever found at all. We want, too, a full account of all peculiar religious ceremonies from all parts of the South, and as many sermons, prayers, and songs, reported verbatim, as can be gathered. With this material it will be possible to reconstruct the religious life and beliefs of the generation that is now passing away, and to preserve for all time the record of what the southern Negroes thought and felt and hoped and believed in those early stages of their development, which we are studying.

Of the Games and Riddles common among the colored people we have already collected quite a number. Many of them, as "King William was King George's son," "London Bridge is burning down," and others of a similar character, show, of course, their English origin, and are played just about in the same way among the colored people as among the English children in the mother country. Others, like "Peep-Squirrel," "Gimme de gourd to drink water," "Rain a little bit, Snow a little bit," leave their origin in greater doubt. A comparison of the whole circle of games and riddles in common use among the colored people with the games and riddles of Europe, Africa, and aboriginal America would be of value, could we complete our collection.

Of Stories we have not thus far collected a great many, but enough have come in to show that this part of the field is extremely fruitful. The chief trouble about making the collection of stories seems to be in the fact that it is much harder for our correspondents to find time to write out a story than it is to send off a few riddles or signs, or the words of a song or notes on customs or dialect. We have, however, on our list such titles as the following: "The Witch Cats," "Why the Tiger is Striped," "Old Hag and Jack Lantern," "Where de Owl fus' come from," "How Brer Rabbit Won de Case," "The Conquest of a Hag," "Brer Rabbit tries to get even with Brer Rooster," "Why Some Men are Black," etc. Stories of this kind, when reported for publication should be given as nearly as possible in the words of the narrator by the cabin fire. No attempt should be made to improve them in any way, for their scientific value depends largely upon their being the truthful record of the words of the original story teller.

In the study of the ancestry of the American Negroes but little progress has been made, and yet it is a matter of as great ethnological importance as any that we have undertaken. While undoubtedly most of the American slaves were imported from the West Coast of Africa there is every reason to believe that they represented a great variety of African tribes. Has a tradition of former tribal relationships been preserved among the descendants of those African importations, or did the horrors of the middle passage blot out all remembrance of a free and savage past? Are there not in many parts of the South to-day Negroes who point with pride to some African chief or medicine man as their ancestor? Have not some families preserved, even in the midst of that weakening of family ties which the system of slavery brought, the remembrance of descent from men or women who were distinguished among the generality of slaves for culture, mental, moral or physical characteristics? It is our wish to gather and preserve all such traditions and remembrances—to make out of the scattered, unwritten history which now lies in the brains and hearts of the old folks an ordered and comprehensive whole that will show to all who have interest in it the past of the Afro-American. Such a picture as this, to be complete, must show, too, the admixture of white and Indian blood that belongs to so many of those who came out of slavery; must give whatever traditions there may be of how that lighter blood was mingled with the darker. Prof. Shaler, of Harvard University, makes the following suggestions:—

"I note at the moment one or two lines of inquiry which you might seek to make.

"First; Are there any survivors of the latter importation of blacks from Africa? Can their children, of pure blood, be identified?

"Second: What proportion of the colored people in particular settlements, the numbers being in each case given, are of mixed blood?

"Third: Are there any families among the Negroes characterized by straight hair along with a normally dark skin? I suspect the existence of some Arab blood among our Negroes, and would like to have evidence on this point."

Work of this kind can only be done by an educated and sympathetic observer in the community in the midst of which he lives and works. But if it is done even in one community with any degree of thoroughness it will be of lasting scientific and historical value.

And now we have gone over the whole ground thus far taken up in the researches of the Folk-Lore Society. It is our hope that some of those who read this article may be moved to help us in our work. Correspondence in regard to the matter may be addressed to Miss A. M. Bacon, SOUTHERN WORKMAN Office, Hampton, Va.

1895

Folk-Lore and Ethnology: Conjuring and Conjure Doctors

by A. M. Bacon

Southern Workman, 24:11 (Hampton, Va., November 1895), 193–194, and 24:12 (December 1895), 209–211.

This article is based on student papers, evidence that the Hampton teachers had realized the value of incorporating the students' own background in their teaching, quite impressive when we remember that Dewey's The School and Society *wasn't published until 1899, and his* Democracy and Education *until 1916. For a full discussion of the practices described here, see N. N. Puckett,* Folk Beliefs of the Southern Negro *(Chapel Hill, 1926).*

Conjuring has not passed out of the folk consciousness. In the 1950's, Richard M. Dorson collected numerous tales of conjure experiences; see his two collections, Negro Folktales in Michigan *(Cambridge, Mass., 1956) and* Negro Tales from Pine Bluff, Arkansas, and Calvin, Michigan *(Bloomington, 1958), both of which have excellent comparative notes. See also* Drums and Shadows: Survival Studies among the Georgia Coastal Negroes, *Savannah Unit of the Georgia Writers' Project, WPA (Athens, Ga. 1940).*

It is difficult here to make any classification of the things used in conjuring which will have any value except as a mere arbitrary distinction for the sake of ease in enumerating and remembering in some intelligible order the great variety of media for the charms cited by the authors of the compositions from which our data are drawn. We will however, for the sake of convenience, classify into

(1.) Poisons.

(2.) Charms.

Of poisons derived from substances known or believed to be poisonous and administered in food or drink a number of cases are cited.

A drink of whiskey is poisoned and offered to the victim; an apple is poisoned and given in church on Sunday. One instance is given of "toad heads, scorpion heads, hair, nine pins and needles baked in a cake and given to a child who became deathly sick." By another of our writers it is said that "some go in the woods and get lizards and little ground hogs and snakes and dry them and then powder them all up together in liquor and give them to drink, or pick a chance and put it in their food so they can eat it." Another case is mentioned of a conjurer who caught a snake, cut his head off, hung him up by his tail and let the blood drop into a can. Then he went out and caught a lizard, killed him, took his blood and mixed it with the snake's blood. This mixture was done up in a bundle and sent to the victim. He drank it up, and in two minutes was lying on the floor speechless. In this case the victim was saved by an old doctor who was brought in and rubbed him about twelve hours. One woman swallowed a lizard in a cup of coffee and was poisoned thereby. In another case cabbage, presumably poisoned, was given to the victim with evil results. Again, horse hair is put into the food or a preparation of poisonous snakes and lizards is mixed with the whiskey. The theory in regard to the poisonous effects of hair is thus stated by a boy whose own hair had been baked in bread and given him to eat. The conjure-doctor told him that if he had eaten it the hair would cling round his heart strings and would have afflicted him so that he would not be able to work and after a while it would kill him. It required no belief in the supernatural whatever to make one afraid of persons whose business it is to devise poisons to place in the food of their victims, and, if the evidence of our collection of compositions is to be trusted, there was on the plantations in the old days a vast amount of just that sort of thing. That the poison did not always produce the desired effect was due rather to a lack of knowledge than to a lack of zeal on the part of the conjurer, and if roots and herbs, snakes and lizards, hairs and other disgusting objects could be worked into the food and drink of the victim it was undoubtedly the most certain way of despatching the business to the satisfaction of his enemy. But this method of revenge, because it was the most direct and certain, was the most easily discovered, and we find that other methods seem to have been more popular. Just as poisoning is less direct and therefore safer than clubbing or shooting, so "fixing" by means of a charm is safer than either, and charms seem to have been relied on for working evil, to a very great extent.

The form of the charm which comes most near to the simple poisoning, of which we have already given examples, is the passing of the spell to the victim by handing to him some conjured article or placing it where he can pick it up. In these examples it is contact alone that transmits the evil; the charmed or poison thing need not be eaten. A sweet potato on a stump in the victim's potato patch has been known to cause pain just as soon as it was touched by the one for whom it was intended. A woman, picking up chips, picked up a small bundle folded in rags; the next chip stuck to her hand and she was conjured. A pair of new shoes just come from the shoe-maker causes such pain that the victim cannot walk. He continues to grow weaker and thinner and to suffer even after the shoes are removed and at last dies of the effect of conjured shoes. A bottle of cologne presented to a girl by her unsuccessful rival puts her eyes out when she smells of it. Something put on the gate-post causes swelling of the hands. One instance is, of a girl who detects her father-in-law putting something into her shoes after she is supposed to have gone to sleep. She burns the shoes and so avoids the trick; the shoes in burning make a noise like a bunch of fire works. In another case a small red bag, (presumably filled with occult miniatures) is fixed to the sole of the victim's foot. In one case a carving knife is conjured, supposing that the cook will be the first person to use it, but the charm goes astray because the seamstress has occasion to use the knife, and the charm goes from it to her. Some conjurers accomplish their ends by throwing hair balls at their victims.

But charms seem to be most frequently conveyed by even more indirect methods than those thus far enumerated. A baby is conjured by the presence in its crib of something all wrapped up in hair and all kinds of other queer looking things. The bundle when burned showed strange variety of colors. A colored man got angry at a woman and tricked her by the following complicated charm. He took some blue cloth and cut out several chickens and sewed them up after filling them with some kind of dust and a lot of needles and pins. He covered these with feathers so that they looked precisely like real chickens, and then sewed them up in his victim's bed. Conjure balls, snakes and all kinds of reptiles are often found in the beds of those who have been "conjured." In other cases the fatal bundle or bottle is secreted in some corner of the room in which the victim lives or is placed in the road over which he most often walks. A charm in the shape of a small rubber ball may be placed in the chimney corner, or poison may be put in a bottle and buried in the path, (in some cases upside down). A sick woman, who had almost pined away to skin and bones, sent for a conjure-doctor. He went at once to the hearth, took up a brick and found sticking in a cloth six pins and needles. He took them up, put salt on them, and threw them in the river. The needles and pins were said to be the cause of so many pains. In other cases poisonous balls of various sizes, filled with roots, herbs and other mixtures, were put in the road. They would have no effect on any but the intended victim. These charms or tricks seem to have been made personal by securing something from the body of the victim, as a strand of his hair, or some earth from his foot prints.

If you fail to get near enough to your victim to place the spell in his room or his hand or his bed or his path, you may yet, if you are skilful, succeed in carrying out your fell design by simply burying your charm under his door-step or in his yard where he may never see it or come in contact with it, but where it can work untold evil to him and his—under the door step if you can, near the house if you can't do that, but failing of that, almost anywhere in the yard will do if the spell is potent. A black bottle containing a liquid mixture and nine pins and nine needles is a favorite charm. Sometimes a bundle containing salt, pepper and a silver five cents; sometimes needles, pins, hairs, snake-heads; again it is salt, red pepper, anvil dust and a kind of root that conjure doctors always carry in their pockets. In the latter case, our informant tell us that "when putting this down they have a ceremony and request the devil to cause this to have the desired effect," specifying in the request the part of the body of the victim which it is desired to injure. A small red flannel bag filled with new pins, small tacks and other things, and buried under the gate-sill made a horse refuse to enter the gate. After working over the horse for an hour, the driver looked under the sill, found the charm and removed it, and the horse walked quietly in at the gate. Jelly-fish taken out of the water, dried, powdered and put into small bags are used for conjuring. In one case, when search was made for the charm there was found in the ground a tin cup seven inches deep and three in diameter, called a "conjure cup." It contained little balls, some like lumps of tar and some like sulphur and other different colors. When burned these balls gave "beautiful blazes." In one case a bottle full of snakes was buried by the doorstep. The first one to come out in the morning stepped over it and fell. A preserve jar found buried in one garden contained "a snake and several other insects and something else wrapped in cloth," which the finder did not open but threw away. In one case, where there was reason to suspect conjuring, a bottle filled with roots, stones, and a reddish powder was found under the doorstep, and in the yard more bottles with beans, nails and the same powder. The man burned them up and got well.

Again a package in the shape of a brick was found and inside of it a "tin trunk and a great many articulate creatures." Another of our writers tells us that "some of their simplest things are salt, pepper, needles, pins, black bottles and all kinds of roots. I have seen one of their roots which they called 'devil's shoe string.' It is a long, wiry-looking root resembling the smallest roots of a sweet potato-vine."

With this variety of gruesome and disgusting things, did the plantation conjurers essay to work evil among the credulous people with whom they were surrounded. The next phase of our study is to inquire what were the evils that were laid to their door as the result of their dealing in roots, herbs, snakes, and mysteries.

The disease which is caused by conjuring may be recognized in its early stages, in the first place by the suddenness of the attack. The victim is seized with a sharp pain in some part of her body; later, swelling and other symptoms follow, but the beginning of the attack can usually be traced to a sharp pain which followed directly upon handling, stepping over, or swallowing the charm. Another, and perhaps the surest sign that the disease is the result of a spell or trick, is that the patient grows worse rather than better under treatment of regular physicians. When this is the case it is well to call in a conjure doctor at once or it may be too late, for there are cases where even after the spell is removed the victim fails to recover from the injuries it has already wrought.

As the disease develops itself the symptoms become more severe and terrible in their nature. In many cases snakes and lizards are seen running up and down under the flesh, or are even known to show their heads from the sufferer's mouth. One example is given of a woman possessed by a lizard that "would run up and down her throat and hollow when she would be a-talking." Another case is of a man whose food did him no good. The conjure doctor told him that he had been conjured and that inside of him were a number of small snakes which ate up the food as fast as he ate it. Another woman who had lizards crawling in her body was obliged to eat very often to keep the lizards from eating her. This possession by reptiles of various kinds seems to be a part in almost every evil wrought by the conjurer, and instances are too numerous and too horrible for a more detailed review of them in this paper. Sometimes when direct evidence of these reptiles fails to appear during the life of the patient, a post mortem brings them to light and establishes the truth of the doctor's diagnosis.

Another evidence that the disease is of a magical origin is in the strange noises made by the patient. Numerous instances are given of sufferers who howled or barked like dogs. One example is given of a woman who "howled like a dog, crowed like a cock, barked like a fox and mewed like a cat and made all sorts of noises before she died." One boy used to walk on all fours and howl like a dog. Another man who was conjured "would have ways like a dog, growling and gritting his teeth."

From these symptoms it is but a brief step to insanity of all kinds, and many cases are cited where the insane patient is regarded as "conjured" by his relative. One woman could not go further than a mile. "When she had walked a mile she would get out of her head so she would have to stop, so she could gather her mind to go back." A girl when conjured "ran wild and drowned herself." One woman "was very sick and almost crazy was conjured to her bed for several months. And now she has some kind of spells that come upon her, when she lies like one dead for about an hour. She cannot bear any kind of medicine to be used about her. She says that she can hear all that is said to her but cannot speak." It is unnecessary to cite all the instances given in the compositions. They are numerous enough to go towards proving that insanity on the plantation was often laid to "conjuration" and consequently took in the patient the form that the belief in conjuration would naturally give it, just as in New Testament times it was believed to be demoniacal possession and took that form in its manifestations.

When it is once decided that the sufferer from mysterious symptoms of any kind has been conjured, there remains no hope except through the conjure doctor. He must be sent for at once, as delay is always dangerous and often fatal. There are few settlements of colored people in which the belief in conjuration is prevalent, in which there is not to be found some person distinguished for his skill as a conjure doctor. Of their personal peculiarities it is not my part to speak. Of that you already have learned through Miss Herron's paper, but of their special methods of procedure when summoned to cure disease, we must try to get some general idea from the mass of testimony presented by the compositions.

The conjure doctor has five distinct services to render to his patient. He must (1) tell him whether he is conjured or not, (2) he must find out who conjured him, (3) he must search for and find the "trick" and destroy it, (4) he must cure the patient, (5) he will if the patient wishes turn back the trick upon the one who made it. But as a rule before he does anything for the patient he demands and receives a large fee. Should he find business slack he will sometimes take it upon himself to secure patients by visiting certain persons and telling them that they have been or are about to be conjured, and often presenting irrefragable proofs in the shape of a pin stuck in the north side of a distant tree, or a bottle dug up at a certain designated spot in the yard; he extracts a payment of money for his services in preventing the evil sure to follow if he is not engaged by a good-sized retainer to prevent it. A conjure doctor summoned to attend a case of mysterious illness in a family will frequently begin his examination by putting a small piece of silver into the mouth or hand of the sufferer. Should the silver turn black, there is no doubt about the diagnosis. The silver piece is not always tried, in some cases the very nature of the seizure proclaims at once to the doctor that it is the work of conjurers. The next step is to study the nature of the disease and search out and destroy the trick by which it was caused. In one case the conjure doctor recognized the disease by the trembling of the patient's fingers as he came in at the door. The poison had not then taken much effect on the patient but the conjure doctor assured the sufferer that, without attention it would kill her. In another case the doctor informed his patient that the charm was fixed to work with the moon and tides. When the tide was coming in he would be worse, when going out he would be better. A case is mentioned of a girl who had been suffering for a long time from a sore and swollen foot, until at last a conjure doctor was called to her relief. "As soon as he saw the foot he said that she was conjured and that it was done by an old man who wanted to marry her, and that it was done at church one night." Then he said, "I will try to cure you in the name of the Lord." Then he asked her for a pin and scratched her foot on the side and got some blood and he rubbed some cream on it and said, "God bless her," and he called her name, and the next morning this girl, who had been ill for nine months, "walked out of doors without crutch or cane." In another case in which a bright silver piece held in the patient's hand had turned perfectly black in five minutes, the patient was cupped three times. In each case the cupping horn came away filled with live lizards, frogs and snakes that had their abode in her. Later she was bathed in an infusion of mullein and moss made with boiling water in a tub. After the bath the water was thrown towards the sunset and this line repeated "As the sun sets in the West so should the works of the Devil end in judgement." This treatment did her good and she recovered rapidly. Another doctor sawed a tree in the middle and put the patient through it four times. He then cupped him and buried the things that came out of him under a tree at sunset. Still another doctor would begin his treatment by making the patient swallow a small piece of silver.

He said the conjuration would stick to the silver and his medicine would cure the person conjured. Another practitioner arrived when sent for with a bottle filled with herbs, roots, and leaves; with these he made a tea which acted as an emetic and the patient threw up a variety of reptiles. Again a conjure doctor came and chewed some roots and did a great many other things. In one light case of tricking the patient was merely given some roots to carry in his pocket and something to rub with.

Either after or before the cure of the patient is well under way, the doctor will make an effort to find the "trick" or "conjure," and identify the miscreant who has caused the trouble. He may be able to tell immediately and without visiting the spot, just where the cause of the trouble is buried. An instance is given of an old man who, visited by a woman who lived twelve miles away, was able to tell the patient after one look at her sore foot exactly the spot in her own yard, where, if she would dig, she would find a large black bottle, containing a mixture, placed there by one of her neighbors to trick her. She went home, dug and found it was as he said. In other cases the detection of the trick seems to be more difficult and the doctor is obliged to have recourse to cards or other means of obtaining the truth. One of our writers tells us of a conjure doctor who, on visiting a patient, cut his cards and told her that she was poisoned by a woman who wanted her place, and that the conjure bottle was under the sill of her door. Every time she stepped over the sill one drop of the poison dried up, and when the last drop dried she would die. The conjure doctors, seemed to have an objection to name the enemy who had cast the spell. In some cases they would simply undertake to describe him; in other cases a more complicated device was resorted to: "They would find a bundle of roots under the door step or floor. After they had found the roots they would ask for a flat iron. They would take the iron and a piece of brown paper and draw the image of the person who put the roots there."

After the enemy has been identified the conjure doctor may be of further use in securing revenge for the injured person. There are many instances cited where the charm has been turned against the one who sent it. This the conjure doctor may do by a variety of devices, some of which easily commend themselves to the ignorant minds with which he deals. It is said that if any one tricks you and you discover the trick and put that into the fire, you burn your enemy, or if you throw it into the running water you drown him. One instance is given of a conjure laid down in the path of a young man. He saw it in time, picked it up with two sticks, carried it into the house, and put it in the fire. This took great effect upon the old man "who danced and ran and hollowed and jumped and did a little of everything, but still the bundle burned," until at last the old man acknowledged everything he had done. Another of our writers tells us that "If the composition used in conjuring can be found and given to the conjure-doctor, he will throw the charm from the person conjured to the one who did it. This affects him so strongly that he will come to the house and ask for something. If he gets it his charm will return, if not it will end on himself." One writer cites the case of a man who had been made lame by a lizard in his leg who was told by a conjure-doctor what to do, and as a result his enemy went about as long as he lived with that lizard in his leg.

And now for the ounce of prevention that is worth the pound of cure in conjuration as in other things. Silver in the shoe or hung around the neck seems to be the most universal counter-charm. A horse shoe nailed over the door or even hidden under the sill will keep out conjurer's spells as well as hags and witches. A smooth stone in the shoe was recommended in one case, in another case, a goose quill filled with quick-silver worn below the knee. In one case where a man had been under the care of a conjure doctor and recovered the doctor would not allow him to visit unless he wore a silver coin in his shoe and a silver ring on his right hand.

1898

A Weddin' and a Buryin' in the Black Belt

by Susan Showers

New England Magazine, XVIII (Boston, 1898), 478–483.

In addition to Miss Showers' interesting descriptions of the marriage and burial ceremonies, this article has two points of especial interest: the peculiar wallpaper and the key game. Among the many beliefs concerned with hags, hag-riding, and witches were a set that indicated that hags were compulsive counters and could be kept in check by objects that took a long time to count. One might protect himself from nocturnal attacks by placing, just inside the door, a handful of sand, a newspaper, a sifter, or a broom; the hag would have to stop to count the grains or letters or holes or straws. One might place a Bible under the pillow—the hag would have to count all the letters before getting down to the business of possession. The computations kept the hag busy until daylight, at which time it had to scoot home or be captured. Folklorist Lydia Parrish papered the walls of her Sea Island cottage with pages from the New York Times*'s financial section; one presumes she was unmolested. For more on the "counting instinct," see N. N. Puckett,* Folk Beliefs of the Southern Negro *([Chapel Hill, 1926], pp. 163–165).*

Games similar to "Run dem Keys" are still current. For one example and an extensive discussion of the function of games, see the prefatory remarks and game # 22, "Sambo Rainey," in J. D. Elder's "Song Games from Trinidad and Tobago," PAFS, *XVI (1965).*

I.

One of our girls was going to be married. We were a little surprised when the news greeted us on our return from our summer vacation. It would be a relief to the discipline of the school,—for little Matilda, though warm-hearted, was a reckless, flyaway sort of child; but it seemed a pity, for she was only sixteen. But marriage at sixteen is not at all uncommon in the Black Belt. The old people, in spite of their own hard experience, think it quite the proper thing, and the young people are only slowly learning better. Often the hard and sordid conditions of life make early marriages almost a necessity. I remember how once in our rambles we came across a poor hut, where we found a girl of fourteen, whom we had known before, now several weeks married.

"I had to, Miss," she said with a sort of stolid pathos. "My folks was dead, and dis am a bad kentry. What could I do? I didn' want toe git married needer, an' my husban' ain' a good man, but I couldn' he'p mysef."

But this was a wedding of a different sort. Great preparations were being made, and the clans were gathering far and near. An invitation came of course, to the School Settlement, and we went. A dilapidated double carriage drawn by a couple of vicious looking but subdued mules was engaged for the occasion from a neighboring farmer. This carriage was considered the very essence of luxury and style. A moonlight drive of an hour brought us to the scene of the festivities.

The house was a tiny board cottage, with a living room containing two beds, and a narrow lean-to at the back. The enclosure in front was swept clear of every spear of grass and trodden down to a hard smoothness, according to the prevailing custom of the "best families." Into this enclosure was crowded a dusky throng of men, women and children, waiting in the moonlight for proceedings to begin. It was a jolly crowd, but not a boisterous one. One pious aunty whispered in our ears that we "would find the doin's different at a weddin' of de worl's people—but dese year is all church folks." The minister, not the magistrate, was to perform the ceremony.

As honored guests, we were allowed to go inside and sit in state in a row of splint bottomed chairs placed along one end of the room. The picture of the little room that the feeble flaring light of the one kerosene lamp revealed is one that I shall not soon forget. The room was neat and tidy, and every effort known to the owners had been made to render it attractive. The walls were freshly papered with old periodicals, and a new set of gay advertising cards had replaced the old ones. The fireplace had been filled with green branches, for it was a warm night, and the floor was freshly swept and scrubbed. The beds were spotless and in perfect order, and around them had been draped fresh white sheets for curtains.

Under the awning made by these curtains sat the frightened little bride to be, with her future husband. She was a slight, graceful mulatto girl, with sharp, clear cut features and crinkly dark brown hair.

Into this was twisted and fastened a skimpy wisp of coarse white muslin to serve for a bridal veil, and around the pretty, delicate head was arranged an ugly wreath of coarse artificial flowers. The bridal dress was a cheap white cotton net threaded with stripes of glittering silver tinsel. A pair of white silk mitts and white shoes completed the outfit.

Yet it looked picturesque enough contrasted with the black suit and blacker face of the bridegroom. We scanned his face with some anxiety, for if our poor flighty child must marry so young, we hoped that she might marry well. It was a kind face, much older than her own, and had no suggestion of brutality or roughness in it.

There were two giggling, self conscious bridesmaids, one in white and the other in pink, which they had tried to make very fine, and two groomsmen also, if I remember rightly.

When the time for the ceremony came, the bridal party filed out into the front yard and grouped themselves, and the ceremony was performed in the moonlight. It seemed as romantic as a leaf out of an old story book. After it was over, the people came up quietly and shook hands with the bride. This quiet and orderly proceeding was quite different from one witnessed by some of us two or three years ago before at a different kind of a wedding. But that was among the "world's people." The ceremony on that occasion was performed by a red faced magistrate in a flannel shirt, who at its conclusion fired a pistol into the air as a signal for the spectators to make a romping chase around the cabin after the bride, the one first catching and kissing her being the next to be married, according to an old sign.

After the handshaking we went inside and into the little back room, where the supper was laid on a long narrow table. Around this gathered the bridal party, the minister, the guests from the school, and such others as could find standing room. The table was covered in every available spot with cakes of all sizes and shapes, plain and decorated, large and small. There must have been forty or fifty of them, to say nothing of the small cakes and biscuits and fried chicken and knick-knacks heaped at each plate. Everything was clean, but such unsystematic profusion would have taken away our appetites if we had any.

It is "cabin custom" that the hostess must never eat with her guests. More than once I have felt awkward enough, on being invited to a dinner, to sit down in state to a groaning board while my hostess waited on me or kept off the flies with a green branch while I ate. Sometimes the latter duty is relegated to some child of the family, and the hostess then gives her undivided attention to your wants, for while she does not eat, you are expected to, and any failure on your part to eat heartily and zealously is considered a slight.

We were therefore not surprised that the bride and groom ate nothing, but stood in solemn silence while we endeavored to do justice to the elaborate display before us. After we left the table, the crowd came, and then there was no holding back, I fancy, from the good things of the feast.

After supper everybody went out into the moonlight again, and "ring games" of different kinds were started. One of these I watched especially, trying to catch the words of the song that accompanied it. Those taking part were arranged in a circle. Two walked up and down the center, while all joined in singing what seemed to be:—

Lonesome without you,
  Lonesome, lonesome;
Lonesome without you,
  Lonesome, lonesome.

The singing was accompanied with rhythmical motions of the feet and body. After a time the two in the center would pair off with others in the circle, new ones taking their places—and so on. I have heard much and read much of the demoralizing effect of these games, of the frenzied excess of physical motion that accompanies them, and of their weakening influence on the moral nature; and I do not doubt that these features sometimes appear where there is no restraining influence to prevent them. I have seen indications of the former sometimes, even among the children, when the games were continued too long; for the negroes are a tropical race and especially susceptible to any rhythmic influence. But here there were no signs of excess of any kind. Even if this moderation were a result of the few years' training in school which a part of those present had had, it was certainly most encouraging. My only possible regret was that some more rational form of amusement could not take the place of one so childish. Apart from that—well, I have seen more suggestion of vulgarity in a country dance in a northern village.

Another game of the same sort was one called "Run dem Keys." A bunch of keys or some other jingling object is passed quickly from hand to hand outside the circle, while one in the center sings, the others joining:

Run dem keys
  Loud, loud,
Run dem keys
  Loud, loud.

Then some one in the circle jingles them and passes them on, all singing:

Back o' me Sophy,
Back o' me, Sophy.

The one in the centre endeavors to find and capture the keys, the others to conceal them and tantalize him. A great deal of good natured fun was got out of this game, and I fancy the fun reached its height after we left, which we did about eleven o'clock, leaving everything in full tide.

It was all very humble and poor and crude we told ourselves on our way homeward; and yet there was a rude poetry in the scene, softened as it was by the mild Southern moonlight. The sunny cheerfulness of the people, who make the best of their hard lives, the delicate prettiness of the bride, which even the tawdry dress could not conceal, the manifest attempts to decorate the little home, all touched us; and so did the ingenuous frankness of the bride, our little Matilda, as she told us in saying good bye that she wasn't half so scared as she thought she would be, that we must tell all the other teachers "howdy" for her, and that she was going to keep her little house fixed up "*all* de time," because the teachers might "slip up" on her any day.

II.

I had never attended a negro funeral. I had heard of some peculiar customs, connected with them, and had learned of the "Burial Societies" so common in the South. I had often been obliged to refuse my pupils in a Virginia school when they asked to be excused because they had "got to turn out," which meant that they belonged to one of these societies and must go or pay a fine unless they could present some good excuse. I suppose that these societies must have grown up out of the poverty or improvidence of a people who had never learned to look ahead. But of the burial customs of the far South I knew nothing.

I was glad therefore of the chance that brought me one day in the way of a country funeral, or rather "buryin'," for there is a distinction. The opportunity came one day when I was out walking with a fellow teacher. We were not directing our steps to any particular spot, and had no further thought as we walked along than to enjoy the soft air and the fragrant smell of the pines,—when all at once we became aware of a hurrying throng of men, women and children, all hastening in the same direction. They seemed to have an object in view, too, another surprise in this sleepy land of procrastination. All had expectant looks on their faces, and many of the dusky, soft-eyed children wore the clean starched pinafores reserved for special occasions.

Upon inquiry we learned that "dey gwine be a buryin' up toe de cemmetry. Bill Shelby way outen de kentry don die las' night an' dey fotch 'im up yeah foh de buryin'." "Up yeah" was indicated by an indefinite sweep of the thumb that conveyed but little idea of the locality to our minds. But we joined the crowd and moved on toward the "cemmetry." We reached it after a scramble of some fifteen or twenty minutes. It was located on a bleak hillside seamed and gashed by rains and washouts which gave the peculiar appearance of desolation so familiar to dwellers in certain sections of the South. Once I had heard an agriculturist allude to this appearance of the country by saying that the "poor hills were skinned and bleeding." On this desolate site was located the cemetery. Some of the graves were marked with a wooden slab, some with a stake only, and many not at all. There was a goodly number decorated with bits of broken glass and china and old bottles—a survival, I fancy of an old heathen custom brought from Africa, for I have heard the missionaries from Africa allude to it. Many of these graves were placed on the steepest part of the slope, and the rains had made sad havoc among them.

"Foh de lan' sakes! look a dem grabes," said one old woman to another as they toiled rheumatically upward. "Seems if dey mout fin' some place toe bury po' cullad folks cepen dis yeah hill."

"Foh de lan' sakes," echoed her companion, "dey don' all be washed away fo' Gabriel don trump 'em up." And it seemed as if they might.

The spot selected for the grave was at the very top of the hill, and thither the people toilsomely repaired. The "onlies' mohner," wife of the deceased, arrived in a rumbling two-wheeled cart, drawn by a mule, and with the rude pine coffin placed away at the back. Sympathetic friends helped the bereaved one to alight, while some of the men gently lowered the coffin and placed it in the new made grave. We were told by a bystander that the "funeral" would take place at some future time when it was convenient for the friends to meet. This is according to southern custom among the Negro folk. Sometimes the "funeral" will be "preached" several months or even a year after the "buryin'." This may be done so that the "mohners" may get together from distant places; that they may prepare suitable clothing, or that the preacher may get ready an appropriate "discourse" for the occasion. Sometimes this custom of holding eulogistic services is taken up in the schools. I remember attending one such service arranged and conducted by students, where the virtues of four deceased classmates were dwelt upon in turn; and one of these had been dead at least three years.

The present congregation was a curious study as it gathered around the hillside grave in the open air. Some of the faces were sympathetic, all were curious. Old age and youth and childhood were all represented. The ignorant everywhere have a morbid curiosity about anything that pertains to the last long sleep; and in the plantation Negro this curiosity reaches an abnormal development, due partly no doubt to his quick sympathy and partly to the atmosphere of superstition in which he lives.

As the gathering represented all ages, so it did all gradations of costume and types of feature. The would be fashionable young lady who had "been to school" was there, and the old aunty in garments of ancient cut patched together from some "barrel" sent down from the North by the benevolent distributor of half worn clothing. The ubiquitous youth in plaid trousers and dangling watch chain was also to be seen, as well as his self-respecting brother in quiet dress. The old men were attired in neatly patched garments or fluttering rags, according to their own foresight or the enterprise of the "old 'oman." Pretty children in white aprons and ragged urchins in rimless hats jostled each other in their efforts to get a better view of the proceedings. The preacher, in his long coat of ministerial cut and well preserved silk hat—that treasured possession of your genuine country preacher—was a conspicuous figure; and so was the shabbily dressed man at his side, with a stoop in his tall, gaunt figure and a burning light in his deep-set eyes as they swept the crowd when he led the singing. I did not find that this man had anything in his life to distinguish him from the others, but his clear cut, severe features and shapely snow white head would have attracted attention anywhere. Add to this that these features were carved in blackest ebony and that his dress was of the commonest and shabbiest, and his figure was all the more striking.

Many uninformed people seem to think that there are only one or two types of either feature or character among the Negroes. Perhaps they know the heavy stolid type, and the jolly, rollicking one, that figure so conspicuously wherever the Negro is introduced into fiction, and they conclude that there are no others. But one could hardly watch a crowd got together at random from any Black Belt county without realizing that here as elsewhere may be found

> Some Village Hampden
> That with dauntless breast

The little tyrant of his
Fields withstood,

so striking are the differences that meet the eye.

The hymn singing would have been a novelty to one not accustomed to the same in the back country churches. The preacher "lined off" the hymn, a couplet at a time: "Hark from the tomb a doleful sound," etc.

It was indeed a "doleful sound" that ascended from that cemetery hill when the people took up the refrain. Many stanzas were sung in a slow, dragging measure; and each couplet was laboriously read out beforehand by the preacher. I have often stood in a country church while the people sang in this way as many as twenty stanzas of some dismal hymn in long meter, without apparent fatigue, while I was ready to drop. I have sometimes thought that such singing must be designed to tone down the emotional zeal of the Negro's religion, for its effect cannot but be depressing. Some of the people swayed softly backward and forward to the music, seeming to find a certain solace in its mournful rhythm.

At last the singing was over. We waited in hushed expectation to hear the solemn words, "Earth to earth, ashes to ashes, dust to dust." After they were spoken, two men came forward silently and began their work of filling up the grave. The crowd stood on tiptoe watching the proceeding; and I think this struck me at the time as the strangest part of the exercises—this morbid curiosity that would not miss a single repulsive detail. The silence was only broken by the sobs of the "onlies' mohner." At last the task was finished, another hymn was lined out and sung, and then the preacher announced that the funeral would probably take place in a few months, as soon as all due preparations had been made.

This announcement seemed to be the signal for a general breaking up. Animation returned to sombre faces, chattering speech to hushed lips. Neighbor shook hands with neighbor, and amidst ejaculations of "How yo' feel?" "Mighty po'ly, thankee!" "Just tolable! Just tolable!" we retraced our steps along the way we had come. The officials who had stood at the outskirts of the crowd to see that the service closed before sunset also moved away—and the buryin' was over.

The cheerful chatter around us could not banish altogether from our minds the weird scene we had witnessed. But we made the effort that was expected of us as "ladies of de college" to talk and listen. Some of the people knew us and greeted us cordially. One stout woman just ahead, smartly dressed in a black satin skirt and red shawl, was proclaiming loudly as she walked: "Yes, I hates trouble mighty bad. I done hab a heap ob it too in my time. But jes gib me peace ob heart an' Ise all right. Peace ob heart, honey, peace ob heart." We happened to know the propounder of this cheerful philosophy as a "pious fraud" of the worst order. Mrs. White, whom we recognized as the mother of one of our school boys bearing the name of Caesar, asked with much solicitude how her baby was gettin' on. We recalled the "baby" as on overgrown youth of nineteen, very black and very simple minded, wont to cross the campus at odd hours carrying on his head baskets of clothing which his mother laundried for his tuition. Like his illustrious namesake, he could direct his activities into many channels. His mother told us with melancholy pride that "Caesar's twin, Agrippa, done die when he was little," that she "done name dem twins arter two kings in de Bible," and that "Caesar was certney a good boy and had done a heap for her." The ties of fraternity and blood are strong among these people, and the love of parents and children is a bright spot against the background of poor circumstance and grinding poverty in which their lives are spent.

Mrs. White told us in her cheerful way about a pretty brown-faced toddler just ahead of us, a "sure enough baby." We learned that he belonged to a numerous family of neglected children who lived, or rather swarmed, in a narrow, crowded lane near the school, through which we had often passed in our walks. His name was King David. Like the David of long ago he had that crowning gift of the gods, beauty. So that those who looked upon him loved him. King David shook his curly head and greeted us with an engaging display of pearly baby teeth and with a warm glow of color in his velvety, brown cheek. The pretty picture lingered in our minds long after the child had gone along, with the sombre picture we had just witnessed.

In one brief hour we had seen the end of life and its beginning, the tears of the mourner and the gay laughter of childhood, the tragedy of life and something of its comedy. As we turned up the lane that led to the school, we thought of that other home where the lights are brighter and the shadows altogether wanting, where, as one of our boys said in his simple prayer, when describing the life hereafter, "it is always 'howdy' and never 'good bye'."

1899

Recent Negro Melodies

by William E. Barton, D.D.

New England Magazine, XIX (Boston, February 1899), 707–719.

This is the last and most interesting article in a series of three published by Barton in Volume XIX of New England Magazine *(the other two were "Old Plantation Hymns" [December 1898], pp. 443–456, and "Hymns of the Slave and the Freedman" [January 1899], pp. 609–624). Later in 1899, he published all three in a single pamphlet, now quite rare, under the title* Old Plantation Hymns: a collection of hitherto unpublished melodies of the slave and the freedman, with historical and descriptive notes, *a title lacking either candor or accuracy.*

Barton did his collecting during a seven-year period as schoolteacher and minister in the South (1880–1887). Many of the songs have white camp-meeting backgrounds, but Barton doesn't seem to have noticed that whites were taken with singing about the same Beyond as his Negro informants. Although Barton has done some textual editing and seems to have glossed over secular singing, his collection is of considerable value; it is one of the largest of the century and, unlike the collections published by Fisk and Hampton, has not been prettified for a white stage.

His comments on the application of church songs to certain kinds of work situations supply us with important links in the musical complex that involves steamboat, rowing, spiritual, railroad, construction, and prison songs. Readers interested in the John Henry tradition might note his description of the men singing while rock-tunneling. If the minor third in "The Christians' Hymn of the Crucifixion" is made major, the melody is similar to the melody of one of the most prevalent worksongs in Southern prisons today, "Hammer Ring"; the two songs have an identical verbal structure. "When the Chariot Comes" is better known nowadays by the other set of lyrics the tune bears: "She'll Be Comin' Round the Mountain."

In two previous articles I have given fifty-four old plantation hymns, including both those of unquestioned antiquity and those which show the influence of the war and the effects of newly found freedom. In the present paper I propose to consider some which show more recent influences.

I cannot pretend, however, that the classification which I have made is strictly chronological. Material is lacking for a hard and fast division of these songs into historical groups. A song which I have recently learned, and which the man who sang it for me assured me was composed by a man well known to him, has all the characteristics of the older melodies. I have selected, in part, the songs that had common or contrasting features in melody or doctrine, and I shall include in this article some songs that were simply left over from the preceding ones. And the so-called "railroad songs" which make up a part of this article, though in their present form modern, represent a very old type of hymn structure, and had their beginnings far back in the days of slavery. No one man made them, nor are they ever written or ever complete. But I have endeavored to follow the general principle of grouping these songs according to their probable age.

Beside the "railroad songs" proper, there are some that are about the railroad. One of these will illustrate how modern influences in the South have affected the content of negro hymns.

To the negro on the levee the steamboat is the greatest thing afloat. But to the negro of the interior the place of the steamer in religious typology is assigned to the locomotive. There are several songs about the Gospel Train, some of which are familiar. The railroad seems so supernatural that it is hard to convince some faithful old souls that heaven is not at one or the other terminus. There is a good old song with this suggestion. It is in triple time, and pronounces "evening" in three sharp syllables.

GIT ON DE EVENING TRAIN

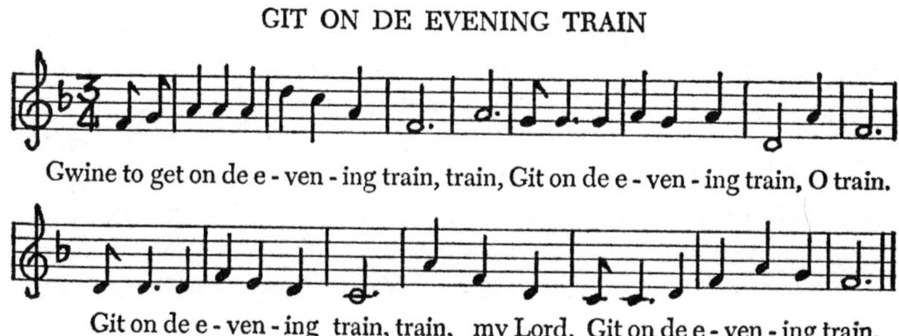

Gwine to get on de e - ven - ing train, train, Git on de e - ven - ing train, O train.
Git on de e - ven - ing train, train, my Lord, Git on de e - ven - ing train.

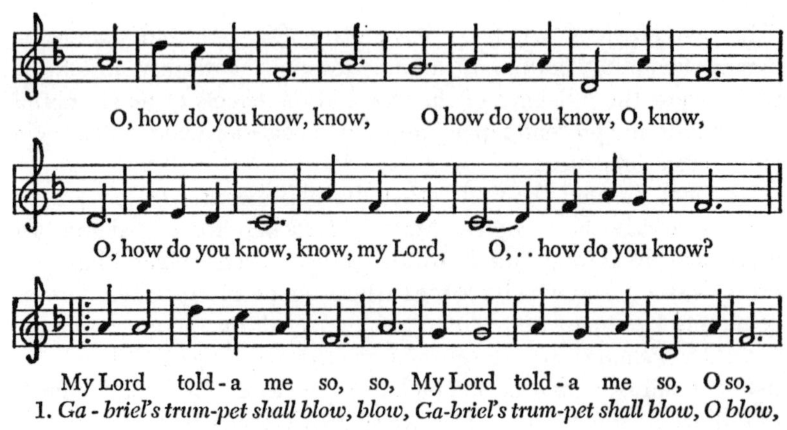
O, how do you know, know, O how do you know, O, know,
O, how do you know, know, my Lord, O, . . how do you know?
My Lord told-a me so, so, My Lord told-a me so, O so,
1. Ga-briel's trum-pet shall blow, blow, Ga-briel's trum-pet shall blow, O blow,

My Lord told-a me so, So, my Lord, My Lord told-a me so.
Ga-briel's trumpet shall blow, Blow, my Lord, Ga-briel's trum-pet shall blow.

2—Old Death stayin' in de grave, grave,
etc.
3—Swing low, chariot, swing low, low, etc.
4—Prayer, prayer is de way, way, etc.
5—Let God's people git 'board, 'board, etc.
6—Gwine to heaven on de mor-en-ing
train, train, etc.
7—My Lord send a me here, here,
My Lord send a me here, to pray.
8—Do thyself a no harm, harm.

Railroad songs are so named from the fact that they are sung by large bodies of men in the construction of railroads and other public works. Not many of them originated on the railroad, but their use in the army building fortifications, and in these more modern kinds of labor, has probably served to elongate them. The wise contractor employing colored men at work of this character lets them sing. The songs require little expenditure of breath, and are long drawn, monotonous chants. They usually have a Scripture theme, and often tell at length a long Scripture story with the negro's own improvements and interpretations thrown in. The refrain comes at considerable and irregular intervals, just often enough to quicken the lagging interest of any who may have dropped out. Only the leader attempts to sing the words, though perhaps a few nearest him catch a strain here and there; but the tune, which often runs along for a dozen verses between *la* and *do*, is hummed by others far and near, and gives the time to which the spades sink into the clay or the picks descend.

To hear these songs, not all of which are religious, at their best, one needs to hear them in a rock tunnel. The men are hurried in after an explosion to drill with speed for another double row of blasts. They work two and two, one holding and turning the drill, the other striking it with a sledge. The sledges descend in unison as the long low chant gives the time. I wonder if the reader can imagine the effect of it all, the powder smoke filling the place, the darkness made barely visible by the little lights on the hats of the men, the echoing sounds of men and mules toward the outlet loading and carting away the rock thrown out by the last blast, and the men at the heading droning their low chant to the *chink! chink!* of the steel. A single musical phrase or a succession of a half dozen notes caught on a visit to such a place sticks in one's mind forever. Even as I write I seem to be in a tunnel of this description and to hear the sharp metallic stroke and the syncopated chant.

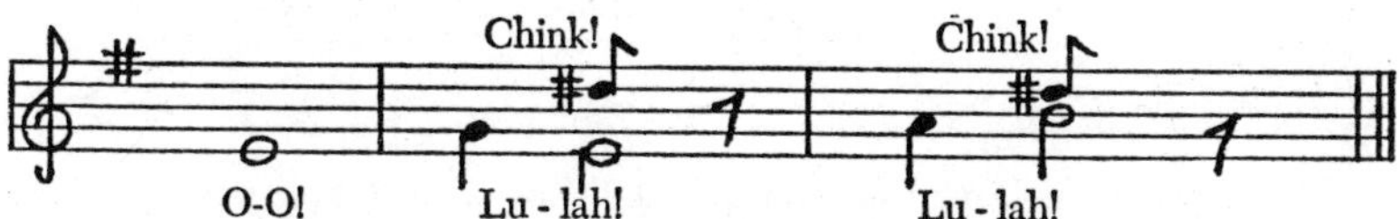

One occasionally hears these long songs in an evening meeting. They are interminable, and the only way to end them is to stop. One of them, a part of which has been published, and the whole of which no one man knows, is "Walk Jerusalem Jes' like John." Different versions of it have been printed, but none like the one I have.

This song throws in almost at random couplets like:

> Walk around from do' to do',
> What to do I did not know;
>
> Walk Jerusalem on Zion's hill,
> Walk about on heaven and earth;
>
> Satan thought he had me fast,
> Thank the Lord I'm free at last.
>
> I bless the Lord I'm going to die,
> I'm going to judgment by and by.
>
> Oh, John he heard the trumpet blow,
> Hills and mountains fall below.

It has no proper end. It goes on at the will of the leader, and, unlike the ordinary hymn, which may be ended either with a stanza or the refrain and usually is meant to end with the latter, this is meant never to end so far as the structure of the song is concerned. It may end with "When I come to die," or "Jes' like John"; but in either case it gives the air of incompleteness, like the old Scotch and Irish songs which ended so often on *re* and were ready to begin again. Some of these songs have a proper end, and may stop with the refrain any time; but the refrain is of variable occurrence, and may come every two lines, or run on for an epitomized biography of some Bible character.

WALK JERUSALEM JES' LIKE JOHN

Walk Je - ru - sa-lem, jes' like John. When I come to die, I want to be

read - y, . . When I come to die. 1. Walk Je - ru - sa - lem, jes' like John,

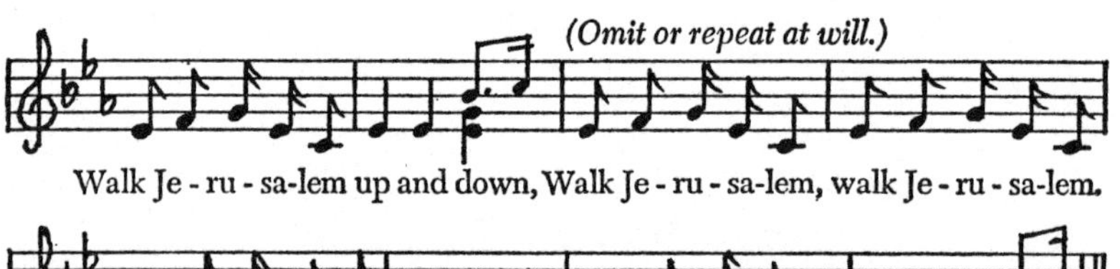
(Omit or repeat at will.)
Walk Je - ru - sa-lem up and down, Walk Je - ru - sa-lem, walk Je - ru - sa-lem.

Walk Je - ru - sa-lem jes' like John, Walk Je - ru - sa - lem round and round.

While the narrative portions of this song and others like it are used as a solo, which is a great saving of breath, there is a humming accompaniment, with many an "Amen" and "Yes," and frequently a chuckle or "holy laugh," especially at any suggestion of giving the devil what is conceived to be his due, or of any sharp turn of Providence for the worsting of sinners. One of these songs, which I have heard both on the railroad and in an evening meeting, is "The New Buryin' Ground."

NEW BURYIN' GROUND

1. { O, my Lord, Good and kind, Take the lit - tle babe, Leave its
To-morrow's the day, First go-in' by, Take the lit - tle babe, To the
O - pen the grave, Let him down, There he's go - in' t'lay Till the }

moth - er be - hind. Judgment day! God's a call-in'! Stars a - fall-in'!
new bur - ry - in' ground.
Judg - ment day.

Char-iot's com - in' down To the new bur - yin' ground! O, Je - sus, come this a -

way! Let not your char-iot wheels de - lay! Want you to live hum-ble-l-humble-l-

Humble your-selves! The bells done rung, Bells done ring, Angels done sing.

O don't it look like a judg-ment day? Gwine to glo-ry an'- a -

hon-or! Praise Jesus! Gwine to glory an'-a-honor! Praise the Lamb!

2–All along down by de watery shore,
De waters run steady, level as a die;
Hearse come down next day gone by;
Take de lill babe to new buryin'
ground.
Yes, I went down to the valley to pray,
Met ole Satan on de way.
Look out, Satan, out my way!
Took my sword an' cut him down;
Satan shot one ball at me:
Missed my soul and got my sin.

Refrain.

3–O' no, brethering, dat ain't all,–
Golden girdle round my waist,

Starry crown upon my head,
Palm of victory in my hand.

Refrain.

4—I went to meeting on a certain day,
Went fo' to hear what de preacher say.
Bout de time dat I got in,
Spoke one word condemned my sin.
Went back home an' counted de cost.
Heard what a treasure I had lost.

Refrain.

5—Yes, mysteree! Come and see!
Heard a great voice shoutin' in de new buryin' ground.
B for book and be forgiven,
Wrote by wise men sent from heaven.
If you want to go to heaven when you dies,
Stop you long tongue from telling lies.
Stars a-fallin'! God's a callin'!
Don't dat look like judgment day?

Refrain.

6—I went down by the tottery sho,
Found a ship all ready to go.
Cap'n he come, troubled in mind,
"Wake up! wake up, you sleep, sleepy man!"
O, cap'n, if it's me,
Pray you cast me overboard!
Cast Brer Jonah overboard;
Whale did swaller Brer Jonah whole.
Three long night, three long days,
Jonah lied in de body of de whale.
Las' words I hear Brer Jonah say,
He had no place to lie his head.
God commanded fish to land,
Cast Brer Jonah on dry sand.
Gourd vine growed all over his head.
Inchworm come long and cut it down.

Refrain.

7—Hit 'em wid de hammer cryin', "Sinner, repent!"
Wrought sorrow in de Jedge-e-ment.
Green trees burn, and why not dry?

Sinner man die, and why not I?
Sea ob glass all full of fire,
I'm gwine to jine God's heavenly choir.
H for Hannah, happy was she,
Lill boy Samuel on her knee.
B for book an' God forgiven,
Young child Jesus came from heaven.

Refrain.

8—Sing ole hymn at new buryin' ground,
Dar gwine lay his body down.
He gave me pree, and sot me free
An' bought my soul from libertee.
Death come along at break of day,
Take de lill baby on his way.
Give me a horn and tell me to blow,
Come along, don't you want to go?
Bell done ring, angels done sing,
God A'mighty bought my heart and
tongue.
Went down hill, fell on my knees,
Help me, Jesus, if you please.

Refrain.

Another of these is "How Long, Watch-a-Man?" The melody of this is worthy of special attention. It is sweet, full, dignified and descriptive. The variations of "Watch-a-man" are very telling, and the repeated and retarded final tonic notes, suggestive of the passing of time as seen by the "Watch-a-man" are fine. It deserves to be fitted with a strong, full harmony and to be widely known. I consider it a gem. It is partly in 3:4 and partly in 4:4 time, and the fitting of these into a smooth, flowing melody in perfect taste is noteworthy. The words are not so good.

HOW LONG, WATCH-A-MAN?

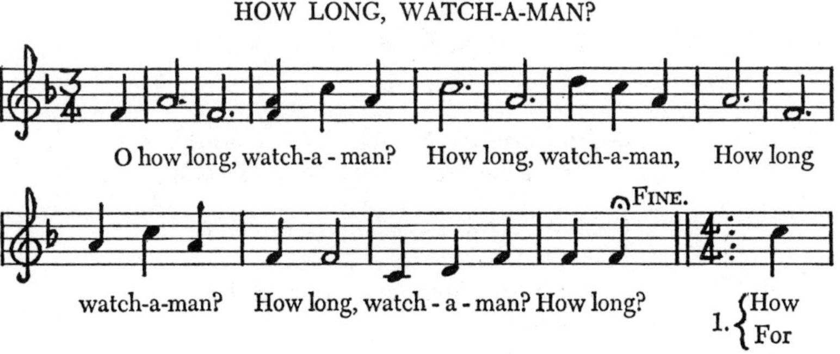
O how long, watch-a - man? How long, watch-a-man, How long
watch-a-man? How long, watch - a - man? How long?
FINE.
1. How
For

D. C.
long did it rain? Can any one tell? How long, watch - a - man? How long?
for - ty days and nights it fell.

2—Oh, dey called ole Noah foolish man.
Built his ark upon dry sand.
Foolish Jews come a-ridin' by,
Hawk and spit on Noah's timber.
My sister done broke de ice an' gone
Sitting in heaven wid 'er raiment on.

Refrain.

3—Watah come up to de cellah door,
Marched an 'slipped on de upper floor,
Den I went up to de winder an' peep out;
I see ole Noah passin' by,
Try an' help me out er my miseree.
I know ole Noah felt and seen,
I b'lieve God A'mighty locked de door.
Come along my muddah to de watah side,
Come along an' be baptized.

Refrain.

4—My dungeon open, my chains flew wide,
Glory to God, I've found him at last.
Brer Jonah lied in de bowels ub de whale,
Brer Jonah prayed in de bowels ub de whale.
De ark got stuck on de mountain-top,
God commanded de rain to stop,
De rainbow show, de sun he shine,
Glory to God, my sins are forgiven.

Refrain.

5—How long was Noah buildin' of de ark?
Mo'n a hundred years he kept to work.

6—How long was Jonah in the bowels of the whale?
For three whole days and nights he sailed.

7—How long will the righteous in heaven
  be?
For ever and ever their Lord they see.

A good many people, no one of whom knew it all, contributed first and last to give the foregoing hymn the degree of completeness which is here shown.

The negro is reluctant to bring a service to a close. When, late at night, the end finally comes, there is often a quotation concerning the heavenly assembly:

Where congregations ne'er break up,
  And Sabbath has no end.

The thought enters several of their own songs, among them one of the interminable ones such as we are now considering. It runs on in narrative form with long or short stanzas, but calls for active and repeated responses in the refrain, "I believe!" The refrain changes, also, from time to time, to suit the tenor of the stanzas, but the end is always the same, "And Sabbath has no end."

SABBATH HAS NO END

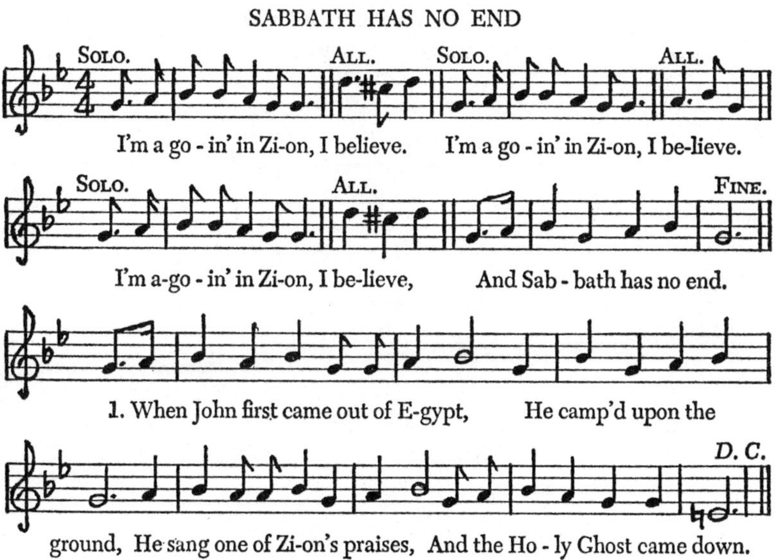
Solo.
All.
Solo.
All.
I'm a go - in' in Zi-on, I believe.
I'm a go - in' in Zi-on, I be-lieve.
Solo.
All.
Fine.
I'm a-go - in' in Zi-on, I be-lieve,
And Sab - bath has no end.
1. When John first came out of E-gypt,
He camp'd upon the
D. C.
ground, He sang one of Zi-on's praises, And the Ho - ly Ghost came down.

2—He done blessed him and cheered him
  And told him not to weep,
For the power was in Christ Jesus
  To raise him from his sleep.

Refrain.

Mighty meeting in Zion,
I believe,
Mighty meeting in Zion,
I believe,
Mighty meeting in Zion,
I believe,
And Sabbath has no end.

3—When Jesus came to the world,
He came to do no harm,
But they placed on him a thorny crown,
And the blood came streaming down.

Refrain.

Wasn't that a shame?
I believe,
Wasn't that a shame?
I believe,
Wasn't that a shame?
I believe,
And Sabbath has no end.

4—Not all the blood of beasts
On Jewish altars slain
Could give a guilty conscience peace,
Or wash away the stain.
Behold he wore the mortgage,
He was Almighty God;
At once they might have 'stroyed him,
But he saved them by his word.

Refrain.

I know, 'twas Jesus,
I believe,
I know, 'twas Jesus,
I believe,
I know, 'twas Jesus,
I believe,
And Sabbath has no end.

5—Want you to look at you dying Saviour.
Want you to look at you dying Lord;
Stand near the cross and view him,
Behold the Lamb of God.
They rebuked him and they scorned
him.

And told him to come down.
Before the cross of suffering,
They changed him for his crown.
Jesus came in many mysterious ways,
His wonders to perform,
He placed his footsteps in the seas,
And rode upon the storm.

Refrain.

I'm going to heaven,
I believe,
I'm going to heaven,
I believe,
I'm going to heaven,
I believe,
And Sabbath has no end.

6—They took my blessed Jesus.
And led him to the whiteoak island.
They hewed him out a yoke.
And they yoked it on to him.
His ankle bones they done give way.
His knees they smote the ground,
And every star shall disappear,
King Jesus shall be mine.

Refrain.

I'm going to Zion,
I believe,
I'm going to Zion,
I believe,
I'm going to Zion,
I believe,
And Sabbath has no end.

7—I met old Judas at the spring.
The history how he talked,—
"For thirty pieces of silver,
I show you where my Jesus walk."

Refrain.

Walked the road to heaven,
I believe,
Walked the road to heaven,
I believe,
Walked the road to heaven,
I believe,
And Sabbath has no end.

8—Mary saw her father coming,
Done run and met him too,
She told him 'bout her brother,
Who was dead and passed away.

Refrain.

Then come forth Lazarus,
I believe,
Then come forth Lazarus,
I believe,
Then come forth Lazarus,
I believe,
And Sabbath has no end.

9—Well, they taken my blessed Jesus,
They led him to the low ground of
sorrow,
They hewed him out a Roman cross,
They placed it on his shoulder.
They speared him long in his side!
They speared him long in his side!
(Wasn't that a shame!)
There came out water and blood!
There came out water and blood!
(O my Lord!)
The blood was for redemption,
The water for baptism.

Refrain.

So we'll rock trouble over,
I believe,
So we'll rock trouble over,
I believe,
So we'll rock trouble over,
I believe,
And Sabbath has no end.

This last hymn I have heard in different places, but the part relating to the crucifixion I have not heard except at religious services. The last of these hymns which I shall give is one that I heard but once. I do not know that it is used as a song to work with, but suspect that the "ham-mer-ring!" which is the constant response, may be used sometimes to time the descent of the pick or sledge. As I heard it, however, it was sung at an evening meeting, a single voice telling the story, repeating twice each line, while the congregation sang a heavy bass "Ham-mer-ring!"

THE CHRISTIANS' HYMN OF THE CRUCIFIXION

Solo.
All.
Solo.
All.
1. O re - pent, sin-ner, Ham-mer-ring!
O re - pent, sin-ner, Ham-mer-ring!'
What de ham-mer say? Ham-mer-ring!
I nailed him down, Ham-mer-ring!
With ten-penny nails, Ham-mer-ring!
Solo.
All.
Solo.
All.
Send for the doc-tor, Ham-mer-ring!
O Je-sus, Ham-mer-ring!
Doc-tor Je-sus, Ham-mer - ring!
They stretch'd him high, Ham-mer-ring!
He bled and groaned. Ham-mer-ring!
I heard them say, Ham-mer-ring!
Solo.
All.
Solo.
All.
You hang me high, Ham-mer-ring!
So sin - ner see, Ham-mer-ring!
Don't weep for me, Ham-mer-ring!
You hang me wide, Ham-mer-ring!
How free I died, Ham-mer - ring!
I go a - way, Ham-mer - ring!
Solo.
All.
Solo.
All.
I'll come a - gain, Ham-mer-ring!
With a band of ang-els, Ham-mer-ring!

2–Mary wept (Ham-mer-ring)
And Martha mourned. (Ham-mer-ring)
If thou'd been there, (Ham-mer-ring)
My brother hadn't died. (Ham-mer-ring)
They buried him, (Ham-mer-ring)
And on the third day (Ham-mer-ring)
He ascended high, (Ham-mer-ring)
To his Father's house. (Ham-mer-ring)
Jesus came, (Ham-mer-ring)
His friend he rise, (Ham-mer-ring)
And found a home (Ham-mer-ring)
Above the skies. (Ham-mer-ring)
O, Lazarus, (Ham-mer-ring)
I know Lazarus! (Ham-mer-ring)
Come forth, Lazarus! (Ham-mer-ring)
Want you to loose him (Ham-mer-ring)
And let him go. (Ham-mer-ring.)

A good many of these railroad songs, I am satisfied, originated in those grewsome vigils, wherein a dozen or more people "sit up" with the dead. The night is largely spent in singing, and the set songs run out long before morning. The family sleep, or are supposed to sleep, often in the same room, and if not there then in a room within easy hearing distance, and the singing is thought to comfort them, as well as to help in keeping the watchers awake and to apply the occasion to the profit of those present. The song about "The New Buryin' Ground" is evidently of this kind. Its references to the little babe that had been taken, the mother left behind, and to the next day as that of the burial, plainly show its original meaning; but it is sung now on other and very different occasions.

These songs are long, low, monotonous croons, wherein the recitative is half sung, half spoken, and the voices other than that of the leader merely hum with occasional ejaculations and an intermittent refrain. The songs are modified by their subsequent uses, but originating, as they do, without a distinct purpose to make a song, they are most irregular in everything but rhythm, which is always such that they can be swayed to and patted with the foot. They afford a good illustration of the way in which the more elaborate songs originate.

There are some of the more recent plantation hymns which have added an element of culture without diminishing religious fervor. One of the best of these is "Were You There When They Crucified My Lord?" It dwells on the details of the crucifixion, and the separate stanzas add only a single line each to the song. It is a tender and beautiful hymn, the climax of its effect depending largely on the hold and slur on the exclamation "O!" with which the third line begins, and the repetition and expression of the word "*tremble! tremble! tremble!*"

WERE YOU THERE?

1. Were you there when they cru-ci-fied my Lord? (Were you there?)
2. Were you there when they nail'd him to the cross? (Were you there?)
3. Were you there when they pierced him in the side? (Were you there?)
4. Were you there when the sun re-fused to shine? (Were you there?)

Were you there when they cru-ci-fied my Lord? O some-times it caus - es me to
Were you there when they nail'd him to the cross? O some-times it caus - es me to
Were you there when they pierced him in the side? O some-times it caus - es me to
Were you there when the sun refused to shine? O some-times it caus - es me to

trem - ble! trem-ble! trem - ble! Were you there when they cru - ci - fied my Lord?
trem-ble! trem-ble! trem - ble! Were you there when they nail'd him to the cross?
trem-ble! trem-ble! trem - ble! Were you there when they pierced him in the side?
trem-ble! trem-ble! trem - ble! Were you there when the sun re - fused to shine?

PETER ON THE SEA

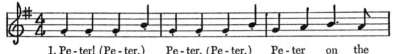

1. Pe - ter! (Pe - ter,) Pe - ter, (Pe - ter,) Pe - ter on the
2. Ga-briel! (Ga-briel,) Ga-briel, (Ga-briel,) Ga-briel, blow your
3. Who did (who did) Jo - nah? (who did?) Who did swal - low
4. Whale did (whale did) Jo - nah! (whale did!) Whale did swal - low
5. Dan - iel (Dan - iel) li - on's (Dan - iel!) Dan - iel in the

sea, sea, sea, sea! Pe - ter, (Pe - ter,) Pe - ter, (Pe - ter,)
trump, trump, trump, trump! Ga - briel, (Ga - briel,) Ga - briel, (Ga - briel,)
Jo - nah, Jo - nah? Who did (who did) Jo - nah? (who did?)
Jo - nah, Jo - nah! Whale did (whale did) Jo - nah! (whale did!)
li - on's, li - on's! Dan - iel (Dan - iel) li - on's (Dan - iel!)

Pe - ter on the sea, sea, sea, sea! Pe - ter, (Pe - ter,)
Ga-briel, blow your, trump, trump, trump, trump! Ga - briel, (Ga - briel,)
Who did swal - low Jo - nah, Jo - nah? Who did (who did)
Whale did swal - low Jo - nah, Jo - nah! Whale did (whale did)
Dan - iel in the li - on's, li - on's! Dan - iel (Dan - iel)

Pe - ter, (Pe - ter,) Pe - ter on the sea, sea, sea, sea!
Ga - briel, (Ga - briel,) Ga-briel, blow your, trump, trump, trump, trump!
Jo - nah? (who did?) Who did swal - low Jo - nah, Jo - nah?
Jo - nah! (whale did!) Whale did swal - low Jo - nah, Jo - nah!
li - on's (Dan - iel!) Dan - iel in the li - on's, li - on's!

Pe - ter on the sea, sea! Pe - ter on the sea, sea, sea!
Ga - briel, blow your trump - et! Ga - briel, blow your trump - et, blow!
Who did swal - low Jo - nah? Who did swal-low Jo - nah? Who?
Whale did swal - low Jo - nah! Whale did swal - low Jo - nah! Whale!
Dan - iel in the li - on's! Dan - iel in the li - on's den!

The foregoing modern song keeps much of the spirit of the older ones. It is in striking contrast with the preceding song. It is a lively staccato, is full of responses, is not in the least shy of the fourth and seventh notes, and is thoroughly up to date except perhaps in its theology. No higher criticism has yet eliminated from negro theology a vestige of the miraculous. Peter on the sea, Gabriel with his trumpet, Jonah and the whale and Daniel in the lion's den are all here in a swift-moving panorama, and with a lively good humor that is nothing less than mirth-provoking.

One of the most interesting places in which I have ever attended worship is a well built and fairly well appointed meeting house erected by the colored people, well out in the country, and adorned with crude frescoes that show a desire to beautify the sanctuary of the Lord. I have been there in summer when the temperature of the day did not exceed that of the meeting and I have been there in winter when the minister announced that he was "cold, brethren; cold two ways, cold in de body and cold speritually"; and yet I have never been wholly disappointed in seeing something worth while. The records of the business meeting of Saturday are read on Sunday morning with a good many exclusions from the church "for immoral conduct," as the charge has invariably read when I have been there; and not infrequently there are people to be received into membership with ecstatic experiences proved by a repetition of them on the spot. The preaching begins very moderately, but as one after another comes to the front, the tide rises until the preacher in charge, who is said to have been the longest settled pastor in Kentucky, rises and begins; and then there is a demonstration. The company has long been swaying back and forth in the rhythm of the preacher's chant, and now and then there has come a shout of assent to the oft repeated text. Each time the preacher's almost incoherent talk becomes articulate in a shout, "I have trod de wine-press," there are cries of "Yes!" "Praise de Lawd!" and "Glory!" from the Amen corner, where sit the "praying brethren," and the Hallelujah corner, where sit the "agonizing sistering." In the earlier demonstrations the men rather lead, but from the time when Aunt Melinda cries out "Nebbah mind de wite folks! My soul's happy! Hallelujah!" and leaps into the air, the men are left behind. Women go off into trances, roll under benches, or go spinning down the aisle with eyes closed and with arms outstretched. Each shout of the preacher is the signal for some one else to start; and, strange to say, though there are two posts in the aisle, and the women go spinning down like tops, I never saw one strike a post. I have seen the pastor on a day when the house would not contain the multitude cause the seats to be turned and take his own position in the door with a third of the audience inside and the rest without, and have heard him provoke the most ecstatic response to a reference to his wife such as this, "O, I love dat yaller woman out dar in dat buggy, but I love my Jesus bettah!" I have seen the minister in grave danger of being dragged out of the pulpit by some of the shouters who in their ecstasy laid hold upon him. I have seen an old man stand in the aisle and jump eighty-nine times after I began to count, and without moving a muscle of his thin, parchment-like face, and without disturbing the meeting.

There is more or less variation in the service at this church, but there is one invariable feature, the collection; and the more white people there are present, the more important is this feature. Two deacons sit at a table in front of the pulpit; a song is sung, and the contributors walk up the aisle and deposit their contributions amid exhortations and plaudits thrown in at the end of the line. Each coin is scrutinized, and there is no opportunity to pass a mutilated coin at par, as some people do in dealing with the Lord, or make a button do duty for legal tender. One day some one started a new fashioned hymn, and the people came up slowly. The preacher interrupted the hymn midway saying "Breddern, dah hain't no money in dat tune. Sing one of de good ole tunes." In response to this suggestion they sang "Jes' gwine ober in de heabenlye lan'." It has a high air, covering only a diminished fifth, and running mostly on the tonic note, but the monotony is broken and a decided character is given to the melody in the refrain, "De heabenlye lan," when from the last syllable of "heabenlye" to "lan' " the voice rises from E flat tonic to D flat, which it holds with a strong accent on a half note filling the last half of the measure.

JES' GWINE OBER IN DE HEABENLYE LAN'

Lively
1 You can hinder me here, but you can't do it there,
For He sits in de heavens, and He answers prayer,
Jes' gwine o - ber in de heabenlye lan'!
REFRAIN.
De heabenlye lan',
Heab-en - lye lan',
Jes' gwine o - ber in de heabenlye lan'!

2—Sinnah jine de church an' he run pretty well,
Jes' gwine ober in de heabenlye lan'!
An' afore six weeks he's on his road to hell,
Jes' gwine ober in de heabenlye lan'!
De heabenlye lan'!
De heabenlye lan'!
Jes' gwine ober in de heabenlye lan'!

3—Hebben is a high an' a lofty place,
Jes' gwine ober in de heabenlye lan'!
But yer can't git dah ef you hain't got de grace,
Jes' gwine ober in de heabenlye lan'!
De heabenlye lan'!
De heabenlye lan'!
Jes' gwine ober in de heabenlye lan'!

4—Satan he's like a snake in de grass,
Jes' gwine ober in de heabenlye lan'!
An' ef you don' mind he'll git you at las',
Jes' gwine ober in de heabenlye lan'!
De heabenlye lan'!
De heabenlye lan'!
Jes' gwine ober in de heabenlye lan'!

5—Way ober yander in de harves' fiel',
Jes' gwine ober in de heabenlye lan'!
De angels are rollin' at de chariot wheel,
Jes' gwine ober in de heabenlye lan'!
De heabenlye lan'!
De heabenlye lan'!
Jes' gwine ober in de heabenlye lan'!

What conception the worshipers have of an angel is patent, for two of them are wrought into the frescoes of the room. The feet of one turn abruptly to the right, and the feet of the other to the left. One of them is cross eyed; both are white. There was every indication that this song brought a good collection.

A good many of the negro songs are written in the pentatonic scale. The same is true of a majority of Scotch songs and the songs of Oriental nations. When Luther W. Mason went to Japan to teach our system of music in the government schools, he sought out melodies common among us that are written in the scale of five notes. The first which he taught and which they received with great pleasure was one that we received from the Orient, I think from India, "There is a happy land." Few of the thousands of thousands who have sung this air all round the world have thought how a part of its hold upon so many million of hearts is its omission of the two notes 4 and 7 from the diatonic scale. Several of the best of the Scotch songs are of this character, as "Auld Lang Syne," and, with the exception of one or two notes which I believe are modern, "Annie Laurie." It is a little strange that just when the breaking up of Primrose and West's minstrel troupe might seem to indicate, and probably does indicate, a decline of interest in the burnt cork show that has been so popular for generations, and still is popular in England, there should be a great increase of so called "coon songs," some of whose airs are very pleasing, arranged for the piano. To any one who desires to write a fair imitation of a characteristic negro melody, one simple rule is good to start with: compose it on the black keys of the piano. It takes more than this rule, however, to make a good negro song, and the best of them are ill adapted to a piano. The violin or banjo fits them best, for they have no frets to distribute the error in tone. A sharp and B flat are not mathematically the same, but they must be represented by one tone on the piano. The negro is able to make this fine discrimination when he uses accidentals and this makes it impossible to represent the tones exactly upon the staff; but the five notes of the simpler scale suffice for most of the hymns. "In Dat Great Day" is an example of a song whose tune is major and which ranges over an octave and a half with no suggestion of a lack of sufficient tone variety. There is great contrast between the startling warning, almost breathless, "Whah you runnin', sinnah?" and the clear, exultant "O Is-a-rel." The entire piece is of great power. It is a negro *Dies Irae*. The use of the major is all the more remarkable because the eschatological theme and the sombre succession of incidents described would naturally suggest the minor.

This song illustrates a way in which the negro varies his melodies.

In theory the song is sung in unison, and there is no harmony proper. But in practice the more independent singers introduce grace notes and slurs, and the higher and lower voices range above and below in fifths and thirds in the more descriptive portions, especially in the latter verses. In this song the melody of "O Isarel! O Isarel!" is given in the first line where those words are used, and in the notes which run nearest the tonic; but as the song proceeds this simple theme is worked out quite elaborately and with much greater variety than the notes here given indicate, but in a manner which they illustrate.

IN DAT GREAT DAY

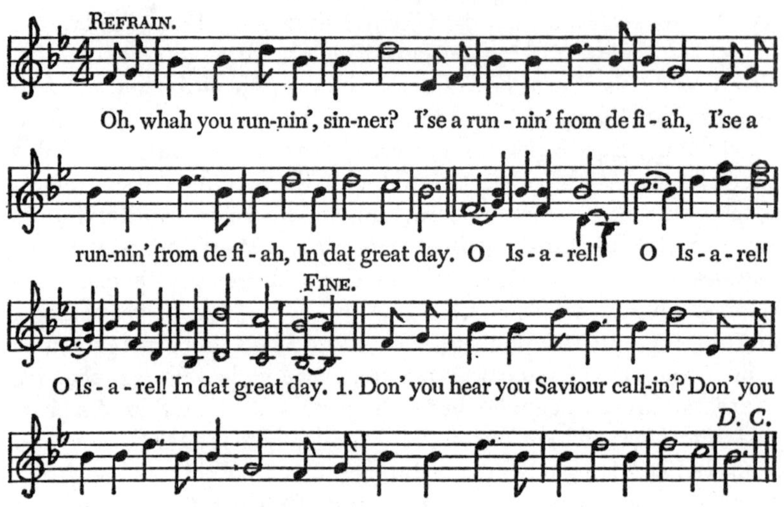

2–Don' you see de dead arisin'? etc.
3–Don' you heah de trumpet soundin'?
4–Don' you see dem tombs a-bustin'?
5–Yes, we'll see our chillen risin'.
6–Don' you see de chariot comin'?
7–Don' you see de sinnah tremblin'?
8–Don' you heah de saints a-shoutin'?

This quaint *Dies Irae* may well be paired with an equally quaint "Hallelujah Chorus." It is a Baptist hymn, "Been down into the Sea." Its exultant hallelujahs suggest, as one hears them, some passages in Handel's great masterpiece. I cannot expect any one to agree with this statement who merely picks out the notes on the piano; but one who hears the piece sung by a great congregation will not think the statement wholly extravagant.

BEEN DOWN INTO THE SEA

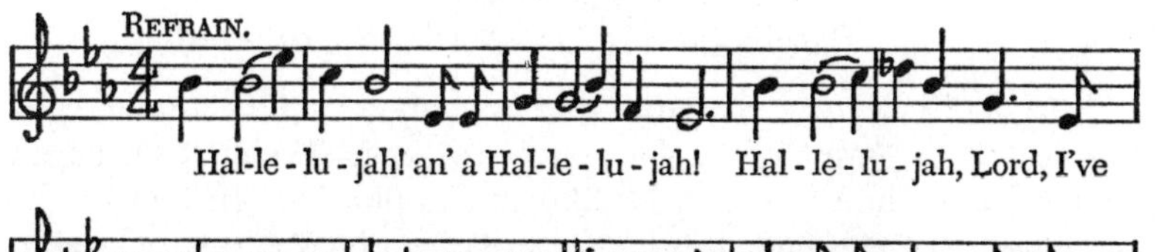
REFRAIN.
Hal-le - lu - jah! an' a Hal-le - lu - jah! Hal - le - lu - jah, Lord, I've
been down in-to the sea. Yes, I've been to the sea, and I've
Yes, I've done been tried in

done been tried, Been down in - to the sea. Hal-le - lu-jah! an' a Hal-le -
Je-sus' name, Been down in - to the sea.

lu-jah! Hal-le - lu - jah, Lord, I've been down in - to the sea.

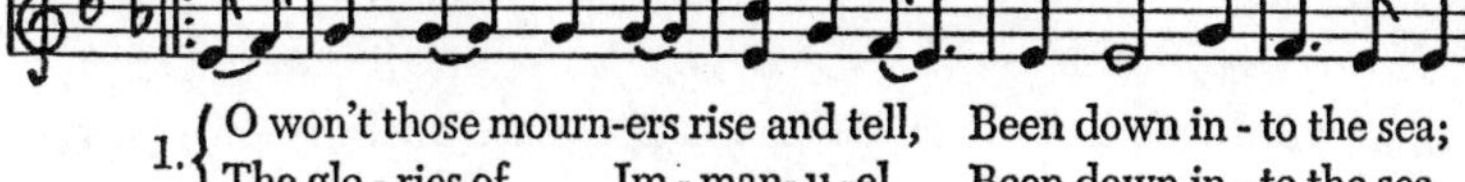
1. O won't those mourn-ers rise and tell, Been down in - to the sea;
The glo - ries of Im - man- u -el, Been down in - to the sea.

2—Hallelujah! an' a hallelujah!
Hallelujah, Lord! I've been down into the sea!
Why don' dem mourners rise an' tell—
Been down into the sea—
The glories of Immanuel?
Been down into the sea!

3—Hallelujah! an' a hallelujah!
Hallelujah, Lord! I've been down into the sea!
I do believe without a doubt—
Been down into the sea—
That a Christian has a right to shout,
Been down into the sea!

4—Hallelujah! an' a hallelujah!
Hallelujah, Lord! I've been down into the sea!

Yes, I've been to the sea and I've been babtized,
  Been down into the sea;
I've been babtized in Jesus' name,
  Been down into the sea!
Hallelujah! an' a hallelujah!
Hallelujah, Lord! I've been down into the sea!

Now and then there is a piece that not only uses the diatonic scale, but makes the most of it. One effective song, "When the Chariot Comes," uses the seven-toned scale, and emphasizes the fact by the prominence of its major thirds. For instance, the first time the word "comes" is used, it is cut into five syllables with emphatic rough breathings, and fitted to a *do-sol-mi-sol-do.*

WHEN THE CHARIOT COMES

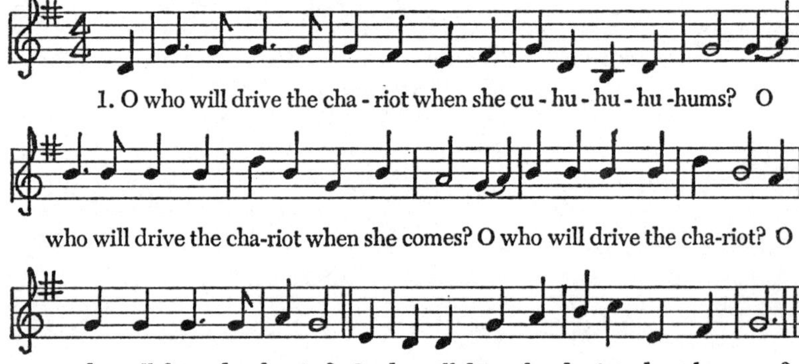
1. O who will drive the cha - riot when she cu - hu - hu - hu -hums? O
who will drive the cha-riot when she comes? O who will drive the cha-riot? O
who will drive the cha-riot? O who will drive the chariot when she comes?

2—King Jesus, he'll be driver, when she cu-hu-hu-hu-hums, etc.

3—She'll be loaded with bright angels, etc.

4—She will neither rock nor totter, etc.

5—She will run so level and steady, etc.

6—She will take us to the portills, etc.

Among the eschatological songs, I do not remember any that have affected me as did the song, "Who's Dat Yandah?" At the end of each inquiry, "Who's dat yandah?" is a rest of two beats in the middle of the measure; and the effect is more startling than the syncopation of a note. It is an emphasized silence of eager and fearful expectancy. It is a pure minor, and runs almost wholly in thirds. This song is so painfully realistic in its tone picturing as to cause an involuntary turning of the head in expectation of some majestic Presence. It starts with a refrain, which is repeated after every stanza and again at the end, as is usually the case where the song opens with the refrain.

WHO'S DAT YANDAH?

REFRAIN.
f
ff
O who's dat yan - dah? an' a who's dat yan - dah? Say, who's dat yan-dah?
FINE
Looks like a' my Lord com-in' in de sky.
1. O, lit-tle did I think He was so nigh,
He spoke, and He made me laugh and cry,
Looks like a' my Lord com-in' in de sky.
f
ff
O who's dat yan - dah? An' a who's dat yan - dah? Say,
D. C.
who's dat yandah? Looks like a' my Lord com-in' in de sky

2—Sinnah, sinnah, you'd bettah pray,
Looks like-a my Lord comin' in de sky!
Or you' soul be los' at de jedgment day,
Looks like-a my Lord comin' in de sky!

3—Wait till I gits in de middle of de air,
Won't be nary sinnah dere.

4—De debbil is a liar and a conjurer, too,
An' ef you don' mind he'll conjure you.

5—I nebbah can fo'git de day,
When Jesus washed my sins away.

6—Washed my haid in de midnight dew,
De mawning star's a witness, too.

7—Sinnahs jines de church, and dey sing and dey shout,
An' afore six months des all turned out.

8—When I was a mourner jes' like you,
My knees got 'quainted wid de hillside, too.

In this and the two preceding articles I have given nearly seventy of these songs. It has been a sincere pleasure to prepare them for preservation in this form. Growing out of the heart experience of the negro, the older ones are absolutely natural and unaffected, and exhibit no attempt to express the religious life in conventional terms. Even their crudest oddities are of interest as data for study in religious and social development, and this is by no means the limit of their value.

I have not counted it a part of my duty to write harmonies for these songs, but have endeavored to preserve the melodies as accurately as possible.

These songs are such excellent exponents of "heart religion" that they are certain to disappear before the swift coming "book religion," save as they are carefully recorded and preserved. I exhort all teachers, pastors and others who are able to secure these songs to do so, with the music wherever possible, and to see that they are suitably preserved in print.

1899

The Survival of African Music in America

by Jeanette Robinson Murphy

Popular Science Monthly, 55 (New York, 1899), 660–672.

In 1895 the Southern Workman *editors had asked their readers to contribute African survivals, but they never pursued the subject further. This is one of the first articles to link explicitly African and American Negro singing styles and customs. In addition, Miss Murphy offers interesting examples of conjure, sending messages by the dead, and commentary on preaching, animal tales, the attitude of the folk toward their folklore, and by her own example gives us a specific instance of Negro-to-white transmission of folklore material and style. The influence of the Negro on American folklore has been extensive, but the channels of transmission are frequently hard to isolate. For this reason, her description of how she learned and performed Negro material is of some importance.*

Fifty years from now, when every vestige of slavery has disappeared, and even its existence has become a fading memory, America, and probably Europe, will suddenly awake to the sad fact that we have irrevocably lost a veritable mine of wealth through our failure to appreciate and study from a musician's standpoint the beautiful African music, whose rich stores will then have gone forever from our grasp.

During my childhood my observations were centered upon a few very old negroes who came directly from Africa, and upon many others whose parents were African born, and I early came to the conclusion, based upon negro authority, that the greater part of their music, their methods, their scale, their type of thought, their dancing, their patting of feet, their clapping of hands, their grimaces and pantomime, and their gross superstitions came straight from Africa.

Some of their later songs, it is true, we must technically call "modified African," but how far the original African song elements have been altered (and usually not for the better) by contact with American life is a question of fact, and can only be settled by a careful comparison of the songs as sung among the natives of Africa and the changed forms in which their modified ones are found today in the South. It must be determined in each case, and cannot be settled by any general theory or formula.

This question of the classification of African music has given rise to more or less discussion. It seems hardly just to call the genuine negro songs "the folk songs of America." We are a conglomerate people, and no one race can claim a monopoly in this matter. English, Scotch, German, French, Italians, and others have brought their own music and their own folklore, and in each case it must be considered distinctly belonging to the nationality that imported it. Why should not the same be true of the genuine negro music? The stock is African, the ideas are African, the patting and dancing are all African. The veneer of civilization and religious fervor and Bible truth is entirely superficial. The African is under it all, and those who study him and his weird music at short range have no difficulty in recalling the savage conditions that gave it birth.

Were I to begin now the study of all the intonations and tortuous quavers of this beautiful music, I fear I should be able to do little toward imitating it; for it was only possible to catch the spirit of it and the reason of it all while my voice had the flexibility of childhood, and the influences of slavery were still potent factors in the daily life of the negroes. I followed these old ex-slaves, who have passed away, in their tasks, listened to their crooning in their cabins, in the fields, and especially in their meeting houses, and again and again they assured me the tunes they sang came from Africa.

Possibly I have an unusual predilection for this imported African music, but to me some of the strange, weird, untamable, barbaric melodies have a rude beauty and a charm beside which, as Cowper says—

> Italian trills are tame.

It is indeed hard to account for the strange misconceptions which prevail as to what really constitutes genuine African music. The "coon songs" which are so generally sung are base imitations. The white man does not live who can write a genuine negro song. At home there used to be a rare old singer, an old Kentucky mammy, whom everybody loved. She once said:

> Us ole heads use ter make 'em up on de spurn of de moment, arter we wrassle wid de Sperit and come thoo. But the tunes was brung from Africa by our granddaddies. Dey was jis 'miliar songs. Dese days dey calls 'em ballots,

but in de ole days dey call 'em spirituals, case de Holy Spirit done revealed 'em to 'em. Some say Moss Jesus taught 'em, and I's seed 'em start in meetin'. We'd all be at the "prayer house" de Lord's Day, and de white preacher he'd splain de word and read whar Ezekial done say—

Dry bones gwine ter lib ergin.

And, honey, de Lord would come a-shining' thoo dem pages and revive dis ole nigger's heart, and I'd jump up dar and den and holler and shout and sing and pat, and dey would all cotch de words and I'd sing it to some ole shout song I'd heard 'em sing from Africa, and dey'd all take it up and keep at it, and keep a-addin' to it, and den it would be a spiritual. Dese spirituals am de best moanin' music in de world, case dey is de whole Bible sung out and out. Notes is good enough for you people, but us likes a mixtery. Dese young heads ain't wuth killin', fur dey don't keer bout de Bible nor de ole hymns. Dey's completely spiled wid too much white blood in 'em, and de big organ and de eddication has done took all de Holy Spirit out en 'em, till dey ain't no better wid der dances and cuttin' up dan de white folks.

The negro usually sang religious music at his work. He was often turned out of church for crossing his feet or singing a "fiddle sing," which is a secular song, but he could steal all the chickens he wanted and never fall from grace. One of the most persistent fancies that the old slaves cherished was that they were the oppressed Israelites, that the Southerners were the cruel Egyptians, and that Canaan was freedom. Bondage was of course their slavery. They believed that some day the Red Sea would come in a sea of blood, which was verified in the civil war. In many of their songs they appropriate Bible prophecies and ideas to themselves. The first song given is a characteristic one, illustrating many peculiarities; and if it did not come from Africa, where did it come from?

It is often asserted at the North that, as a rule, the negro was punished if he prayed or received religious instruction. On the contrary, many fine plantations had their "prayer houses," where a white minister was employed to hold services and to instruct them in the Bible. In nearly every section they were permitted and encouraged to hold their own meetings. That this is true is attested by these same thousands of "spirituals," all of which are filled with Bible texts. Some of the most devout Christians were, and are yet, the old "mammies" and "uncles" who lived all the closer to the heavenly Father because of their simplicity and lack of learning. The deeply religious and better class of old negroes maintain that the reason that this music is so fascinating to whites and blacks is because it is God's own music inspired by the Holy Spirit. There is indeed a wonderful power in some of these songs, and the charm undoubtedly lies in the fact that they are founded on Bible texts.

DONE FOUND DAT NEW HIDIN' PLACE
1. Who dat.. yon - der dressed in white?.. Must be de
2. Who dat.. yon - der dressed in black?.. Must be de
3. Jes on-ly could see lee-tle ba - by to - day—.. An - gel done
4. When I was down in E - gypt's land,.. Heard a mighty
portamento.
chil- lun ob de Is - rael - ite... Done found dat new hid - in' place!
nig - gers a - turn-in' back! Done found dat new hid - in' place!
drug her thoo de twelve pearly gates! Done found dat new hid - in' place!
talkin' 'bout de promised land— Done found dat new hid - in' place!
Who dat.. yon - der dressed in red-.... Must be de
God don't talk like a nat-er - al man—... Talk so a
Pur - ti - est ting what eb-ber I done.... Was to
And when we get on Ca - naan's shore... We'll
chil-lun dat a Mos-es led!.. Done found dat new hid - in' place!
sin-ner can a - un-der - stand— Done found dat new hid - in' place!
git religion when I was young— Done found dat new hid - in' place!
shout and sing for-eb-ber more— Done found dat new hid - in' place!
Refrain.
portamento.
Come a - long— Done found dat new hid - in' place!
Ise so gla - ad 'm Done found dat new hid - in' place!

No one questions the remarkable hold the genuine negro music has upon the Anglo-Saxon race, as is evidenced by the success of the

Jubilee singers years ago and of the Hampton students now. The negroes have simply used the weird African melodies as a fascinating vehicle for Bible truths.

Most students of English hymnology have observed a similar fact in their own religious poetry. One of the most powerful devotional hymns in the language—How Firm a Foundation, Ye Saints of the Lord—is largely indebted for its perpetuity to the fact that almost every line is taken directly from the Bible.

To illustrate the power of this music upon the colored people themselves, I may be permitted to give this little bit of personal experience:

A few nights ago I went to pay a visit to an old "mammy" from Charleston. All her family sat round the room when they found I was from the South. The eldest daughter said: "Bress le Lord! I'm glad to see you! The Norf am no place for people what's been used to eberyting. Nuffin but wuk, wuk, wuk; all's jes money. No fun, nor lub, nor Jesus Christ nowhar! Why, dey'll jes meet you and pass de time ob day, and dey'll let you go away widout eber stoppin' to ax yer ef you's prepared to die, and how's your soul. Why, I neber seed no stranger in Charleston 'thout axin' 'em, how's der soul comin' on? De niggers heah ain't got no Holy Spirit and dey is singing no 'count songs—dese white songs from books."

At this juncture I quietly began to sing, "I don't want to be buried in de Storm." Suddenly they all began to sing and pat with me, and quickly adapted their different versions to mine. They lost no time in getting happy. They all jumped up and down in a perfect ecstasy of delight, and shouted, "I feel like de Holy Spirit is right on my hade!"

Another one exclaimed: "People! dem songs makes de har rise up. Mine a-risin' now."

We all had a good time, and I felt greatly complimented when the head of the house explained enthusiastically: "You does shore sing 'em good; and for a white lady you is got a good deal of de Holy Spirit in you, honey"; and before I left the house they had tried to convince me that God has surely blessed this music by taking a hand in forming it himself.

We find many of the genuine negro melodies in Jubilee and Hampton Song Books, but for the uninitiated student of the future there is little or no instruction given, and the white singer in attempting to learn them will make poor work at their mastery; for how is he, poor fellow, to know that it is bad form not to break every law of musical phrasing and notation? What is there to show him that he must make his voice exceedingly nasal and undulating; that around every prominent note he must place a variety of small notes, called "trimmings," and he must sing tones not found in our scale; that he must on no account leave one note until he has the next one well under control? He might be tempted, in the *ignorance* of his twentieth-century education, to take breath whenever he came to the end of a line or verse! But this he should never do. By some mysterious power, to be learned only from the negro, he should carry over his breath from line to line and from verse to verse, even at the risk of bursting a blood-vessel. He must often drop from a high note to a very low one; he must be very careful to divide many of his monosyllabic words in two syllables, placing a forcible accent on the last one, so that "dead" will be "da—*ade*," "back" becomes "ba—*ack*," "chain" becomes "ch—*ain*."

♩=84
accel.
1. Ma-ry and Marthy had a cha-*ain*— Walk Jerus'lem jis like Job! An'a
2. I tell you bredderin, for a fac'— Walk Jerus'lem jis like Job! If you
3. Some says Pe-ter and some says Paul—Walk Jerus'lem jis like Job! But dey
eb'- ry link was a Je-sus Na-*ame*! Walk Jerus'lem jis like Job!
ebber leabs de debbil you musn't turn back! Walk Jerus'lem jis like Job!
ain't but one God saves us all— Walk Jerus'lem jis like Job!
Refrain.
When I comes ter die . . . I want ter be . . . . . read - y; When
accel.
I comes ter die, ... Gwine ter walk Jeru-s'lem jis like Job!

He must also intersperse his singing with peculiar humming sounds —"hum-m-m-m." He will have to learn that the negro never neglects his family relations in his songs, and seldom considers his "spirityul" finished until he has mentioned his father and mother and sister and brother, and his preacher.

A beautiful custom prevails among them of sending messages by the dying to friends gone before into heaven. When a woman dies some friend or relative will kneel down and sing to the soul as it takes its flight. This song contains endless verses, conveying love and kisses to Aunt Fannie and Uncle Caesar and "Moss Jesus." With omissions it is used upon other occasions with fine effect.

RIDE ON, JESUS
CHORUS. ♩=72.
Ride on, Je-sus, Ride on, Je-sus, Ride on, Conq'ring King; I
want to go to Heaven in de morn - in' 1. See my mud-der,
Oh, yes! Tell her for me, Oh yes! Ride my hoss in de
bat-tle ob de field, I want to go to Heaven in de morn - in'!

Old Mary, who sang this, was a nurse in our family. She, like most negroes, had no ideas how old she really was. She never worried, though the heavens should fall, and this ignorance as to when their birthdays rolled round may account for their longer lives here and in Africa, and for their not showing their age. She found great difficulty in arranging her religion to suit her morals, and once, in my childish innocence, I remonstrated with her for getting "baptisted" so many times, and she exclaimed indignantly: "I's a Methodist wid a Baptist faith. I gits baptisted ebery summer when de water am rale warm, and I gits turned out ebery winter fur dancin' and stealin', and you would too, child, ef you was a nigger."

A few days ago I asked one of the most scholarly and noted ministers of the colored race, who was visiting in New York, about the negro music. He is very black, and his parents were pure Africans. He said that undoubtedly the tunes came directly from Africa, that his father said he had sung them at home in Africa, and that the tunes were almost supernatural in their hold upon the people. He continued: "Upon condition that you will never tell my name, I'll give you an incident which will prove to you that many of our race are still under the influences of voodooism, and that although I am, as you see, a professed Christian, all the African practices hold a powerful charm for me which I can't shake off." Knowing well his reputation and position, I was startled. He went on and said:

"And this may serve you some time, as it is a true story of my own weakness. Once the bishop ordered me to the city of ———, where I was to have charge of a run-down church. The first prayer-meeting night the members locked me out, and came with shotguns to the church steps and said they were tired of ministers, that they had had four, and would not have a fifth minister. By dint of eloquence and superior education I obtained their consent to enter the church. Well, I tried faithfully to attract them. I never had more than a handful, and for six months all seemed dead set against me. I could not draw. Completely discouraged, I was in my study praying when the door opened and a little conjure man came in and said softly: 'You don't understand de people. You must get you a hand as a friend to draw 'em. Ef you will let me fix you a luck charm you'll git 'em.' In my desperation, I told him to fix it. He brought the charm back in a few days, and said, 'Now, you must feed it wid alcohol, whisky, or spirits, and never let it git dry, and always wear it nex' your heart when you enters or leaves de church.'

"It was only an ugly piece of red flannel, and I hate to confess it, but I obeyed his instructions. I always felt for it before I went down on my knees to pray. The next Sunday the church was full of people. The following Sabbath there was not standing room. For four years the aisles were crowded every Sunday. I knew it was not the gospel's power, but that wretched 'luck ball.' When the bishop sent me to another church he wrote and said: 'When you came they tried to drive you away with shotguns; here, now twenty men write me begging to have you stay. Now you draw beyond any minister in the city! How is this?' I was ashamed to tell him. I opened the charm, and found these things in it. It was a large piece of red flannel, with a horseshoe magnet fastened flat to it. In the center of the space in the magnet was a bright silver dime. On one side were sewed two needles, on the other side of the money one needle. Below it were two more needles. The whole was covered with what looked and tasted like gunpowder. I tore it up and threw it away, and have never been able to draw an audience since.—You want one? Well, I'll try to get one for you."

"Indeed I want one! What lecturer would not?"

I give this as an instance of the peculiar persistency of African ideas even in enlightened, civilized, Christian minds.

There is a Mrs. R—— in a side street in a Northern town whom I lately visited. She was the most prominent member in the Baptist colored church. She was the leading singer. Another singer got jealous of her power to holler the loudest; besides, she wanted to get her washing away from her as well as her husband, and, worst of all, *conjured* her. At last the first singer fell sick, and the doctor could do nothing to relieve her. A conjure woman called, and for twenty-five dollars undertook the case. She came in and moaned a few incantations in an unknown tongue. She carried a satchel, and took from it a glass, poured some gin into it and drank a little, and then, holding her hand over it, said:

"Mrs. R——, look inside yourself and tell me what you see."

Mrs. R—— was hypnotized, I suppose, and said, "I see pizen, and snakes a-crawlin'."

"That's right! It's the lady across the way has put the spell on you, and she has cut your shape out in red flannel and stuck it full of pins and needles and biled it. She's trickin' you, and killin' you. But I'll throw it back on her—scatter your spell to the four winds. She has killed a snake and taken the blood and mixed it with wine, and in twenty-four hours it turned into snakes and you drank it and you were going crazy, and your home would have been gone."

It is needless to say the sick woman recovered.

She showed the caul she was born with tied up in a bundle in her stocking. The neighbors were always trying to touch the lump so they could put spells on people and be healed from diseases. The conjure woman also makes luck balls for sale. She tells her customers they must always wear them next their skin on the right side, and keep them wet with "feedin' medicine."

I was so fortunate as to discover the contents of one of her balls. Corn, twine, pepper, a piece of hair from under a black cat s foot, a piece of rabbit's right foot, and whisky—all put into a red flannel bag. This was all inclosed in a buckeye biscuit. She puts loadstones in some of them to draw away a lover from a girl. She also takes roots of several different herbs and flowers and makes them into love powders, and gives them to a darkey lassie to throw upon her truant lover to bring him back to her waiting heart.

It is not to be disputed that Africa has touched in many ways and in divers places the highest civilization of the Old World. I am fully persuaded that in the near future scientific researches will discover among native African tribes traditions which disclose the real parentage of many of the weird stories concerning the Creation and the Flood which are now current among their descendants in this country. The same may be said of "Brer Rabbit" and the "Tar baby," "Brer Fox," "Brer Dog," "Brer Wolf," and all that other wonderful fraternization with animal nature which simple savage life and unbridled childish imagination suggest. In many instances they will be found absolutely identified with those that are now told in the wilds of Africa.

To show the existence of this belief among the negroes themselves, I will quote from an old negress, whom I know well, named "Aunt Lucinda":

"Dis is an ole tale. Hit done come down since de Flood. Why, chile, de Bible didn't git eberyting by a good deal—cose it didn't: Us niggers done tole dis in Africk, and Moss John done say de Bible say ef it got all de words Jesus say hit couldn't holt 'em. And dere's lots of tales de Bible didn't git. Dis one now be 'bout de hammer and de ark:

"One time God done tole Moss Nora to build him a ark, case de people fo de Flood was a singin' and a cuttin' up and a givin' entertainments, and God wanted to raise up a better people to a sarve him, and so Moss Nora had to build de ark tight, so de few people wouldn't drown. God tole him to take a he and a she of every kind and fix de jistes tight so de ark wouldn't leak water when de Flood came. De people sat around on de benches a-pokin' fun at him, and dey say, 'Moss Nora, what you doin' ?'

"He says, 'I's a-hammerin' de jistes tight.'

"And de people say, 'What dat you doin' ?'

"And Moss Nora say, 'I got this ark to build, and I gwine to build it.'

"And de people kep' a-pokin' fun. Dey say, 'Moss Nora, what dat hammer say?'

"And he say, 'What it sound to you like it say, humph?'

"And de people laugh and say it soun' like it say nuffin but 'Tim—tam! tim—tam!'

"And Moss Nora say: 'Dot's whar you fotch up wrong. I got ter build this ark so tight de water won't leak thoo, and de people won't fall out, and dat hammer don't say "Tim—tam," no sich ting. Hit say ebery time I hits de jistes, "Repent! repent!" '

"Dere's a spiritual what goes long wid it too, honey, 'bout de hammer and de nails, but I don't know it. Hit's a ole, ole story dat we been singin' since de Flood—jes come down from mouf to mouf. Hist de Window is a ole tune, but not ole like dis one. Hit come jis like I tole you."

In regard to one song, at least, I have irrefragable proof of its African origin. Mrs. Jefferson Davis tells me her old nurse was a full-blooded African named Aunt Dinah. She would lovingly put her little charge to sleep with this doggerel:

FADDING, GIDDING

Fad-ding, gid-ding, fad-ding go; San - té mo - lé, san - té mo - lé;
Fad-ding, gid-ding, fad-ding go; Eb-er sence I born ma' han' 'tan' so.

Aunt Dinah would also sing it pleadingly when begging for a present. She would begin the supplication with hands clinched tight, and open them quickly at the last line. She declared that she always sang it in this exact manner in her old African home whenever she was asking a favor, but she was never able to tell the meaning of any part of it except the last line, the African of which she had forgotten, but which meant that all black races are born with wide-open palms ready and waiting for other peoples to pour rich gifts into them. This she translated in her apt, crude way: "Eber since I born, my hand stand so!"

She had a relative named Moses, I think, who had three deep gashes radiating from each eye. Of these he was very proud, as he said they indicated that he was of the king's blood.

Ten days have elapsed since the above was written. I feel like crying, "Eureka!" I have found my proof! After a diligent search for a real live African, I have found an educated convert to Christianity, who has been absent only two years from the wilds of the west coast of Africa. In broken English he sang for me several songs sung by the savages of the native Mendi tribe. The tunes sounded much like songs I know, but I could not take them down during this interview. All the songs I sang he said seemed very familiar—in certain portions especially so.

I was especially interested in the description he gave of a peculiar ceremony common among the wildest Bushmen and the Yolloff tribe. My informant grew up and played with them a great deal when a child. He says the death of a young boy they consider an affront to the living—an affront which they never forgive. It is singular that among some of our Indian tribes a similar notion prevails. The friends meet around the corpse and exclaim, while they chant and sing and dance, in a high-pitched voice: "Why did you die? Were you too proud to stay with us? You thought yourself too good to stay with us. To whom do you leave all your things? We don't want them! Take them with you if you are so stuck up; we'll bury them with you!"

They work themselves into a perfect fury, and one gets a whip and flogs the corpse until it is horribly mutilated. Then the few who have really been friends to the child in their crude way draw near and begin to sing:

Anasa yi.
Anasa papa,

which this native African assured me meant, as nearly as he could translate it:

Find out how mother is.
Find out how papa is.

The curious identity of the name for father in this African dialect and our own he could not explain.

Even while the relatives were thus speaking kindly to the departed child, others would come up with whips, and with blows spitefully exclaim: "Tell my father's sister I am happy. Speak to her for me." This they said, mocking the relatives for sending messages.

What better proof is required of the origin of the peculiar custom of the negroes in our own Southland of sending communications by the dead? He also gave me new stories of Brother Conch, and a tale of a rabbit and a pitch-man.

He says he has heard a savage tribe often sing to the beat of a peculiar drum, as they started to pillage and destroy a neighboring tribe, these words, which he could not translate:

Zo, whine, whine,
Zo, bottom balleh.
Zo, whine, whine,
Zo, bottom balleh.

Some of the tribes are followers of Mohammed. After they have broken their fast, they sing this hymn to their God:

Li, li, e li li,
Moo moo dooroo, soo moo li.

I then sang for him a part of "Gawd bless dem Yankees, dey'll set me free," and when I came to the humming, which we all know is the marked peculiarity of the negro singing, he stopped me and said, "Whenever you hum that way it means 'Hush!' and among

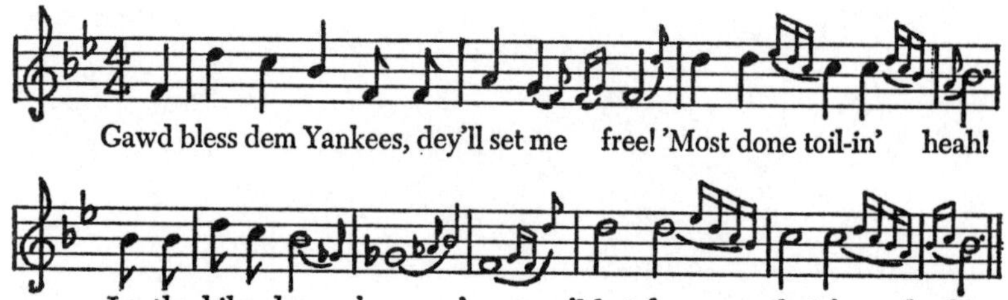
Gawd bless dem Yankees, dey'll set me free! 'Most done toil-in' heah!
Leetle chiler-den, 'm.. 'm.. 'Most done toil - in'.. heah!

the tribes I have known it always comes in baby songs." He then sang this one, which a heathen woman used to sing to his little sister "Amber":

> Amber in a wa,
> Keen yah feenyah ma,
> Amber in a bamboo carri,
> Amber eeka walloo.
> Um, um, um.

A rough translation of this means: "Amber, be quiet and I'll give you something. I'm not going to flog you. You are quiet, so I thank you. Hush, hush, hush!"

Appendix I: *A Slaveholder's Primer*

The whip-cracking image of plantations peppered with Simon Legrees is too easy; it lets us quickly anger and damn old Simon to hell and back, and in the process forget that the life of the average slave was not one of gratuitous brutality (though it sometimes was), but something far worse—cold and methodical manipulation by rational owners who considered the slave in the same category as farm machinery and livestock. The slave didn't even have the single comfort of the long-term convict: a date, however far removed, when he would be released. To give some idea of how considered was the treatment accorded by "reasonable men," I append here two articles from *De Bow's Review*, an ante bellum monthly published in New Orleans. Like a slaveholder's Dr. Spock, everything is worked out, even how much fiddling time is to be allowed.

1851

Management of Negroes upon Southern Estates

by "A Mississippi Planter"

De Bow's Review, X (New Orleans, June 1851), 621–627.

In regard to the planter's comments on fiddling, Herbert Halpert wrote: "I find the limitation on fiddling till midnight on Saturday, with required worship service on Sunday, even more significant on the folkways of the white masters. This is part of the Devil and fiddler tradition: that the Devil would appear to fiddlers and dancers who carried on past midnight, i.e., desecrated the Sabbath."

[We regard this as a practical and valuable paper for the planters, and hope that those of them who have been experimenting in the matter, will give us the results.]—EDITOR.

Some very sensible and practical writer in the March No. of "The Review," under the "*Agricultural Department*," has given us an article upon the *management of negroes*, which entitles him to the gratitude of the planting community, not only for the sound and useful information it contains, but because it has opened up this subject, to be thought of, written about, and improved upon, until the comforts of our black population shall be greatly increased, and their services become more profitable to their owners. Surely there is no subject which demands of the planter more careful consideration than the proper treatment of his slaves, by whose labor he lives, and for whose conduct and happiness he is responsible in the eyes of God. We very often find planters comparing notes and making suggestions as to the most profitable modes of tilling the soil, erecting gates, fences, farm-houses, machinery, and, indeed, everything else conducive to their comfort and prosperity; but how seldom do we find men comparing notes as to their mode of feeding, clothing, nursing, working, and taking care of those human beings intrusted to our charge, whose best condition is slavery, when they are treated with humanity, and their labor properly directed! I have been a reader of agricultural papers for more than twenty years, and while I have been surfeited, and not unfrequently disgusted, with those chimney-corner theories (that have no practical result, emanating from men who are fonder of using the pen than the plough-handle) upon the subject of raising crops, and preparing them for market, I have seldom met with an article laying down general rules for the management of negroes, by which their condition could be ameliorated, and the master be profited at the same time. One *good article* upon this subject, would be worth more to the master than a hundred theories about "rotations" and "scientific culture"; and infinitely more to the slave than whole volumes dictated by a spurious philanthropy looking to his emancipation. For it is a fact established beyond all controversy, that when the negro is treated with humanity, and subjected to constant employment without the labor of thought, and the cares incident to the necessity of providing for his own support, he is by far happier than he would be if emancipated, and left to think, and act, and provide for himself. And from the vast amount of experience in the management of slaves, can we not deduce some general, practical rules for their government, that would add to the happiness of both master and servant? I know of no other mode of arriving at this great desideratum, than for planters to give the public their rules for feeding, clothing, housing and working their slaves, and of taking care of them when sick, together with their plantation discipline. In this way, we shall be continually learning something new upon this vitally interesting question, filled, as it is, with great responsibilities; and while our slaves will be made happier, our profits from their labor will be greater, and our consciences be made easier.

I would gladly avail myself of the privilege of contributing my mite to the accomplishment of this end, by giving my own system of management, not because there is anything novel in it—that it is better, or differs essentially from that of most of my neighbors—but because it may meet the eye of some man of enlarged experience who will necessarily detect its faults, and who may be induced to suggest the proper corrections, and for which I should feel profoundly grateful. To begin, then, I send you my plantation rules, that are printed in the plantation book, which constitute a part of the contract made in the employment of the overseer, and which are observed, so far as my constant and vigilant superintendence can enforce them. My first care has been to select a proper place for my "Quarter," well protected by the shade of forest trees, sufficiently thinned out to admit a free circulation of air, so situated as to be free from the impurities of stagnant water, and to erect comfortable houses for my negroes. Planters do not always reflect that there is more sickness, and consequently greater loss of life, from the decaying logs of negro houses, open floors, leaky roofs, and crowded rooms, than all other causes combined; and if humanity will not point out the proper remedy, let self-interest for once act as a virtue, and prompt him to save the health and lives of his negroes, by at once providing comfortable quarters for them. There being upwards of 150 negroes on the plantation, I provide for them 24 houses made of hewn post oak, covered with cypress, 16 by 18, with close plank floors and good chimneys, and elevated two feet from the ground. The ground *under* and around the houses is swept every month, and the houses, both inside and out, white-washed twice a year. The houses are situated in a double row from north to south, about 200 feet apart, the doors facing inwards, and the houses being in a line, about 50 feet apart. At one end of the street stands the overseer's house, workshops, tool house, and wagon sheds; at the other, the grist and saw-mill, with good cisterns at each end, providing an ample supply of pure water. My experience has satisfied me, that spring, well, and lake water are all unhealthy in this climate, and that large under-ground cisterns, keeping the water pure and cool, are greatly to be preferred. They are easily and cheaply constructed, very convenient, and save both doctors' bills and loss of life. The negroes are never permitted to sleep before the fire, either lying down or sitting up, if it can be avoided, as they are always prone to sleep with their heads to the fire, are liable to be burnt, and to contract disease: but beds with ample clothing are provided for them, and in them they are *made to sleep*. As to their habits of amalgamation and intercourse, I know of no means whereby to regulate them, or to restrain them; I attempted it for many years by preaching virtue and decency, encouraging marriages, and by punishing, with some severity, departures from marital obligations; but it was all in vain. I allow for each hand that works out, four pounds of clear meat and one peck of meal per week. Their dinners are cooked for them, and carried to the field, always with vegetables, according to the season. There are two houses set apart at mid-day for resting, eating, and sleeping, if they desire it, and they retire to one of the weather-sheds or the grove to pass this time, not being permitted to remain in the hot sun while at rest. They cook their own suppers and breakfasts, each family being provided with an oven, skillet, and sifter, and each one having a coffee-pot, (and generally some coffee to put in it,) with knives and forks, plates, spoons, cups, &c., of their own providing. The wood is regularly furnished them; for, I hold it to be absolutely mean, for a man to require a negro to work until daylight closes in, and then force him to get wood, sometimes half a mile off, before he can get a fire, either to warm himself or cook his supper. Every negro has his hen-house, where he raises poultry, which he is not permitted to sell, and he cooks and eats his chickens and eggs for his evening and morning meals to suit himself; besides, every family has a garden, paled in, where they raise such vegetables and fruits as they take a fancy to. A large house is provided as a nursery for the children, where all are taken at daylight, and placed under the charge of a careful and experienced woman, whose sole occupation is to attend to them, and see that they are properly fed and attended to, and above all things to keep them as dry and cleanly as possible, under the circumstances. The suckling women come in to nurse their children four times during the day; and it is the duty of the nurse to see that they do not perform this duty until they have become properly cool, after walking from the field. In consequence of these regulations, I have never lost a child from being burnt to death, or, indeed, by accidents of any description; and although I have had more than thirty born within the last five years, yet I have not lost a single one from teething, or the ordinary summer complaints so prevalent amongst the children in this climate.

I give to my negroes four full suits of clothes with two pair of shoes, every year, and to my women and girls a calico dress and two handkerchiefs extra. I do not permit them to have "truck patches" other than their gardens, or to raise anything whatever for market; but in lieu thereof, I give to each head of a family and to every single negro on Christmas day, five dollars, and send them to the county town under the charge of the overseer or driver, to spend their money. In this way, I save my mules from being killed up in summer, and my oxen in winter, by working and hauling off their crops; and more than all, the negroes are prevented from acquiring habits of trading in farm produce, which invariably leads to stealing, followed by whipping, trouble to the master, and discontent on the part of the slave. I permit no spirits to be brought on the plantation, or used by any negro, if I can prevent it; and a violation of this rule, if found out, is always followed by a whipping, and a forfeiture of the five dollars next Christmas.

I have a large and comfortable hospital provided for my negroes when they are sick; to this is attached a nurse's room; and when a negro complains of being too unwell to work, he is at once sent to the hospital, and put under the charge of a very experienced and careful negro woman, who administers the medicine and attends to his diet, and where they remain until they are able to work again. This woman is provided with sugar, coffee, molasses, rice, flour and tea, and does not permit a patient to taste of meat or vegetables until he is restored to health. Many negroes relapse after the disease is broken, and die, in consequence of remaining in their houses and stuffing themselves with coarse food after their appetites return, and both humanity and economy dictate that this should be prevented. From the system I have pursued, I have not lost a hand since the summer of 1845, (except one that was killed by accident,) nor has my physician's bill averaged fifty dollars a year, notwithstanding I live near the edge of the swamp of Big Black River, where it is thought to be very unhealthy.

I cultivate about ten acres of cotton and six of corn to the hand, not forgetting the little wheat patch that our correspondent speaks of, which costs but little trouble, and proves a great comfort to the negroes; and have as few sour looks and as little whipping as almost any other place of the same size.

I must not omit to mention that I have a good fiddler, and keep him well supplied with catgut, and I make it his duty to play for the negroes every Saturday night until 12 o'clock. They are exceedingly punctual in their attendance at the ball, while Charley's fiddle is always accompanied with Ihurod on the triangle, and Sam to "pat."

I also employ a good preacher, who regularly preaches to them on the Sabbath day, and it is made the duty of every one to come up clean and decent to the place of worship. As Father Garritt regularly calls on Brother Abram, (the foreman of the prayer meetings,) to close the exercises, he gives out and sings his hymn with much unction, and always cocks his eye at Charley, the fiddler, as much as to say, "Old fellow, you had your time last night; now it is mine."

I would gladly learn every negro on the place to read the bible, but for a fanaticism which, while it professes friendship to the negro, is keeping a cloud over his mental vision, and almost crushing out his hopes of salvation.

These are some of the leading outlines of my management, so far as my negroes are concerned. That they are imperfect, and could be greatly improved, I readily admit; and it is only with the hope that I shall be able to improve them by the experience of others, that I have given them to the public.

Should you come to the conclusion that these rules would be of any service when made known to others, you will please give them a place in the "Review."

A Mississippi Planter.

RULES AND REGULATIONS FOR THE GOVERNMENT OF A SOUTHERN PLANTATION

1. There shall be a place for everything, and everything shall be kept in its place.

2. On the first days of January and July, there shall be an account taken of the number and condition of all the negroes, stock and farming utensils, of every description, on the premises, and the same shall be entered in the plantation book.

3. It shall be the duty of the overseer to call upon the stock-minder once every day, to know if the cattle, sheep and hogs have been seen and counted, and to find out if any are dead, missing, or lost.

4. It shall be the duty of the overseer, at least once in every week, to see and count the stock himself, and to inspect the fences, gates, and watergaps on the plantation, and see that they are in good order.

5. The wagons, carts, and all other implements, are to be kept

under the sheds, and in the houses where they belong, except when in use.

6. Each negro-man will be permitted to keep his own axe, and shall have it forthcoming when required by the overseer. No other tool shall be taken or used by any negro, without the permission of the overseer.

7. Humanity, on the part of the overseer, and unqualified obedience on the part of the negroes are, under all circumstances, indispensable.

8. Whipping, when necessary, shall be in moderation, and never done in a passion; and the driver shall in no instance inflict punishment, except in the presence of the overseer, and when, from sickness, he is unable to do it himself.

9. The overseer shall see that the negroes are properly clothed and well fed. He shall lay off a garden of at least six acres, and cultivate it as part of his crop, and give the negroes as many vegetables as may be necessary.

10. It shall be the duty of the overseer to select a sufficient number of the women, each week, to wash for all. The clothes shall be well washed, ironed and mended, and distributed to the negroes on Sunday morning; when every negro is expected to wash himself, comb his head, and put on clean clothes. No washing or other labor will be tolerated on the Sabbath.

11. The negroes shall not be worked in the rain, or kept out after night, except in weighing or putting away cotton.

12. It shall be the duty of the driver, at such hours of the night as the overseer may designate, to blow his horn, and go around and see that every negro is at his proper place, and to report to the overseer any that may be absent; and it shall be the duty of the overseer, at some hour between that time and day-break, to patrol the quarters himself, and see that every negro is where he should be.

13. The negro children are to be taken, every morning, by their mothers, and carried to the houses of the nurses; and every cabin shall be kept locked during the day.

14. Sick negroes are to receive particular attention. When they are first reported sick, they are to be examined by the overseer, and prescribed for, and put under the care of the nurse, and not put to work until the disease is broken and the patient beyond the danger of a relapse.

15. When the overseer shall consider it necessary to send for a physician, he shall enter in the plantation book the number of visits, and to what negro they are made.

16. When any negro shall die, an hour shall be set apart by the overseer for his burial; and at that hour all business shall cease, and every negro on the plantation, who is able to do so, shall attend the burial.

17. The overseer shall keep a plantation book, in which he shall register the birth and name of each negro that is born; the name of each negro that died, and specify the disease that killed him. He shall also keep in it the weights of the daily picking of each hand; the mark, number and weight of each bale of cotton, and the time of sending the same to market; and all other such occurrences, relating to the crop, the weather, and all other matters pertaining to the plantation, that he may deem advisable.

18. The overseer shall pitch the crops, and work them according to his own judgment, with the distinct understanding that a failure to make a bountiful supply of corn and meat for the use of the plantation, will be considered as notice that his services will not be required for the succeeding year.

19. The negroes, teams, and tools, are to be considered as under the overseer's exclusive management, and are not to be interfered with by the employer, only so far as to see that the foregoing rules are strictly observed.

20. The overseer shall, under no circumstances, create an account against his employer, except in the employment of a physician, or in the purchase of medicines; but whenever anything is wanted about the plantation, he shall apply to his employer for it.

21. Whenever the overseer, or his employer, shall become dissatisfied, they shall, in frank and friendly manner, express the same, and, if either party desires it, he shall have the right to settle and separate.

1851

Management of Negroes

by "A Small Farmer"

De Bow's Review, XI (New Orleans, October 1851), 369–372.

J. D. B. De Bow, Esq.—Your number for June contains an article upon this subject, "Management of Negroes upon Southern Estates," and whilst I agree with the writer in the main, I have also some notions of my own, which you are at liberty to use.

The public may desire to know the age of the writer, the length of time he has been managing negroes, and how long he has tried the mode of management he recommends. It is sufficient to say, I have had control of negroes in and out of the field for thirty years, and have been carrying out my present system, and improving it gradually, for twenty years.

I do not deem it needful to follow "a planter," nor shall I strike a blow at book-farming or theories, as I am an advocate for both, believing that even an error has its advantages, as it will frequently elicit inquiry and a good article in reply, whereas a statement of facts will sometimes pass unnoticed.

Housing for negroes should be good; each family should have a house, 16 by 18 feet in the clear, plank floor, brick chimney, shingle roof; floor, elevated 2 feet above the earth. There should be no loft, no place to stow away anything, but pins to hang clothes upon. Each house should be provided with a bedstead, cotton mattress, and sufficient bed-clothes for comfort for the heads of the family, and also for the young ones.

Clothing should be sufficient, but of no set quantity, as all will use, or waste what is given, and many be no better clad with four suits than others with two. I know families that never give more than two suits, and their servants are always neater than others with even four.

My rule is, to give for winter a linsey suit, one shirt of best toweling, one hat, one pair of shoes, a good blanket, costing $2 to $2.50, every other year, (or I prefer, after trying three years, a comfort.) In the summer, two shirts, two pair pants, and one straw hat. Several of my negroes will require two pair pants for winter, and occasionally even a third pair, depending mostly upon the material. Others require another shirt and a third pair of pants for summer. I seldom give two pair of shoes.

Food is cooked by a woman, who has the children under her charge. I do not regard it as good economy, to say nothing of any feeling, to require negroes to do any cooking after their day's labor is over.

The food is given out daily, a half pound to each hand that goes to the field, large and small, water carriers and all; bread and vegetables without stint, the latter prepared in my own garden, and dealt out to the best advantage, endeavoring to have something every day in the year. I think four pounds of clear meat is too much. I have negroes here that have had only a half pound each for twenty years, and they bid fair to outlive their master, who occasionally forgets his duty, and will be a gourmand. I practice on the plan, that all of us would be better to be restrained, and that health is best subserved by not over-eating.

My cook would make cotton enough to give the extra one pound. The labor in making vegetables would make another pound. I say this to show I do not dole out a half pound per day from parsimony.

My hours of labor, commencing with pitching my crop, is from daylight until 12 M.; all hands then come in and remain until 2 o'clock, P.M., then back to the field until dark. Some time in May we prolong the rest three hours; and if a very hot day, even four hours. Breakfast is eaten in the field, half an hour to an hour being given; or they eat and go to work without being driven in and out—all stopping when my driver is ready.

I give all females half of every Saturday to wash and clean up, my cook washing for young men and boys through the week. The cabins are scoured once a week, swept out every day, and beds made up at noon in summer, by daylight in winter. In the winter, breakfast is eaten before going to work, and dinner is carried to the hands.

I do not punish often, but I seldom let an offence pass, making a lumping settlement, and then correct for the servant's remembrance. I find it better to whip very little. Young ones being rather treacherous in their memory, pulling an ear, or a sound box, will bring every thing right. I am almost afraid I will subject myself to the "chimney corner theorist's" animadversion, if I say more, but I will risk it. Put up a hewed log-house, with a good substantial door, lock and key, story 12 feet high, logs across above, so as to make a regular built jail. Have air holes near the ceiling well protected by iron bars. The first negro that steals, or runs away, or fights, or who is hard to manage in order to get a day's work, must be locked up every night as soon as he comes in from work, and turned out next morning; kept up every Sunday. Negroes are gregarious; they dread solitariness, and to be deprived from the little weekly dances and chit-chat. They will work to death rather than be shut up. I know the advantage, though I have no jail, my house being a similar one, yet used for other purposes.

I have a fiddle in my quarters, and though some of my good old brethren in the church would think hard of me, yet I allow dancing; ay, I buy the fiddle and encourage it, by giving the boys occasionally a big supper.

I have no overseer, and do not manage so scientifically as those who are able to lay down rules; yet I endeavor to manage so that myself, family and negroes may take pleasure and delight in our relations.

It is not possible in my usual crude way to give my whole plans, but enough is probably said. I permit no night-work, except feeding stock and weighing cotton. No work of any kind at noon, unless to clean out cabins, and bathe the children when nursing, not even washing their clothes.

I require every servant to be present each Sabbath morning and Sabbath evening at family prayers. In the evening the master or sometimes a visitor, if a professor, expounds the chapter read. Thus my servants hear 100 to 200 chapters read each year anyhow. One of my servants, a professor, is sometimes called on to close our exercises with prayer.

Owning but a few slaves, I am probably able to do a better part by them than if there were one or two hundred. But I think I could do better if I had enough to permit me to systematize better.

I would keep a cook and a nurse. I would keep a stock feeder, whose whole duty should be to attend to stock in general, to clean out the stable, have troughs filled with food, so that the plow hands would have nothing to do but water, clean down, and tie up the teams. I would build a house large enough, and use it for a dance-house for the young, and those who wished to dance, as well as for prayer meetings, and for church on Sunday—making it a rule to be present myself occasionally at both, and my overseer always. I know the rebuke in store about dancing, but I cannot help it. I believe negroes will be better disposed this way than any other. I would employ a preacher for every Sabbath. One of my negroes can read the Bible, and he has prayer-meeting every Sabbath at four o'clock, P.M.—all the negroes attend regularly, no compulsion being used.

I have tried faithfully to break up immorality. I have not known an oath to be given for a long time. I know of no quarrelling, no calling harsh names, and but little stealing. "Habits of amalgamation" I cannot stop; I can check it, but only in the name. I am willing to be taught, for I have tried everything I know. Yours, truly,

A SMALL FARMER.

P.S.—I endeavor to have regularity on going to bed; forbid sitting or lying by the fire after bed-time. I require fire makers to be up before day in winter, but forbid getting up before day, trotting off to the field, and waiting for daylight, as some persons are said to do.

I forbid my driver from keeping hands in the field when there is an appearance of rain.

My negroes get baits of fresh meat occasionally, but always seasoned high with red pepper. At times I give molasses, sugar, coffee and flour, generally laying out about $10 per hand for such luxuries.

APPENDIX II: *Further Reading*[1]

A.

The recent paperback reprints of Melville Herskovits' *The Myth of the Negro Past** (Boston, 1958) and Gunnar Myrdal's *An American Dilemma** (New York, 1964) have once again made generally available some of the most interesting thinking on the cultural background and role of the American Negro. The bibliography in the Herskovits reprint has more than 130 entries not in the 1941 edition. Harvey Wish recently edited an interesting anthology of writings by Southern whites, abolitionists, and former slaves, *Slavery in the South* (New York, 1964). Miles Mark Fisher's *Negro Slave Songs in the United States** (Ithaca, 1953; paperback reprint, New York, 1963) is frequently suggestive, though Fisher's textual interpretations are peculiar and unreliable. E. Franklin Frazier's *The Negro in the United States,** (rev. ed.; New York, 1957) is an excellent reference work.

Charles Haywood's *A Bibliography of North American Folklore and Folksong** (New York, 1951), for all its annoying errors, is still the most comprehensive bibliography we have. Many references to minstrelsy can be found in Carl Wittke's *Tambo and Bones* (Durham, 1930). Two bibliographical articles worth consulting are Damon S. Foster, "The Negro in Early American Songsters,"* *Papers of the Bibliographical Society of America*, XXVIII, Pt. 2 (1934), 132–163; and Dena J. Epstein, "Slave Music in the United States before 1860, a Survey of Sources,"* Music Library Association *Notes* (Spring, 1963), pp. 195–212, and (Summer, 1963), pp. 377–390. Two other important lists are George Herzog, "Research in Primitive and Folk Music in the United States: A Survey," American Council of Learned Societies *Bulletin 24* (April 1936); and Julius Metfessel (compiler and annotator), *The Folk Music of the Western Hemisphere: A List of References in the New York Public Library* (New York, 1925),

[1] All volumes and articles marked with an asterisk have useful bibliographies.

first issued under the same title in the *Bulletin of the New York Public Library*, 28:11 (November 1924), 779–830, and 28:12 (December 1924), 864–889.

B. A. Botkin's *Lay My Burden Down: A Folk History of Slavery* (Chicago, 1945) presents selections from interviews made among former slaves by members of the Federal Writers Project. Like much primary material, it is a delightful corrective to some of the excesses found in a few of the more academic discussions.

One might examine with profit some of the many articles dealing with minstrelsy, for they display the folklore about folklore mentioned earlier, among them R. P. Nevin's "Stephen C. Foster and Negro Minstrelsy," *Atlantic Monthly*, XX (November 1867), 608–616, and Ralph Keeler's "Three Years as a Negro Minstrel," *Atlantic Monthly*, XXIV (July 1869), 71–85. Many contemporary biographies and autobiographies by whites offer rich materials. Thomas Wentworth Higginson's *Army Life in a Black Regiment* (Boston, 1869; paperback reprint, Boston, 1962) is particularly readable; Fanny Kemble's well-known *Journal of a Residence on a Georgia Plantation in 1838–1839* (New York, 1863) includes many penetrating, though frequently emotional, insights into plantation life. Edward L. Pierce's "The Freedman at Port Royal" (*Atlantic Monthly*, XXI [September 1863], 291–315) is a well-balanced and well-written account of an area important in the activities of many Northern abolitionists, among them W. F. Allen, C. P. Ware, and Lucy McKim Garrison, editors of the first major collection of Negro folksong—*Slave Songs of the United States* (New York, 1868; reprinted 1929 and 1951).

George Pullen Jackson's *White and Negro Spirituals** (New York, 1943) documents the case for the white-to-Negro theory of the development of spirituals. Newman I. White's *American Negro Folk-Songs** (Cambridge, Mass., 1928; reprint, Hatboro, Pa., 1965) presents a more moderate aspect of the theory, and also includes several other intelligent and suggestive discussions about Negro folksong. Both Jackson and White have excellent bibliographies. At the other end of the scale from Jackson is H. E. Krehbiel, whose *Afro-American Folksongs* (New York, 1914) attempts to prove just how nonwhite the songs are. By far the best anatomy of the guerrilla warfare among the various partisan groups asserting claims to the origin of Negro song is D. K. Wilgus' "The Negro-White Spiritual," in *Anglo-American Folksong Scholarship Since 1898** (New Brunswick, N. J., 1959).

Newbell Niles Puckett's *Folk Beliefs of the Southern Negro* (Chapel Hill, 1926) is the only book-length study of American Negro superstitions and beliefs; it is valuable both as a collection and an analysis, and well repays examination. One of the best regional collections of such material is *Drums and Shadows: Survival Studies among the Georgia Coastal Negroes*, Savannah Unit of the Georgia Writers' Project, WPA (Athens, Ga., 1940); in addition to a considerable quantity of excellent collectanea, the editors have included a long appendix of parallel customs and beliefs from African collections.

Many of the thirty volumes written by Joel Chandler Harris included adaptations of folklore material. Harris has been the subject of numerous articles and books, among them Stella Brewer Brookes's *Joel Chandler Harris, Folklorist* (Athens, Ga., 1950). A starting list of Harris' works and editions and related biography and criticism can be found in Robert E. Spiller, *et al.* (eds.), *Literary History of the United States: Bibliography* ([3d ed., rev. New York, 1963], pp. 131–133, 540–542).

The several early articles on folklore of the Sea Island Negroes have been completed by an excellent series of regional studies made much later. *Drums and Shadows* has been cited above; some other collections and studies from the region are Guy B. Johnson, *Folk Culture on St. Helena Island, South Carolina* (Chapel Hill, 1930); Charles C. Jones, Jr., *Negro Myths from the Georgia Coast* (Columbia, S.C., 1888; reprinted 1925); Lydia Parrish, *Slave Songs of the Georgia Sea Islands* (New York, 1942; reprinted, Hatboro, Pa., 1965); Augustine T. Smythe, *et al., The Carolina Low-Country* (New York, 1942); and A. M. H. Christensen, *Afro-American Folk-Lore: Told round Cabin Fires on the Sea Islands of South Carolina* (Boston, 1892).

The *Memoirs of the American Folklore Society* is a rich source of documented texts of African and New World Negro folklore, particularly the following: Heli Chatelain, "Folk-Tales of Angola," *MAFS* I (1894); Alcée Fortier, "Louisiana Folk-Tales," *MAFS* 3 (1895); Elsie Clews Parsons, "The Folk-Tales of Andros Islands, Bahamas," *MAFS* 13 (1918); Elsie Clews Parsons, "Folk-Lore from the Cape Verde Islands," *MAFS* 15 (1923); Elsie Clews Parsons, "Folk-Lore of the Sea Islands, South Carolina," *MAFS* 16 (1923); Martha Warren Beckwith, "Jamaica Anansi Stories," *MAFS* 17 (1924); C. M. Doke, "Lamba Folk-Lore," *MAFS* 20 (1927); Martha Warren Beckwith, "Jamaica Folk-Lore," with music recorded in the field by Helen Roberts, *MAFS* 21 (1928); Arthur Huff Fauset, "Folklore from Nova Scotia," *MAFS* 24 (1931); Elsie Clews Parsons, "Folk-Lore of the Antilles, French and English," *MAFS* 26, Pt. III (1943). J. D. Elder's

"Song Games of Trinidal and Tobago" (*PAFS* 16 [1964]) includes interesting commentary on a number of items found in American Negro tradition.

One might examine also some of the more important collections of African folklore. William Bascom's "Folklore Research in Africa" (*JAF*, LXXVII [1964], 12–31) includes a survey of scholarship concerning verbal arts and an extensive bibliography of collections.

For other articles and books on Negro folklore—and there have been many—consult the annual bibliographies in *Journal of American Folklore* and *Southern Folklore Quarterly*, the bibliographies in the items marked with an asterisk above, and the annotations in *MAFS*.

Beginning with its first volume, the *Journal of American Folklore* expressed considerable interest in the folklore of the Negro. Because the *Journal* is generally available, none of its articles has been included in this anthology. The following chronological list of all articles on American Negro folklore and most articles on African folklore appearing in *JAF*, Vols. I—XIII (1888–1900), may give some indication of what the professional folklorists were finding of interest during the last thirteen years of the nineteenth century.

B.

Articles in the *Journal of American Folklore*, 1888–1900.

1888

Newell, W. W., "Myths of Voodoo Worship and Child Sacrifice in Hayti," I:1, 16–30.

Fortier, Alcée, "Customs and Superstitions in Louisiana, I:2, 136–140.

———, "Louisiana Nursery Tales," I:2, 140–145. (Two tales with translations.)

Fowke, Gerard, "Brer Rabbit and Brer Fox: How Brer Rabbit was Allowed to Choose His Death," I:2, 148–149. (Text without commentary.)

Newell, W. W. "*Negro Myths from the Georgia Coast*, by Charles C. Jones, Jr," I:2, 169–170. 'Review.)

1889

Fortier, Alcée, "Louisiana Nursery Tales, II," II:4, 36–40. (Two more Creole patois stories, with translations.)

Newell, W. W., "Reports of Voodoo Worship in Hayti and Louisiana," II:4, 41–47.

"Notes and Queries: Reports Concerning Voodooism," II:6, 232–233.

Bergen, Mrs. Fanny D., "On the Eastern Shore," II:7, 295–300. (Miscellanea from Maryland.)

1890

Owen, Mary A., "Ole Rabbit an' de Dawg He Stole," III:9, 135–138. (Dialect tale.)

Pendleton, Louis, "Notes on Negro Folk-lore and Witchcraft in the South," III:10, 201–207. (Georgia material: a Tar Baby story less pleasant than Harris'; metempsychosis; voodoo; conjuring; Devil tales.)

"Concerning Negro Sorcery in the United States," III:11, 281–287. (Newspaper items clipped by Stewart Culin: voodoo; enchanted girls; conjure bags; invisible white doctor who steals blood; charms; clairvoyants.)

Clarke, Mary Olmsted, "Song Games of Negro Children in Virginia," III:11, 288–290.

Chamberlain, A. F., "Negro Creation Legend," III:11, 302. (God, making Negro, Chinaman, and Indian, exhausts his lump of earth. He seizes a butterfly and removes the wings, making the first Frenchman, then makes the first Englishman from an ant. "And consequently the Englishman and the Frenchman, having proceeded from animate beings, instead of coming from a lump of earth, have always made their way in the world better than the rest.")

1891

Edwards, Charles L., "Some Tales from Bahama Folk-lore," IV:12, 47–54.

"Record of Folklore and Mythology," IV:13. (Two notes, the first unsigned but probably by W. W. Newell, commenting on Mary Pamela Milne-Homes' *Mama's Black Nurse Stories* [pp. 180–181]; the second, signed by Newell, concerning Vôdu and Hoodoo, and a confluence of practice and a confusion of terms [pp. 181–182].)

Bolton, H. Carrington, "Decoration of Graves of Negroes in South Carolina," IV:14, 214.

Edwards, Charles L., "Some Tales from Bahama Folk-lore: Fairy Stories," IV:14, 247–252.

Newton, Mary Mann-Page, "Notes and Queries: Aunt Debora Goes Visiting: A Sketch from Virginia Life," IV:15, 354–356. (A fatuous piece that unintentionally exemplifies the Mammy-syndrome cliché.)

1892

Ingersoll, Ernest, "Notes and Queries: Decoration of Negro Graves," V: 68–69. (Negroes in Columbia, S.C., place broken utensils on graves.)

Lee, Collins, "Some Negro Lore from Baltimore," V:17, 111–112. (A list of superstitions.)

Thanet, Octave, "Folk-Lore in Arkansas," V:17, 121–125. (Br'er Rabbit's immorality "is the reflection of the African religion, which interferes less with morals than any I know. Br'er Rabbit, indeed, personifies the obscure ideals of the Negro race. He has a sort of futility in 'scheminess' that is very African; so is the simple-minded vanity that is always getting him in the snare. But the enemy against whom he is pitted is so much stupider than he that the main impression made is of amazing arts and resources," p. 122. Because the writer's bigotry is so unencumbered by observation, this article is more entertaining than annoying.)

Kane, Helen P., "Notes and Queries: Reception to the Dead," V:17, 148. (This is the entire note: "Among certain Negroes, locality unknown, a custom prevails of a reception by a dead person. The corpse is dressed as if for a festival, in its best clothing; the usher announces, 'The corpse will now receive his friends'; and those present enter and depart with greetings and farewells, given as if the dead person were capable of comprehending.")

Newell, W. W., "*Afro-American Folk-Lore: Told round Cabin Fires on the Sea Islands of South Carolina*, by A. M. H. Christensen," V:18, 258–260. (Review.)

"Negro Superstitions concerning the Violin," V:19, 329–330 (from Boston *Transcript*, October 1892).

"Folk-Lore Scrap-Book: Superstitions of Negroes in New Orleans," V:19, 330–332.

1893

Gerber, A., "Uncle Remus Traced to the Old World," VI:23, 245–257. (African and European parallels for Uncle Remus stories; stories learned from white masters "have undergone greater changes than the tales from Africa, yet that is nothing but natural. The African tales were merely transferred to another soil, the European changed both climate and race," p. 256.)

"Demoniacal Possession in Angola, Africa," VI:23, 258.

Meikleham, Randolph, "Notes and Queries: A Negro Ballad," VI:23, 300–301. (A rhyme and song without commentary.)

Bacon, Alice Mabel, "Notes and Queries: Proposal for Folk-Lore Research at Hampton, Va.," VI:23, 305–309.

D[orsey], J. O[wen], "*Old Rabbit the Voodoo and Other Stories*, by Mary Alicia Owen," VI:23, 322–324. (Review.)

1894

"Folk-Lore Scrap-Book: Beliefs of Southern Negroes Concerning Hags," VII:24, 66–67. (From *Southern Workman*, March 1894. If you stick a fork into the floor below a chair in which your visitor sits, you pin her hag-spirit to the floor and she cannot leave until the fork is removed; charms, etc.)

Banks, Frank D., "Plantation Courtship," VII:25, 147–149. (Sentimentalia in dialect.)

Christensen, Mrs. Abigail M. H., "Notes and Queries: Spirituals and 'Shouts' of Southern Negroes," VII:25, 154–155.

Moore, Ruby Andrews, "Superstitions from Georgia," VII:27, 305–306. (White and Negro.)

Backus, E. M., "Cradle-Songs of Negroes in North Carolina," VII:27, 310.

"Folk-Lore Scrap-Book: Mortuary Customs and Beliefs of South Carolina Negroes," VII:27, 318–319. (From Atlanta *Constitution* article by Mary A. Waring.)

1895

"Folk-Lore Scrap-Book: Courtship Formulas of Southern Negroes," VIII:29, 155–156. (From *Southern Workman.*)

Chatelain, Heli, "Some Causes of the Retardation of African Progress," VIII:30, 177–184. (Seclusion; climate; lack of a system of writing; polygamy; slavery; fear of witchcraft.)

"Folk-Lore Scrap-Book: Negro Superstitions in South Carolina," VIII:30, 251–252. (Mary A. Waring's articles in Atlanta *Constitution.*)

1896

Chatelain, Heli, "Angolan Customs," IX:32, 13–18. (Marriage; adultery; oaths; ordeals; funerals; drinking . . .)

Bates, William C., "Creole Folk-Lore from Jamaica," IX:32, 38–42. (Seventy-six proverbs.)

McLennan, Marcia, "Notes and Queries: Origin of the Cat; a Negro tale," IX:32, 71. (Sin to kill a cat because it comes from Jesus' right-hand glove.)

Williams, Alfred M., "A Miracle Play in the West Indies," IX:33, 117–120.

Bates, William C., "Creole Folk-Lore from Jamaica, II," IX:33, 121–126. (Four "Nancy" stories. Long note by W. W. Newell follows the article, pp. 126–128.)

Hawkins, John, "An Old Mauma's Folk-Lore," IX:33, 129–131.

Moore, Ruby Andrews, "Folk-Lore Scrap-Book: Conjuring and Conjure-Doctors in the Southern United States," IX:33, 143–147; continued in IX:34, 224–226. (From *Southern Workman.*)

Johnston, Mrs. William Preston, "Two Negro Tales," IX:34, 194–198.

"Negro Hymn of the Judgment Day," IX:34, 210.

Backus, E. M., "Notes and Queries: Negro Ghost Stories," IX:34, 228–230.

Smith, Pamela Coleman, "Two Negro Stories from Jamaica," IX:35, 278.

Trowbridge, Ada Wilson, "Negro Customs and Folk-Stories of Jamaica," IX:35, 279–287.

1897

Chatelain, Heli, "African Folk-Life," X:36, 21–34. (Interesting ethnographic article, particularly the comments on African slavery.)

"Folk-Lore Scap-Book: A Voodoo Festival near New Orleans," X:36, 76. (From New Orleans *Times-Democrat*, June 24, 1896.)

Backus, Mrs. E. M., "Negro Hymns from Georgia," X:37, 116. (This is one of a long series of unannotated songs with which Mrs. Backus peppered *JAF* for several issues. Others appear in X:38, 202 and 216; X:39, 264; XI:40, 22 and 60; XII:47, 272.)

"Folk-Lore Scrap-Book," X:38, 240–241. (Two stories, untitled, from *Southern Workman.*)

Hall, Julien A., "Notes and Queries: Negro Conjuring and Tricking," X:38, 241–243.

Whitney, Annie Weston, "De Los' Ell an' Yard," X:39, 293–298. (Provenience of a Negro expression.)

1898

Bullock, Mrs. Waller R., "The Collection of Maryland Folklore," XI:40, 7–16. (Some Negro sayings and stories.)

Bacon, Alice Mabel, "Work and Methods of the Hampton Folk-Lore Society," XI:40, 17–21.

Minor, Mary Willis, "Notes and Queries: How to Keep Off Witches," XI:40, 71.

"Folk-Lore Scrap-Book: Two Negro Tales Concerning the Jay," XI:

40, 74–75. (Two tales sent to *Southern Workman* by Susan Showers.)

"Folk-Lore Scrap-Book: Divination in South Africa," XI: 42, 231–234.

Backus, Emma M., "Animal Tales from North Carolina," XI:42, 284–292. (Seven stories.)

Bogg, Mrs. E. T., "Notes and Queries: De Secon' Flood Story of a Negro Nurse," XI:43, 237–238.

1899

Backus, Emma M., "Tales of the Rabbit from Georgia Negroes," XII: 45, 108–115. (Six Br'er Rabbit tales.)

Bergen, Fanny D., "Notes and Queries: Two Negro Witch-Stories," XII:45, 145–146, and "Louisiana Ghost Story," XII:45, 146–147.

"Various Ethnographic Notes: African Masks and Secret Societies," XII:46, 208–209, and "Mumbo Jumbo," XII:46, 209–211.

"Folk-Lore Scrap-Book: Irishman Stories told by Negroes," XII:46, 226–230.

Steiner, Roland, "Superstitions and Beliefs from Central Georgia," XII:47, 261–271. (139 Negro and white superstitions.)

"Folk-Lore Scrap-Book: Cures by Conjure Doctors," XII:47, 288–289 (from *Southern Workman*) and "Modern Conjuring in Washington," XII:47, 289–290 (from Washington *Post*).

Newell, W. W., "Notes and Queries: Negro Superstitions of European Origin," XII:47, 294–295.

1900

Backus, Emma M., "Folk-Tales from Georgia," XIII, 19–32. (Eight animal, one tree, one boy.)

Packwood, Mrs. L. H. C., "Cure for an Aching Tooth," XIII, 66–67. (Carry blood from aching tooth to north side of pine tree at sundown.)

Steiner, Roland, "Sol Lockheart's Call," XIII, 67–70. (In this description of a man's call to preach there is a story about transferring chills and fever to a persimmon tree.)

C.

Articles in *Southern Workman*, 1893–1901.

[Except for those articles marked with an asterisk, all entries below were published in the "Folk-Lore and Ethnology" section of *Southern Workman*.]

1893

Rathburn, F. G., "The Negro Music of the South," 22:11, 174* (A letter to the editor of the New York *Herald* from the director of music at Hampton. See Preface to "Folk-Lore and Ethnology," *Southern Workman.*)

1894

23:1, 15–16. (A report on the first monthly meeting of the Hampton Folk-Lore Society, Dec. 11, 1893. The topic was "Popular Signs and Superstitions." Several samples are given.)

"Hags and their Ways," 23:2, 26–27. (Dream signs; general discussion of hags' activities; story of a woman who captured a hag's skin; variants of the game "Hully Gully.")

Bedford, The Reverend, "Another Tribute to the Negro Melodies," 23:3, 45.

23:3, 46–47. (Superstitions from Bradley, S. C.; more ways to handle hags; a few riddles.)

23:4, 65–66. (A letter from Phillis Wheatley's sister, Mrs. Chloe Cabot Thomas; folk medicine from Washington, D.C.)

23:5, 84–86. (Dream and plant lore from Asheville, N.C.; Hampton paper on children's games.)

23:7, 131–133. (Address by W. W. Newell, "The Importance and Utility of the Collection of Negro Folk-Lore."—a general paper by Anna J. Cooper.)

23:8, 149–150. ("Bre'r Rabbit and Bre'r Elephant," "The Donkey, The Dog, The Cat and the Rooster," "The Eagle and the Fish-hawk.")

23:10, 179–180. (Man bargains with the Devil, cats take him away in seven years; old man disfigured by giant cat; preacher story.)

23:12, 209–210. (Riddles from South Carolina; cures; fortune telling; dreams; hags; proverbs.)

1895

Banks, Frank D., "Old Time Courtship," 24:1, 14–15. (Also more courting riddles from Portia Smiley, Calhoun, Alabama.)

"Negro Folk-Songs," 24:2, 30–32. (A paper given and performed by several Hampton students at the 1894 AFS meeting. A corn song, "Run, Nigger, Run," and "Juba.")

24:3, 49–50. (To cure a drunkard, 'Take a live eel, skin it, put the skin in some liquor and give it to the drunkard. He will never drink again." Other medical techniques; nurses' signs; tests for criminals; hag lore, with cats.)

"Sermon and Prayers of the Negroes," 24:4, 59–61.

24:5, 78–79. (Courtship dialogue; signs and superstitions; riddles.)

Herron, Leonora, "Conjuring and Conjure Doctors," 24:7, 117–118. (Based on earlier work by Hampton students.)

24:8, 154–156. (Request for folklore contributions; reprinted in this anthology.)

Bacon, A. M., "Conjuring and Conjure Doctors," 24:11, 193–194, and 24:12, 209–211. (Reprinted in this anthology.)

1896

25:1, 15–16. ("A Religious Song of the Yoruba People, West Africa," by H. F. Smith; "Courtship Customs," by Portia Smiley; "Superstitions about Animals" and "Weather-Lore," by J. H. Evans.)

25:2, 37–38.* (Reviews of Alcée Fortier, *Louisiana Folk-Tales*, and Charles L. Edwards, *Bahama Songs and Stories*.)

25:2, 38–39. ("Courtship in Old Virginia," a dialogue play; "The Rhode Island Vampire," which notes similarity to hag riding.)

25:3, 61. ("Brer Rabbit Outdone"—Brer Rooster tricks him into cutting off his leg, later tricks him into starving to death.)

25:4, 82. ("The Ceremony of the 'Foot Wash' in Virginia"; "Why the Tiger is Striped.")

Smiley, Portia, "The Foot-Wash in Alabama," 25:5, 101–102. (Also a tale, "Why the Fox's Mouth is Sharp, Why the Possum has no Hair on his Tail, and Why the Rabbit has a Short Tail and White Spot on his Forehead.")

25:7, 144–147. (An address to the annual meeting of the Hampton Folk-Lore Society by W. H. Scarborough, quite similar to his article "Negro Folk-Lore and Dialect," *Arena*, 17 [January 1897], 186–192.)

Chatelain, Heli, "Folk-Lore in an African's Life," 25:8, 164–166.*

25:9, 185–186. (John tricks other slaves about cursing master; story of the Marsh Light, based on superstition that if you turn a pocket facing the Will-o'-the-Wisp inside out it won't hurt you, but John is caught between three of them; Brer Wolf and Brer Rabbit get a cow and Brer Rabbit tricks the wolf. Also a Creole tale from W. H. Scarborough, "Compair Bouki and Compair Lapin.")

25:10, 205–206. ("How Brer Wolf Divide de Hog," "How Brer Wolf Caught Brer Rabbit," "Creole Proverbs," and, from W. H. Scarborough, "Proverbs and Sayings from Africa and the West Indies.")

"A Difficult Courtship," 25:11, 226. (A courting play.)

1897

"Beliefs and Customs Connected with Death and Burial," 26:1, 18–19.

"Some Conjure Doctors we have Heard Of," 26:2, 37–38. (Verbatim transcriptions of student essays from the files: "Amenities of the Profession," "Tricking a Steamboat," "A False Messiah," "Devil Worship.")

26:3, 58. ("Why the Terrapin has Red Eyes," "Why the Mole has no Eyes," "Where de Owl Fus' Come From.")

26:4, 78–79. ("A Race for a Wife"—a variant of the Riding Horse tale—and "The Hog Thief.")

26:6, 122–123. (Two ghost stories.)

26:8, 163. (Extracts from student compositions: "Slave marriages," "Wednesday Night, Wife Night," "How the slaves cooked and ate," "How they were dressed.")

"Morality and Religion in Slavery Days," 26:10, 210. (Has a few brief humorous tales.)

"Fish Stories," 26:11, 229–230. (Sambo is warned against fishing on Sundays, disobeys, catches a talking monster which instructs him to take itself home to cook and eat; Sambo does, then bursts; second story is about Simon hooking Mollie Gohead.)

26:12, 249. ("The rabbit and the busards" and "The rabbit and the girl," both stories from Alabama.)

1898

Showers, Susan, "How the Jays Saved their souls" and "The Jay and the Martin," 27:1, 17–18.

Jefferson, Thomas, "The Indian Legend of the Mammoth," 27:2, 35.* (Reprinted from his *Notes on Virginia.*)

Barnette, V. G., and Herbert, C. H., "Why the Dog Cannot Talk" and "Why the Rabbit has a Short Tail," 27:2, 36–37.

Showers, Susan, "Snakes and Conjure Doctors," 27:2, 37.

27:3, 57. ("The Rich Ghost" and "The Boy and the Ghost.")

27:4, 76–77. ("Why the Rabbit has a Short Tail and the Dog a Wide Mouth," "The Goose and the Snake." Also "A Navajo Indian Story of the Creation," by J. C. Walker.)

27:6, 124–125. ("A Ghost Story" and "Story of a Fox and a Pig"—pig tricks fox into barrel, scalds him to death.)

"Proverbs and Sayings," 27:7, 145–146.

"Searching for Hidden Treasure," 27:10, 209–210.

Showers, Susan, "How the Rabbit and the Frog Caught a Deer," 27: 11, 230.

Hill, Jesse, "The Lost Tree: An Indian Legend," 27:12, 250.*

Davis, Daniel Webster, "Conjuration," 27:12, 251–252.

1899

28:1, 32–33. ("Why the Crab has no Head," "Why the Buzzard Eats Carrion," "Why there are Moles," "Why Hens are Afraid of Owls," "The Snail's Smartness," old sayings.)

Davis, Daniel Webster. "Echoes from a Plantation Party," 28:2, 54–59.* (Describes slave parties, tale telling, riddles, songs, etc. Eight ring-play texts.)

Moton, R. R., "Sickness in Slavery Days," 28:2, 74–75.

Walker, John G., "Handicraft of the Southwestern Indians," 28:3, 111–112.*

28:3, 112–113. (The Trick Bone of a cat; how to conjure; conjuration remedies; courtship; why the wren does not fly high; Brer Rabbit beats Brer Fox.)

28:4, 151–154. ("Watch Meeting"—description of New Year's ceremony, prayers, three hymns.)

28:5, 190–194. (Indian tale; Irishman tales.)

28:5, 194–196.* (Reviews of Charles W. Chestnutt, *The Conjure Woman*, and Martha S. Gielow, *Mammy's Reminiscences, and other Sketches.*)

"Editorial: Folk-Lore Department," 28:6, 201.* (Response to negative reaction to language in Irishman stories in previous issue. Editorial says the texts have to be verbatim if they are to be meaningful.)

"The Fool Hunter," 28:6, 230–232.

Anderson, W. T., "Jack and the King," 28:6, 232–233.

28:6, 234–237. (Review of Mary H. Kingsley, *West African Studies.*)

28:8, 314–315. (Conjure cures.)

28:11, 449–450. ("A Negro Ghost Story"; "Don't" superstitions from Tidewater Virginia; "Birds of Ill Omen," from the New York *Sun.*)

1900

Showers, Susan, "Alabama Folk-Lore," 29:3, 179–180, and 29:7, 443–444.* (Proverbs; supersitions; medicines; ring games.)

1901

Conrad, Georgia Bryan, "Reminiscences of a Southern Woman," 30:2,

77–80; 30:3, 167–171; 30:5, 252–257; 30:6, 357–359; 30:10, 409–411.*

30:2, 128–129.* (Review of Howard Weeden, *Songs of the Old South*, by L. A. S., and review of Virginia Frazer Boyle, *Devil Tales*, by S. H. S.)

Sherrard, Virginia B., "Recollections of My Mammy," 30:2, 86–87.* (Mostly sentimentalia, but the article includes the comment that the mammy sang "Lord Lovell" to the children.)

Dowd, Jerome, "Sermon of an Ante-Bellum Negro Preacher," 30:11, 655–658.*

D.

Some Other Articles on Negro Folklore in Nineteenth-Century Periodicals.

Allen, W. F., "Southern Negro Folklore," *The Dial*, I (Chicago, 1881), 183–185.

Babcock, W. H., "Carols and Child-Lore at the Capital," *Lippincott's Magazine*, XXXVIII (1886), 320–342.

———, "Games of Washington Children," *American Anthropologist*, I (1888), 243–284.

———, "Song Games and Myth Dances at Washington," *Lippincott's Magazine*, XXXVII (1886), 239–257.

Barton, William E., D. D., "Hymns of the Slave and the Freedman," *New England Magazine*, XIX (1899), 609–624.

———, "Old Plantation Melodies," *New England Magazine*, XIX (1898), 443–456.

Bergen, F. D., "Uncle Remus and Folklore," *Outlook*, 48 (1893), 427–428.

Chamberlain, A. F., "Negro Dialect," *Science*, XII (1888), 23–24.

Elam, William Cecil, "Lingo in Literature," *Lippincott's Magazine*, LV (1895), 286–288.

Haskell, Marion Alexander, "Negro 'Spirituals'," *Century Magazine*, n.s. 36 (1899), 577–581.

Hopkins, Isabella, "In the M. E. African," *Scribner's Monthly*, XX (1880), 422–429.

Krehbiel, Henry Edward, "Folk Music Studies," New York *Tribune*, 1899, *passism*.

Nathanson, Y. S., "Negro Melodies and National Music," *Music Review*, II (1893), 514–516.

Scarborough, W. H., "Negro Folk-lore and Dialect," *Arena*, 17 (1897), 186–192.

Shaler, N. W. "An Ex-Southerner in South Carolina," *Atlantic Monthly*, XXVI (1870), 53–61.
"Slave Songs of the United States," *Living Age*, 96 (1866), 230–242.
"Slave Songs of the United States," *Nation*, V (Nov. 21, 1867), 411.
Tonsor, Johann, "Negro Music," *Music*, III (1892–1893), 119–122.
Vance, L. J., "Plantation Folk Lore," *Open Court*, II (1888), 1028–1032, 1074–1076, 1092–1095.
Wood, Henry Cleveland, "Negro Camp-Meeting Melodies," *New England Magazine*, n.s. VI (1892), 60–64.

Index of Authors, Titles of Articles, and Periodicals

Index of Songs and Verses

Titles (indicated by quotation marks) are listed in this index wherever they appear in the essays, the Introduction, or Prefaces; a title followed by a text is indicated by an asterisk after the page number. First lines are given for all songs and verses appearing without titles and for those songs for which the first line might be more helpful for identification than the title given by the original author. When neither title nor first line seemed particularly helfpul, the chorus line is indexed also (indicated by parenthetical *ch.*). Tunes are indicated by a double asterisk.

THE NEGRO AND HIS FOLKLORE

IN NINETEENTH-CENTURY PERIODICALS